CONTENTS

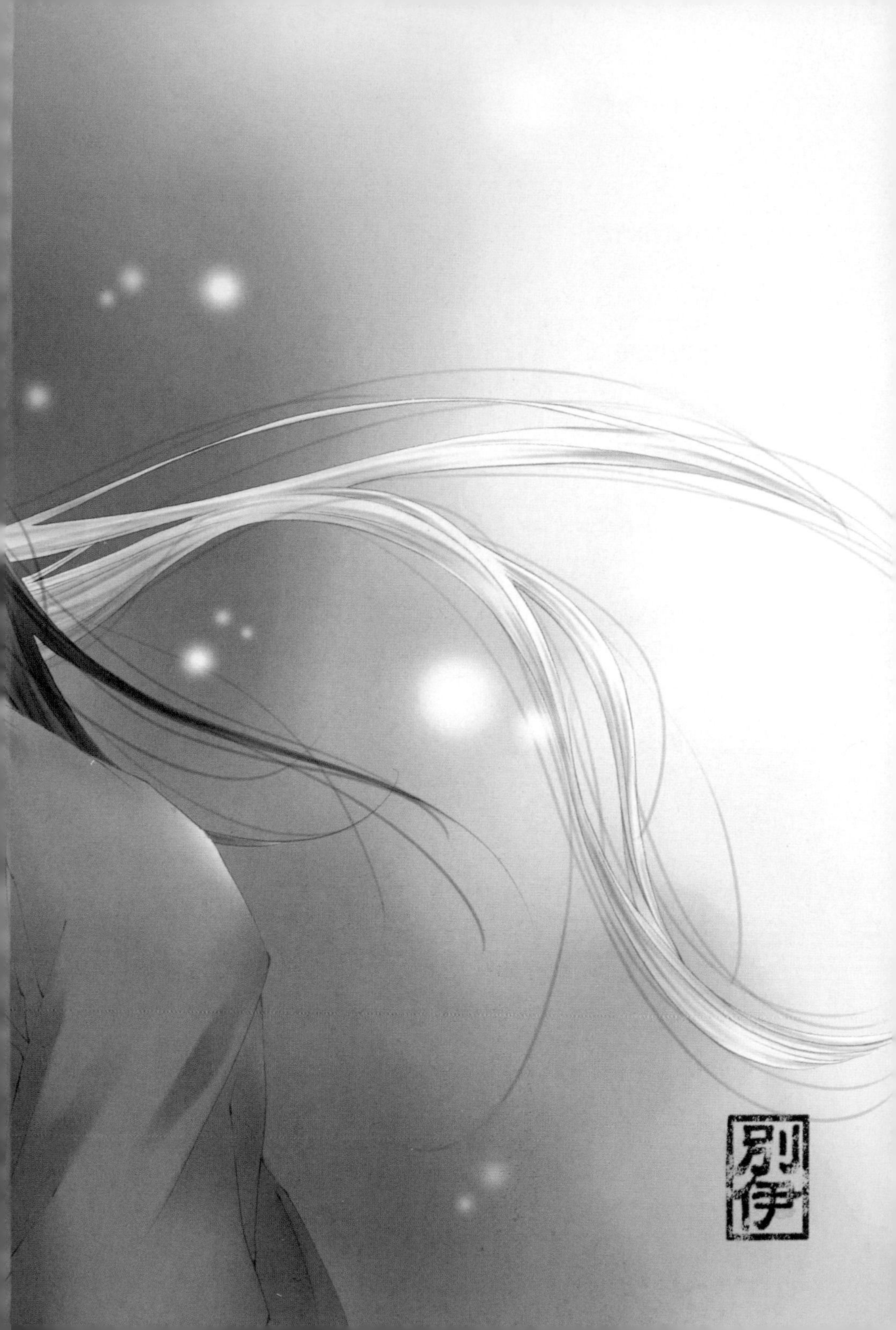
別伝

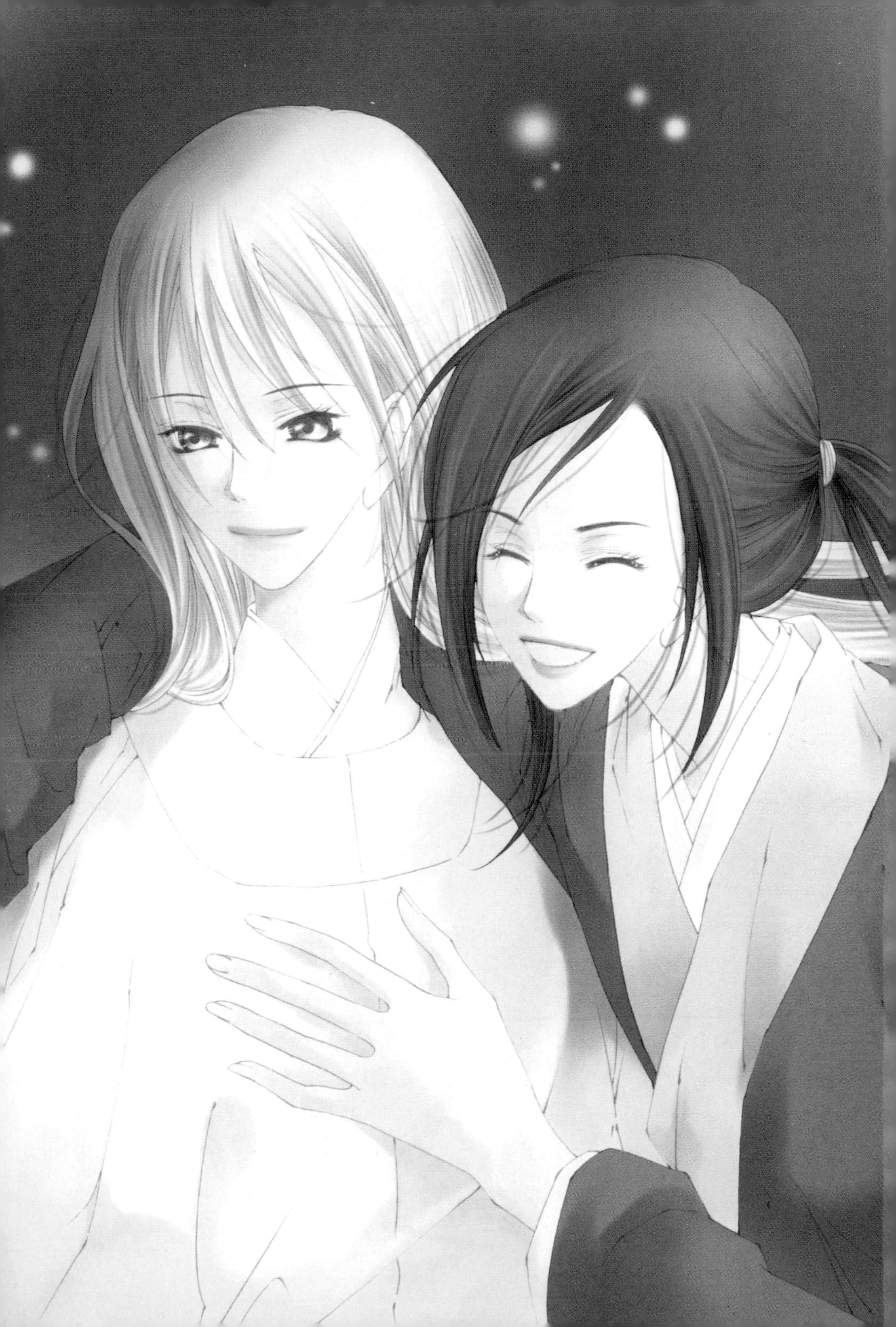

6 JiUn Yun

"TO PADONG WHILE
READING A BOOK IN CHANGGU"
HE LI

COLD NIGHT, UNDER THE DIM LAMP
    AND SOFT SOUND OF INSECTS,
THE SMELL OF MEDICINE FILLS
    THE ROOM.
YOU PITY THIS WEAK ME,
AND REMAIN BY MY SIDE IN SPITE
    OF ALL THE HARDSHIP.

TIME
AND
AGAIN

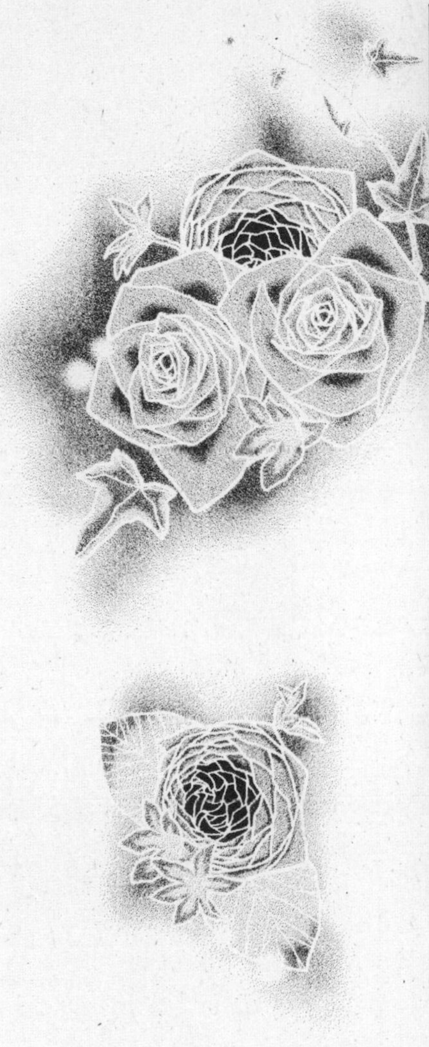

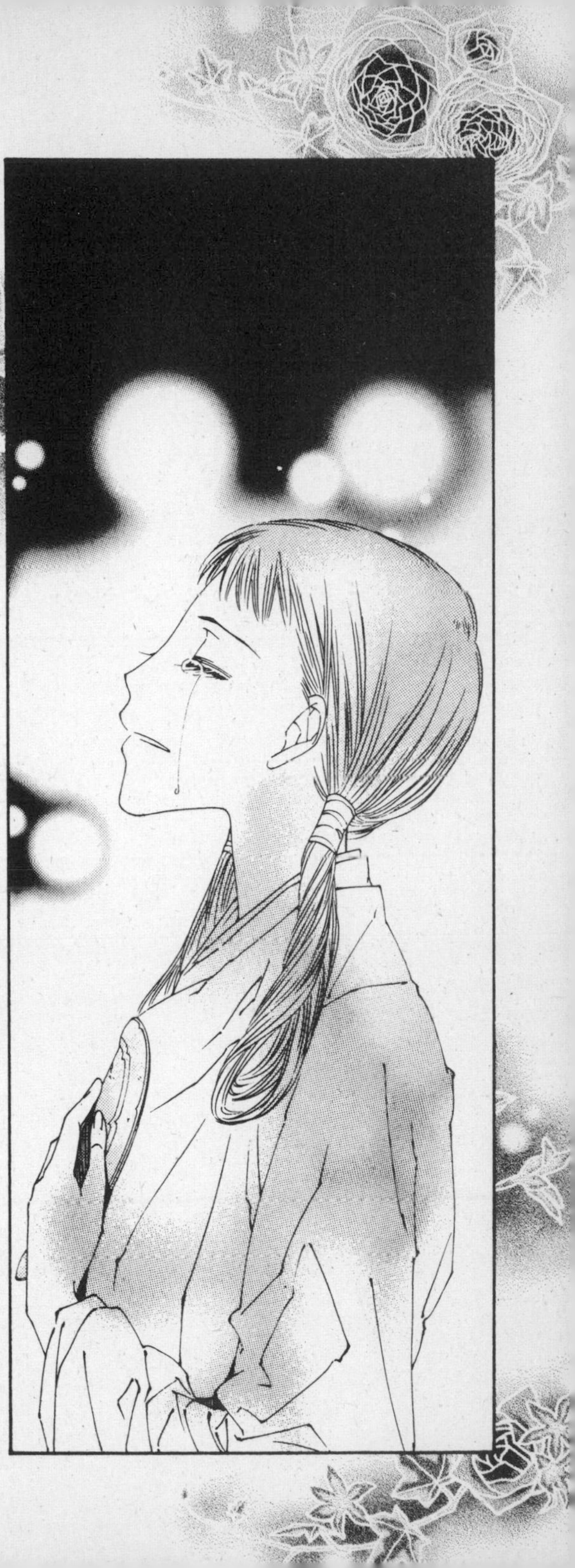

CHAPTER NINETEEN
SADNESS

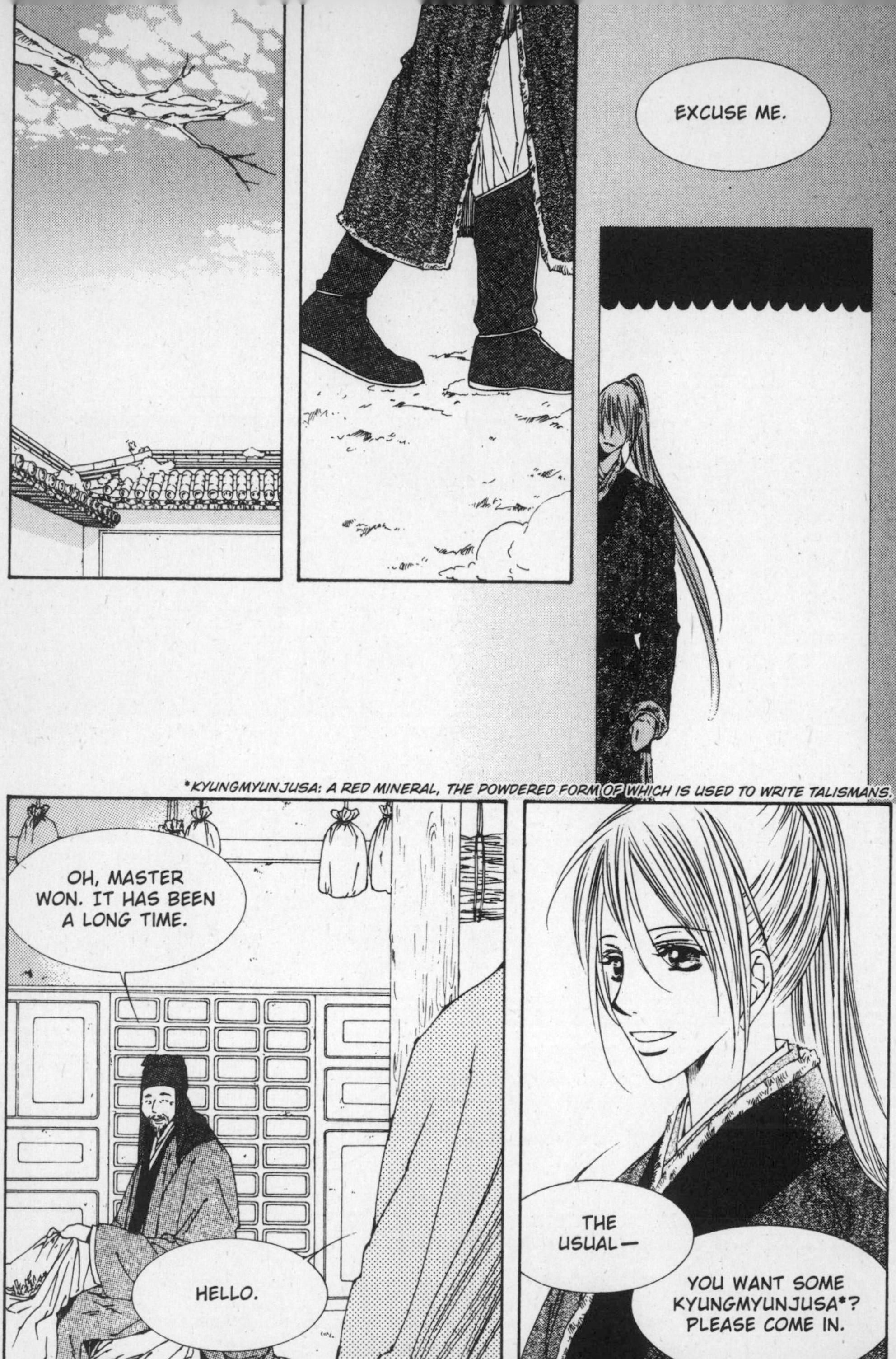
EXCUSE ME.
OH, MASTER WON. IT HAS BEEN A LONG TIME.
HELLO.
THE USUAL—
YOU WANT SOME KYUNGMYUNJUSA*? PLEASE COME IN.
*KYUNGMYUNJUSA: A RED MINERAL, THE POWDERED FORM OF WHICH IS USED TO WRITE TALISMANS.

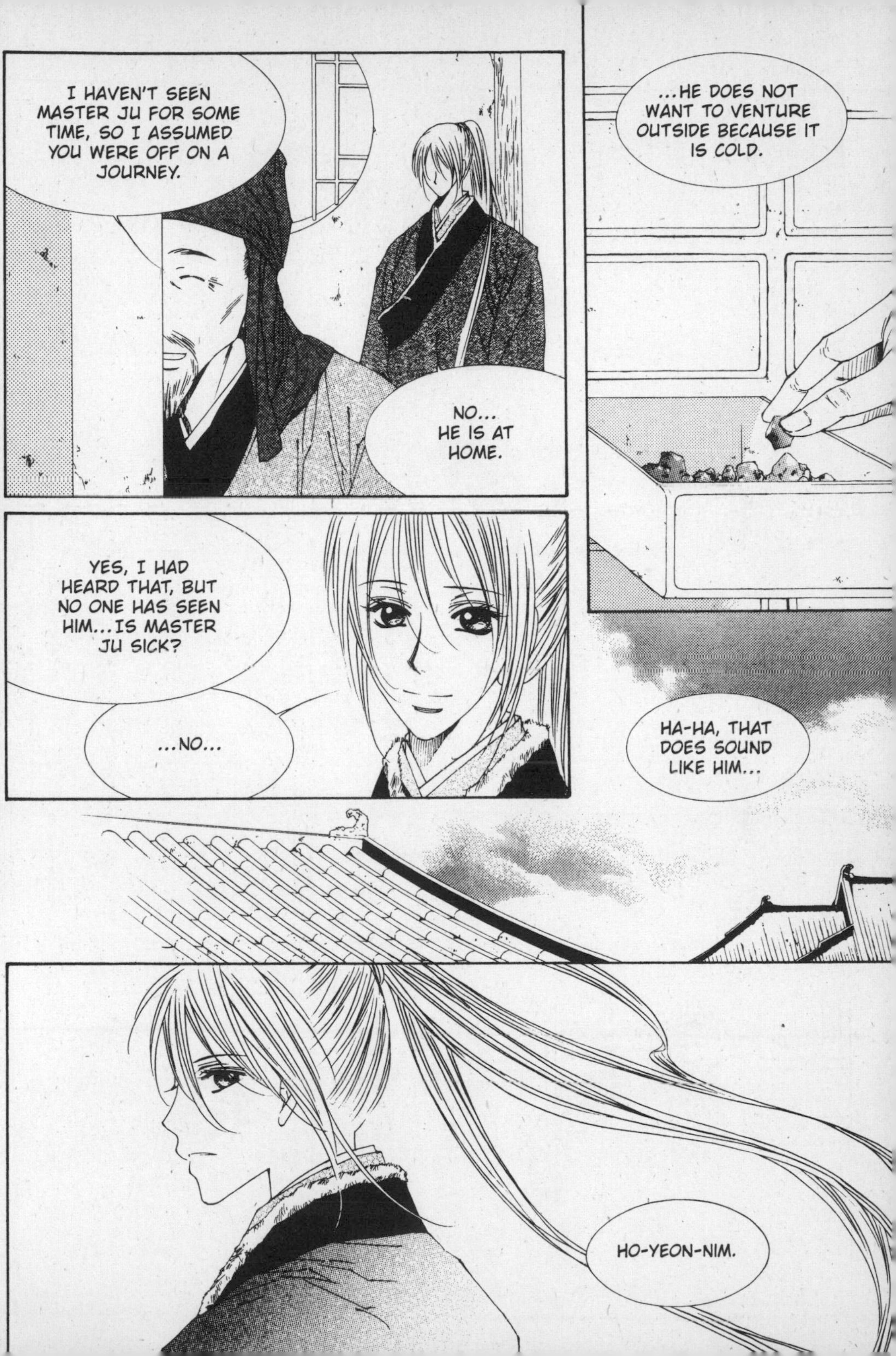
I HAVEN'T SEEN MASTER JU FOR SOME TIME, SO I ASSUMED YOU WERE OFF ON A JOURNEY.
NO... HE IS AT HOME.
YES, I HAD HEARD THAT, BUT NO ONE HAS SEEN HIM...IS MASTER JU SICK?
...NO...
...HE DOES NOT WANT TO VENTURE OUTSIDE BECAUSE IT IS COLD.
HA-HA, THAT DOES SOUND LIKE HIM...
HO-YEON-NIM.

IT WAS TRYING TO ENTER BAEK-ON-NIM'S QUARTERS.

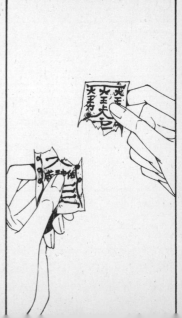

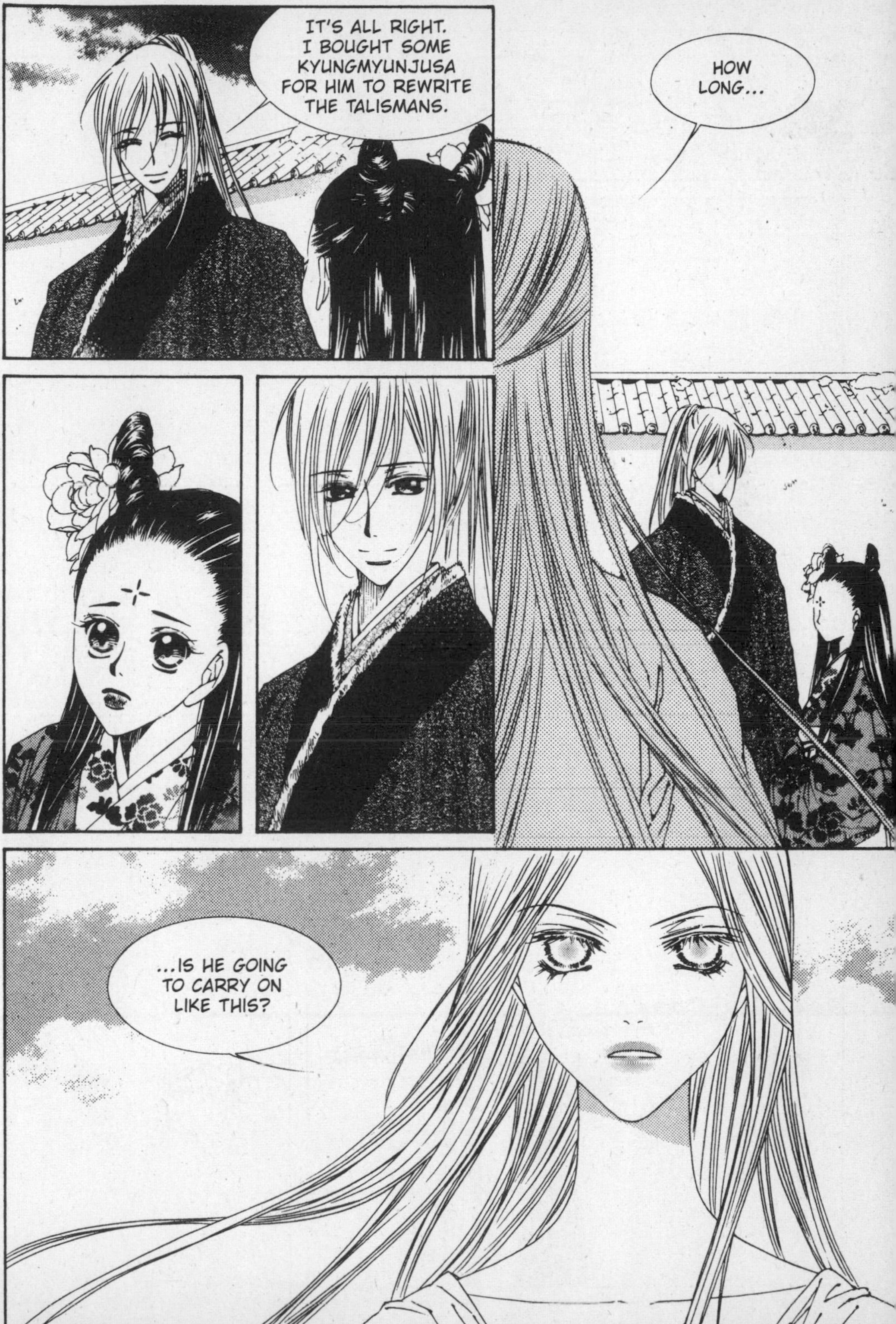
IT'S ALL RIGHT. I BOUGHT SOME KYUNGMYUNJUSA FOR HIM TO REWRITE THE TALISMANS.
HOW LONG...
...IS HE GOING TO CARRY ON LIKE THIS?

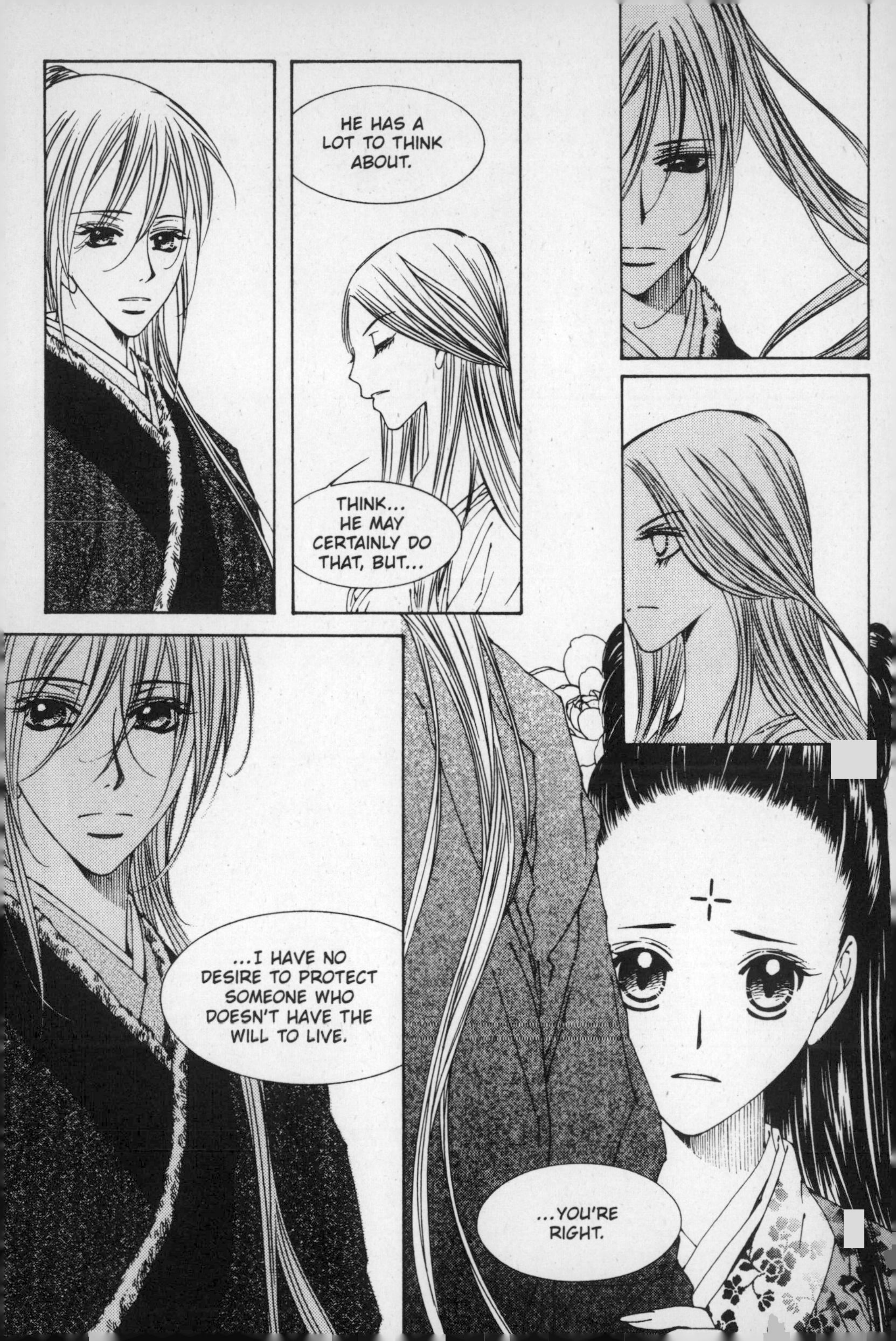
HE HAS A LOT TO THINK ABOUT.
THINK... HE MAY CERTAINLY DO THAT, BUT...
...I HAVE NO DESIRE TO PROTECT SOMEONE WHO DOESN'T HAVE THE WILL TO LIVE.
...YOU'RE RIGHT.

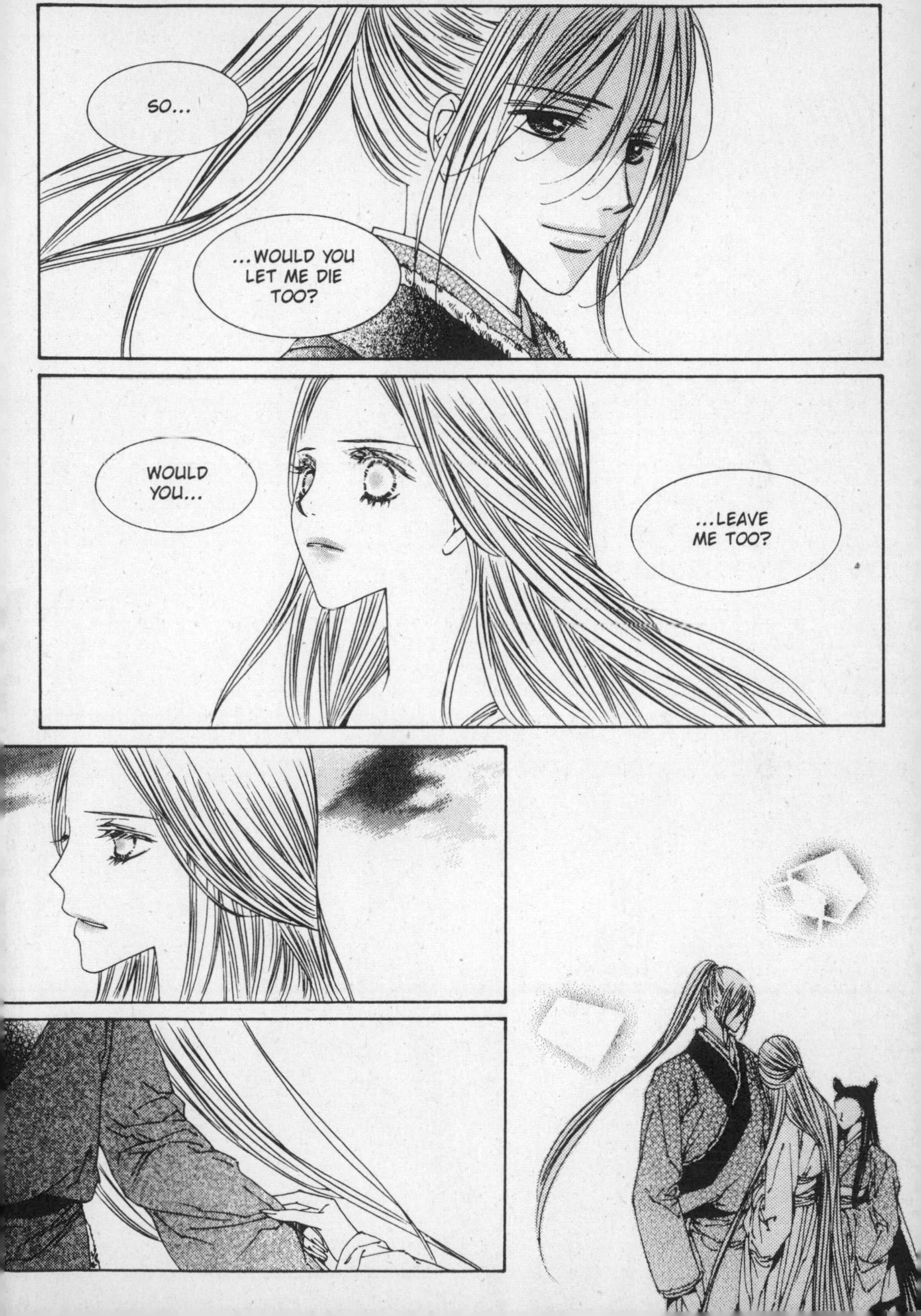
SO...
...WOULD YOU LET ME DIE TOO?
WOULD YOU...
...LEAVE ME TOO?

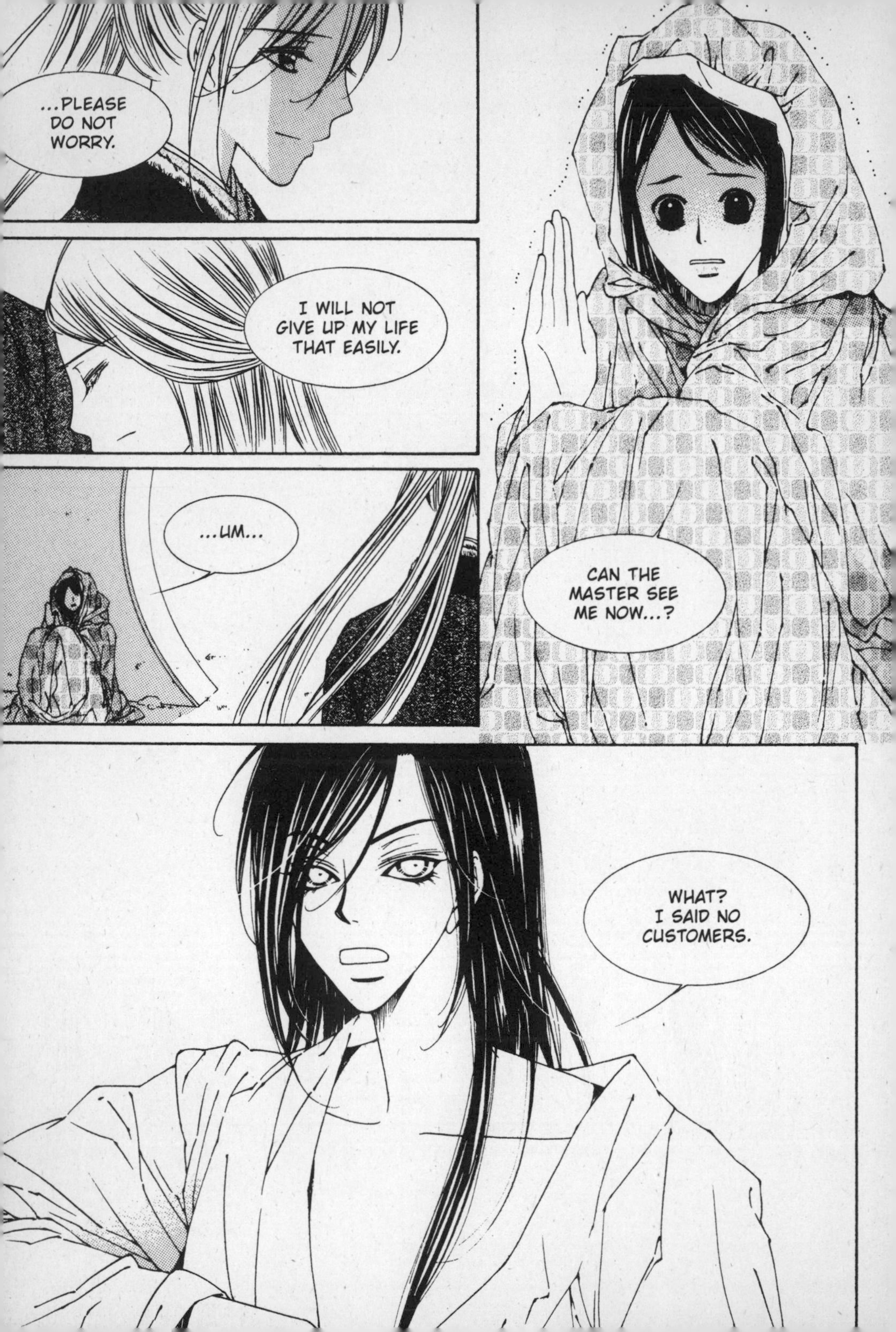
...PLEASE DO NOT WORRY.
I WILL NOT GIVE UP MY LIFE THAT EASILY.
...UM...
CAN THE MASTER SEE ME NOW...?
WHAT? I SAID NO CUSTOMERS.

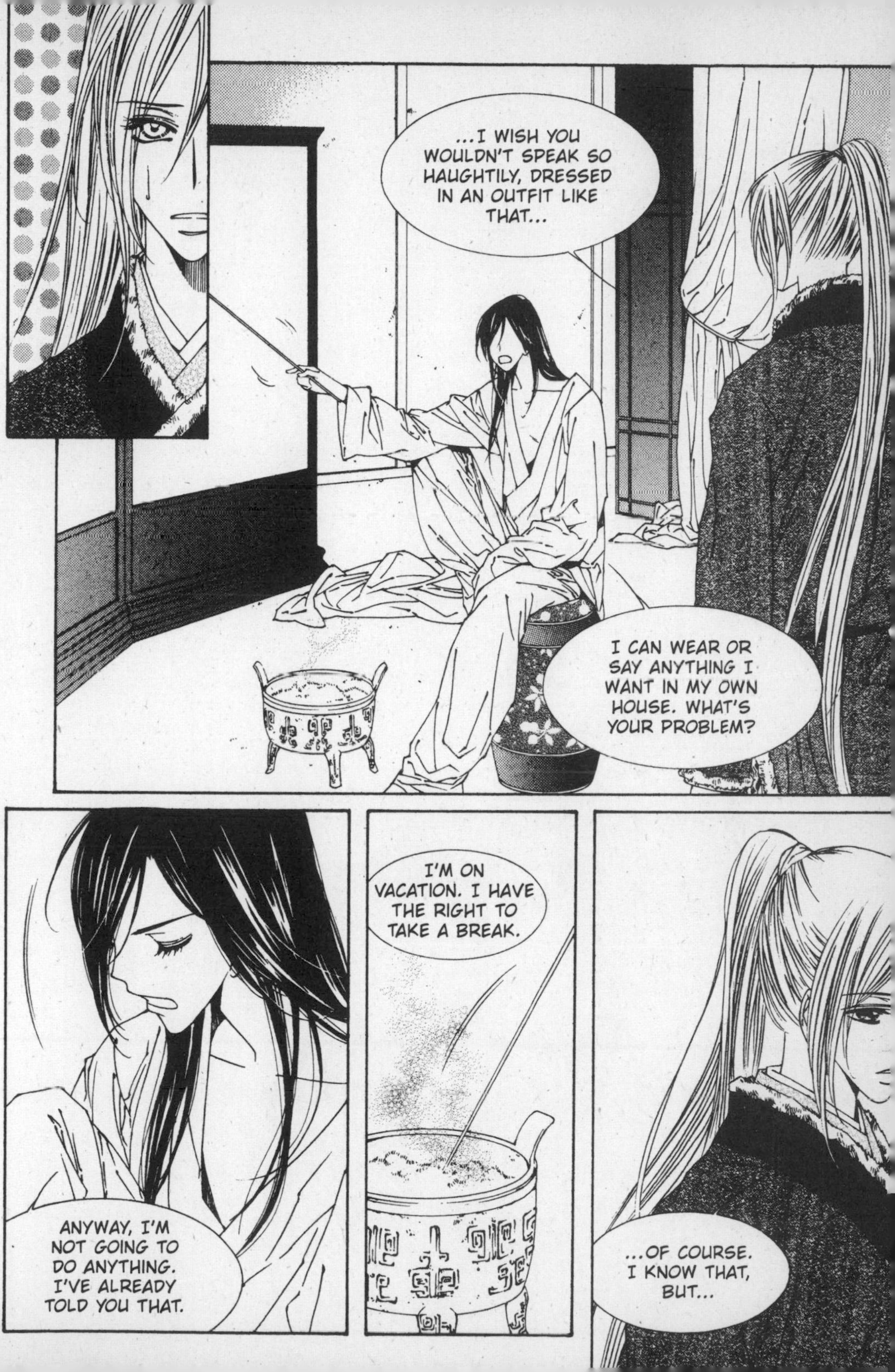
...I WISH YOU WOULDN'T SPEAK SO HAUGHTILY, DRESSED IN AN OUTFIT LIKE THAT...
I CAN WEAR OR SAY ANYTHING I WANT IN MY OWN HOUSE. WHAT'S YOUR PROBLEM?
ANYWAY, I'M NOT GOING TO DO ANYTHING. I'VE ALREADY TOLD YOU THAT.
I'M ON VACATION. I HAVE THE RIGHT TO TAKE A BREAK.
...OF COURSE. I KNOW THAT, BUT...

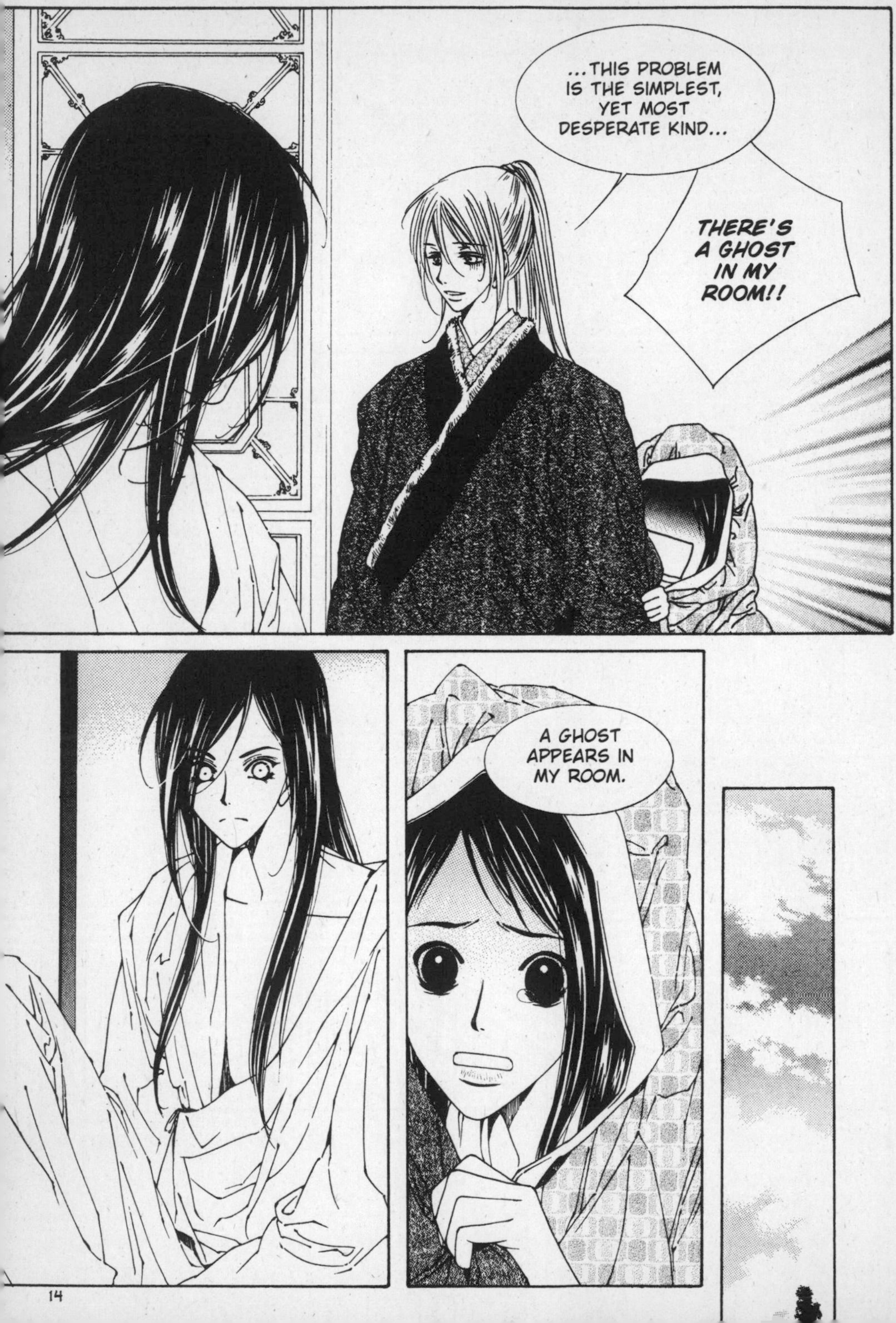
...THIS PROBLEM IS THE SIMPLEST, YET MOST DESPERATE KIND...
THERE'S A GHOST IN MY ROOM!!
A GHOST APPEARS IN MY ROOM.

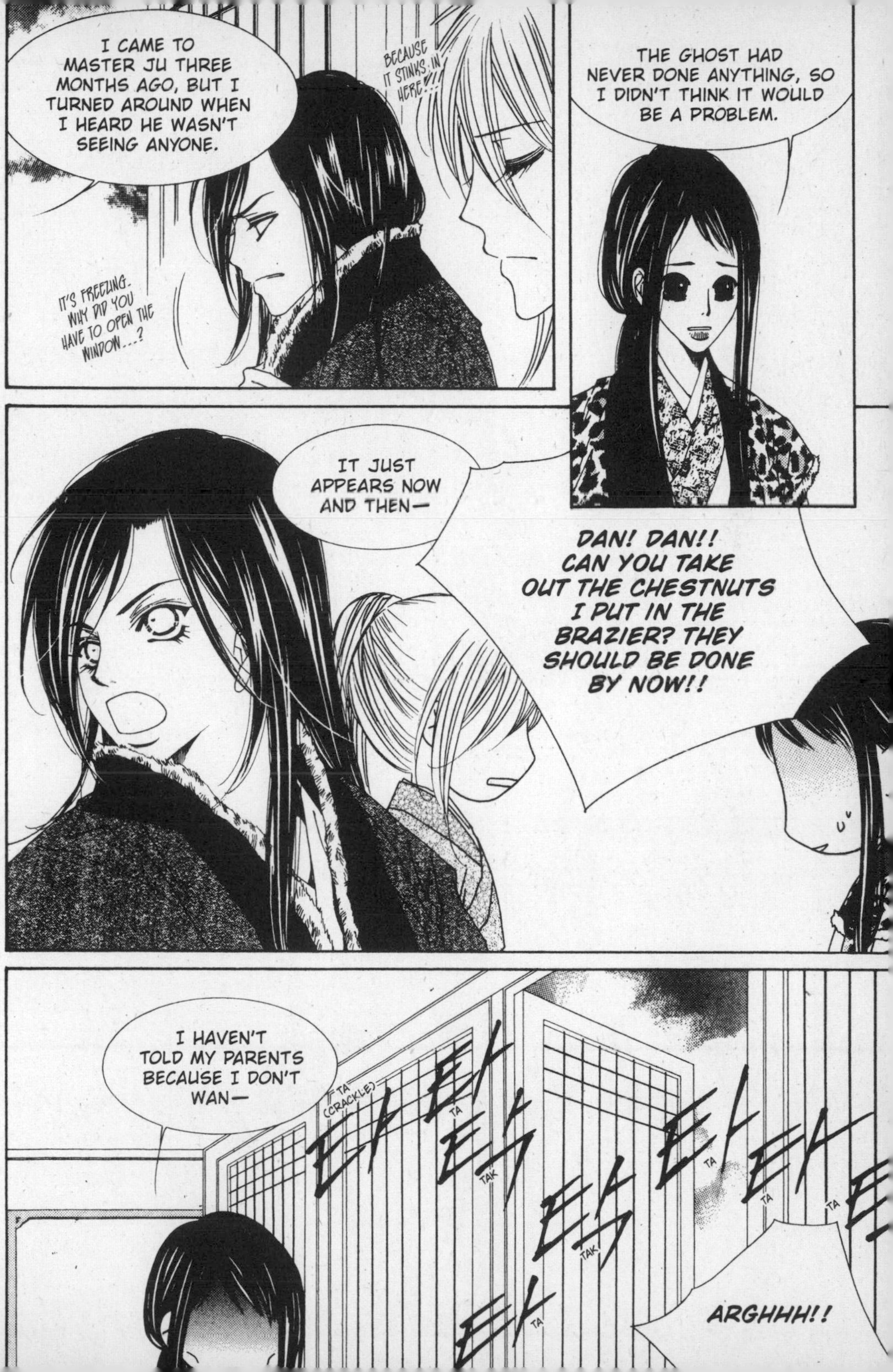
I CAME TO MASTER JU THREE MONTHS AGO, BUT I TURNED AROUND WHEN I HEARD HE WASN'T SEEING ANYONE.
IT'S FREEZING. WHY DID YOU HAVE TO OPEN THE WINDOW...?
BECAUSE IT STINKS IN HERE!!...
THE GHOST HAD NEVER DONE ANYTHING, SO I DIDN'T THINK IT WOULD BE A PROBLEM.
IT JUST APPEARS NOW AND THEN—
DAN! DAN!! CAN YOU TAKE OUT THE CHESTNUTS I PUT IN THE BRAZIER? THEY SHOULD BE DONE BY NOW!!
I HAVEN'T TOLD MY PARENTS BECAUSE I DON'T WAN—
TA (CRACKLE)
TA
TAK
TA
TAK
TA
TA
TA
TA
ARGHHH!!

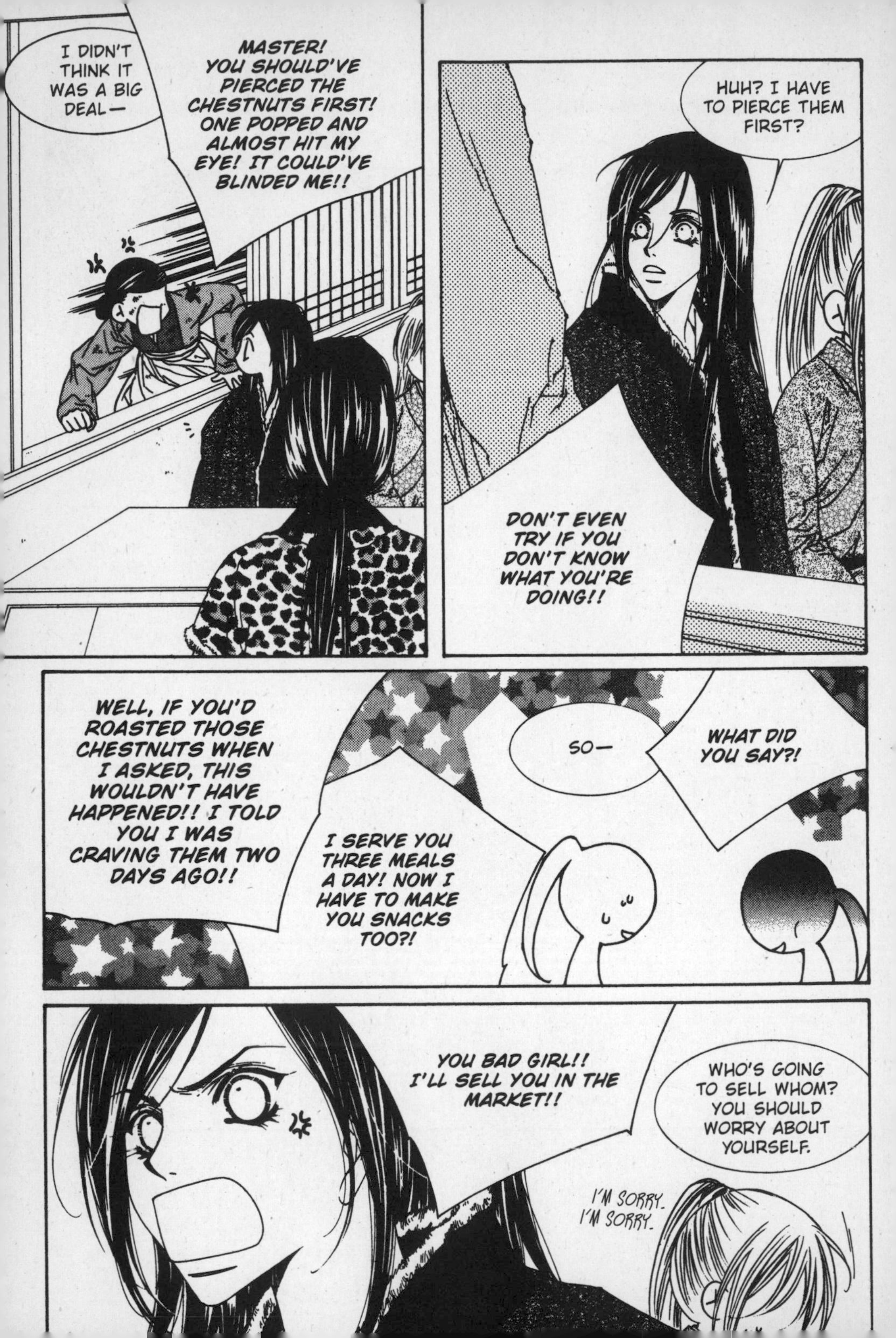
I DIDN'T THINK IT WAS A BIG DEAL—
MASTER! YOU SHOULD'VE PIERCED THE CHESTNUTS FIRST! ONE POPPED AND ALMOST HIT MY EYE! IT COULD'VE BLINDED ME!!
HUH? I HAVE TO PIERCE THEM FIRST?
DON'T EVEN TRY IF YOU DON'T KNOW WHAT YOU'RE DOING!!
WELL, IF YOU'D ROASTED THOSE CHESTNUTS WHEN I ASKED, THIS WOULDN'T HAVE HAPPENED!! I TOLD YOU I WAS CRAVING THEM TWO DAYS AGO!!
I SERVE YOU THREE MEALS A DAY! NOW I HAVE TO MAKE YOU SNACKS TOO?!
SO—
WHAT DID YOU SAY?!
YOU BAD GIRL!! I'LL SELL YOU IN THE MARKET!!
WHO'S GOING TO SELL WHOM? YOU SHOULD WORRY ABOUT YOURSELF.
I'M SORRY. I'M SORRY.

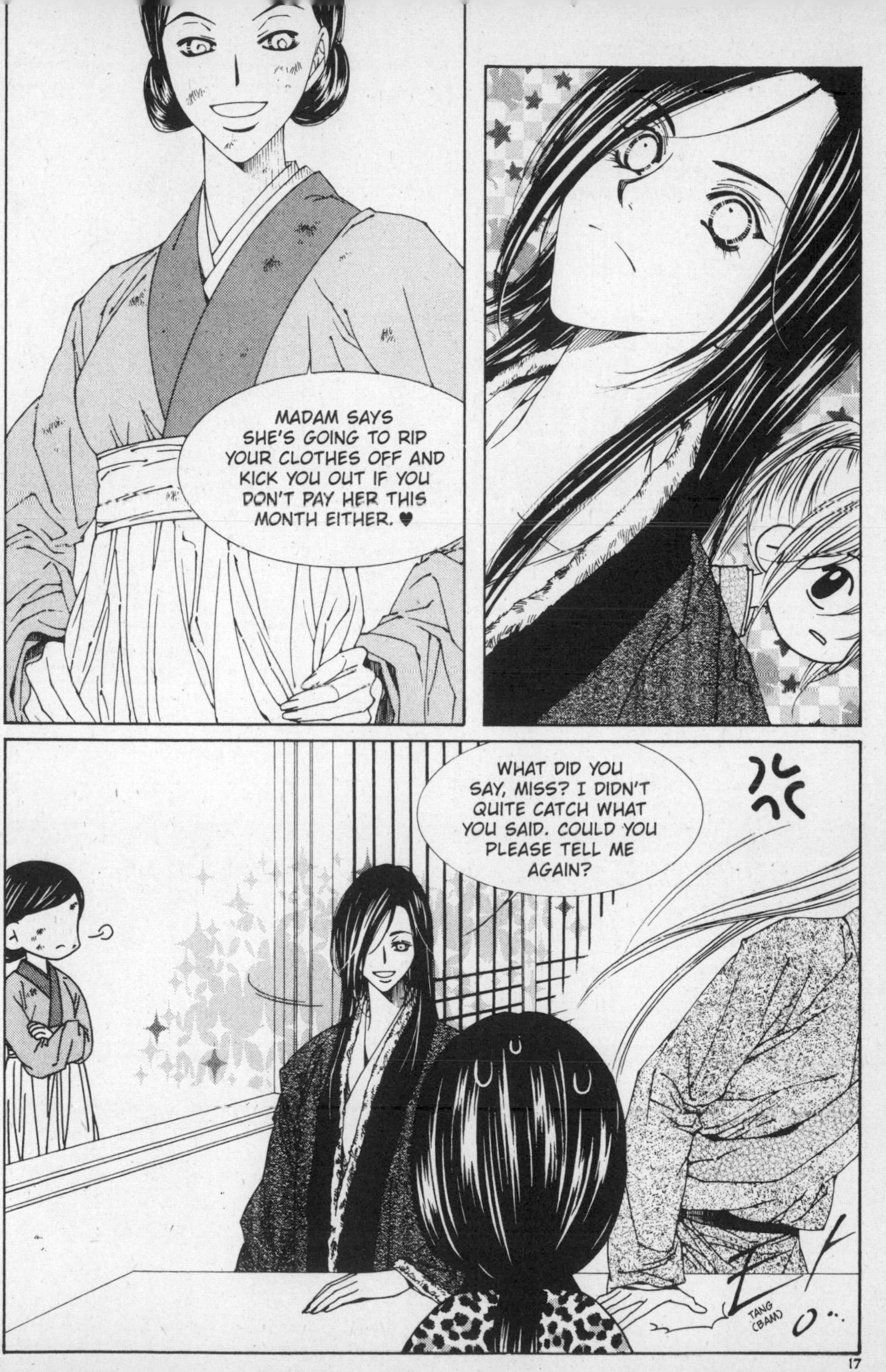
MADAM SAYS SHE'S GOING TO RIP YOUR CLOTHES OFF AND KICK YOU OUT IF YOU DON'T PAY HER THIS MONTH EITHER. ♥
WHAT DID YOU SAY, MISS? I DIDN'T QUITE CATCH WHAT YOU SAID. COULD YOU PLEASE TELL ME AGAIN?
TANG (BAM)

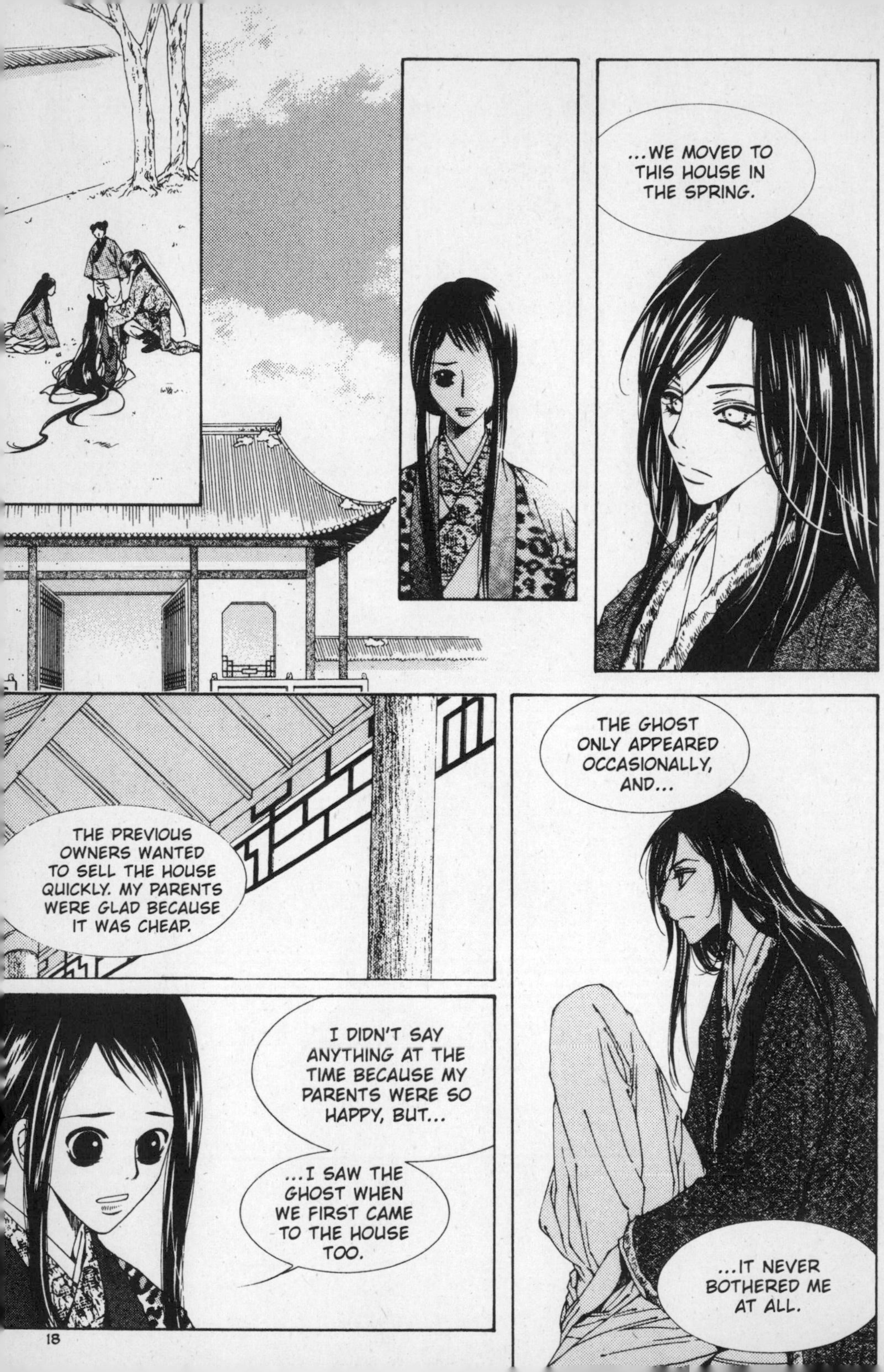
...WE MOVED TO THIS HOUSE IN THE SPRING.
THE PREVIOUS OWNERS WANTED TO SELL THE HOUSE QUICKLY. MY PARENTS WERE GLAD BECAUSE IT WAS CHEAP.
THE GHOST ONLY APPEARED OCCASIONALLY, AND...
I DIDN'T SAY ANYTHING AT THE TIME BECAUSE MY PARENTS WERE SO HAPPY, BUT...
...I SAW THE GHOST WHEN WE FIRST CAME TO THE HOUSE TOO.
...IT NEVER BOTHERED ME AT ALL.

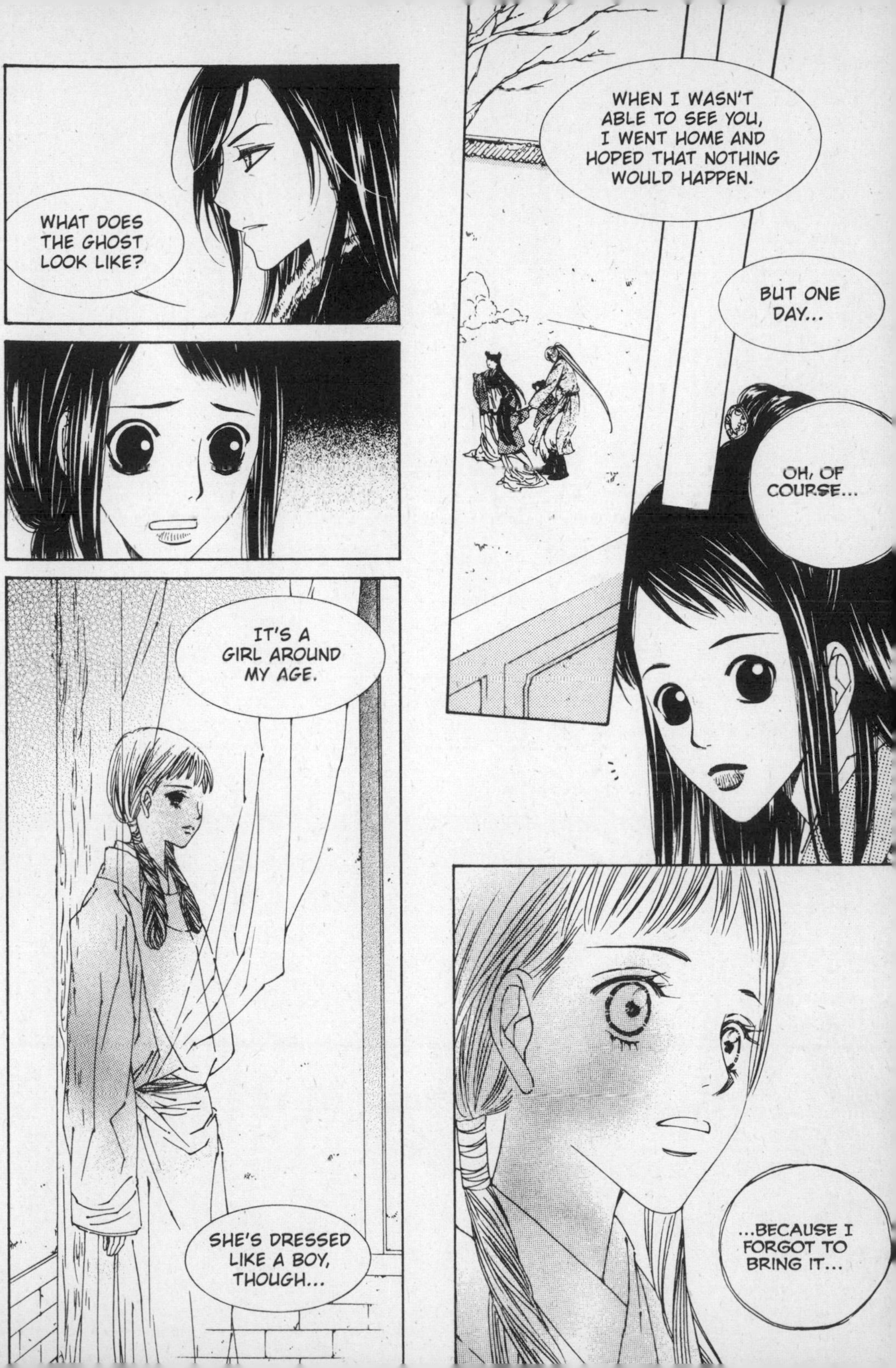
WHAT DOES THE GHOST LOOK LIKE?
IT'S A GIRL AROUND MY AGE.
SHE'S DRESSED LIKE A BOY, THOUGH...
WHEN I WASN'T ABLE TO SEE YOU, I WENT HOME AND HOPED THAT NOTHING WOULD HAPPEN.
BUT ONE DAY...
OH, OF COURSE...
...BECAUSE I FORGOT TO BRING IT...

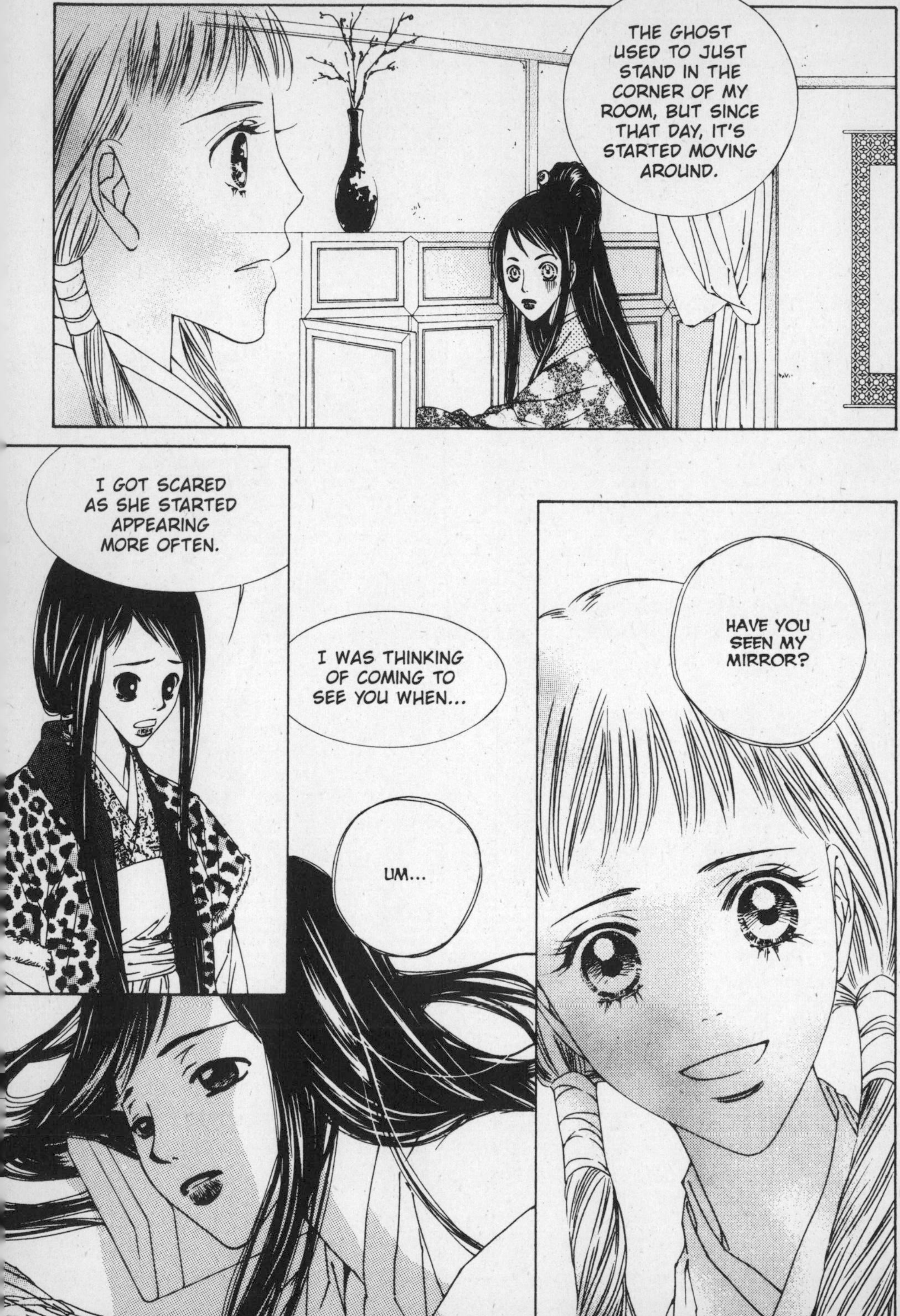
THE GHOST USED TO JUST STAND IN THE CORNER OF MY ROOM, BUT SINCE THAT DAY, IT'S STARTED MOVING AROUND.
I GOT SCARED AS SHE STARTED APPEARING MORE OFTEN.
I WAS THINKING OF COMING TO SEE YOU WHEN...
UM...
HAVE YOU SEEN MY MIRROR?

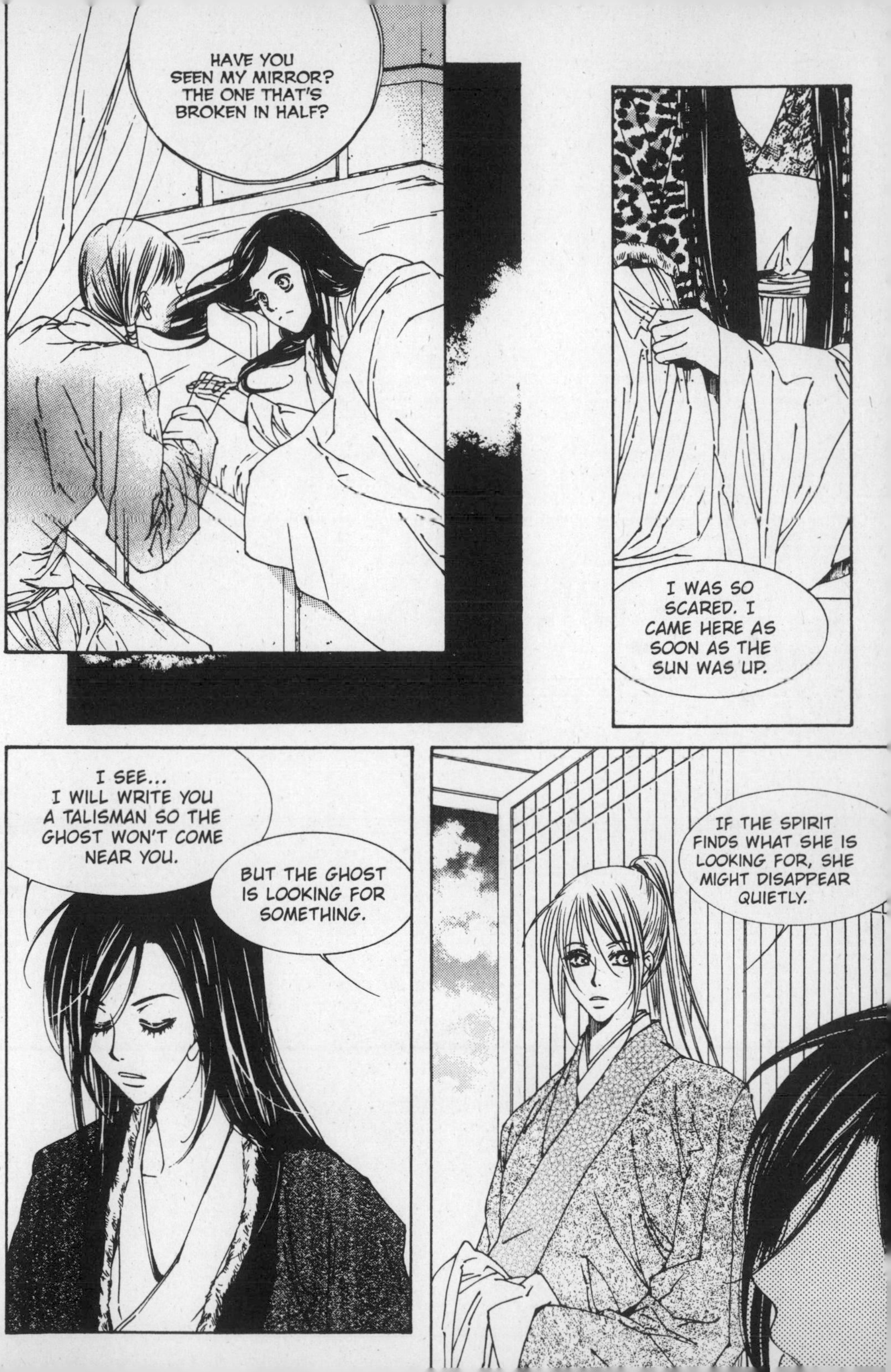
HAVE YOU SEEN MY MIRROR? THE ONE THAT'S BROKEN IN HALF?
I WAS SO SCARED. I CAME HERE AS SOON AS THE SUN WAS UP.
I SEE... I WILL WRITE YOU A TALISMAN SO THE GHOST WON'T COME NEAR YOU.
BUT THE GHOST IS LOOKING FOR SOMETHING.
IF THE SPIRIT FINDS WHAT SHE IS LOOKING FOR, SHE MIGHT DISAPPEAR QUIETLY.

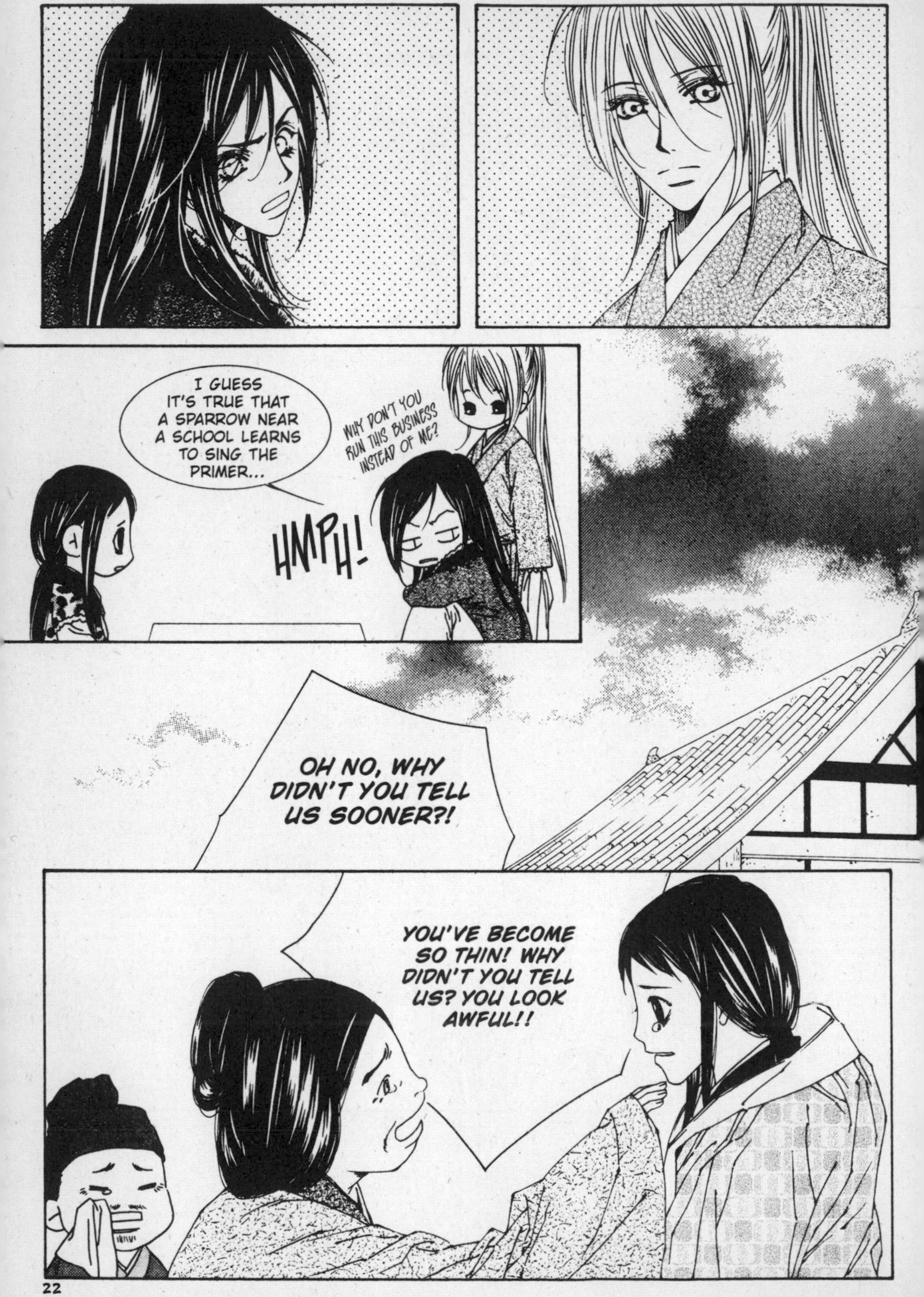
I GUESS IT'S TRUE THAT A SPARROW NEAR A SCHOOL LEARNS TO SING THE PRIMER...
WHY DON'T YOU RUN THIS BUSINESS INSTEAD OF ME?
HMPH!
OH NO, WHY DIDN'T YOU TELL US SOONER?!
YOU'VE BECOME SO THIN! WHY DIDN'T YOU TELL US? YOU LOOK AWFUL!!

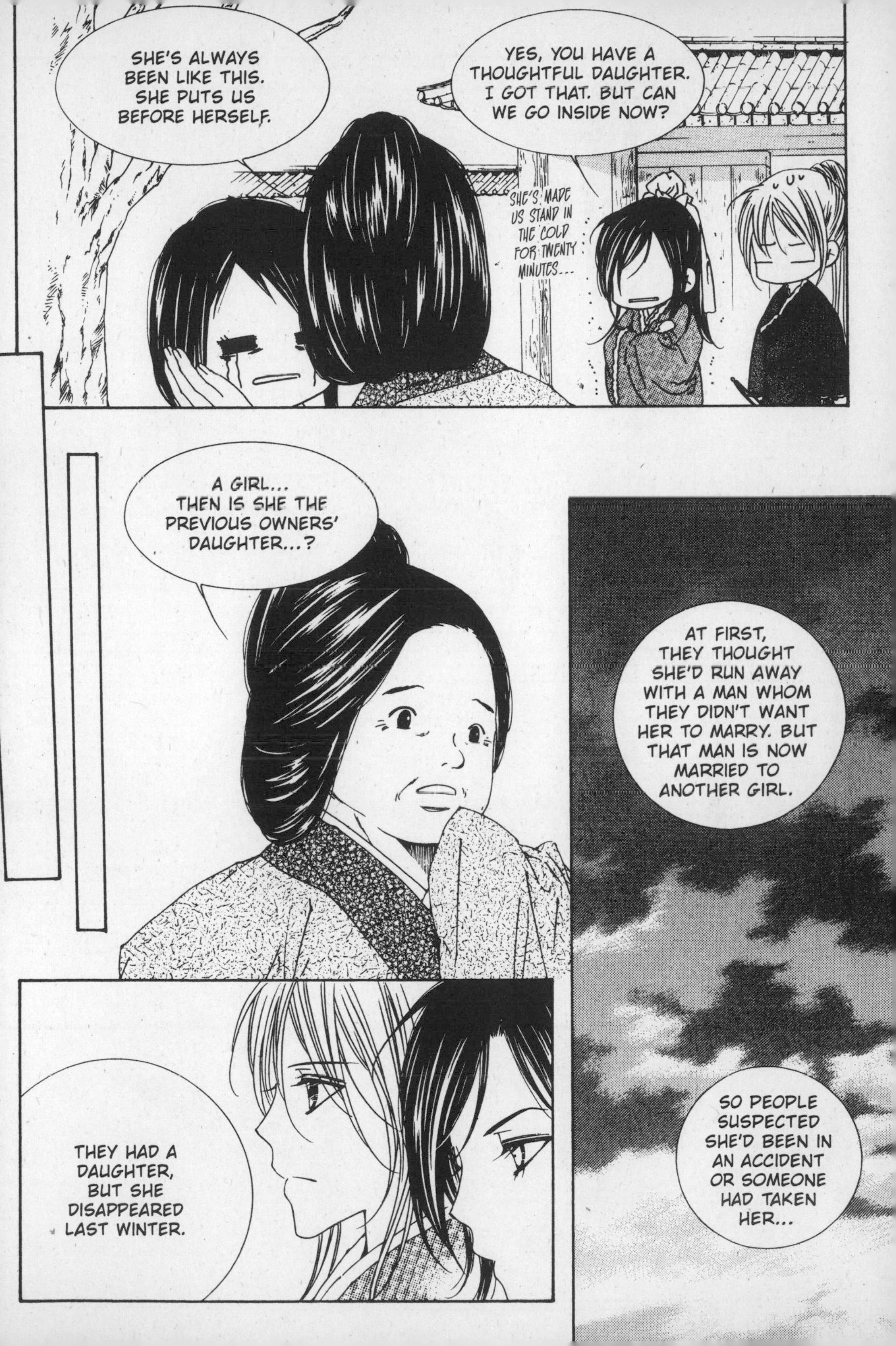
SHE'S ALWAYS BEEN LIKE THIS. SHE PUTS US BEFORE HERSELF.
YES, YOU HAVE A THOUGHTFUL DAUGHTER. I GOT THAT. BUT CAN WE GO INSIDE NOW?
SHE'S MADE US STAND IN THE COLD FOR TWENTY MINUTES...
A GIRL... THEN IS SHE THE PREVIOUS OWNERS' DAUGHTER...?
THEY HAD A DAUGHTER, BUT SHE DISAPPEARED LAST WINTER.
AT FIRST, THEY THOUGHT SHE'D RUN AWAY WITH A MAN WHOM THEY DIDN'T WANT HER TO MARRY. BUT THAT MAN IS NOW MARRIED TO ANOTHER GIRL.
SO PEOPLE SUSPECTED SHE'D BEEN IN AN ACCIDENT OR SOMEONE HAD TAKEN HER...

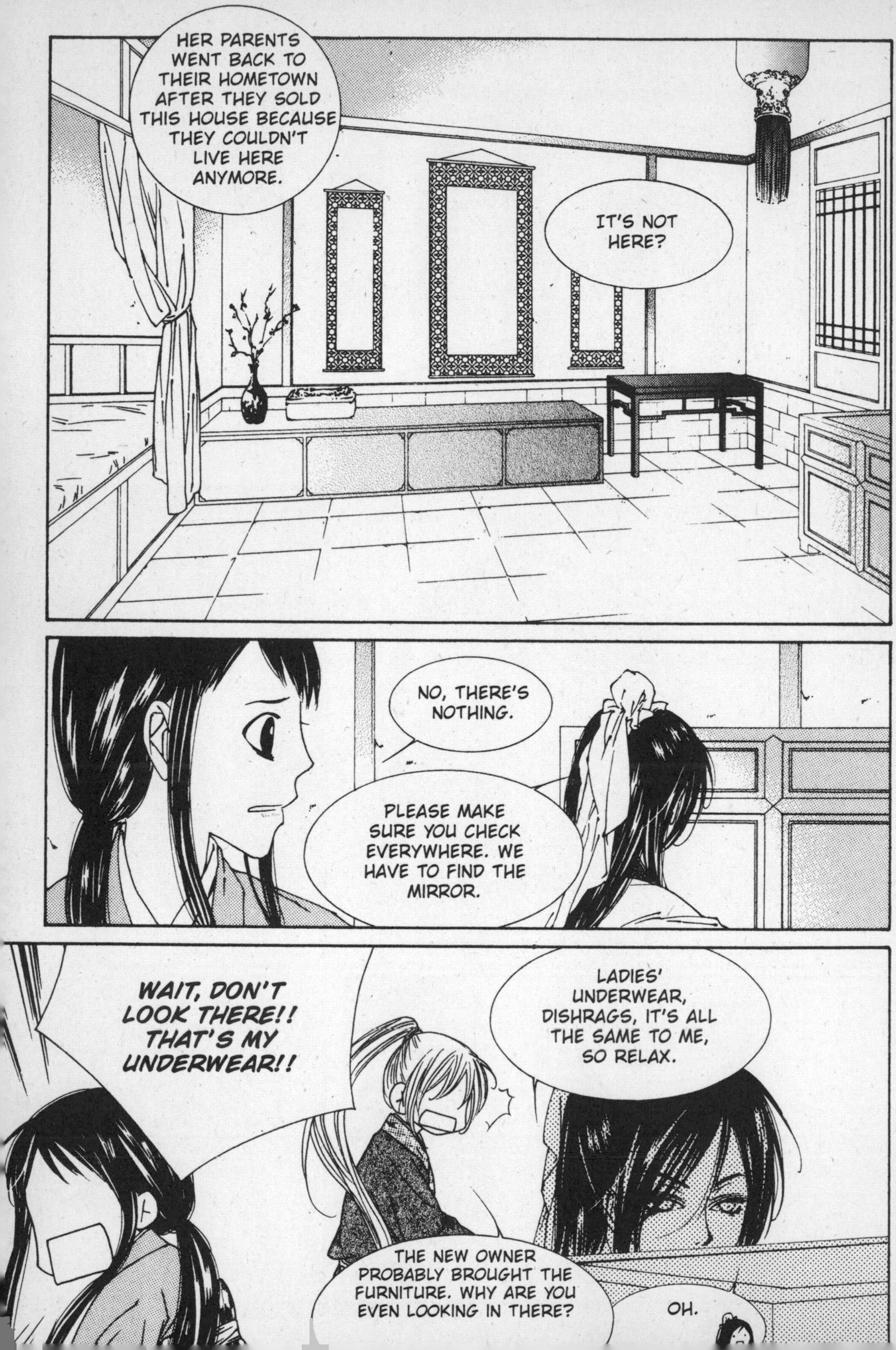
HER PARENTS WENT BACK TO THEIR HOMETOWN AFTER THEY SOLD THIS HOUSE BECAUSE THEY COULDN'T LIVE HERE ANYMORE.
IT'S NOT HERE?
NO, THERE'S NOTHING.
PLEASE MAKE SURE YOU CHECK EVERYWHERE. WE HAVE TO FIND THE MIRROR.
WAIT, DON'T LOOK THERE!! THAT'S MY UNDERWEAR!!
LADIES' UNDERWEAR, DISHRAGS, IT'S ALL THE SAME TO ME, SO RELAX.
THE NEW OWNER PROBABLY BROUGHT THE FURNITURE. WHY ARE YOU EVEN LOOKING IN THERE?
OH.

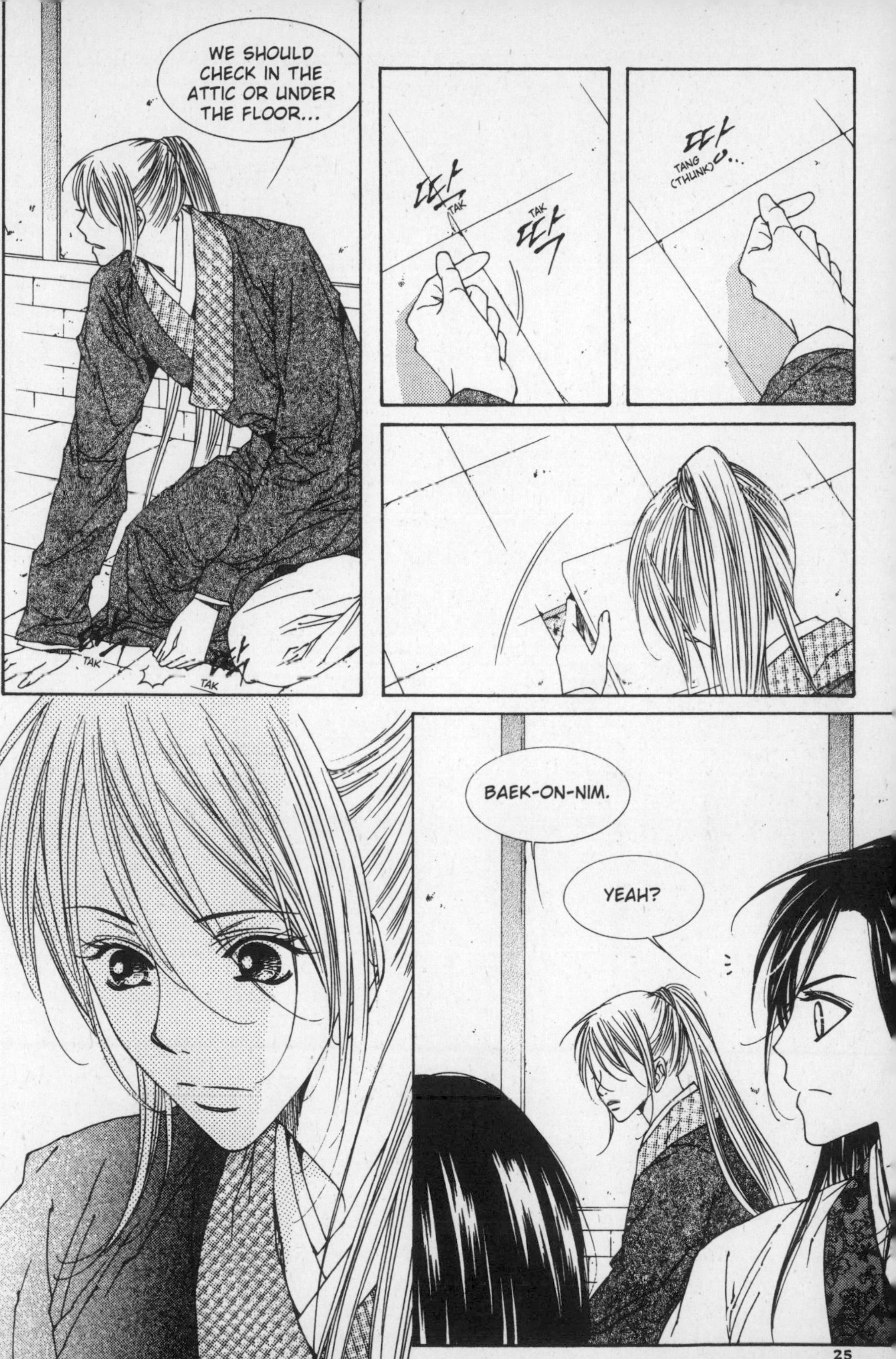
WE SHOULD CHECK IN THE ATTIC OR UNDER THE FLOOR...
TAK
TAK
딱 TAK
TAK 딱
땅 TANG (THUNK)...
BAEK-ON-NIM.
YEAH?

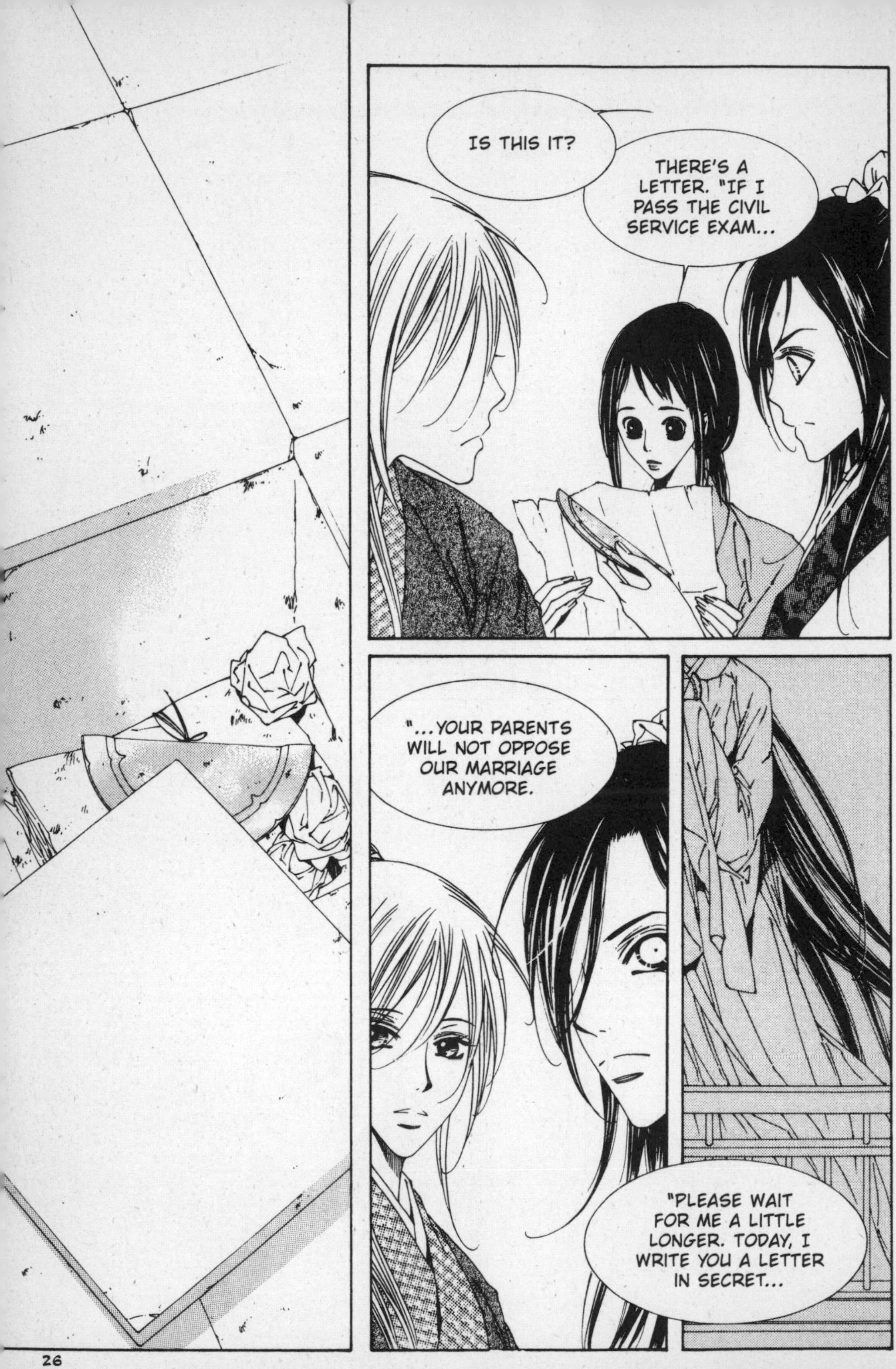
IS THIS IT?
THERE'S A LETTER. "IF I PASS THE CIVIL SERVICE EXAM...
"...YOUR PARENTS WILL NOT OPPOSE OUR MARRIAGE ANYMORE.
"PLEASE WAIT FOR ME A LITTLE LONGER. TODAY, I WRITE YOU A LETTER IN SECRET...

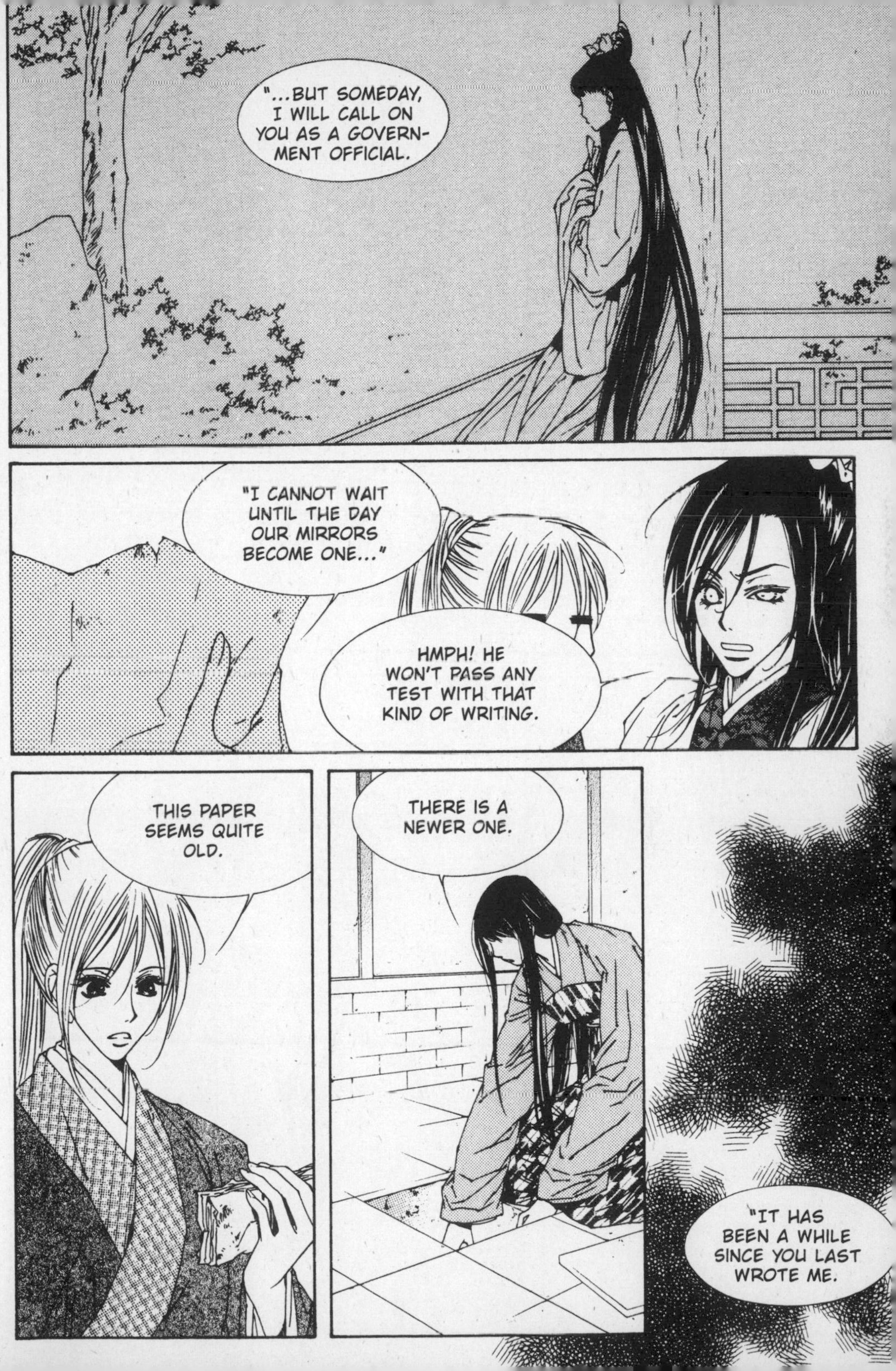
"...BUT SOMEDAY, I WILL CALL ON YOU AS A GOVERNMENT OFFICIAL.
"I CANNOT WAIT UNTIL THE DAY OUR MIRRORS BECOME ONE..."
HMPH! HE WON'T PASS ANY TEST WITH THAT KIND OF WRITING.
THIS PAPER SEEMS QUITE OLD.
THERE IS A NEWER ONE.
"IT HAS BEEN A WHILE SINCE YOU LAST WROTE ME.

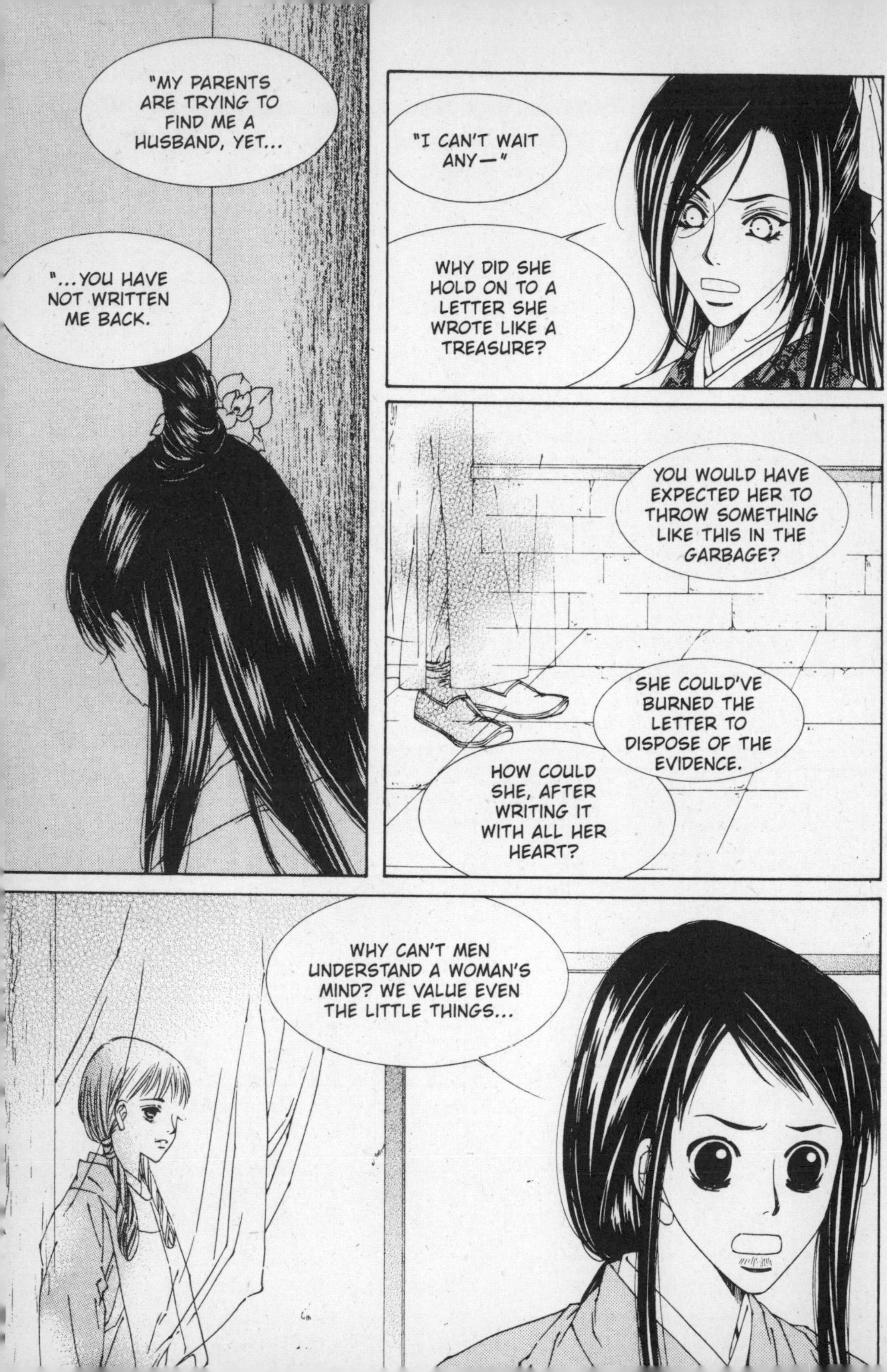
"MY PARENTS ARE TRYING TO FIND ME A HUSBAND, YET...
"...YOU HAVE NOT WRITTEN ME BACK.
"I CAN'T WAIT ANY—"
WHY DID SHE HOLD ON TO A LETTER SHE WROTE LIKE A TREASURE?
YOU WOULD HAVE EXPECTED HER TO THROW SOMETHING LIKE THIS IN THE GARBAGE?
SHE COULD'VE BURNED THE LETTER TO DISPOSE OF THE EVIDENCE.
HOW COULD SHE, AFTER WRITING IT WITH ALL HER HEART?
WHY CAN'T MEN UNDERSTAND A WOMAN'S MIND? WE VALUE EVEN THE LITTLE THINGS...

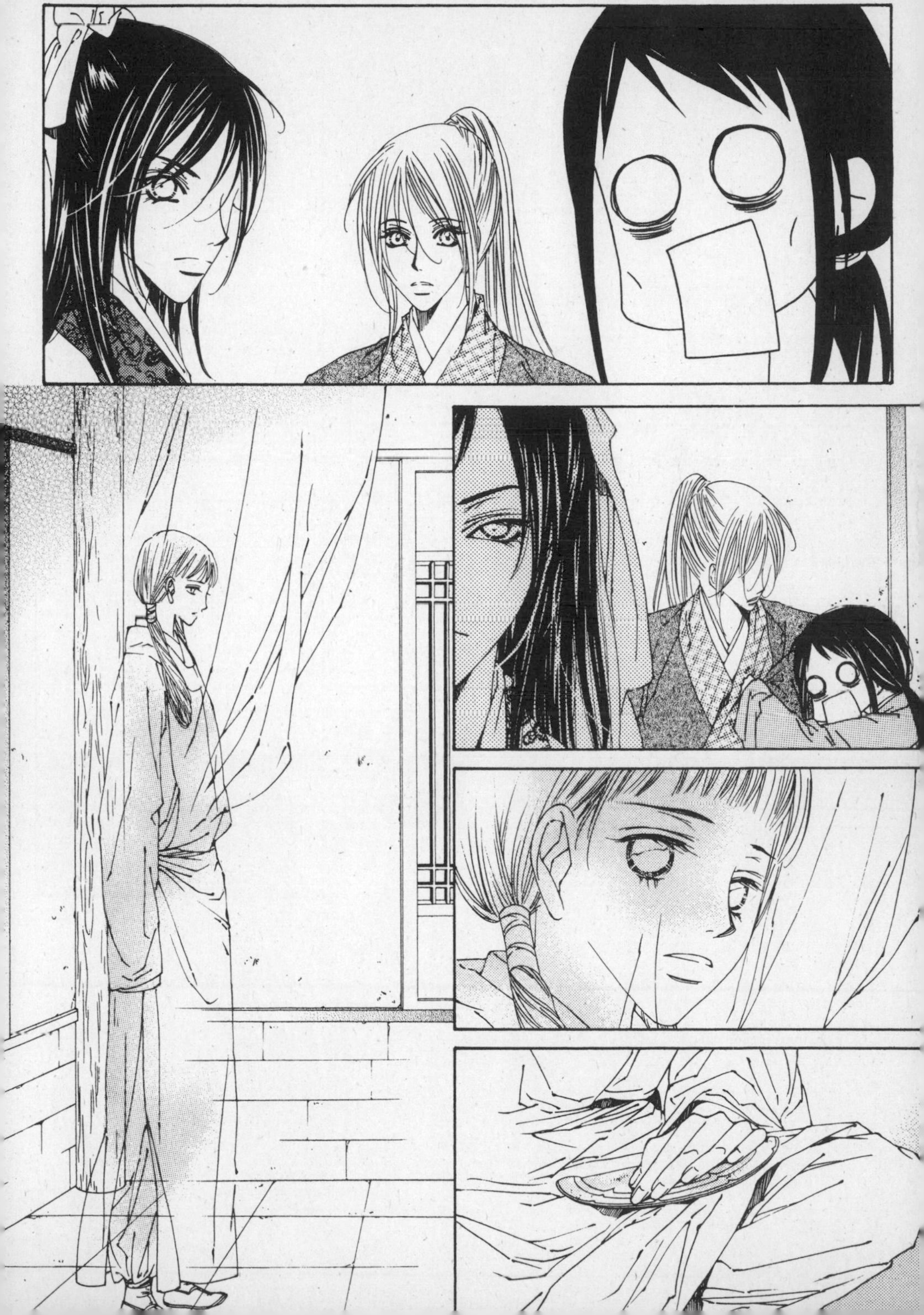

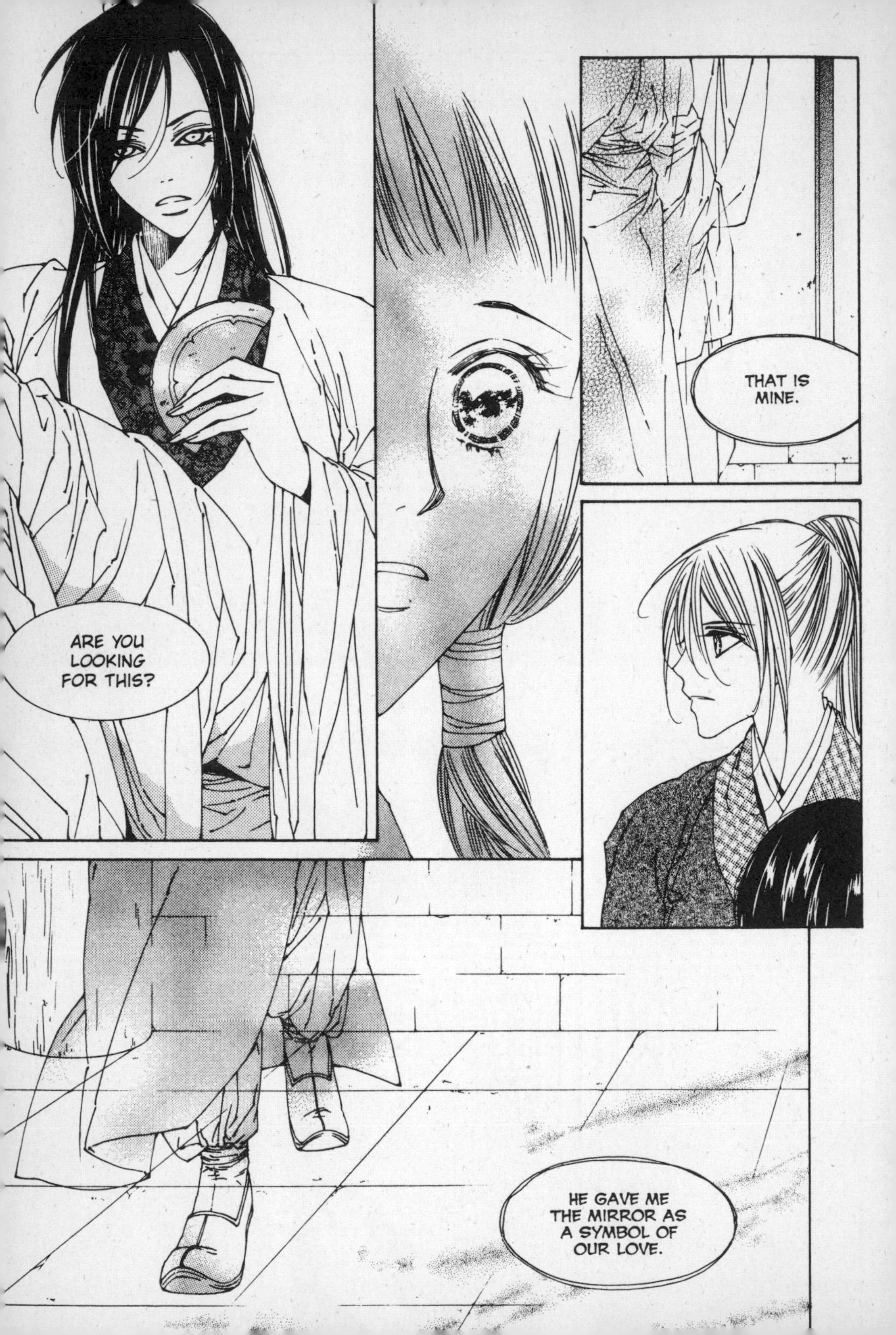
ARE YOU LOOKING FOR THIS?
THAT IS MINE.
HE GAVE ME THE MIRROR AS A SYMBOL OF OUR LOVE.

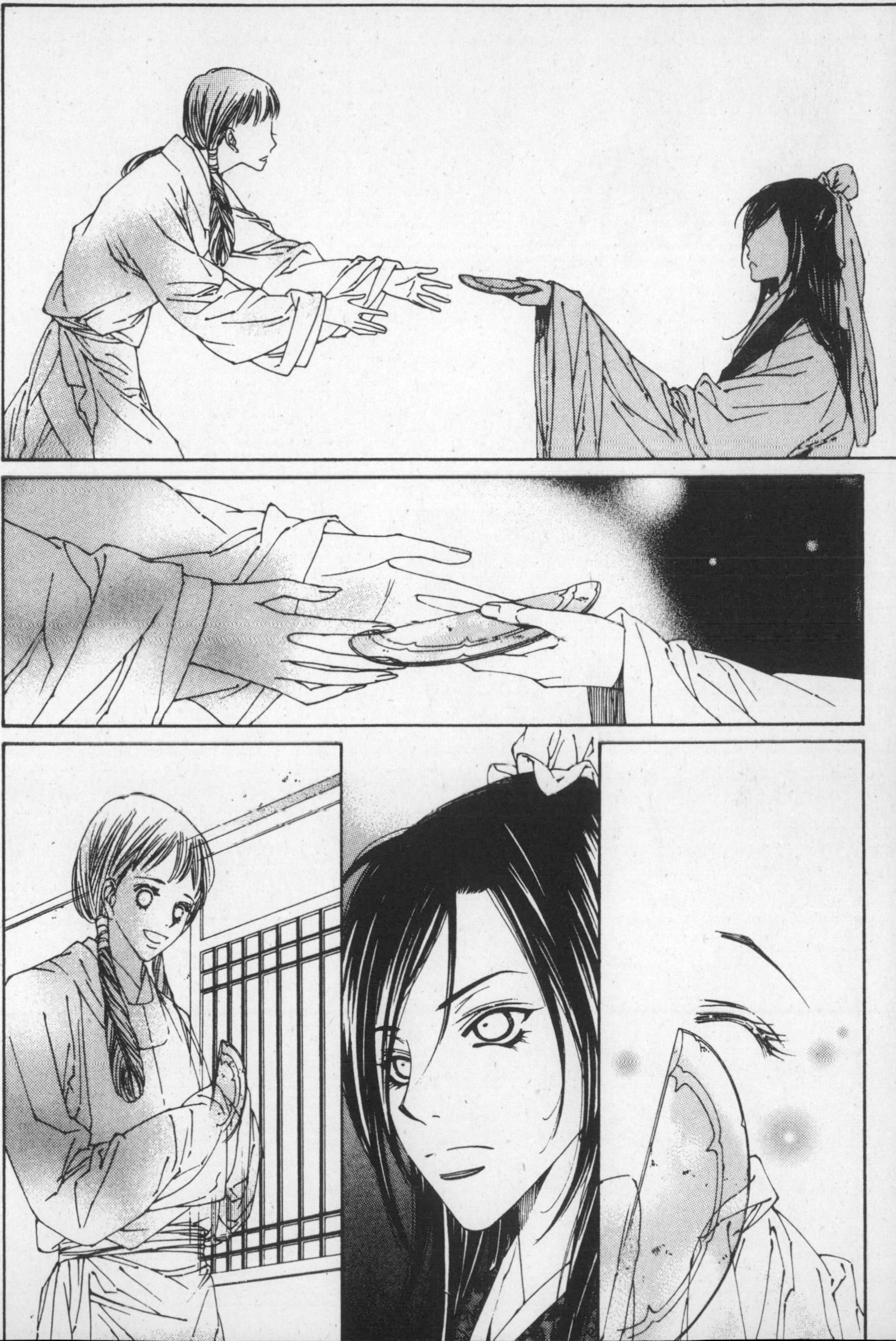

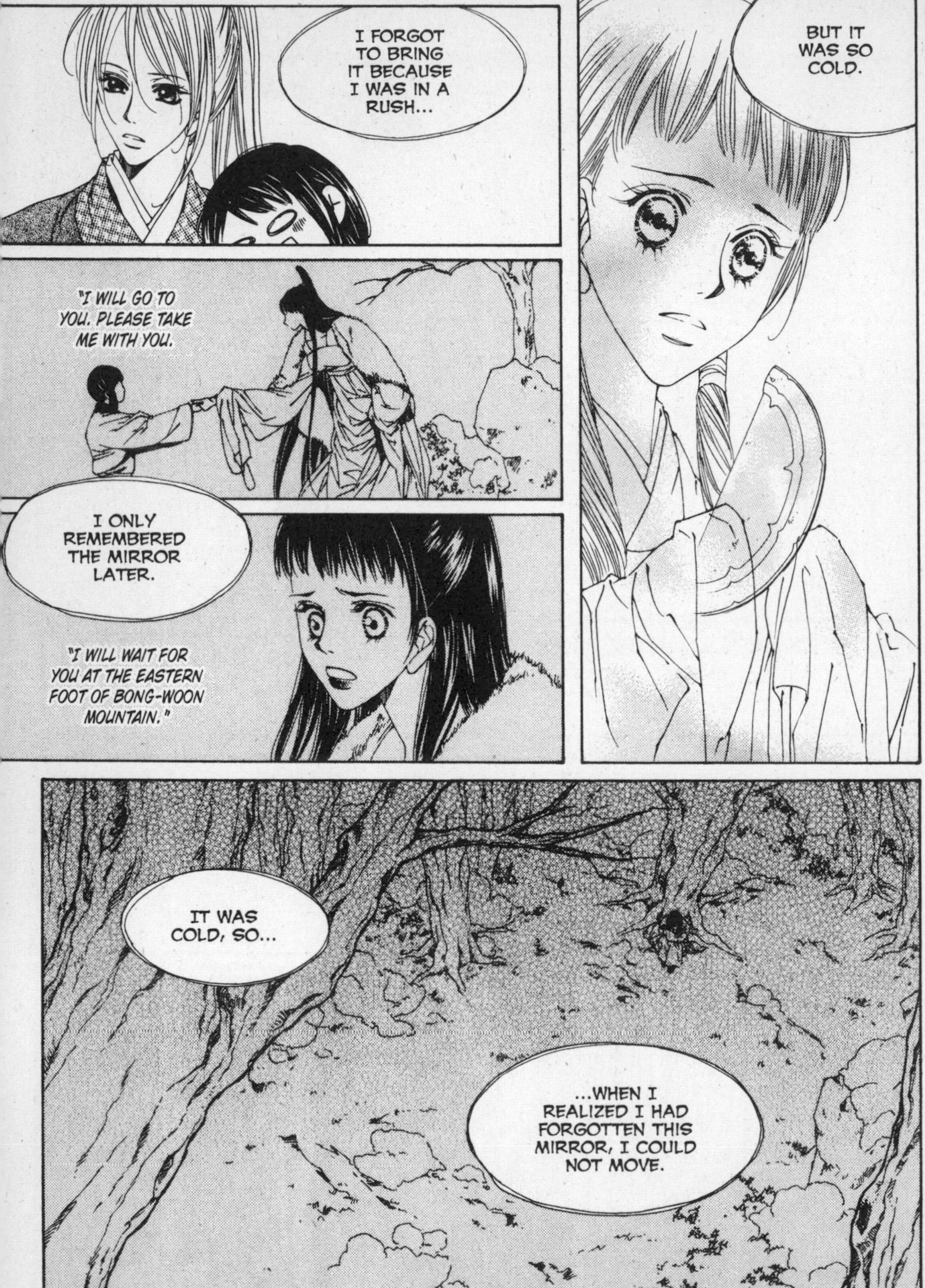
I FORGOT TO BRING IT BECAUSE I WAS IN A RUSH...
"I WILL GO TO YOU. PLEASE TAKE ME WITH YOU.
I ONLY REMEMBERED THE MIRROR LATER.
"I WILL WAIT FOR YOU AT THE EASTERN FOOT OF BONG-WOON MOUNTAIN."
BUT IT WAS SO COLD.
IT WAS COLD, SO...
...WHEN I REALIZED I HAD FORGOTTEN THIS MIRROR, I COULD NOT MOVE.

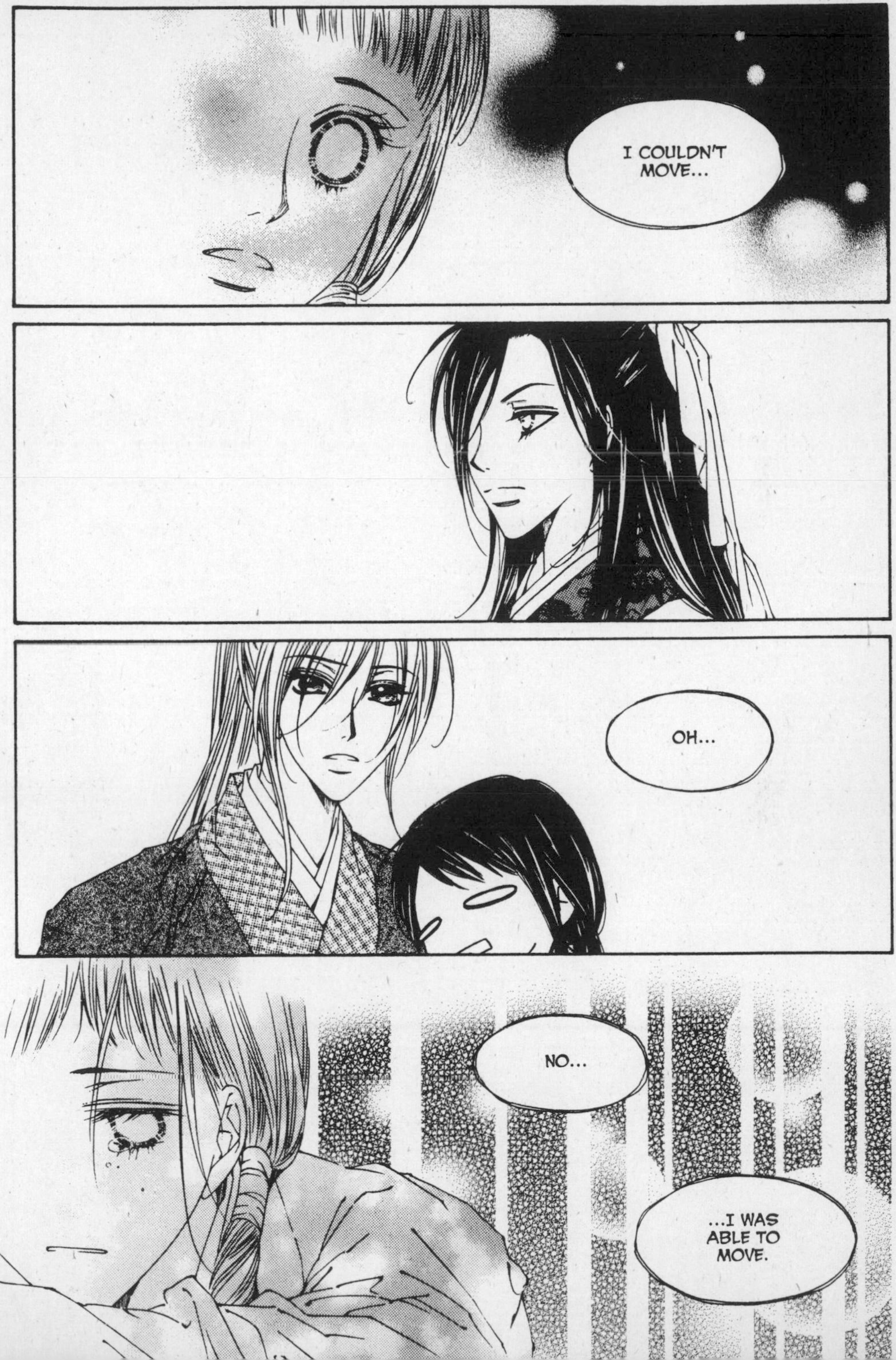
I COULDN'T MOVE...
OH...
NO...
...I WAS ABLE TO MOVE.

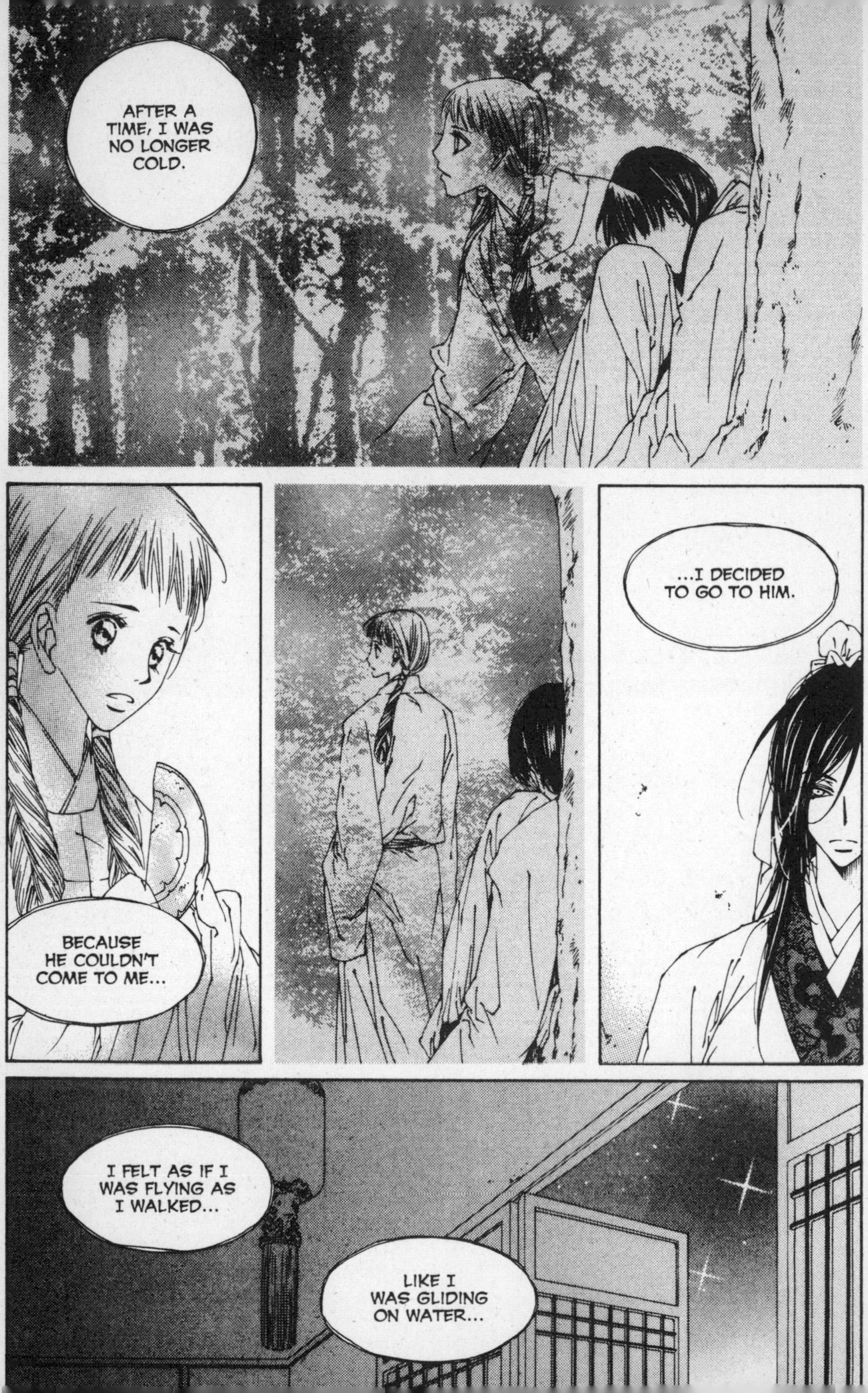
AFTER A TIME, I WAS NO LONGER COLD.
BECAUSE HE COULDN'T COME TO ME...
...I DECIDED TO GO TO HIM.
I FELT AS IF I WAS FLYING AS I WALKED...
LIKE I WAS GLIDING ON WATER...

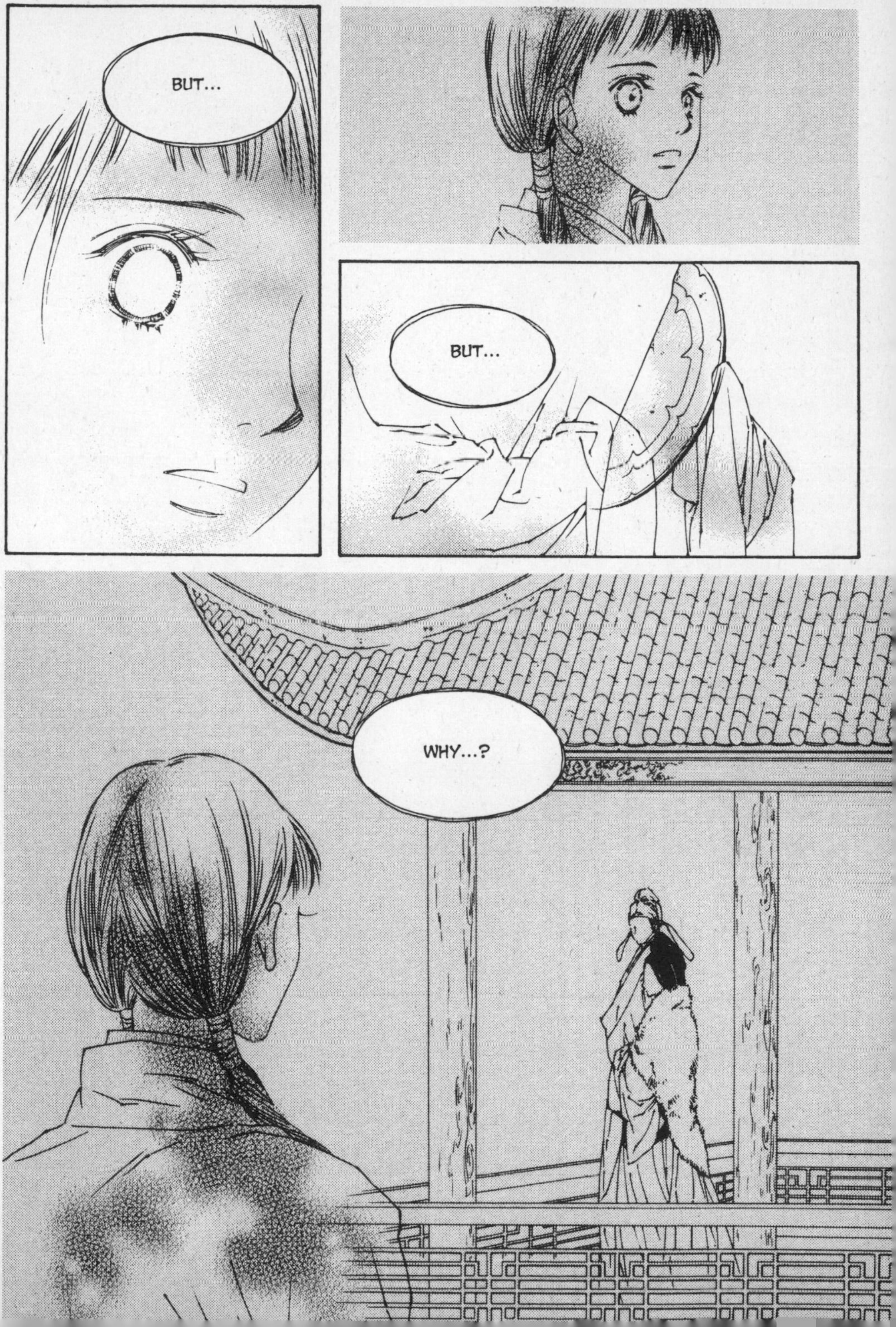
BUT...
BUT...
WHY...?

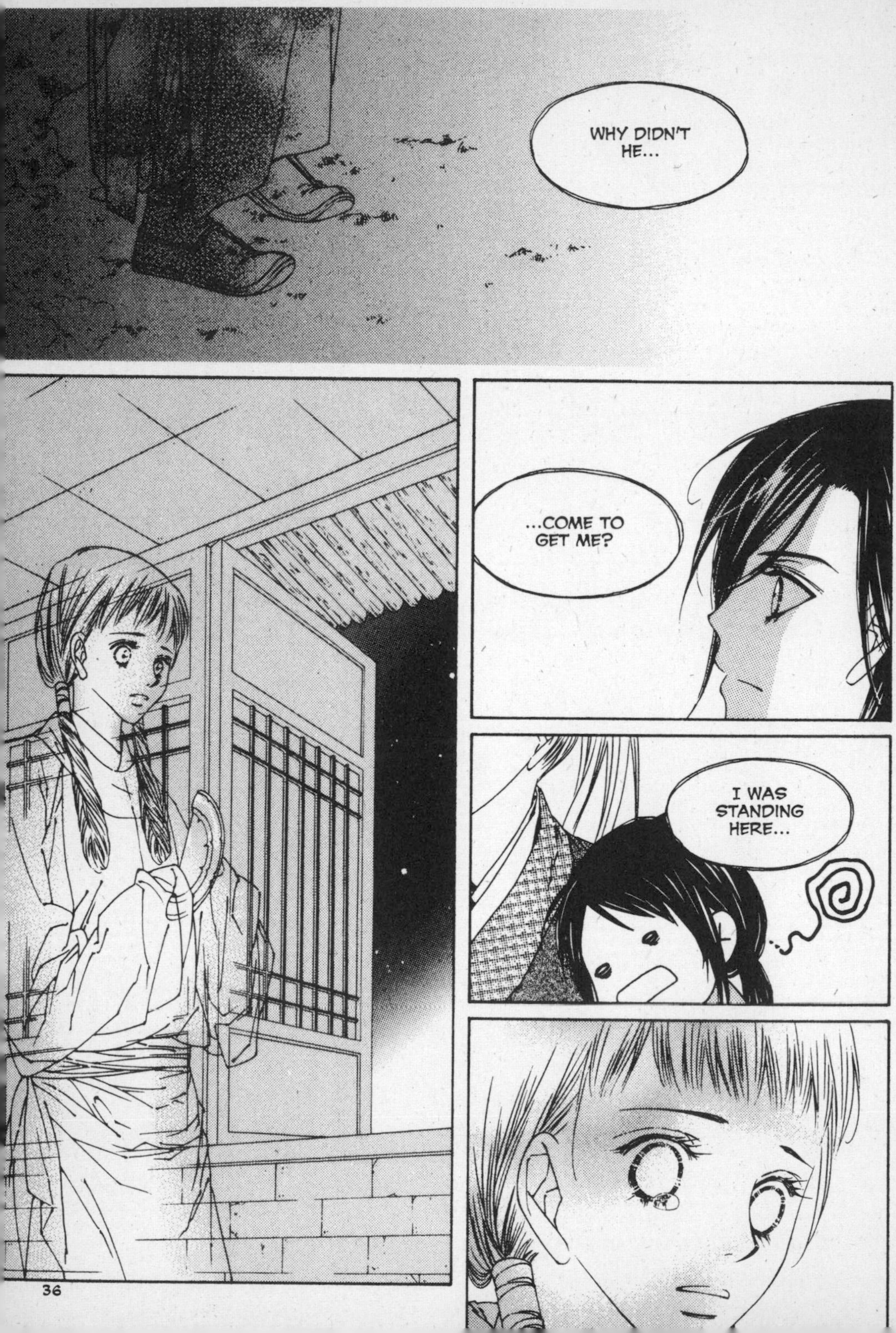
WHY DIDN'T HE...
...COME TO GET ME?
I WAS STANDING HERE...

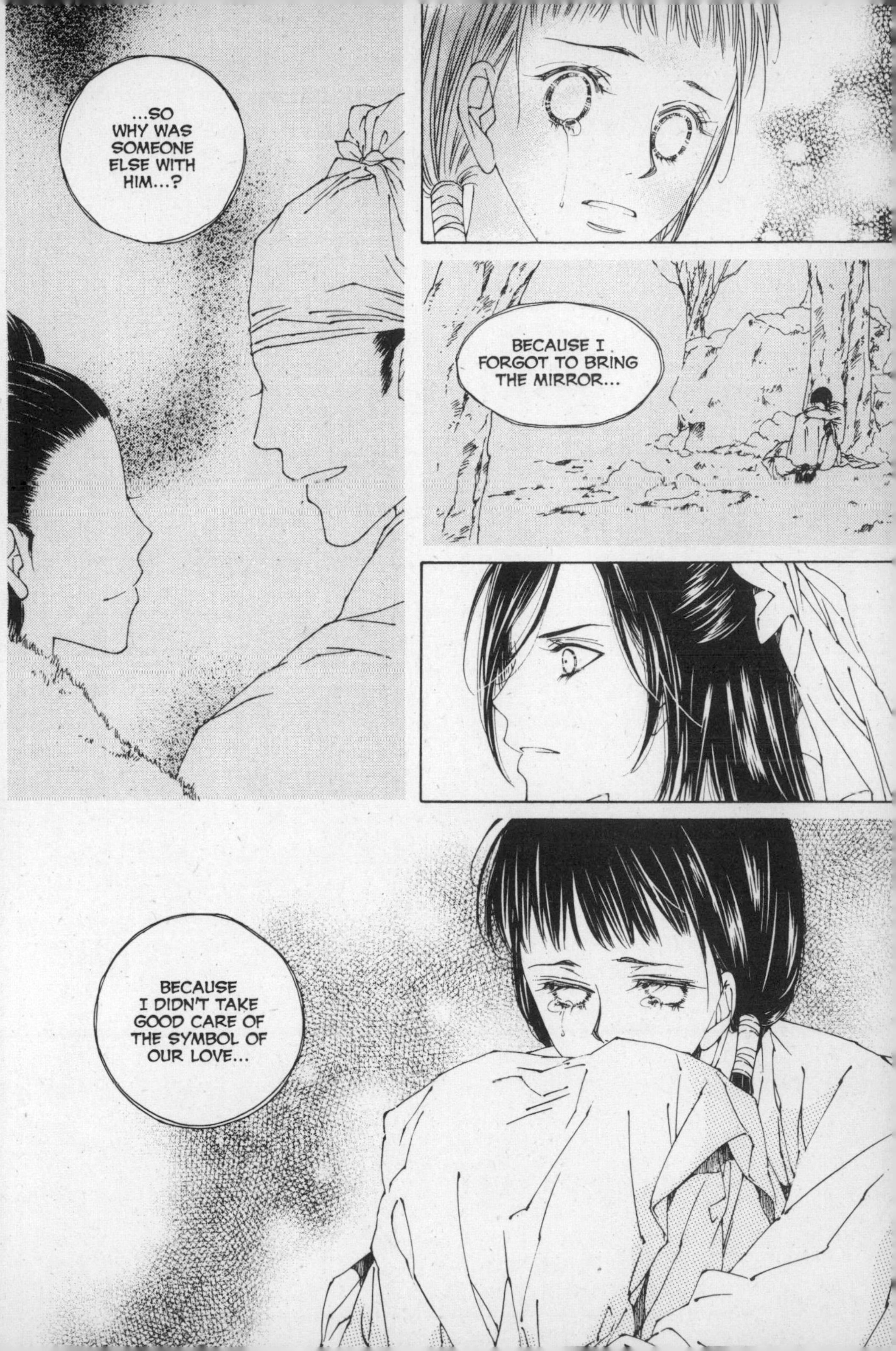
...SO WHY WAS SOMEONE ELSE WITH HIM...?
BECAUSE I FORGOT TO BRING THE MIRROR...
BECAUSE I DIDN'T TAKE GOOD CARE OF THE SYMBOL OF OUR LOVE...

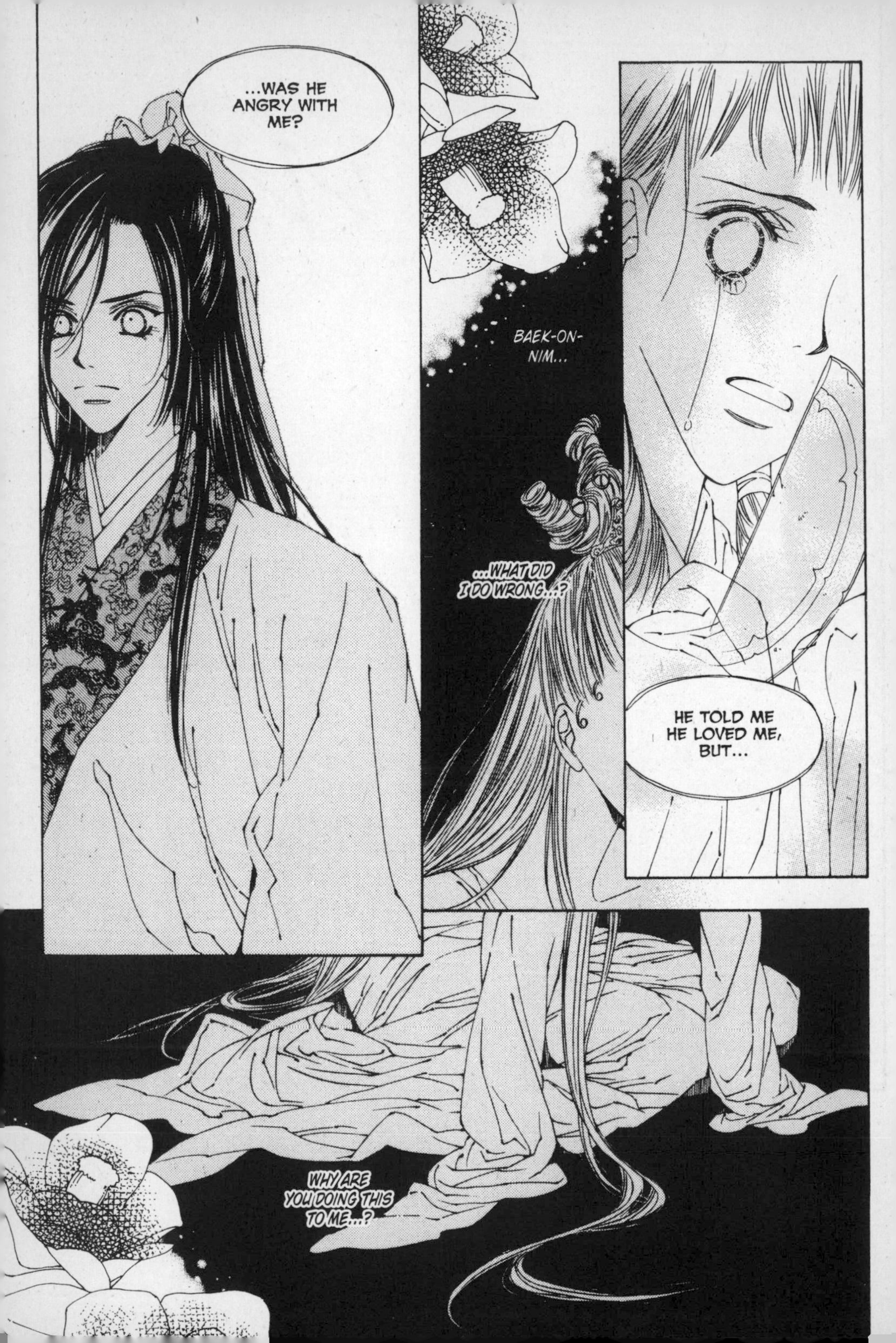
...WAS HE ANGRY WITH ME?
BAEK-ON-NIM...
...WHAT DID I DO WRONG...?
HE TOLD ME HE LOVED ME, BUT...
WHY ARE YOU DOING THIS TO ME...?

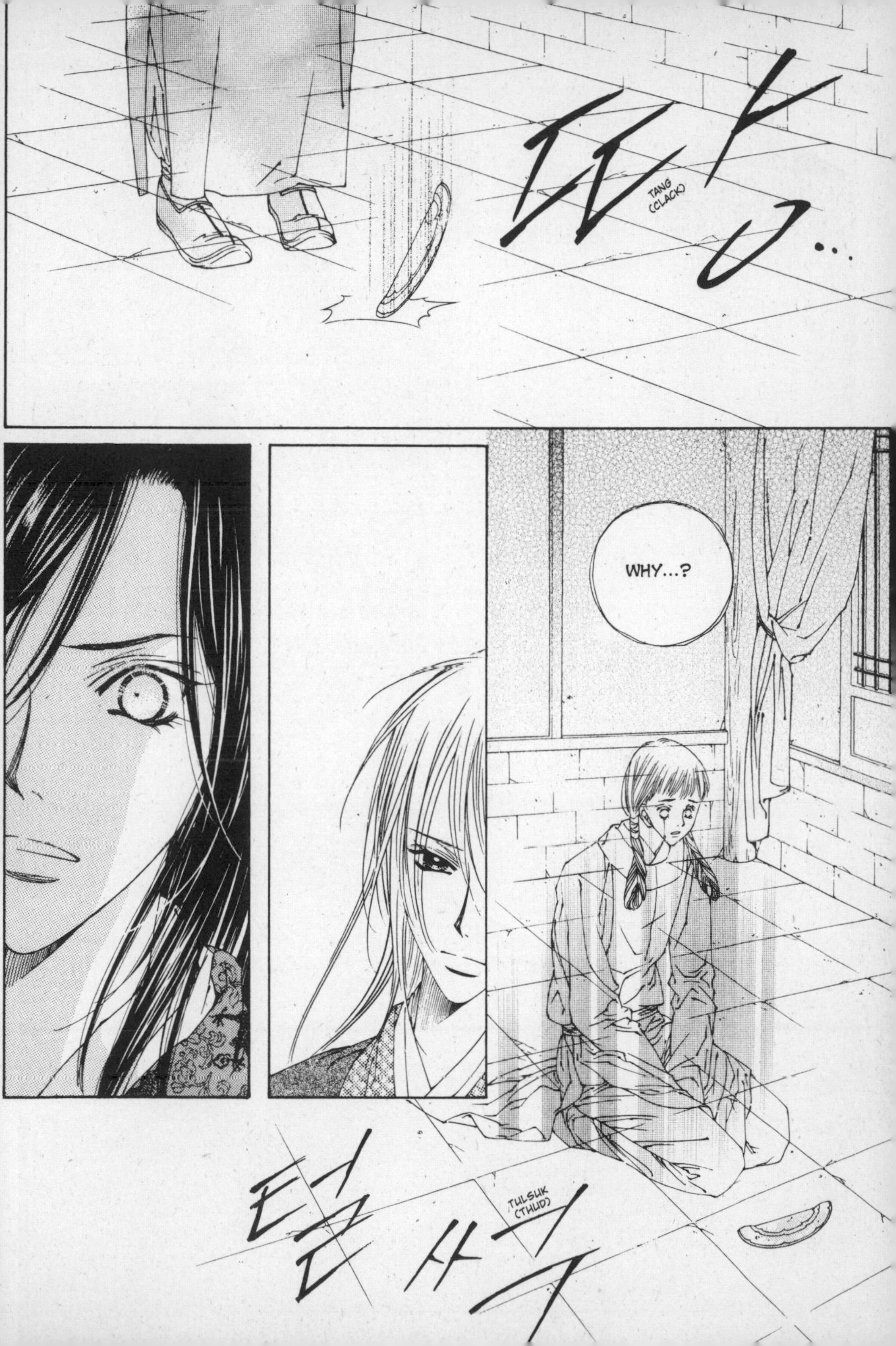
땅..
TANG (CLACK)
WHY...?
털썩
TULSUK (THUD)

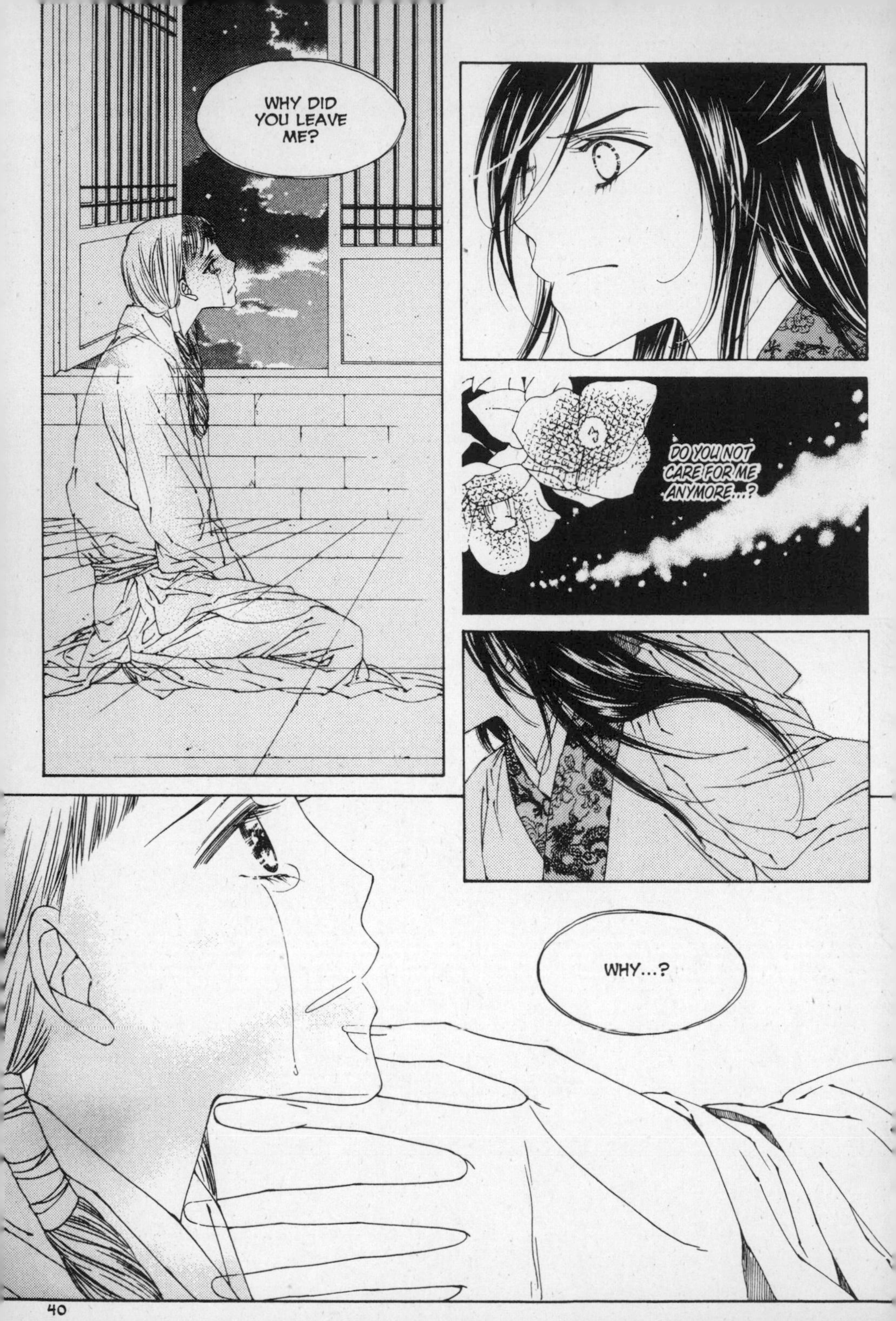
WHY DID YOU LEAVE ME?
DO YOU NOT CARE FOR ME ANYMORE...?
WHY...?

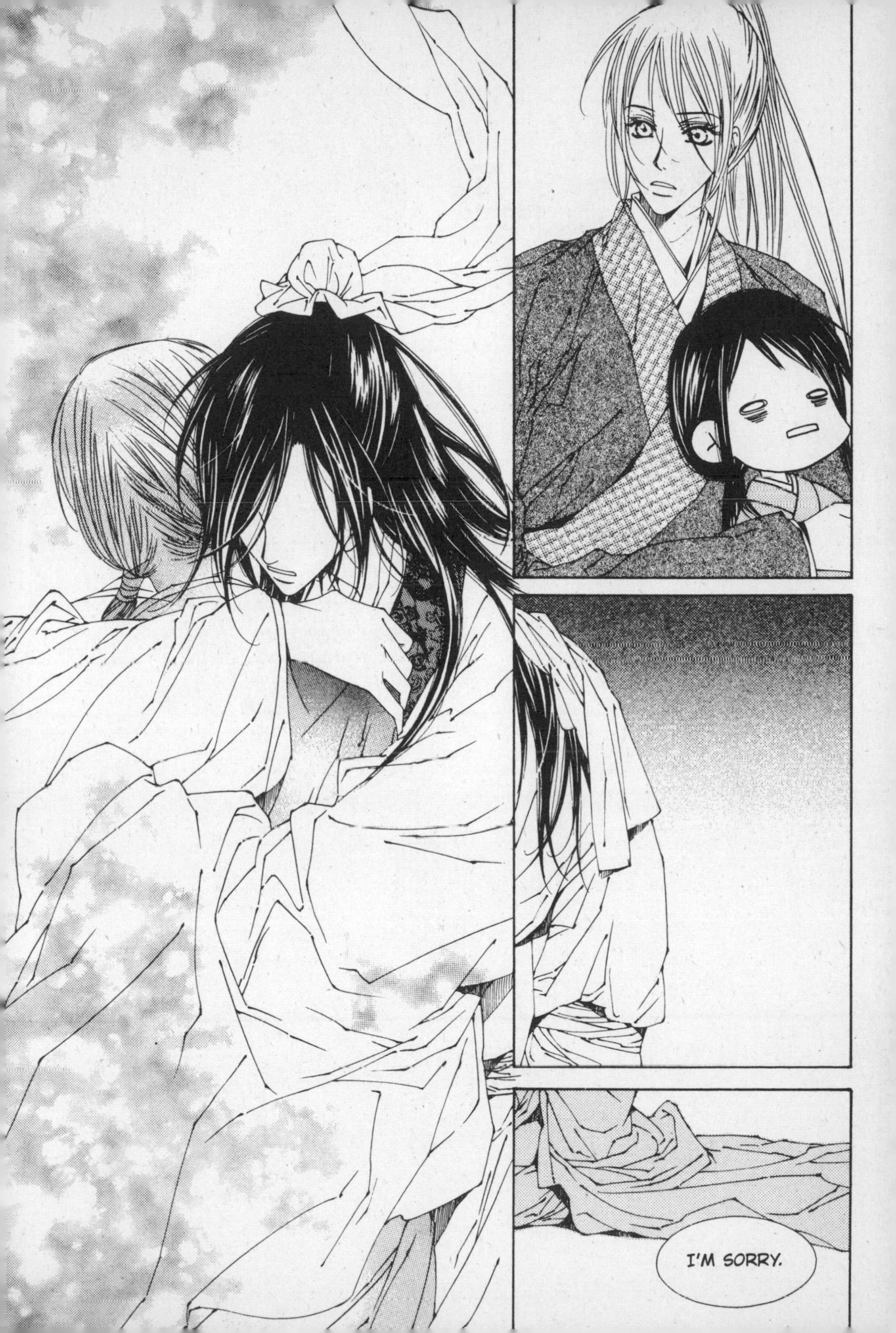
I'M SORRY.

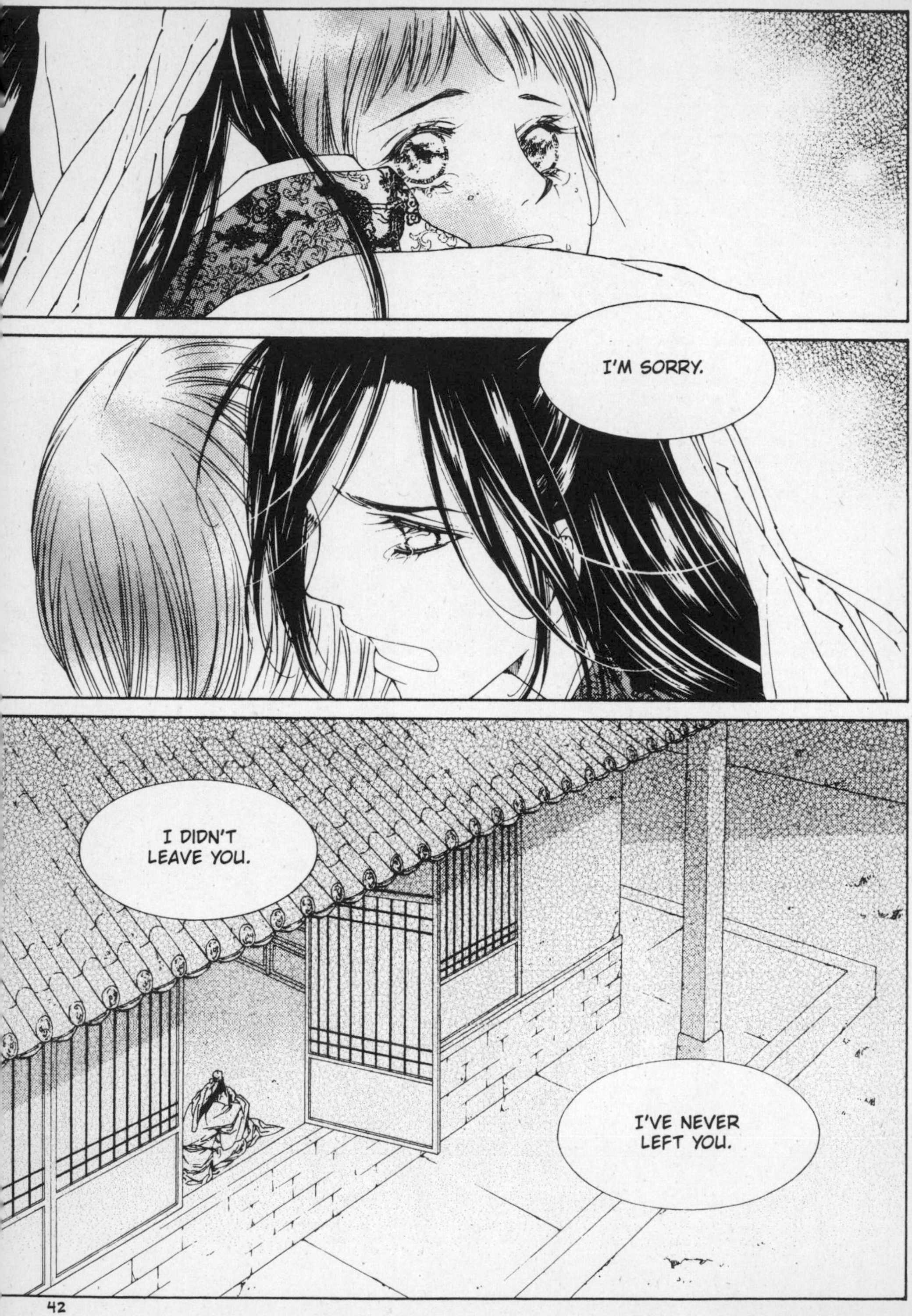
I'M SORRY.
I DIDN'T LEAVE YOU.
I'VE NEVER LEFT YOU.

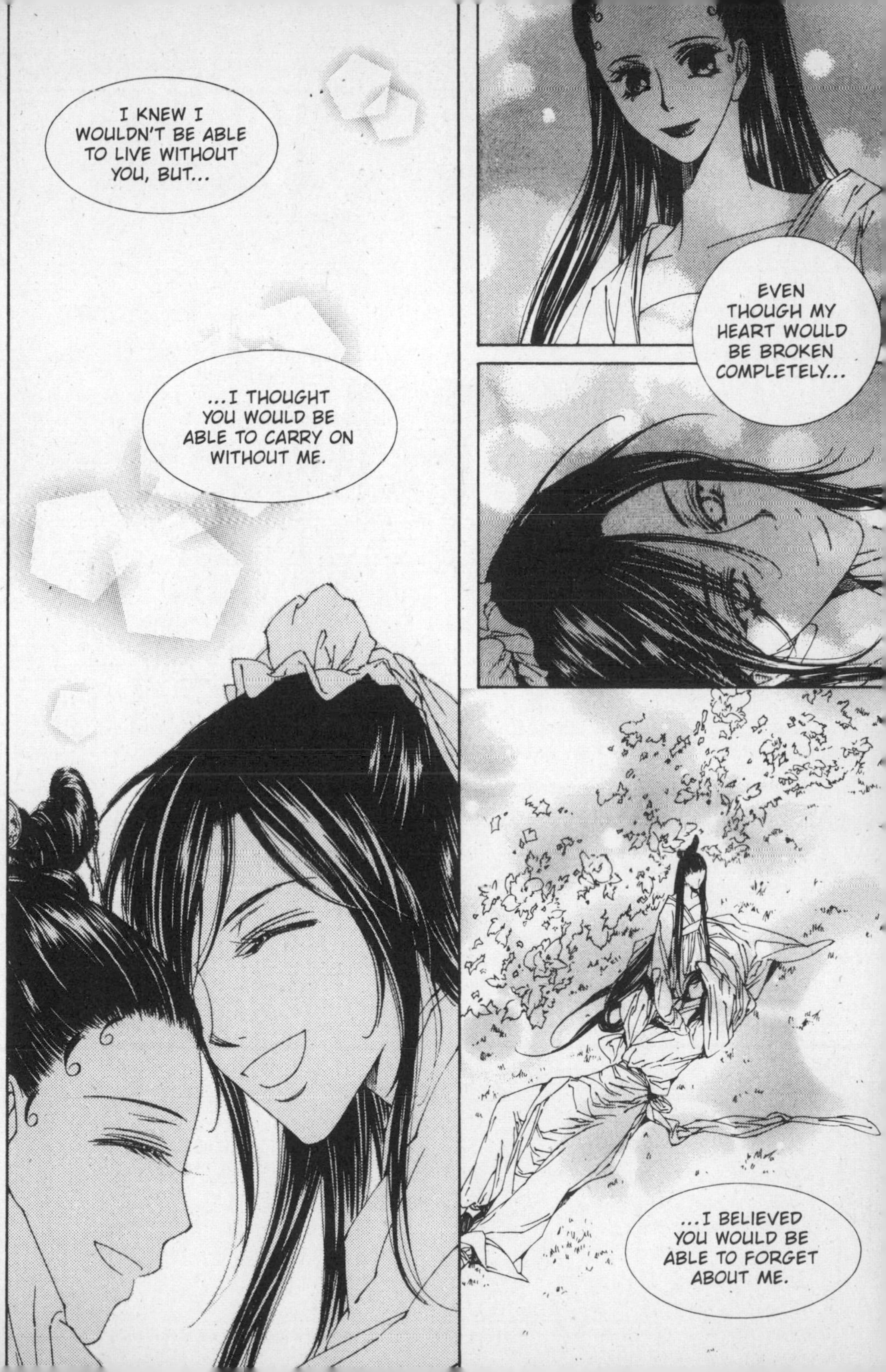
I KNEW I WOULDN'T BE ABLE TO LIVE WITHOUT YOU, BUT...
...I THOUGHT YOU WOULD BE ABLE TO CARRY ON WITHOUT ME.
EVEN THOUGH MY HEART WOULD BE BROKEN COMPLETELY...
...I BELIEVED YOU WOULD BE ABLE TO FORGET ABOUT ME.

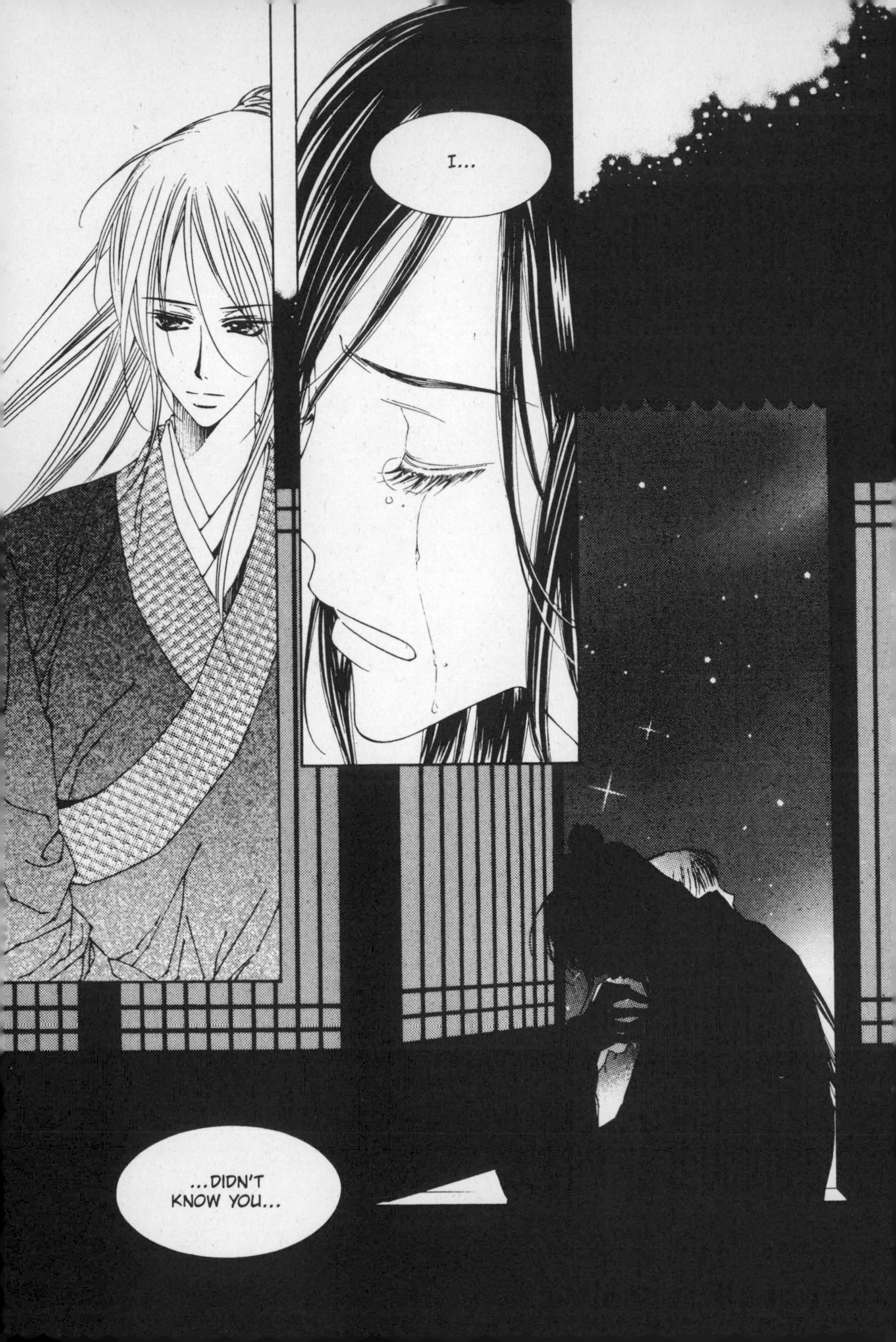
I...
...DIDN'T KNOW YOU...

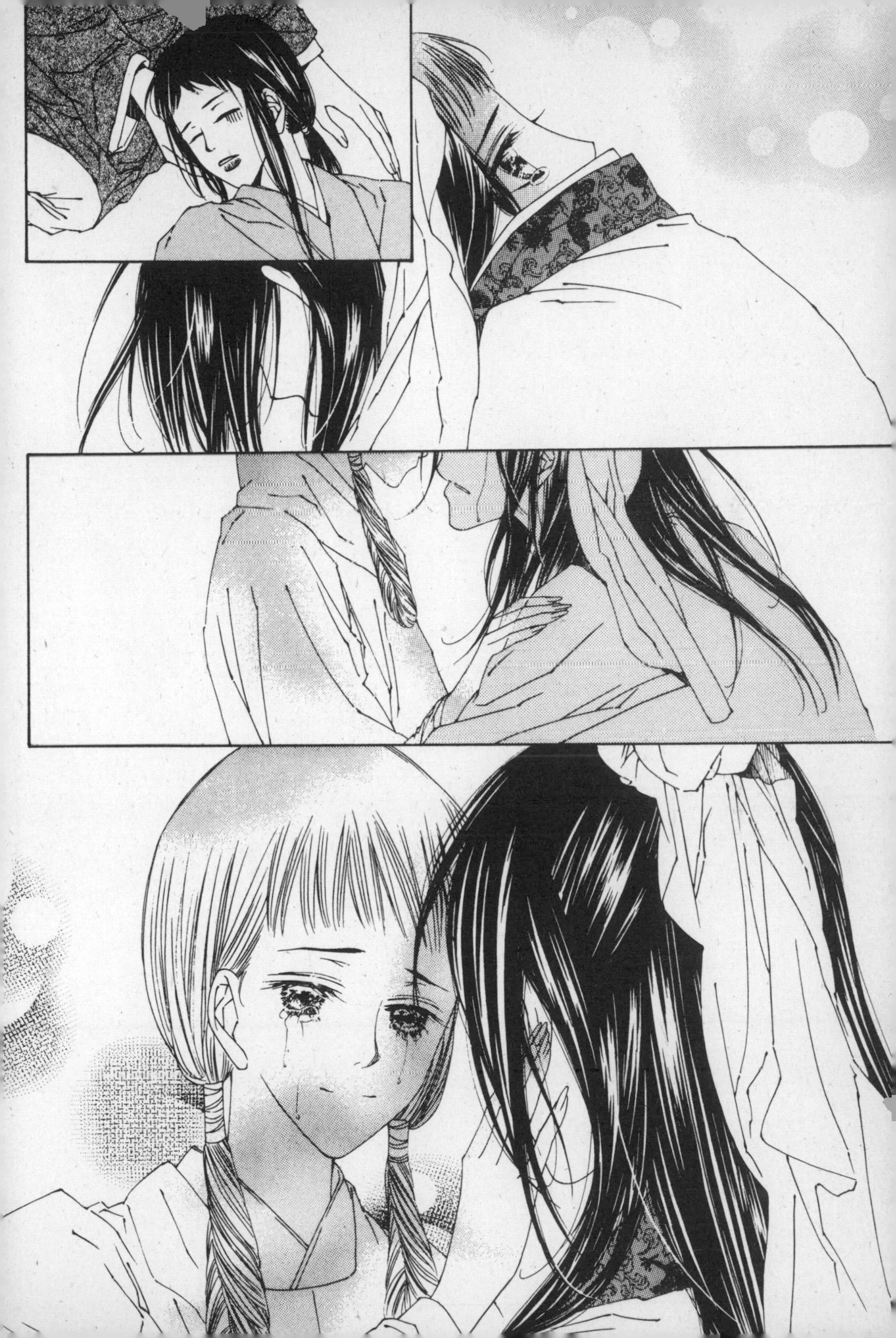

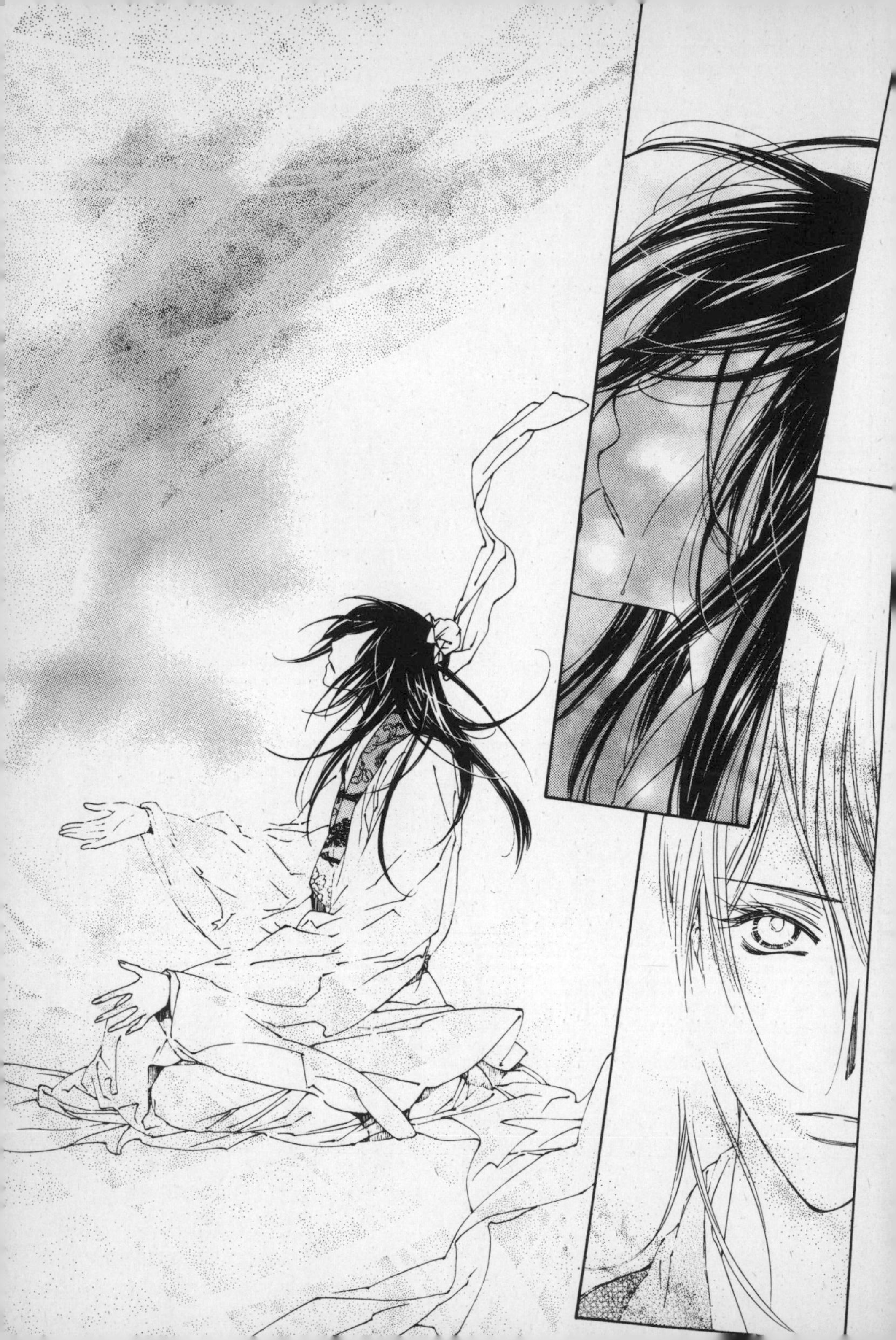

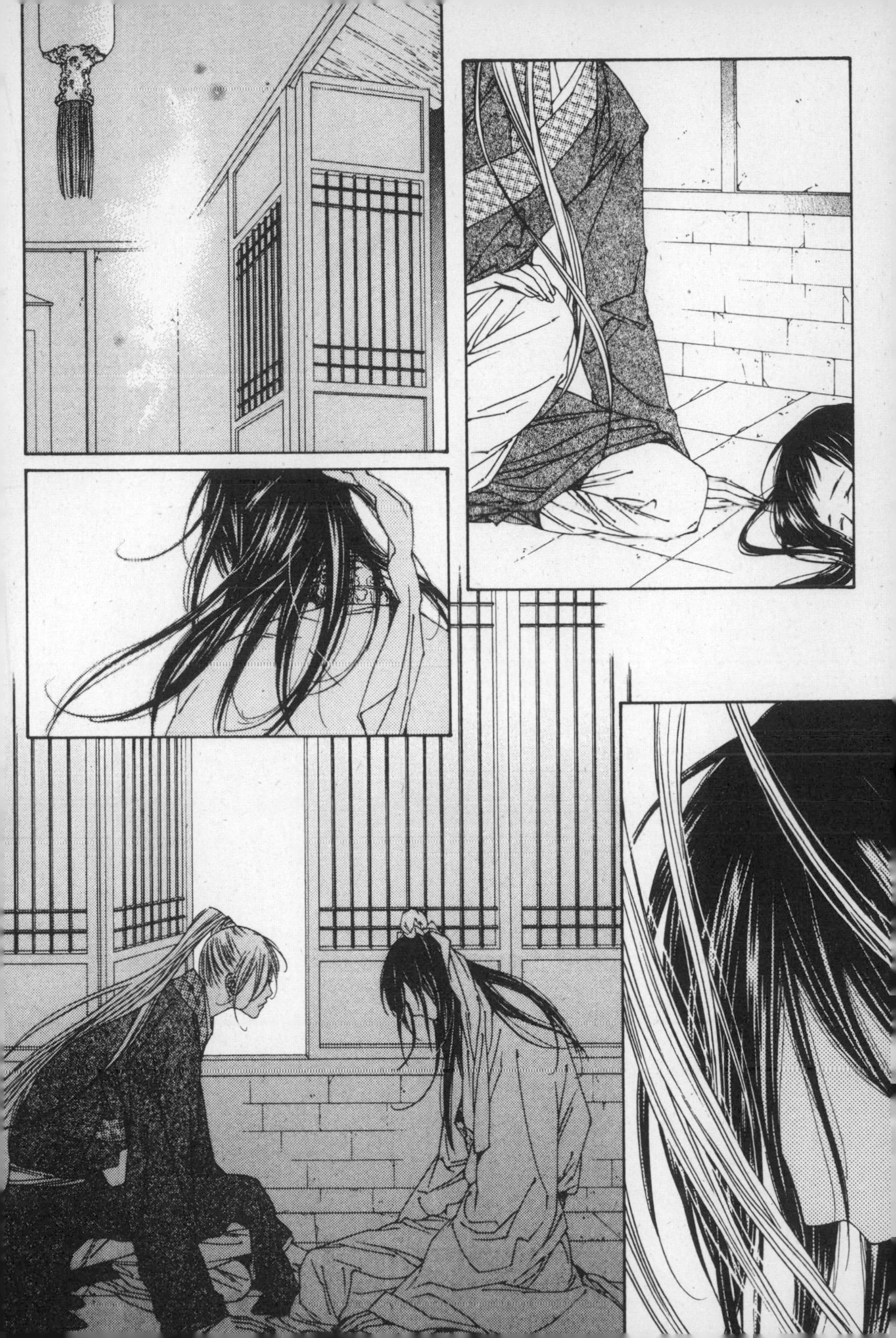

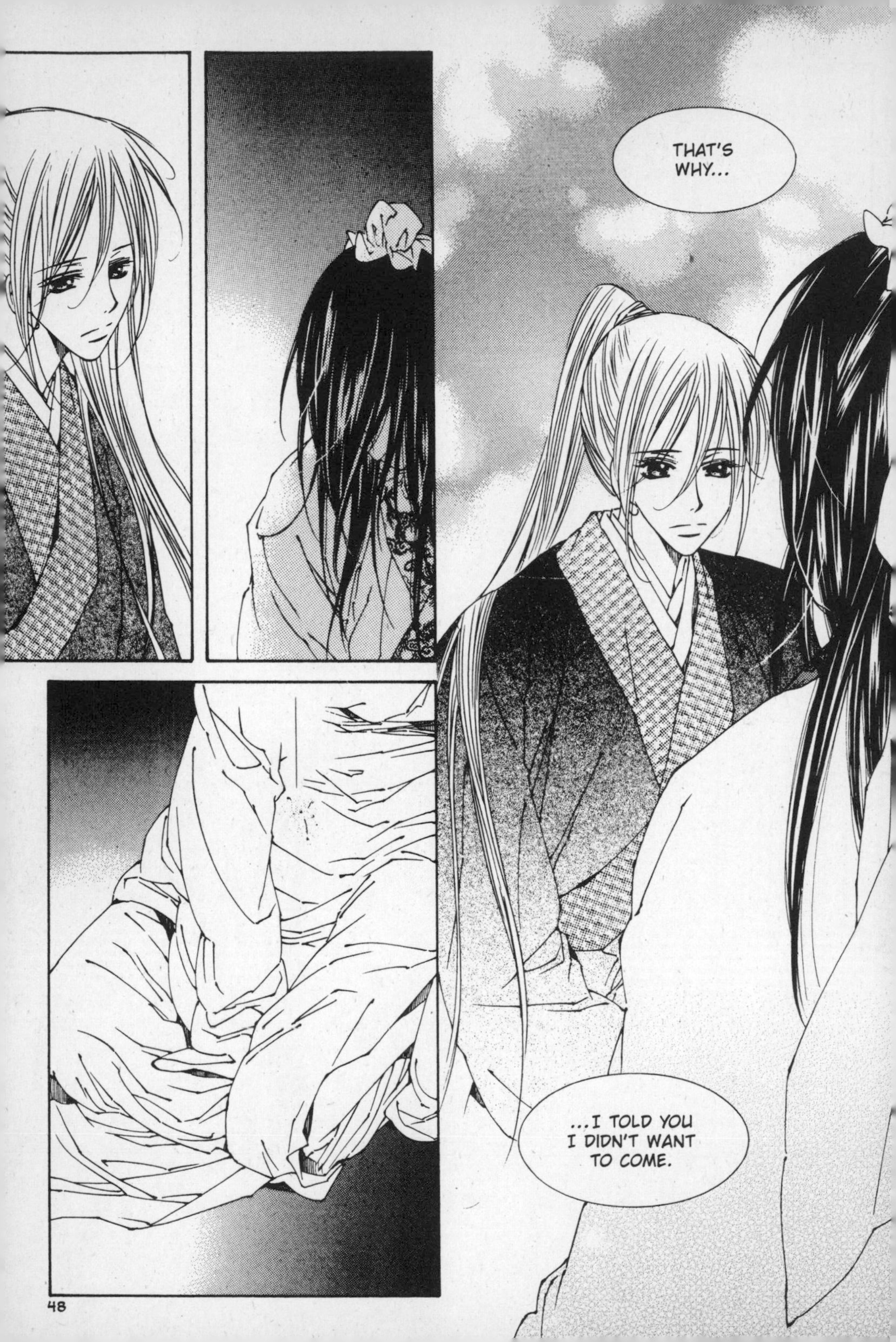
THAT'S WHY...
...I TOLD YOU I DIDN'T WANT TO COME.

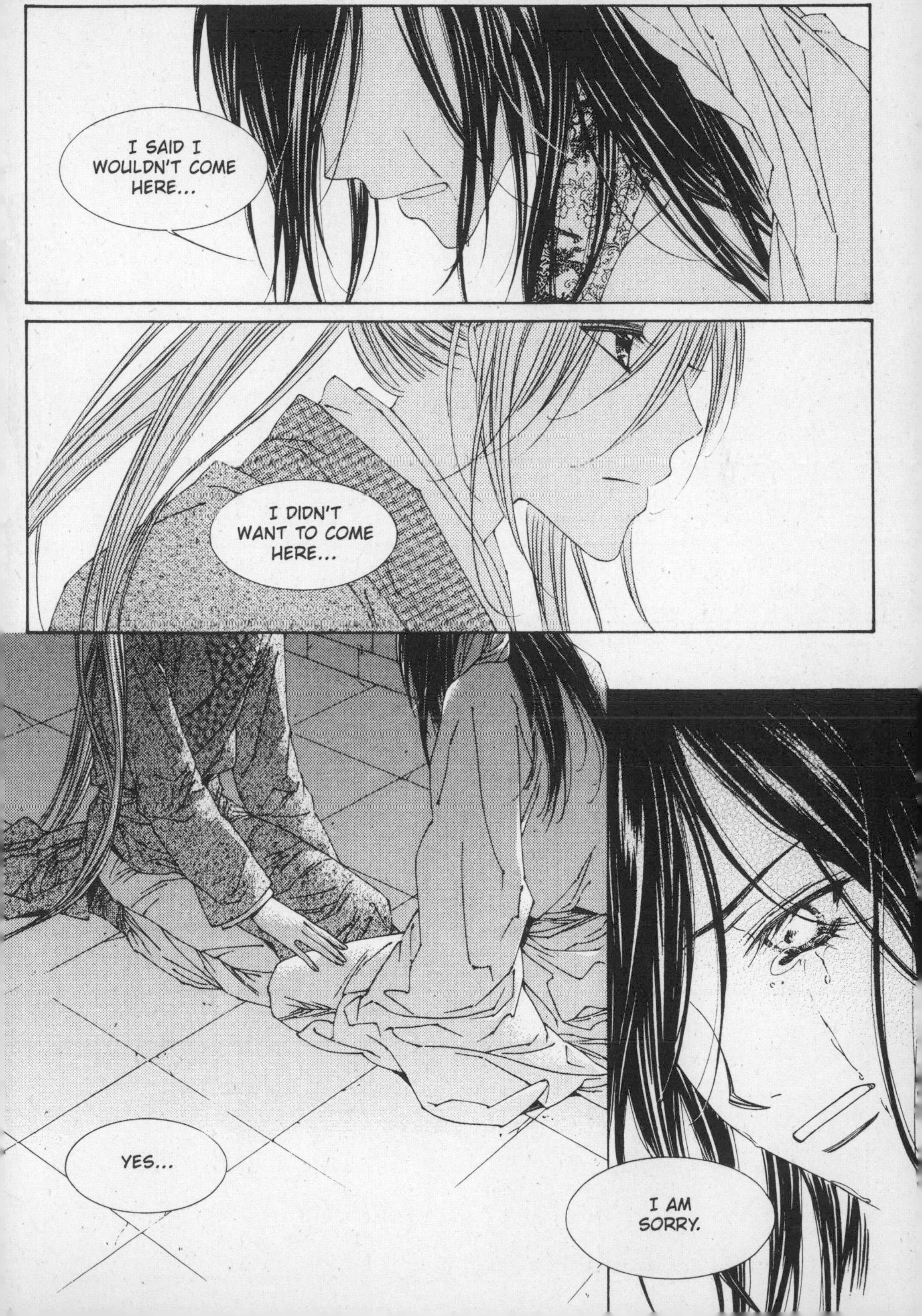
I SAID I WOULDN'T COME HERE...
I DIDN'T WANT TO COME HERE...
YES...
I AM SORRY.

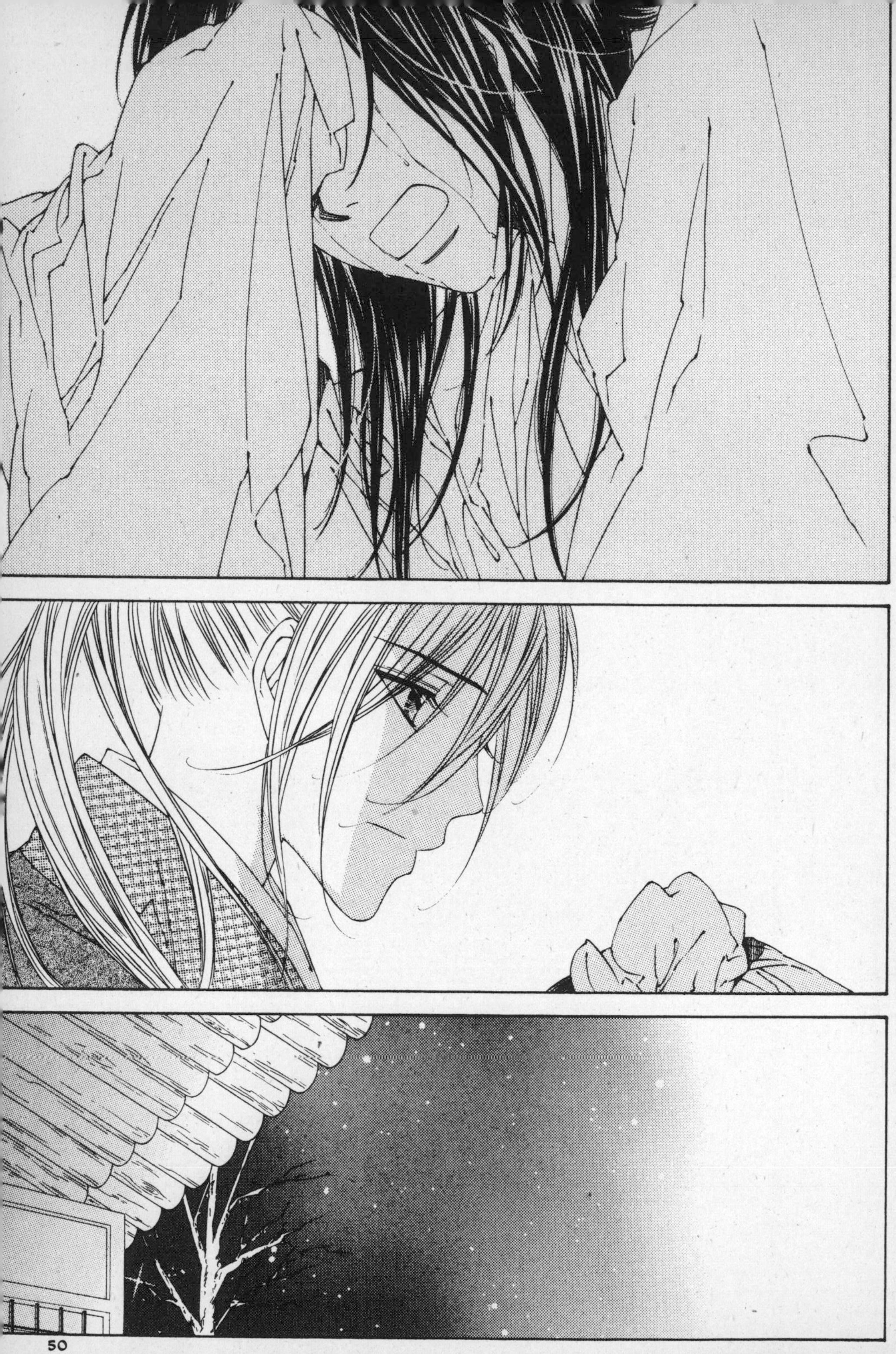

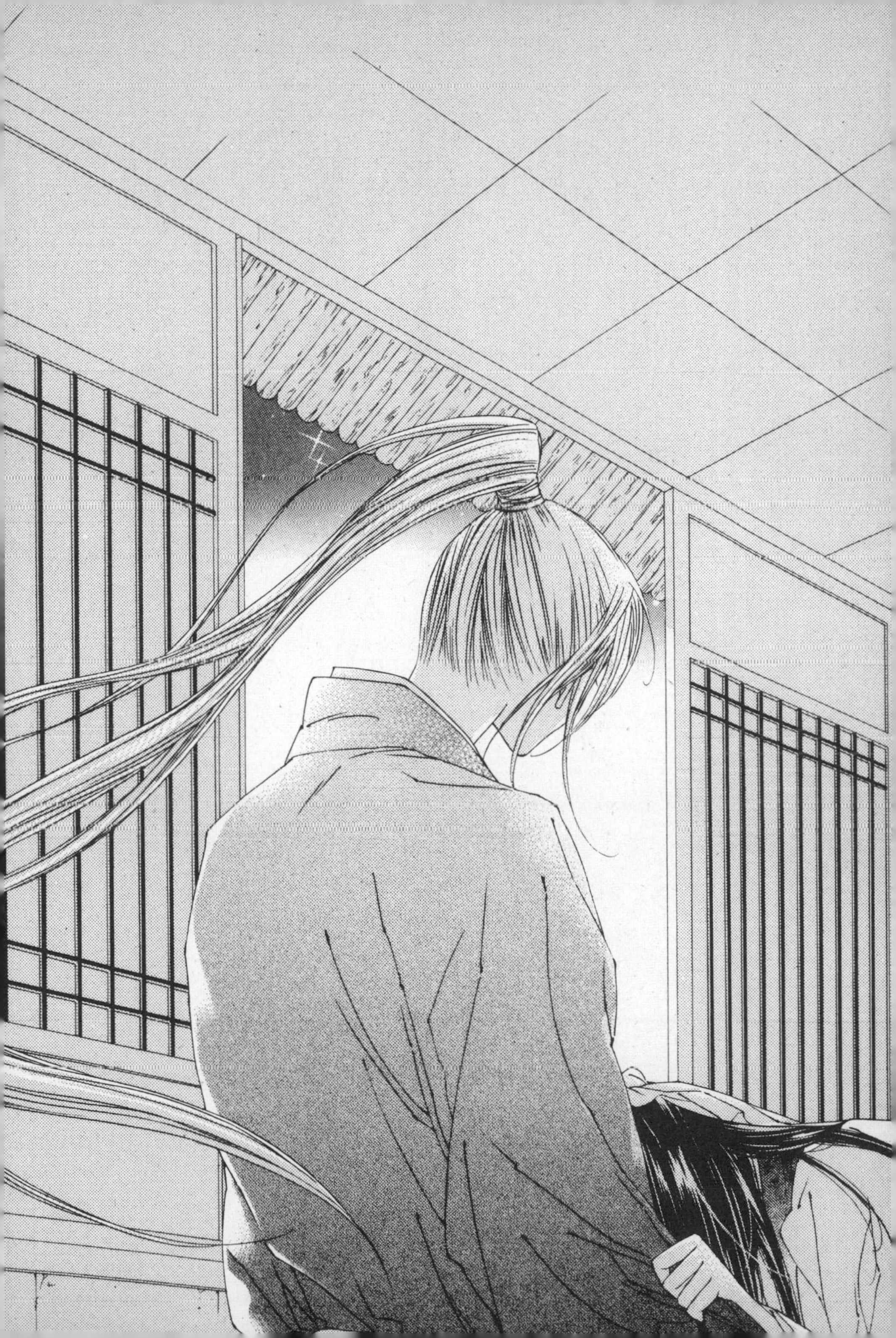

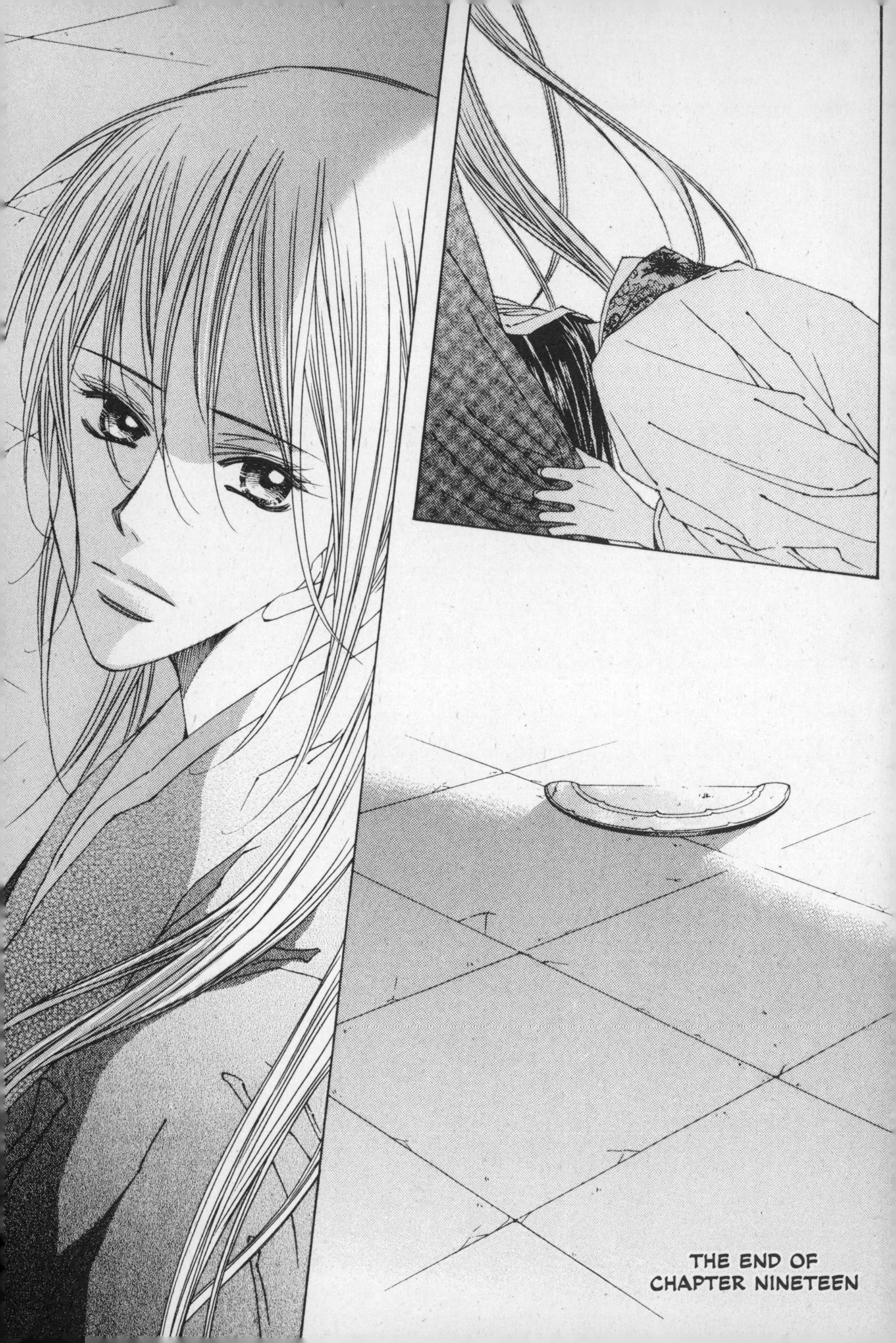
THE END OF
CHAPTER NINETEEN

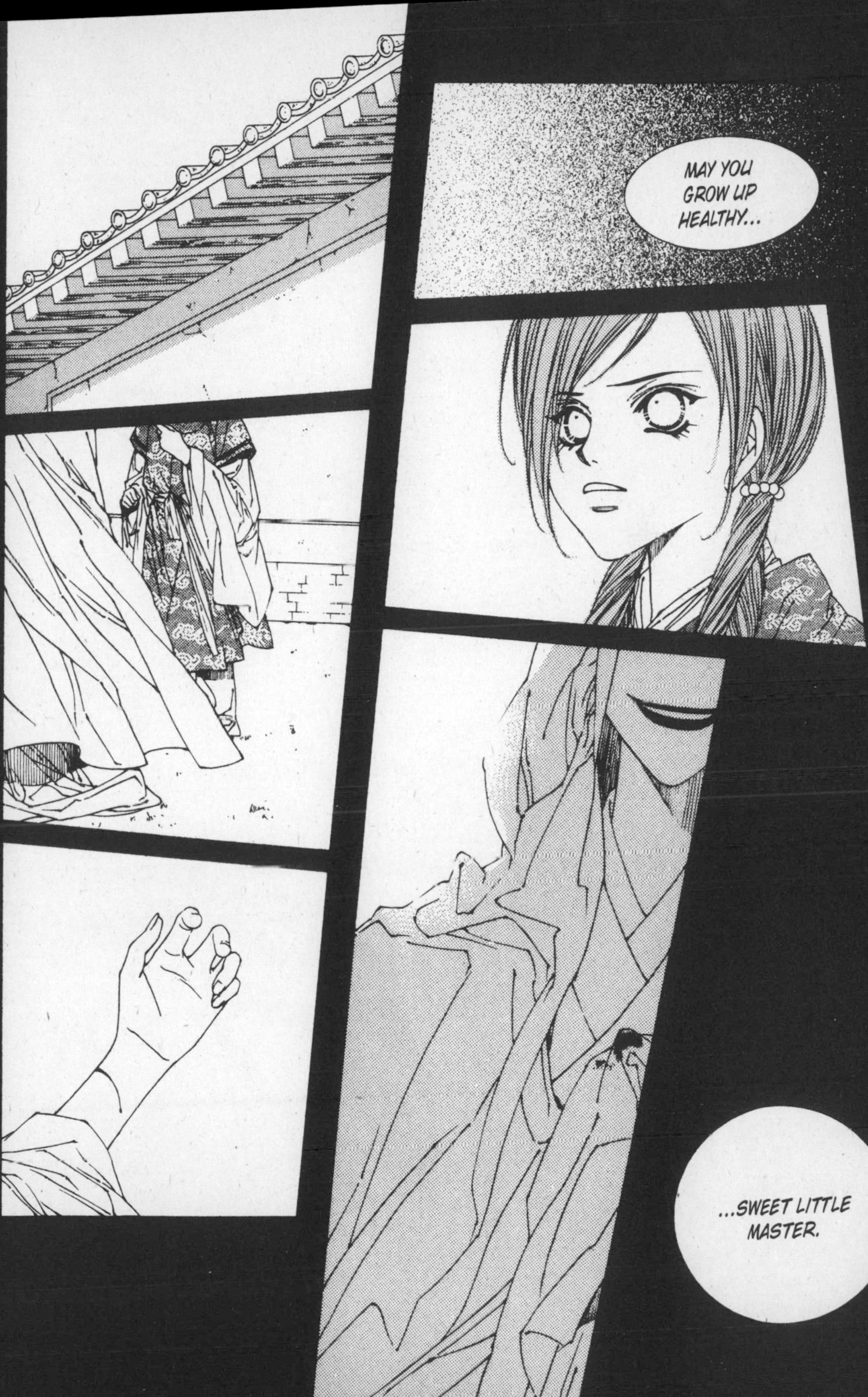
MAY YOU GROW UP HEALTHY...
...SWEET LITTLE MASTER.

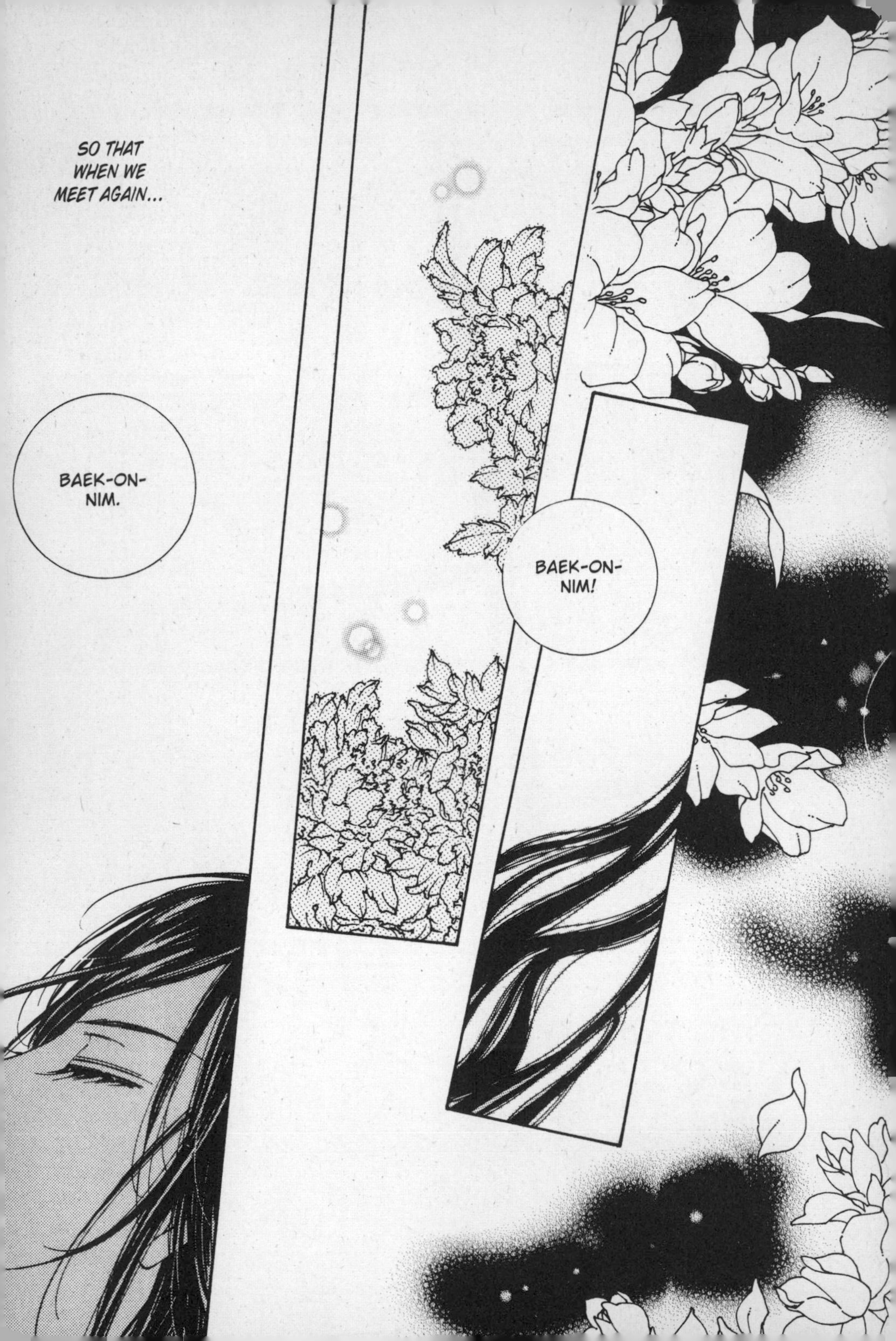
SO THAT WHEN WE MEET AGAIN...
BAEK-ON-NIM.
BAEK-ON-NIM!

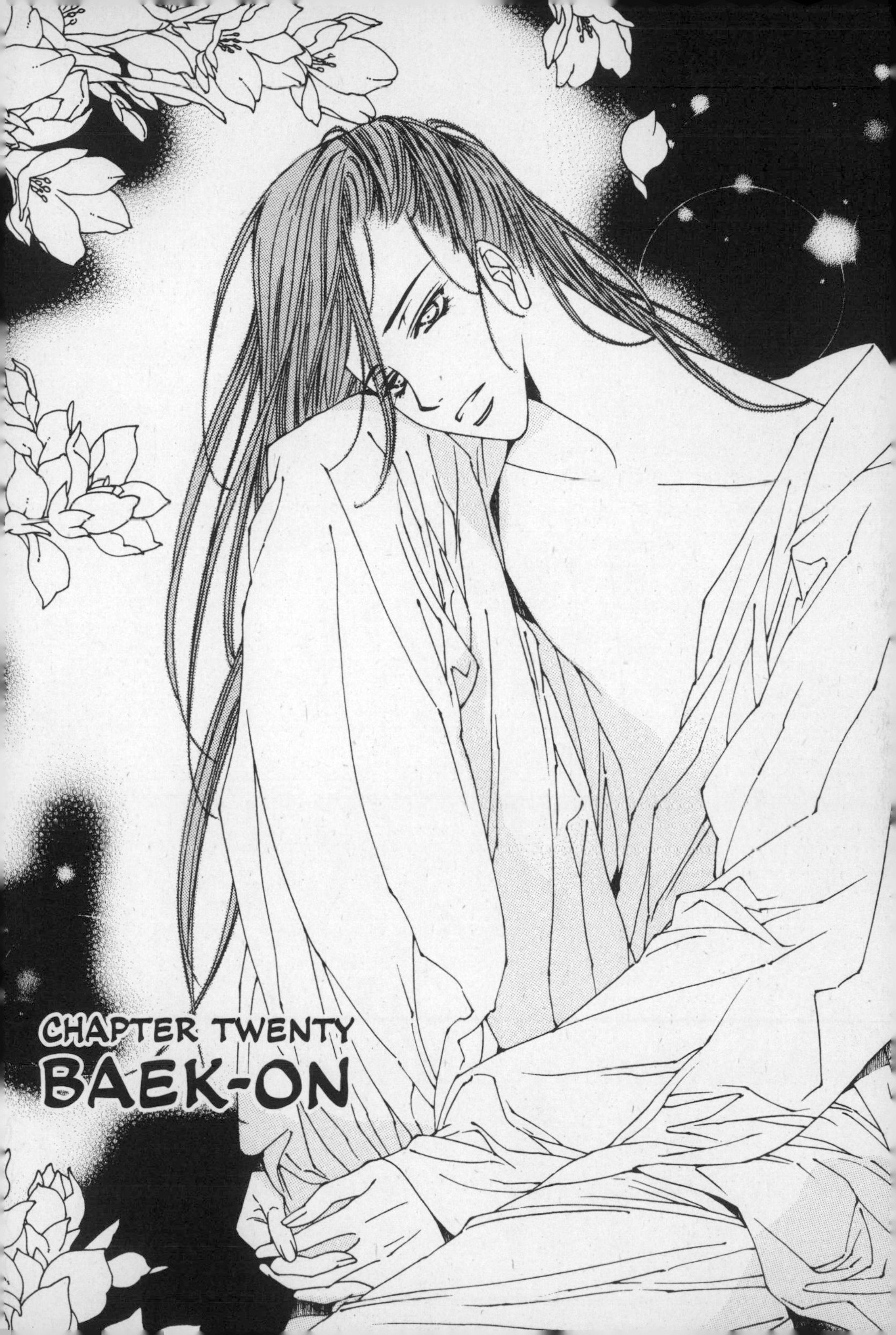
CHAPTER TWENTY
BAÉK-ON

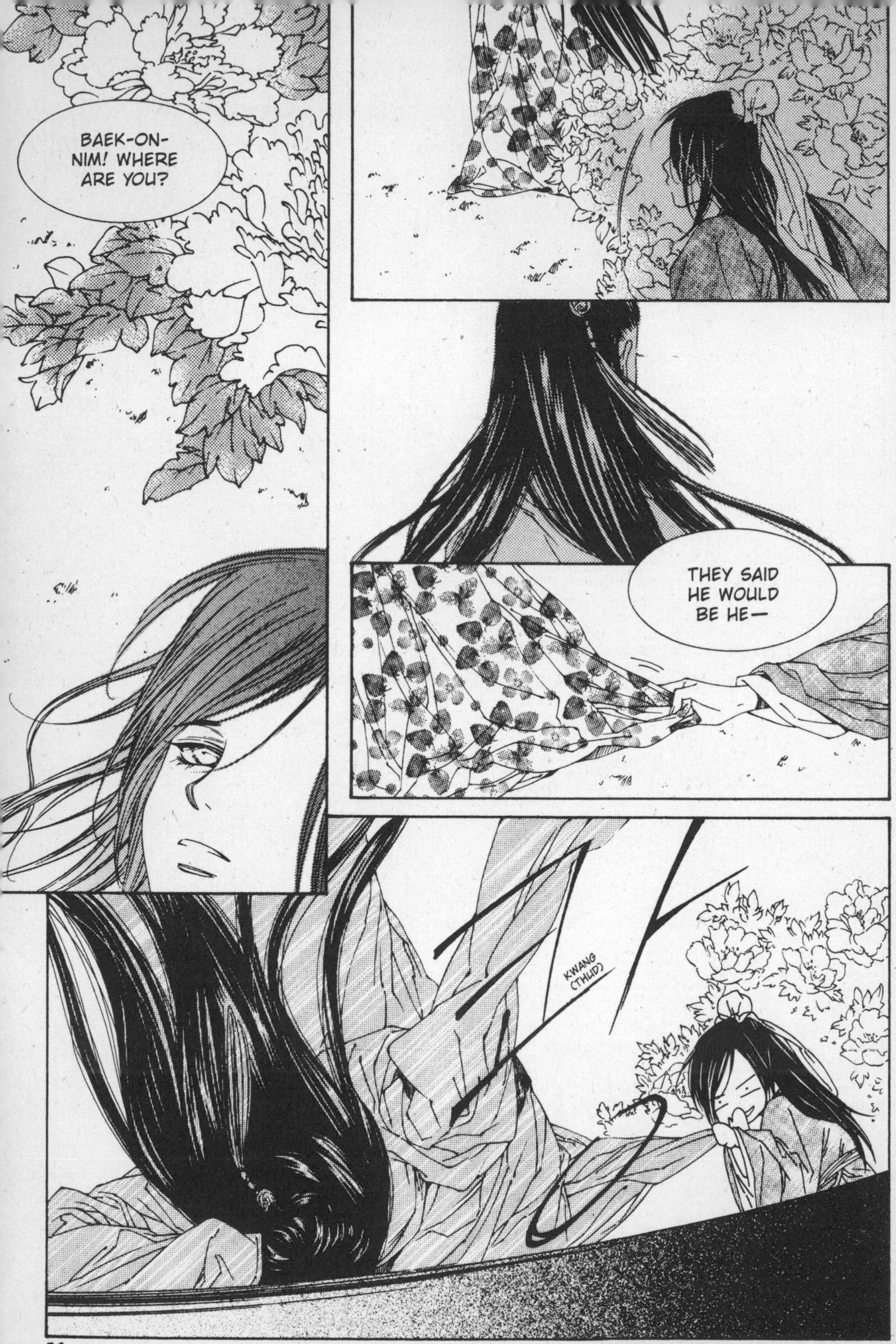
BAEK-ON-NIM! WHERE ARE YOU?
THEY SAID HE WOULD BE HE—
KWANG (THUD)

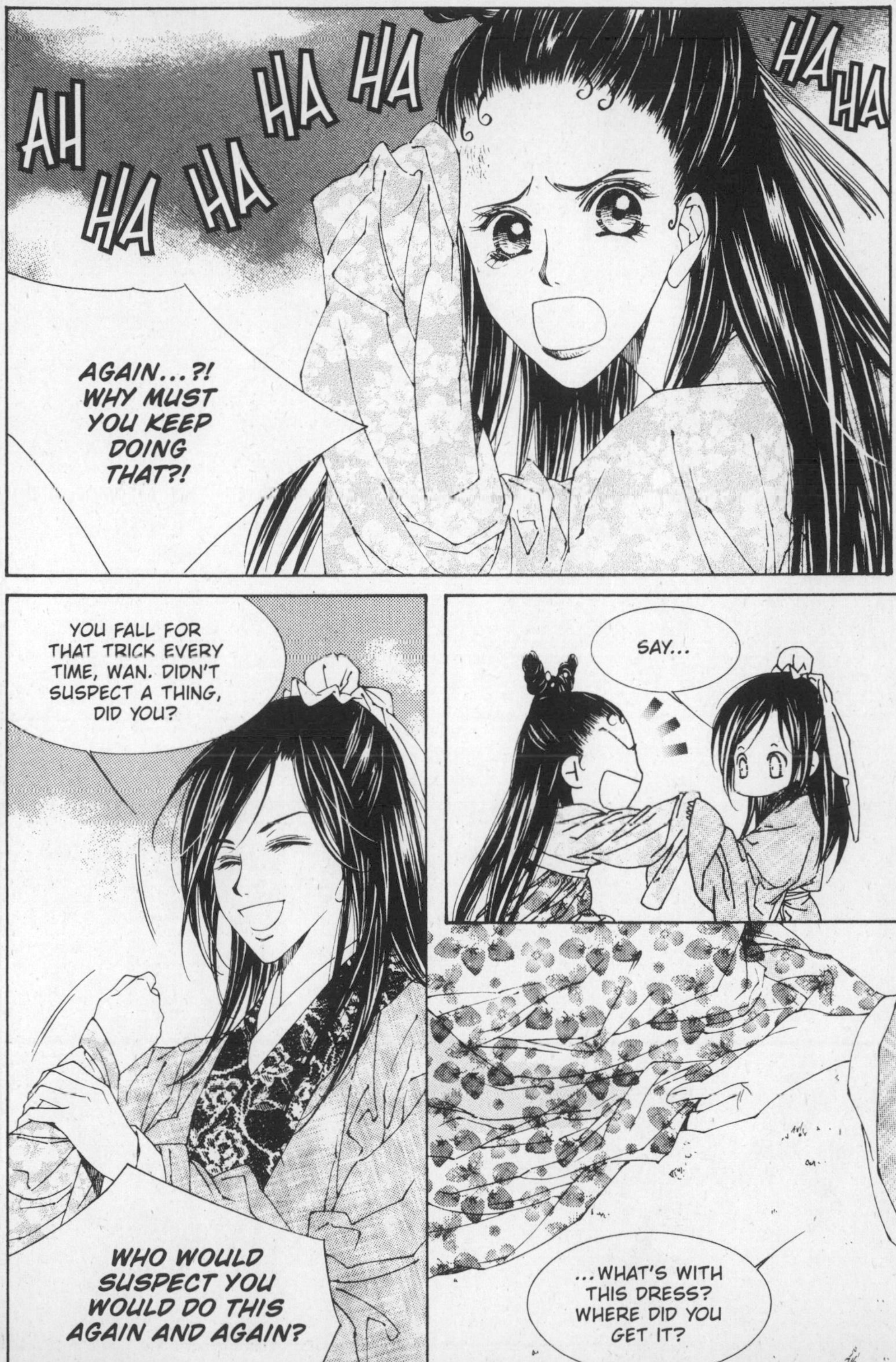
AH HA HA HA HA HA
AGAIN...?! WHY MUST YOU KEEP DOING THAT?!
HA HA HA
YOU FALL FOR THAT TRICK EVERY TIME, WAN. DIDN'T SUSPECT A THING, DID YOU?
WHO WOULD SUSPECT YOU WOULD DO THIS AGAIN AND AGAIN?
SAY...
...WHAT'S WITH THIS DRESS? WHERE DID YOU GET IT?

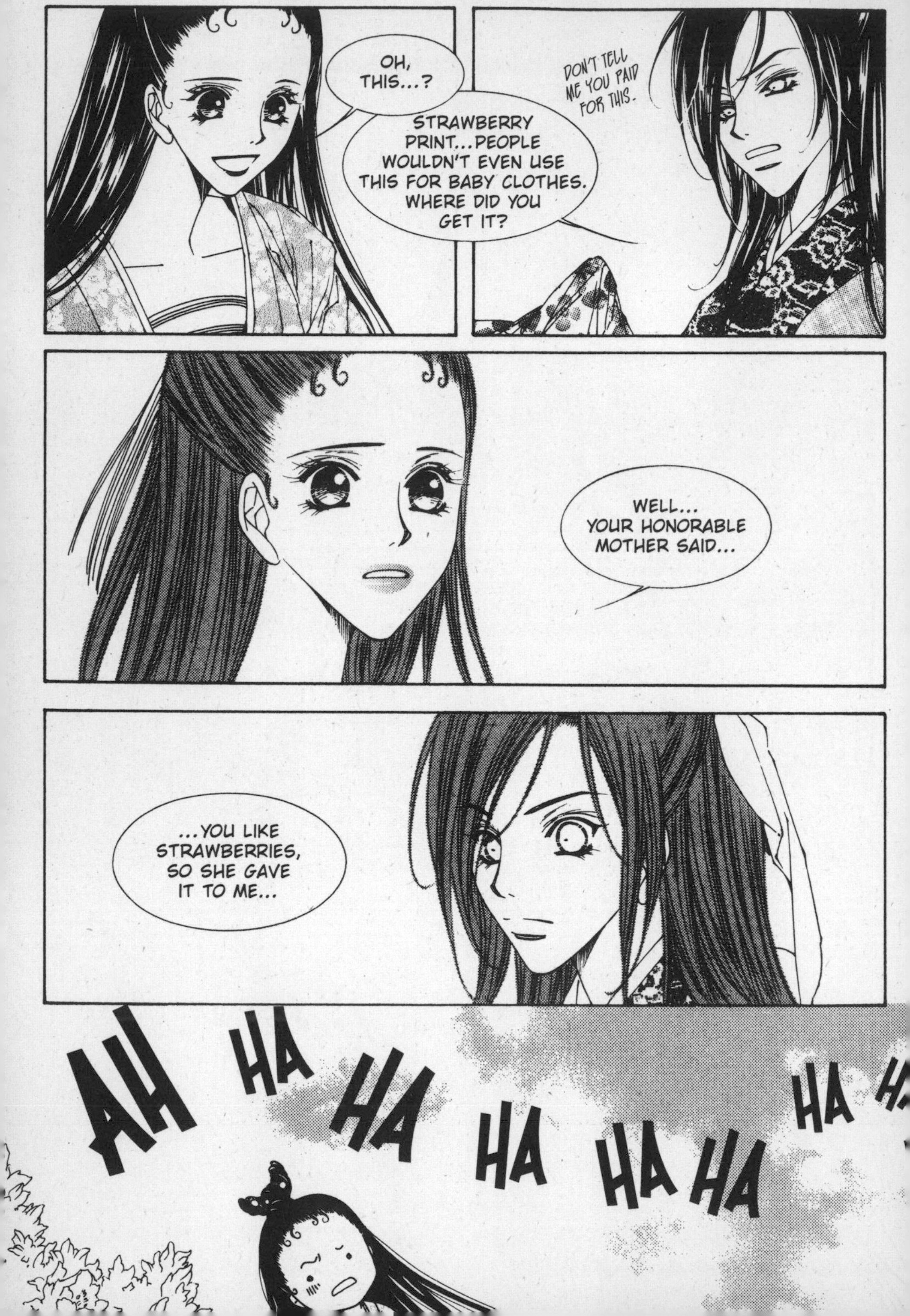
OH, THIS...?
STRAWBERRY PRINT...PEOPLE WOULDN'T EVEN USE THIS FOR BABY CLOTHES. WHERE DID YOU GET IT?
DON'T TELL ME YOU PAID FOR THIS.
WELL... YOUR HONORABLE MOTHER SAID...
...YOU LIKE STRAWBERRIES, SO SHE GAVE IT TO ME...
AH HA HA HA HA HA HA HA

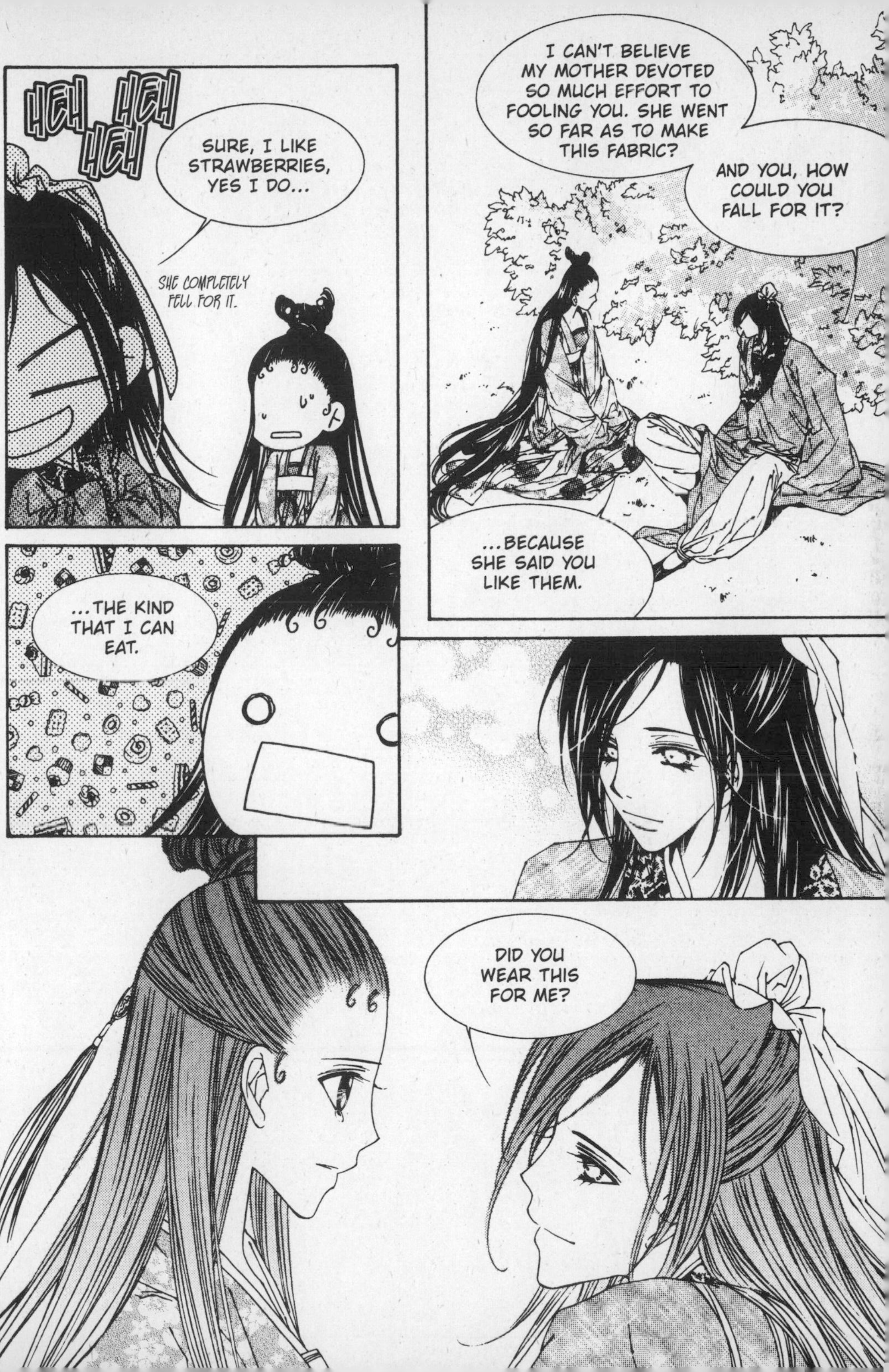
HEH HEH HEH
SURE, I LIKE STRAWBERRIES, YES I DO...
SHE COMPLETELY FELL FOR IT.
I CAN'T BELIEVE MY MOTHER DEVOTED SO MUCH EFFORT TO FOOLING YOU. SHE WENT SO FAR AS TO MAKE THIS FABRIC?
AND YOU, HOW COULD YOU FALL FOR IT?
...BECAUSE SHE SAID YOU LIKE THEM.
...THE KIND THAT I CAN EAT.
DID YOU WEAR THIS FOR ME?

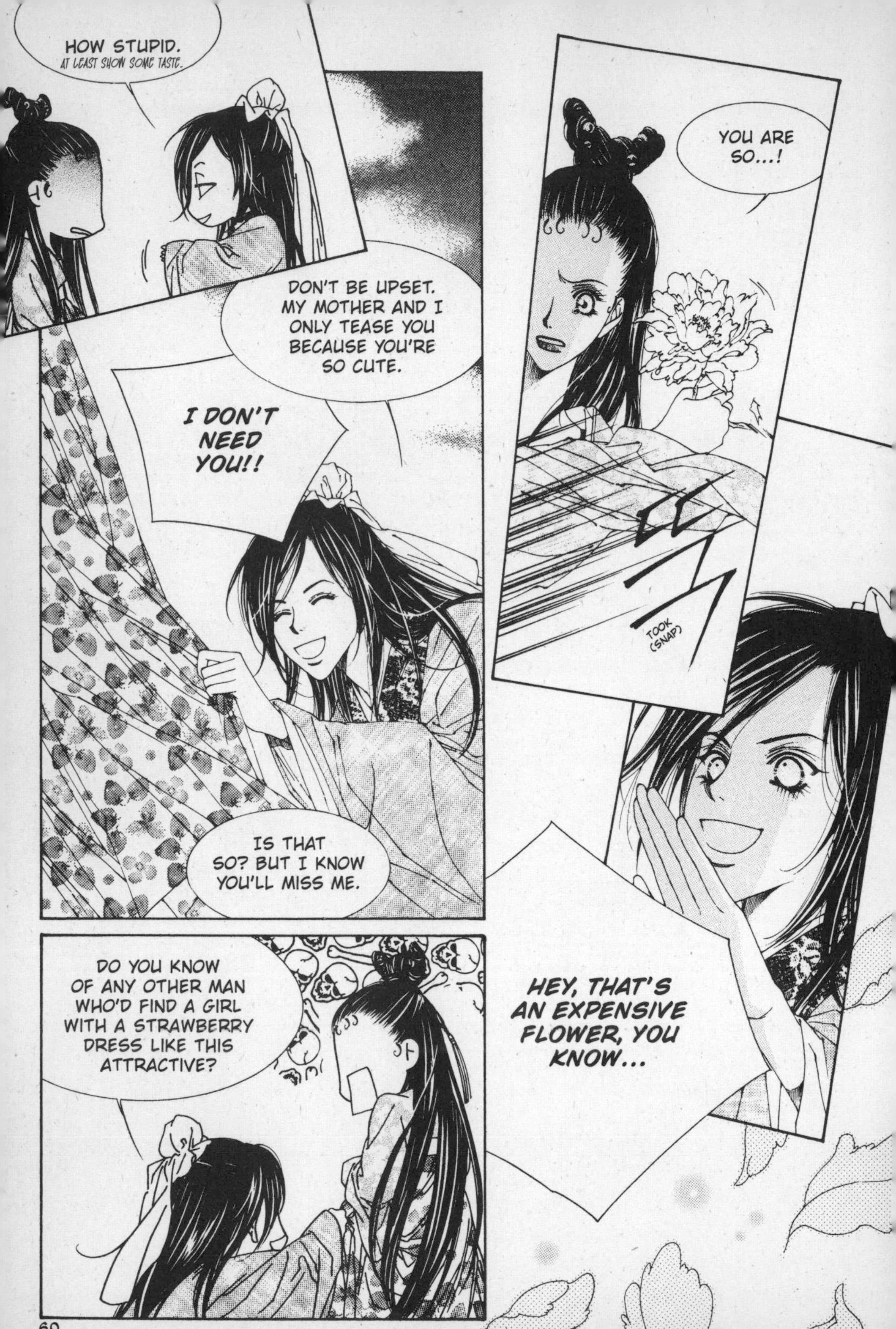
HOW STUPID.
AT LEAST SHOW SOME TASTE...
YOU ARE SO...!
DON'T BE UPSET. MY MOTHER AND I ONLY TEASE YOU BECAUSE YOU'RE SO CUTE.
I DON'T NEED YOU!!
IS THAT SO? BUT I KNOW YOU'LL MISS ME.
DO YOU KNOW OF ANY OTHER MAN WHO'D FIND A GIRL WITH A STRAWBERRY DRESS LIKE THIS ATTRACTIVE?
TOOK (SNAP)
HEY, THAT'S AN EXPENSIVE FLOWER, YOU KNOW...

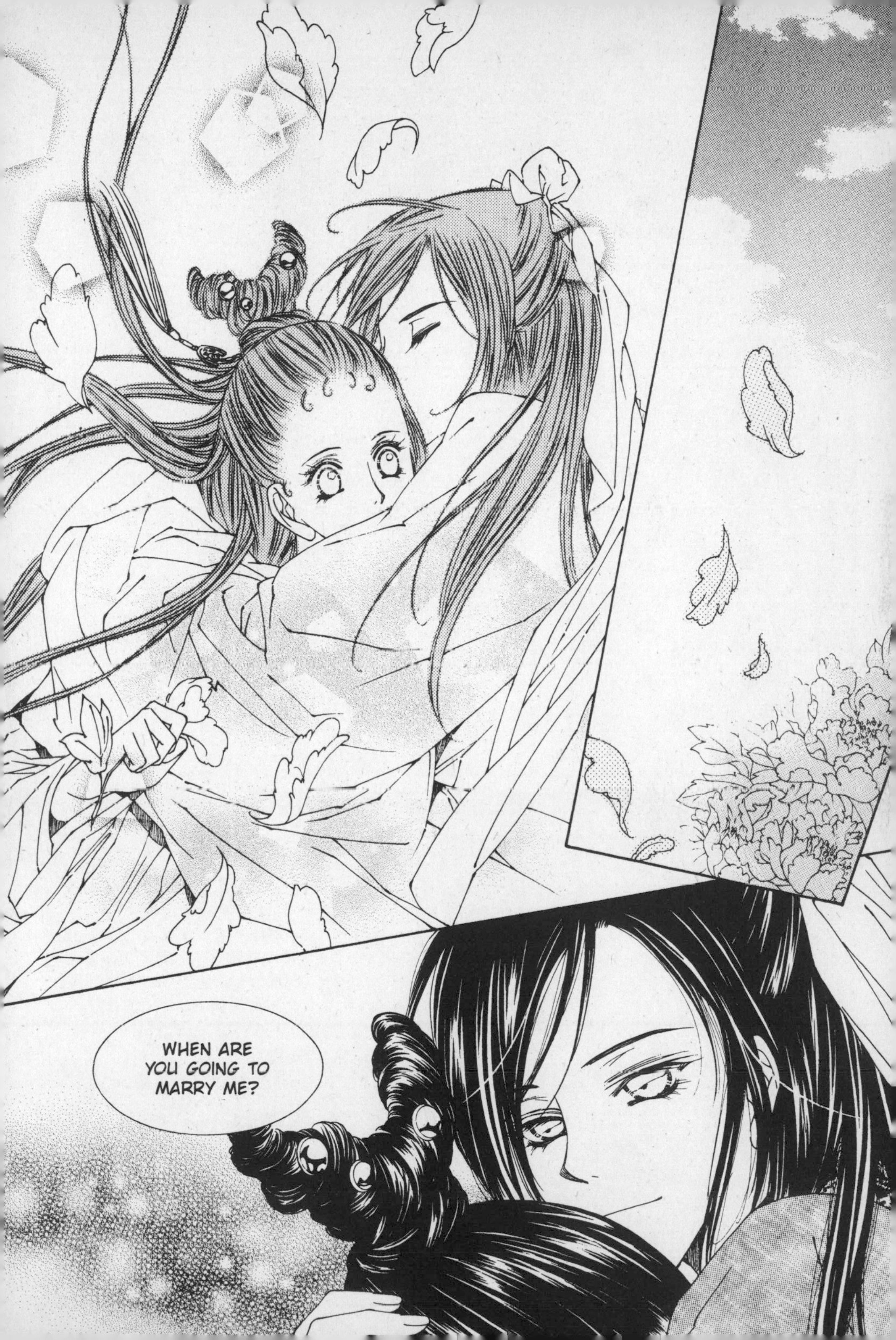
WHEN ARE YOU GOING TO MARRY ME?

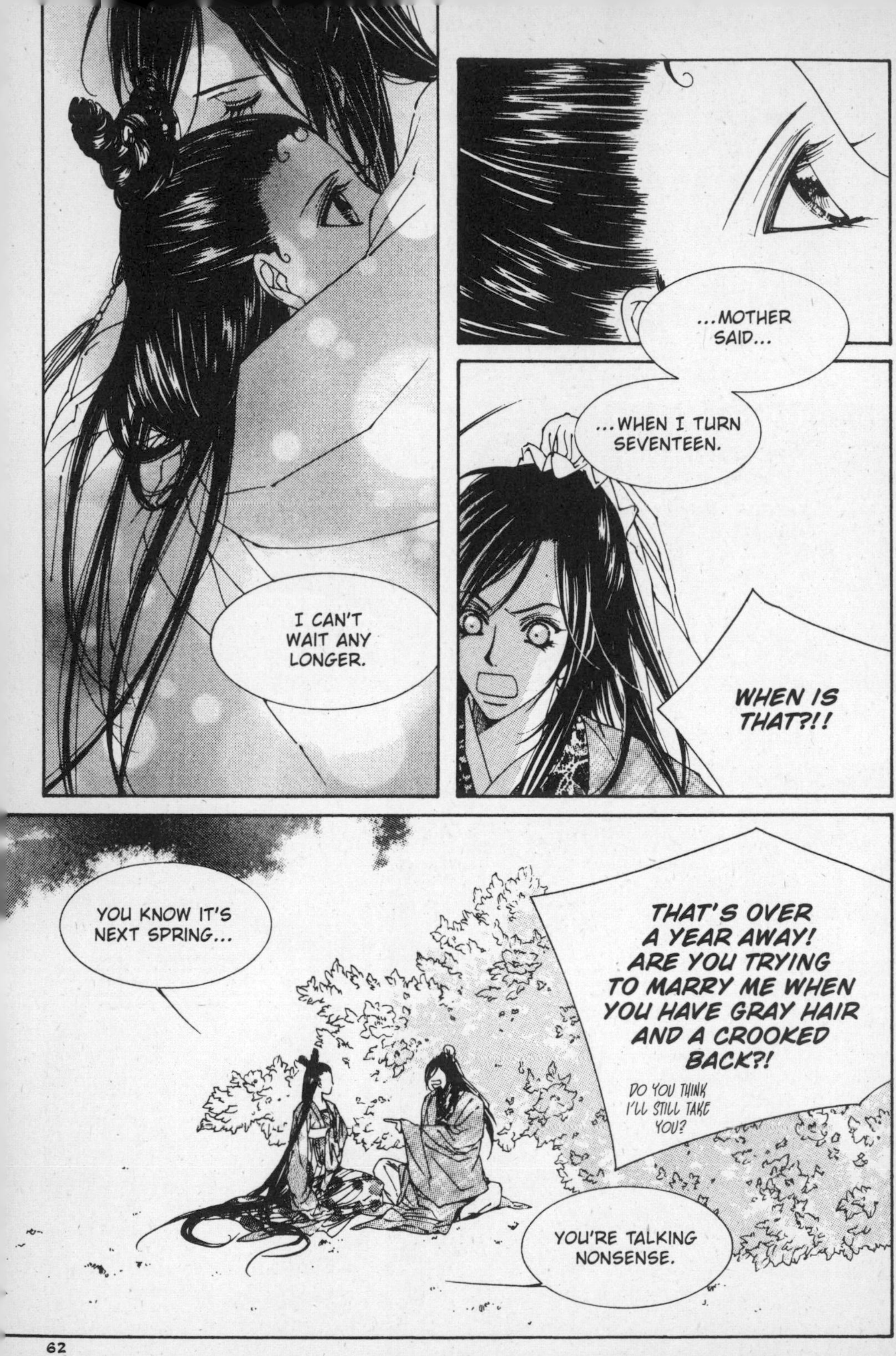
I CAN'T WAIT ANY LONGER.
...MOTHER SAID...
...WHEN I TURN SEVENTEEN.
WHEN IS THAT?!!
YOU KNOW IT'S NEXT SPRING...
THAT'S OVER A YEAR AWAY! ARE YOU TRYING TO MARRY ME WHEN YOU HAVE GRAY HAIR AND A CROOKED BACK?!
DO YOU THINK I'LL STILL TAKE YOU?
YOU'RE TALKING NONSENSE.

*GAENYUN: FIFTEEN YEARS OLD. THE AGE AT WHICH A GIRL CAN MARRY.

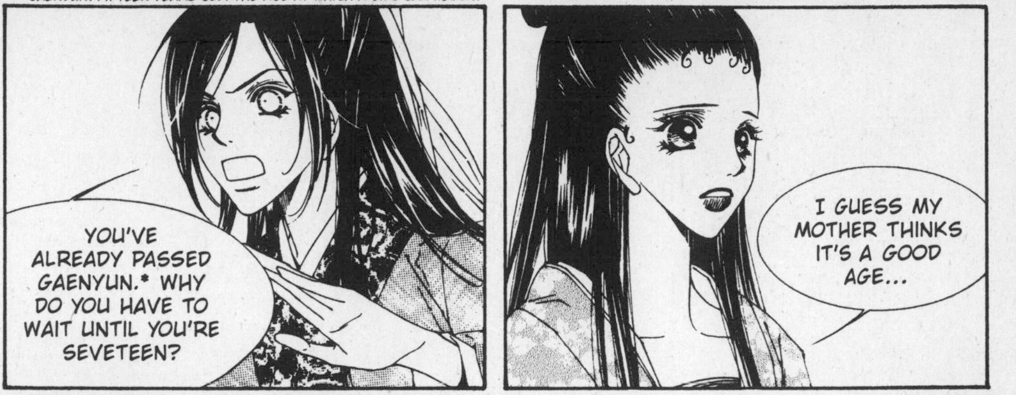
YOU'VE ALREADY PASSED GAENYUN.* WHY DO YOU HAVE TO WAIT UNTIL YOU'RE SEVETEEN?
I GUESS MY MOTHER THINKS IT'S A GOOD AGE...

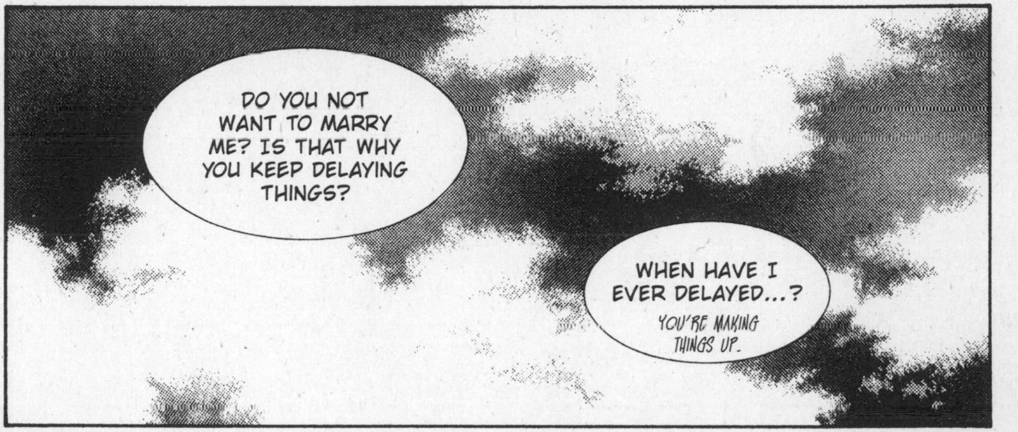
DO YOU NOT WANT TO MARRY ME? IS THAT WHY YOU KEEP DELAYING THINGS?
WHEN HAVE I EVER DELAYED...?
YOU'RE MAKING THINGS UP.

*NAPPAE: WEDDING PRESENTS WHICH THE GROOM SENDS THE BRIDE.

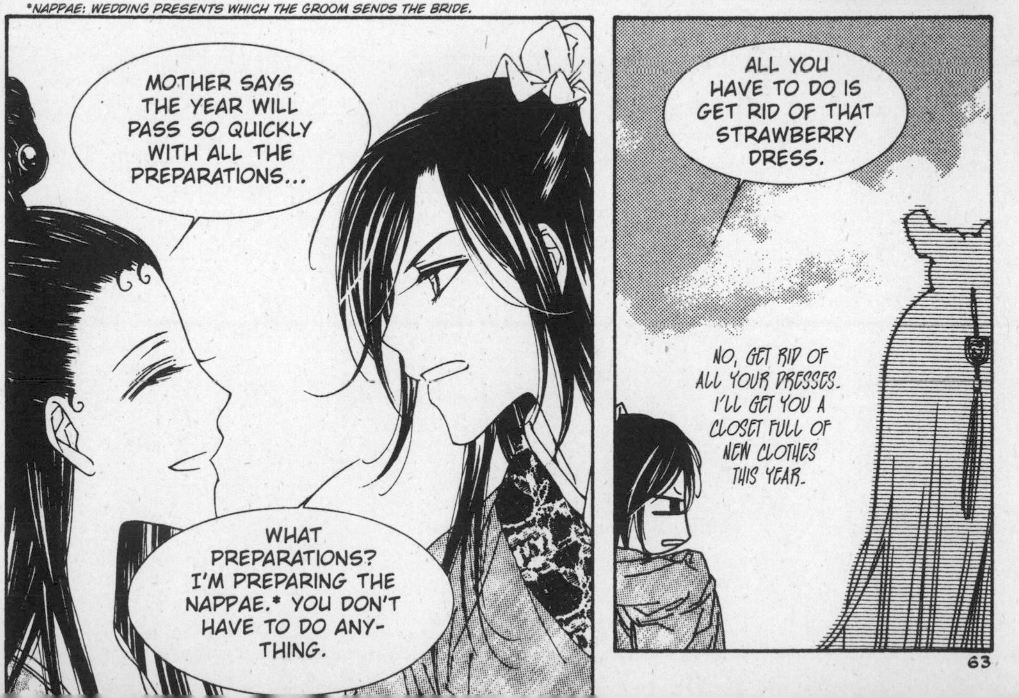
MOTHER SAYS THE YEAR WILL PASS SO QUICKLY WITH ALL THE PREPARATIONS...
WHAT PREPARATIONS? I'M PREPARING THE NAPPAE.* YOU DON'T HAVE TO DO ANY-THING.
ALL YOU HAVE TO DO IS GET RID OF THAT STRAWBERRY DRESS.
NO, GET RID OF ALL YOUR DRESSES. I'LL GET YOU A CLOSET FULL OF NEW CLOTHES THIS YEAR.

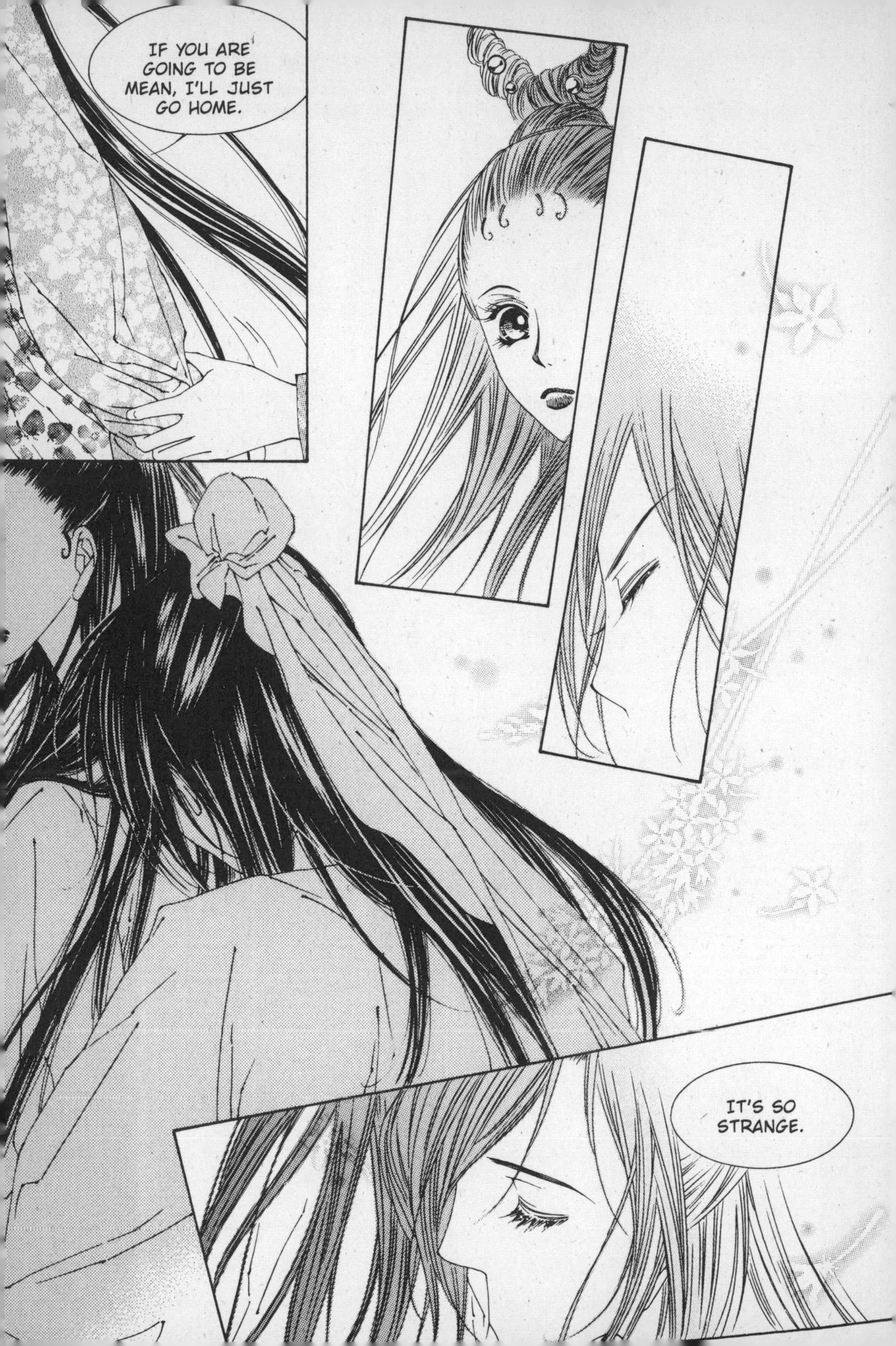
IF YOU ARE GOING TO BE MEAN, I'LL JUST GO HOME.
IT'S SO STRANGE.

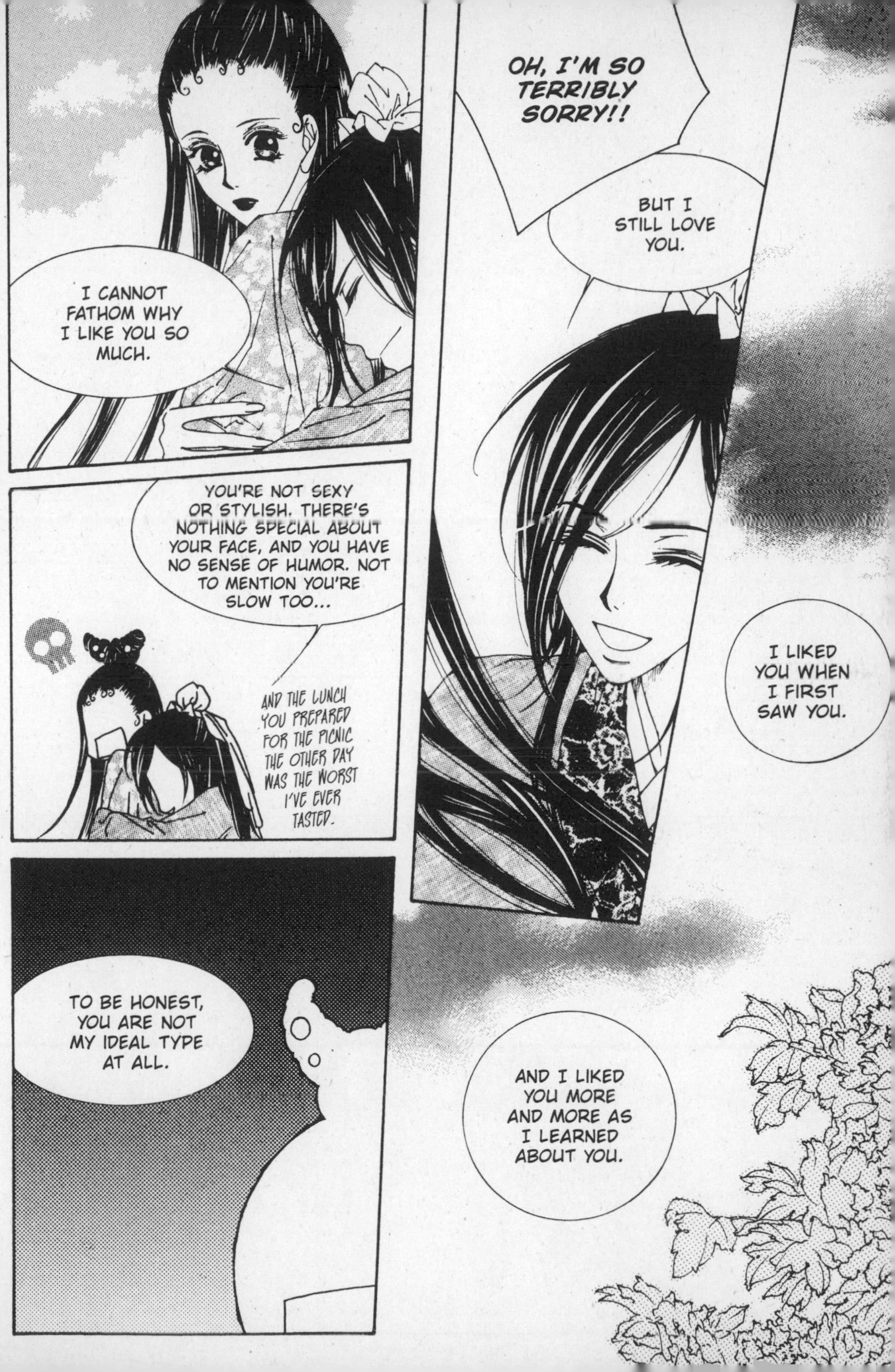
I CANNOT FATHOM WHY I LIKE YOU SO MUCH.
YOU'RE NOT SEXY OR STYLISH. THERE'S NOTHING SPECIAL ABOUT YOUR FACE, AND YOU HAVE NO SENSE OF HUMOR. NOT TO MENTION YOU'RE SLOW TOO...
AND THE LUNCH YOU PREPARED FOR THE PICNIC THE OTHER DAY WAS THE WORST I'VE EVER TASTED.
TO BE HONEST, YOU ARE NOT MY IDEAL TYPE AT ALL.
OH, I'M SO TERRIBLY SORRY!!
BUT I STILL LOVE YOU.
I LIKED YOU WHEN I FIRST SAW YOU.
AND I LIKED YOU MORE AND MORE AS I LEARNED ABOUT YOU.

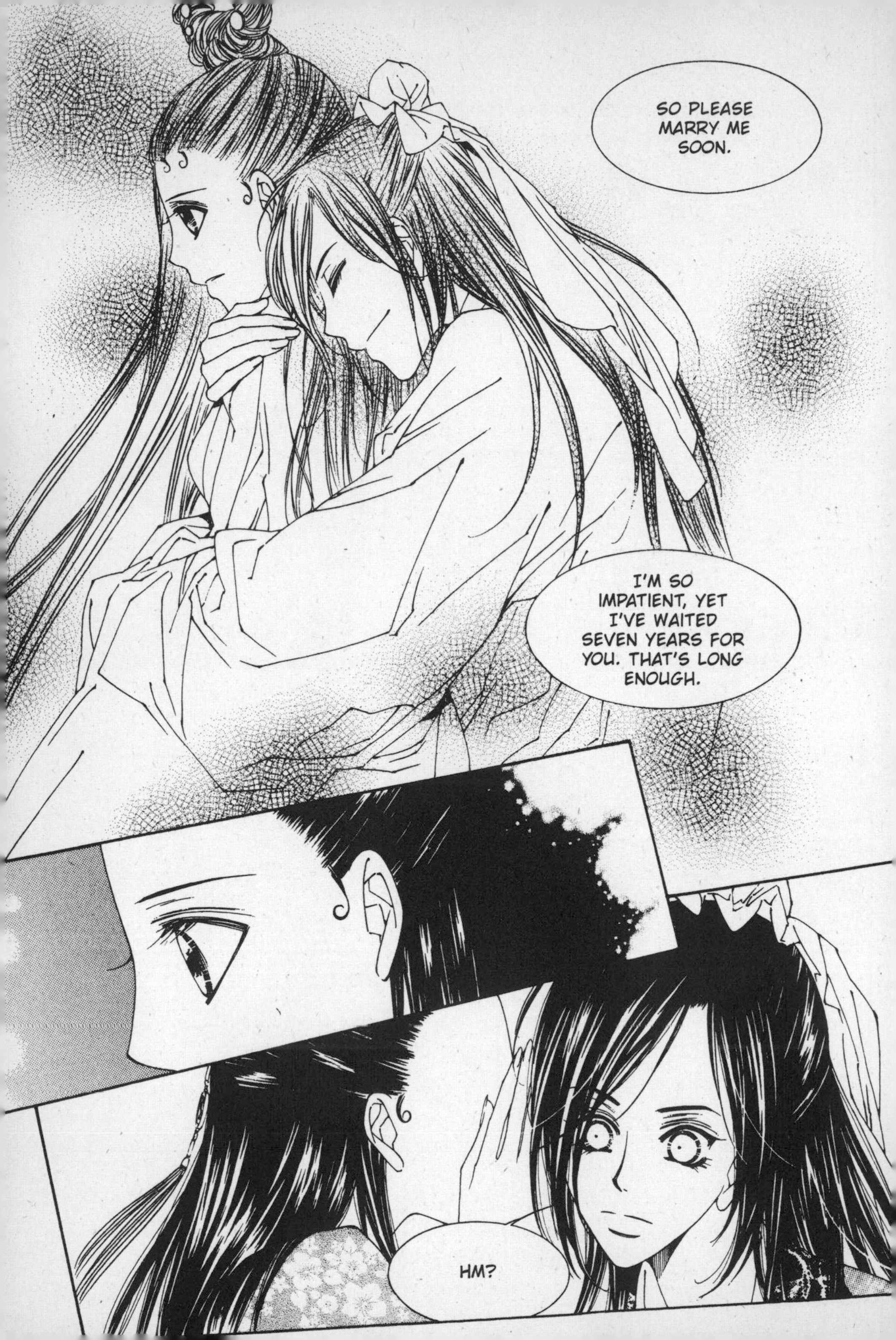
SO PLEASE MARRY ME SOON.
I'M SO IMPATIENT, YET I'VE WAITED SEVEN YEARS FOR YOU. THAT'S LONG ENOUGH.
HM?

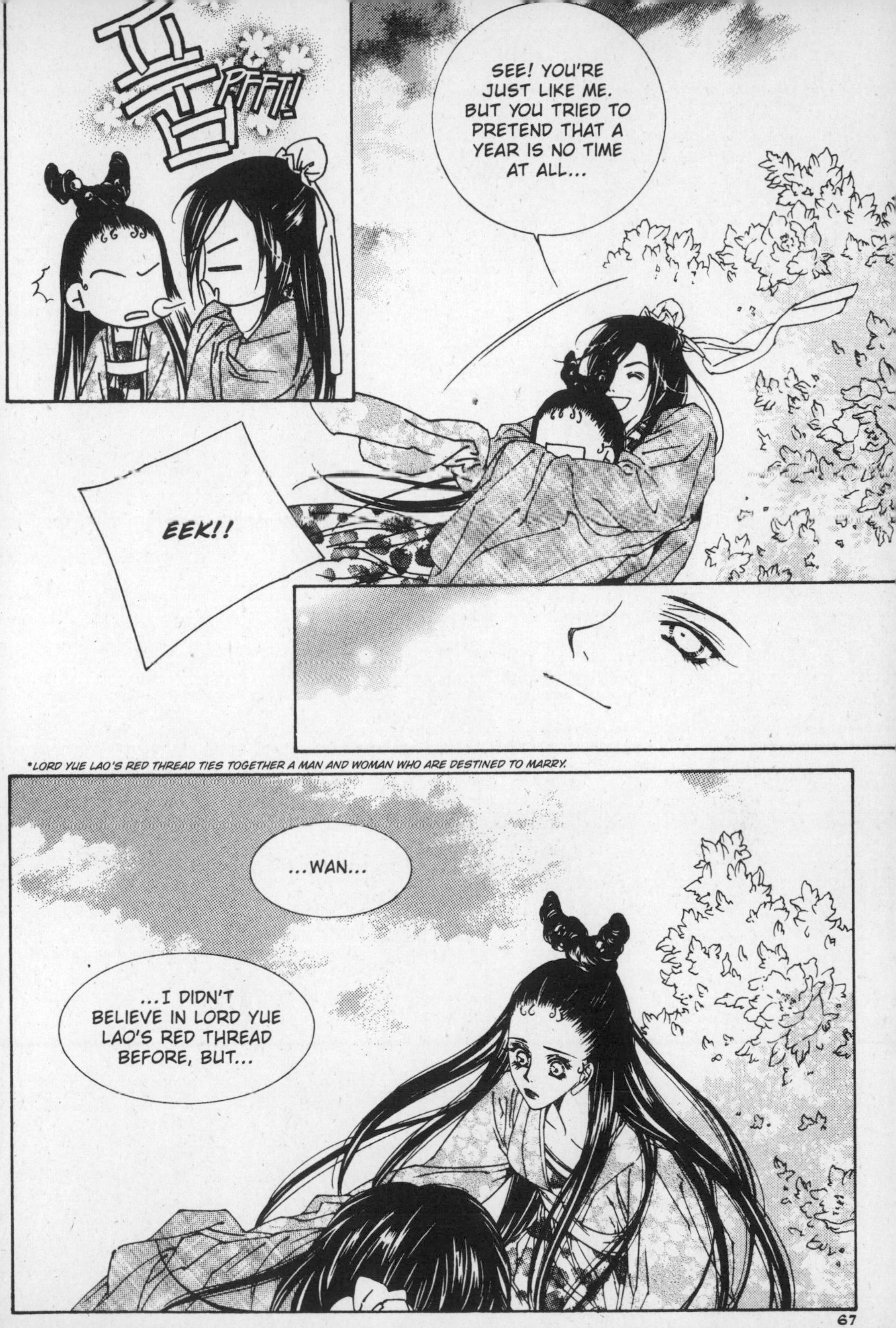
PFFT!
SEE! YOU'RE JUST LIKE ME. BUT YOU TRIED TO PRETEND THAT A YEAR IS NO TIME AT ALL...
EEK!!
...WAN...
...I DIDN'T BELIEVE IN LORD YUE LAO'S RED THREAD BEFORE, BUT...

*LORD YUE LAO'S RED THREAD TIES TOGETHER A MAN AND WOMAN WHO ARE DESTINED TO MARRY.

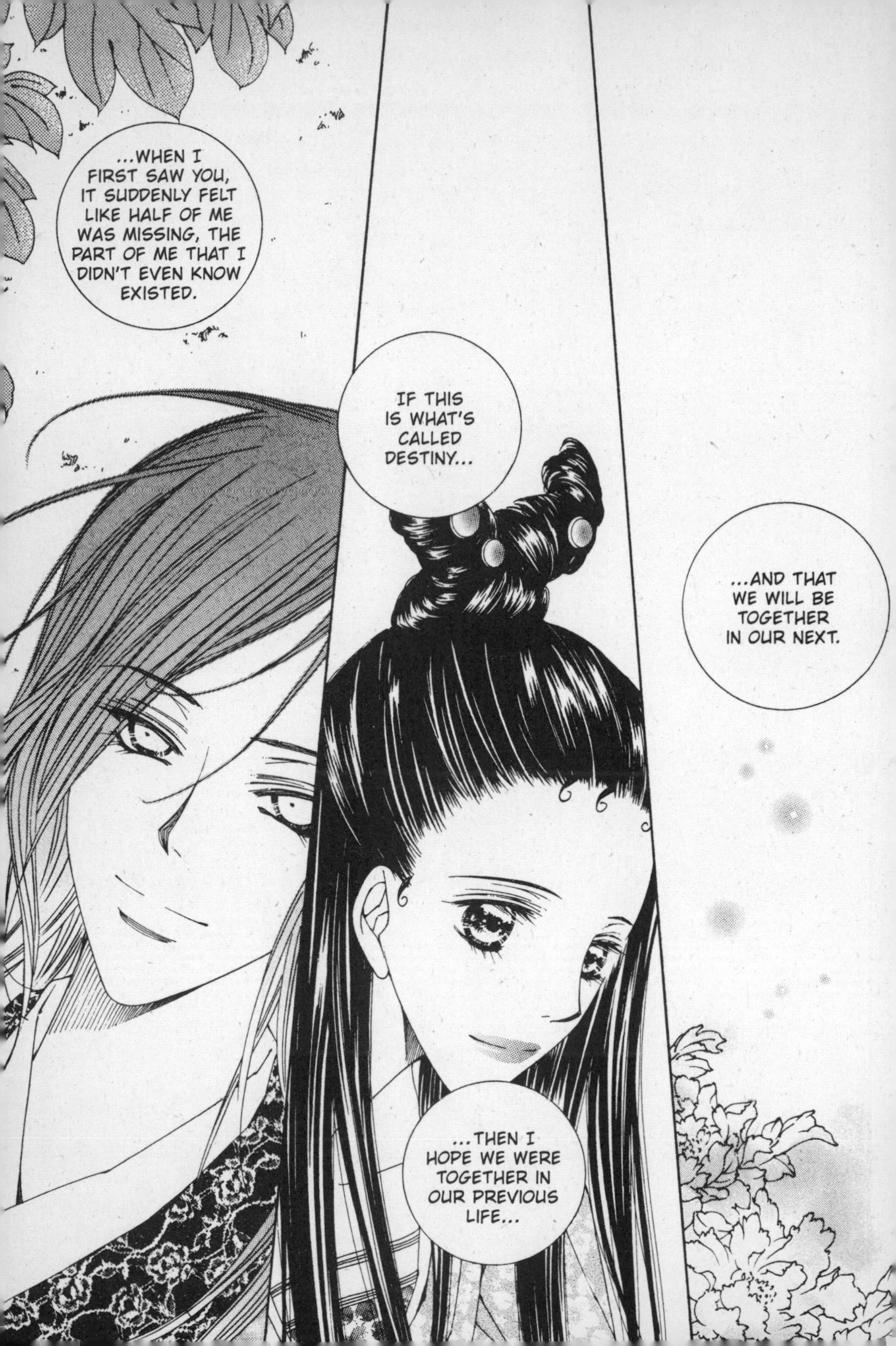
...WHEN I FIRST SAW YOU, IT SUDDENLY FELT LIKE HALF OF ME WAS MISSING, THE PART OF ME THAT I DIDN'T EVEN KNOW EXISTED.
IF THIS IS WHAT'S CALLED DESTINY...
...THEN I HOPE WE WERE TOGETHER IN OUR PREVIOUS LIFE...
...AND THAT WE WILL BE TOGETHER IN OUR NEXT.

MOTHER...

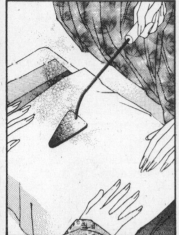

...ARE THOSE FATHER'S CLOTHES?

YES.

I HUNG THEM OUT BECAUSE THE SUN WAS QUITE NICE TODAY.

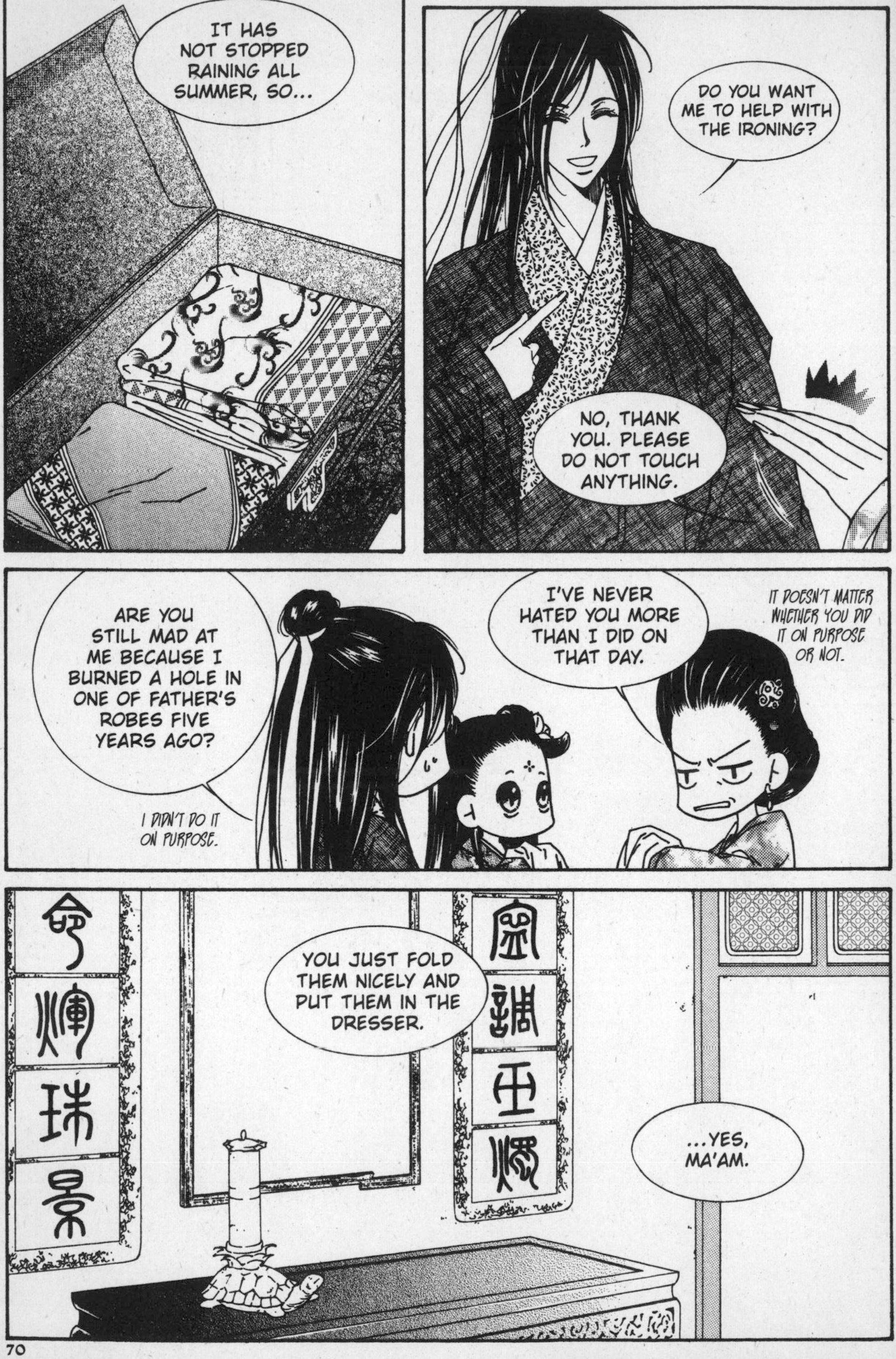
IT HAS NOT STOPPED RAINING ALL SUMMER, SO...
DO YOU WANT ME TO HELP WITH THE IRONING?
NO, THANK YOU. PLEASE DO NOT TOUCH ANYTHING.
ARE YOU STILL MAD AT ME BECAUSE I BURNED A HOLE IN ONE OF FATHER'S ROBES FIVE YEARS AGO?
I DIDN'T DO IT ON PURPOSE.
I'VE NEVER HATED YOU MORE THAN I DID ON THAT DAY.
IT DOESN'T MATTER WHETHER YOU DID IT ON PURPOSE OR NOT.
YOU JUST FOLD THEM NICELY AND PUT THEM IN THE DRESSER.
...YES, MA'AM.

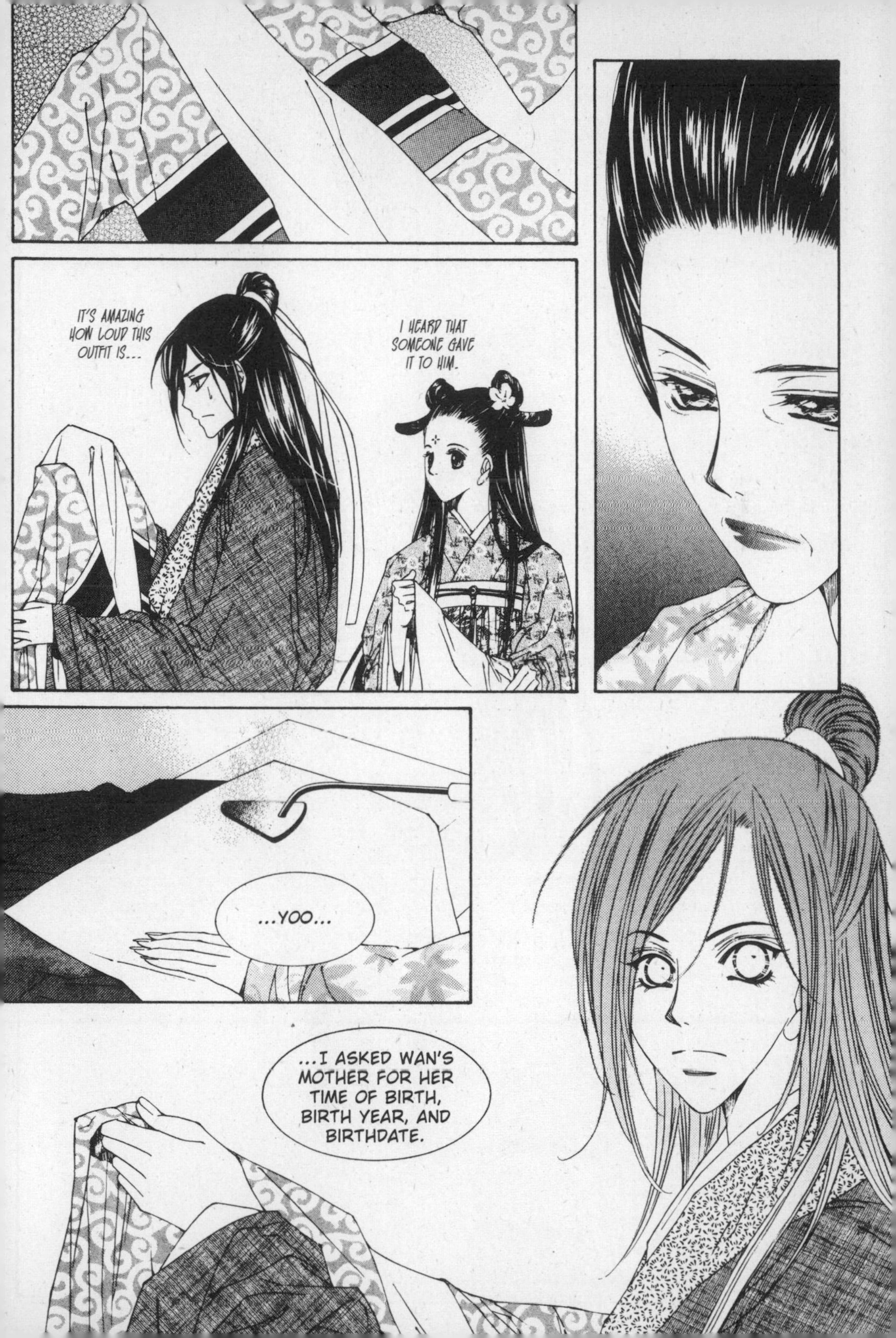
IT'S AMAZING HOW LOUD THIS OUTFIT IS...
I HEARD THAT SOMEONE GAVE IT TO HIM.
...YOO...
...I ASKED WAN'S MOTHER FOR HER TIME OF BIRTH, BIRTH YEAR, AND BIRTHDATE.

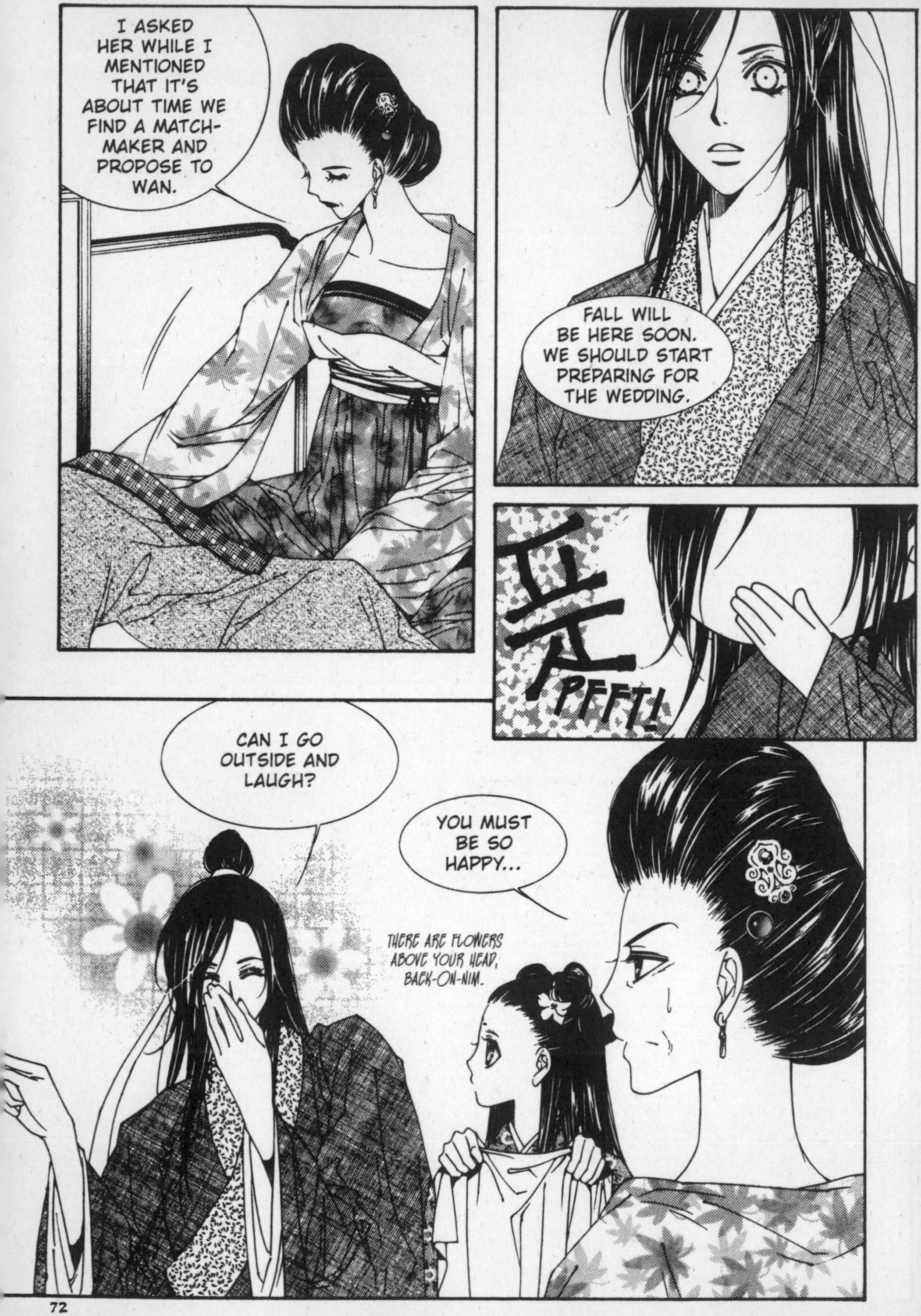
I ASKED HER WHILE I MENTIONED THAT IT'S ABOUT TIME WE FIND A MATCH-MAKER AND PROPOSE TO WAN.
FALL WILL BE HERE SOON. WE SHOULD START PREPARING FOR THE WEDDING.
푸ㅅ
PFFT!
CAN I GO OUTSIDE AND LAUGH?
YOU MUST BE SO HAPPY...
THERE ARE FLOWERS ABOVE YOUR HEAD, BAEK-ON-NIM.

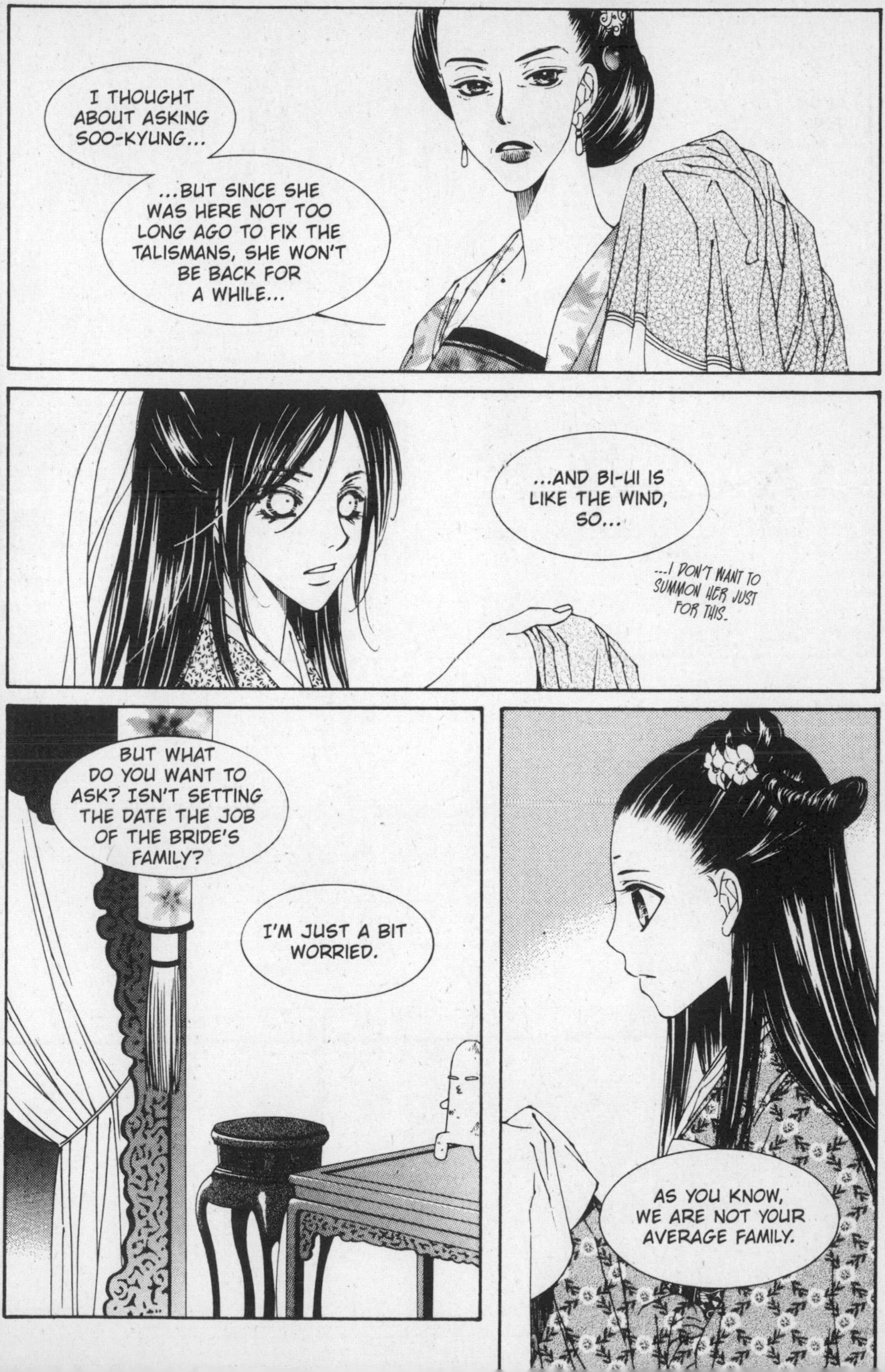
I THOUGHT ABOUT ASKING SOO-KYUNG...
...BUT SINCE SHE WAS HERE NOT TOO LONG AGO TO FIX THE TALISMANS, SHE WON'T BE BACK FOR A WHILE...
...AND BI-UI IS LIKE THE WIND, SO...
...I DON'T WANT TO SUMMON HER JUST FOR THIS.
BUT WHAT DO YOU WANT TO ASK? ISN'T SETTING THE DATE THE JOB OF THE BRIDE'S FAMILY?
I'M JUST A BIT WORRIED.
AS YOU KNOW, WE ARE NOT YOUR AVERAGE FAMILY.

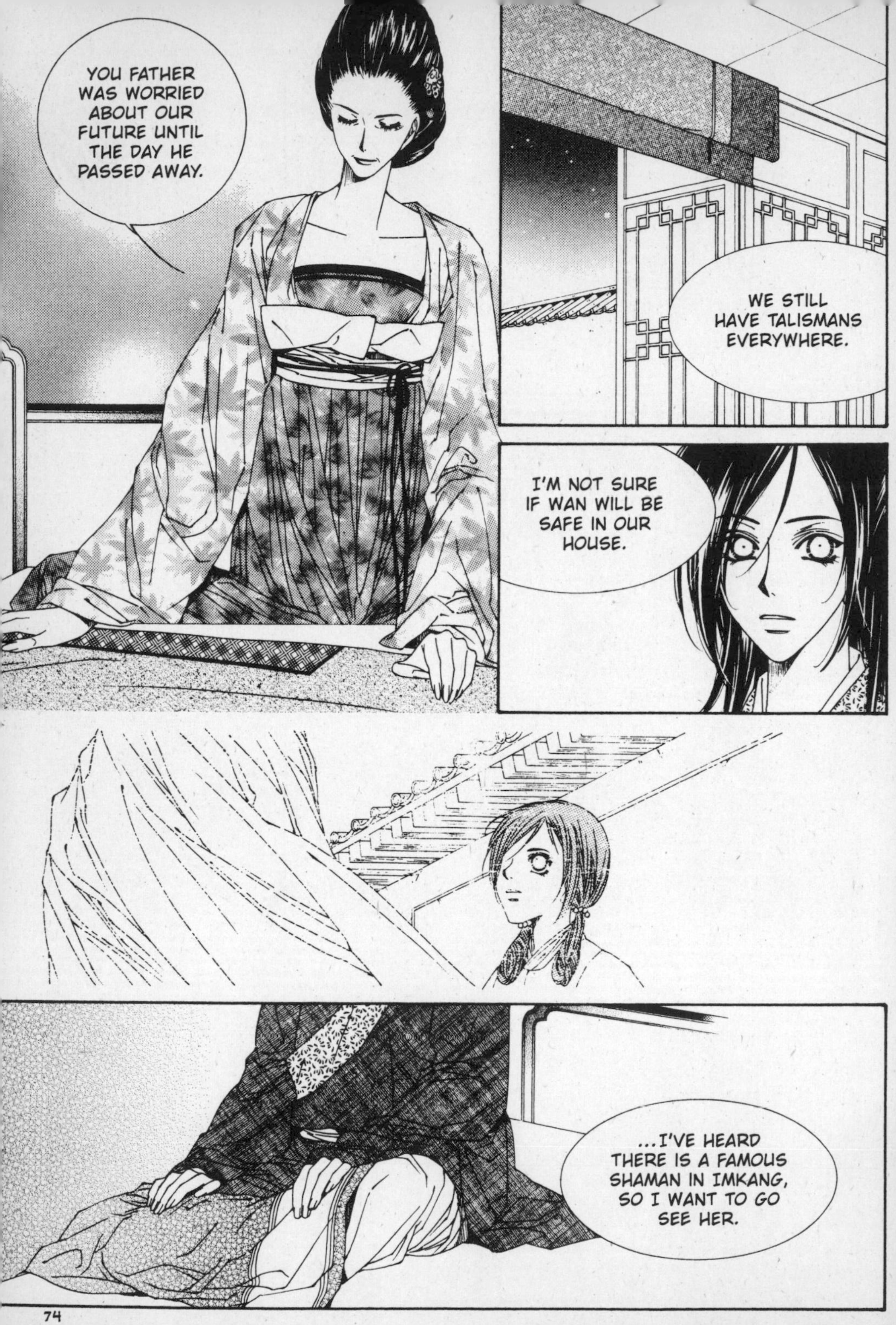
YOU FATHER WAS WORRIED ABOUT OUR FUTURE UNTIL THE DAY HE PASSED AWAY.
WE STILL HAVE TALISMANS EVERYWHERE.
I'M NOT SURE IF WAN WILL BE SAFE IN OUR HOUSE.
...I'VE HEARD THERE IS A FAMOUS SHAMAN IN IMKANG, SO I WANT TO GO SEE HER.

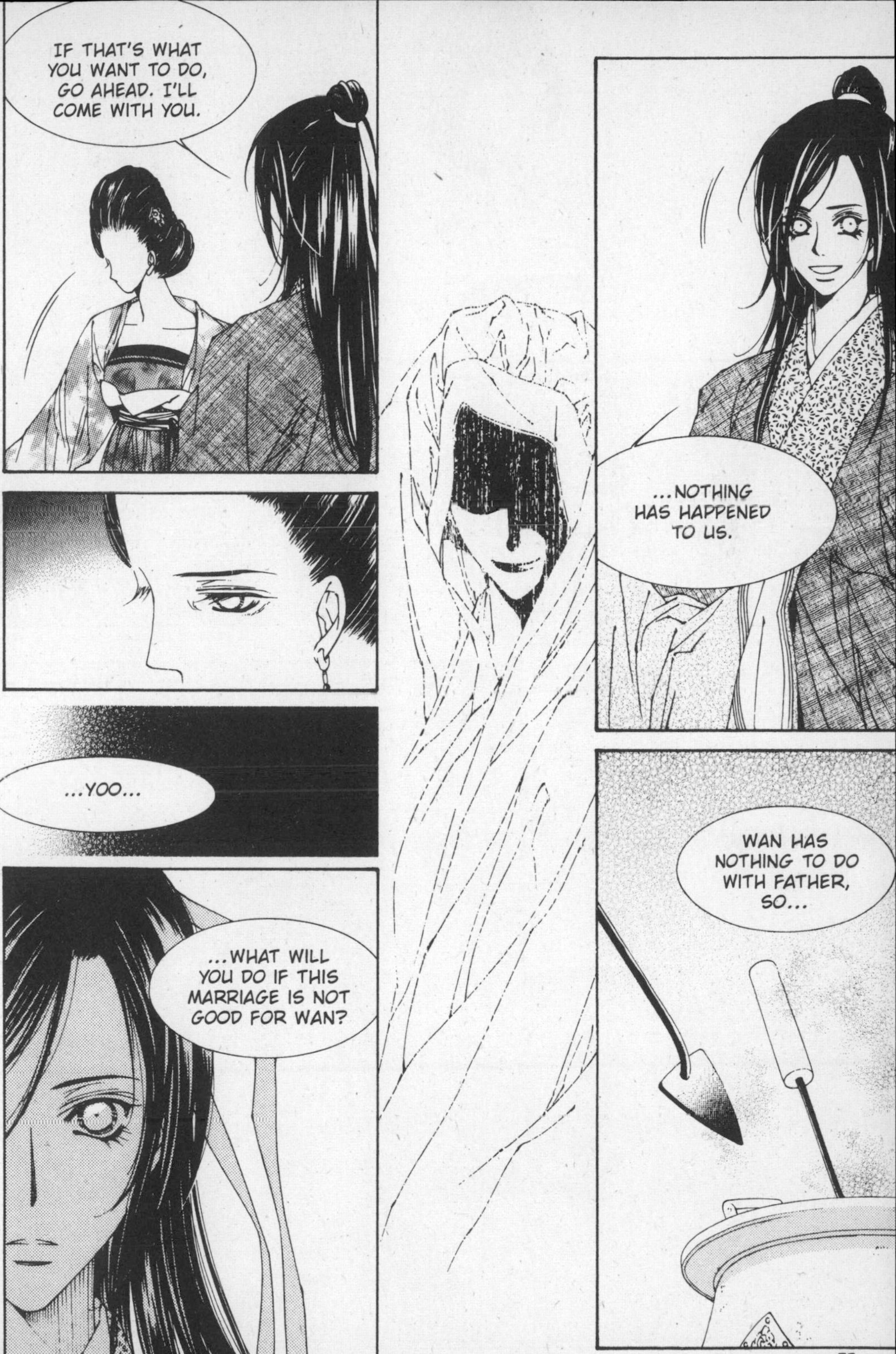
IF THAT'S WHAT YOU WANT TO DO, GO AHEAD. I'LL COME WITH YOU.
...YOO...
...WHAT WILL YOU DO IF THIS MARRIAGE IS NOT GOOD FOR WAN?
...NOTHING HAS HAPPENED TO US.
WAN HAS NOTHING TO DO WITH FATHER, SO...

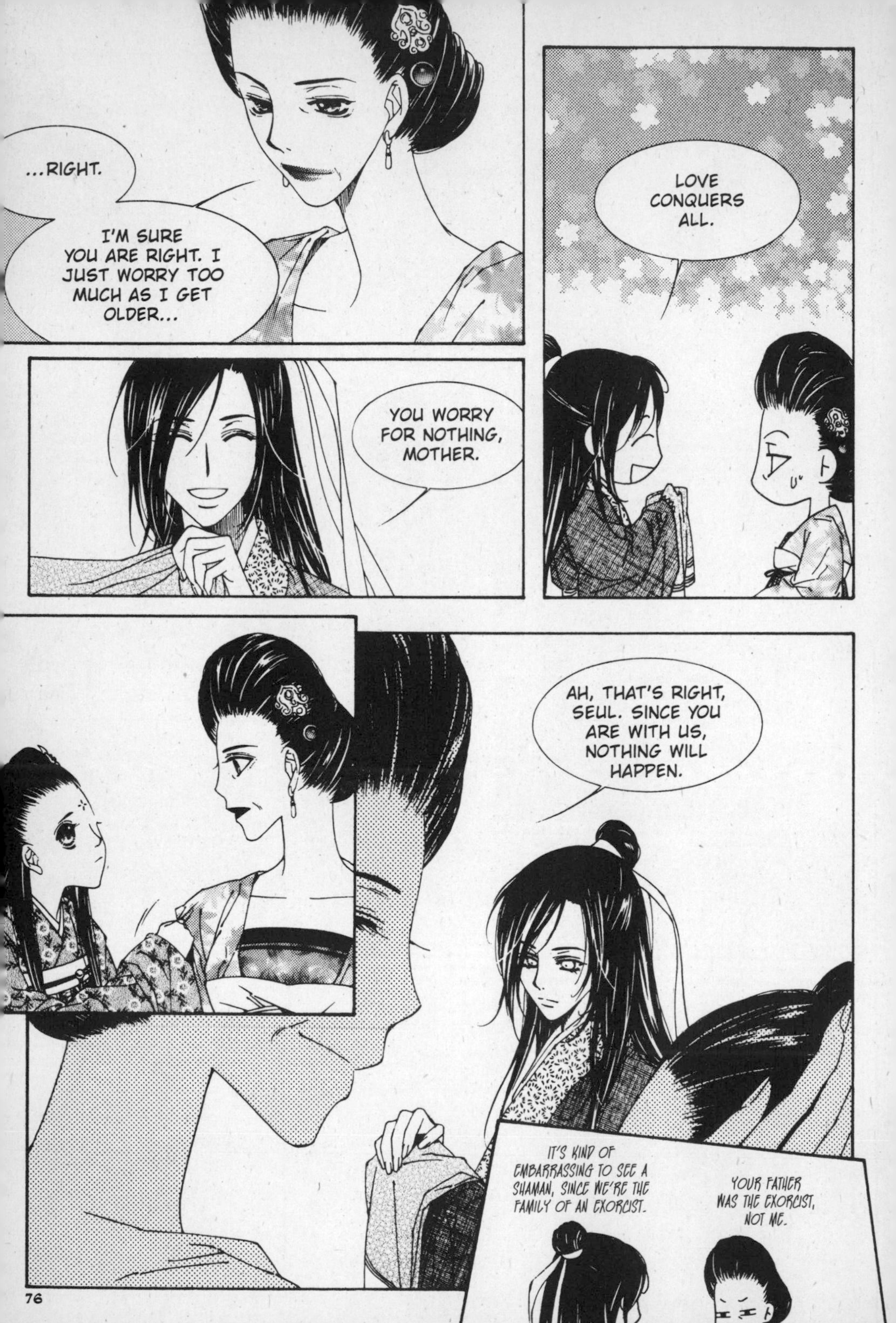

...RIGHT.
I'M SURE YOU ARE RIGHT. I JUST WORRY TOO MUCH AS I GET OLDER...
LOVE CONQUERS ALL.
YOU WORRY FOR NOTHING, MOTHER.
AH, THAT'S RIGHT, SEUL. SINCE YOU ARE WITH US, NOTHING WILL HAPPEN.
IT'S KIND OF EMBARRASSING TO SEE A SHAMAN, SINCE WE'RE THE FAMILY OF AN EXORCIST.
YOUR FATHER WAS THE EXORCIST, NOT ME.

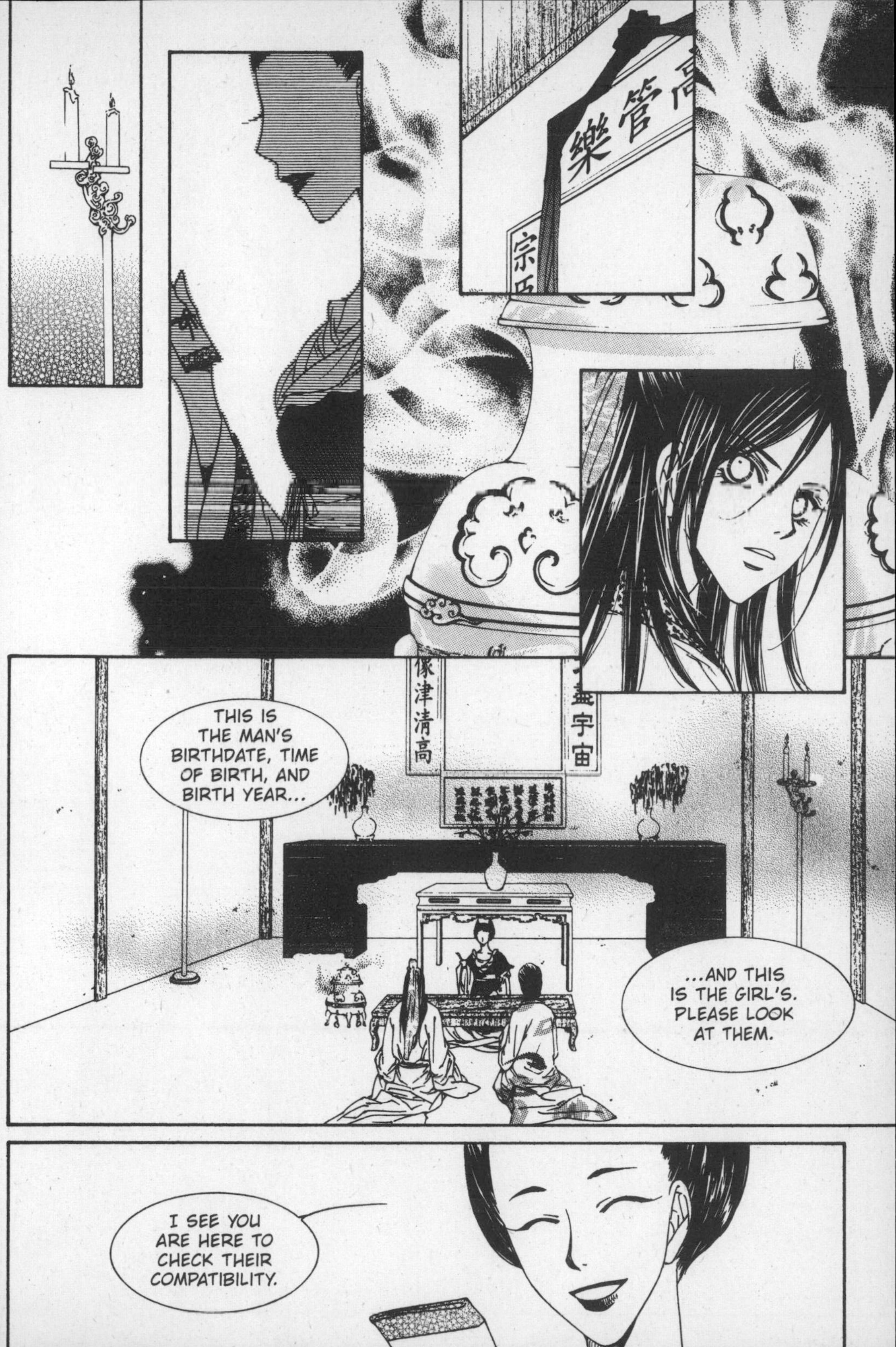
THIS IS THE MAN'S BIRTHDATE, TIME OF BIRTH, AND BIRTH YEAR...
...AND THIS IS THE GIRL'S. PLEASE LOOK AT THEM.
I SEE YOU ARE HERE TO CHECK THEIR COMPATIBILITY.

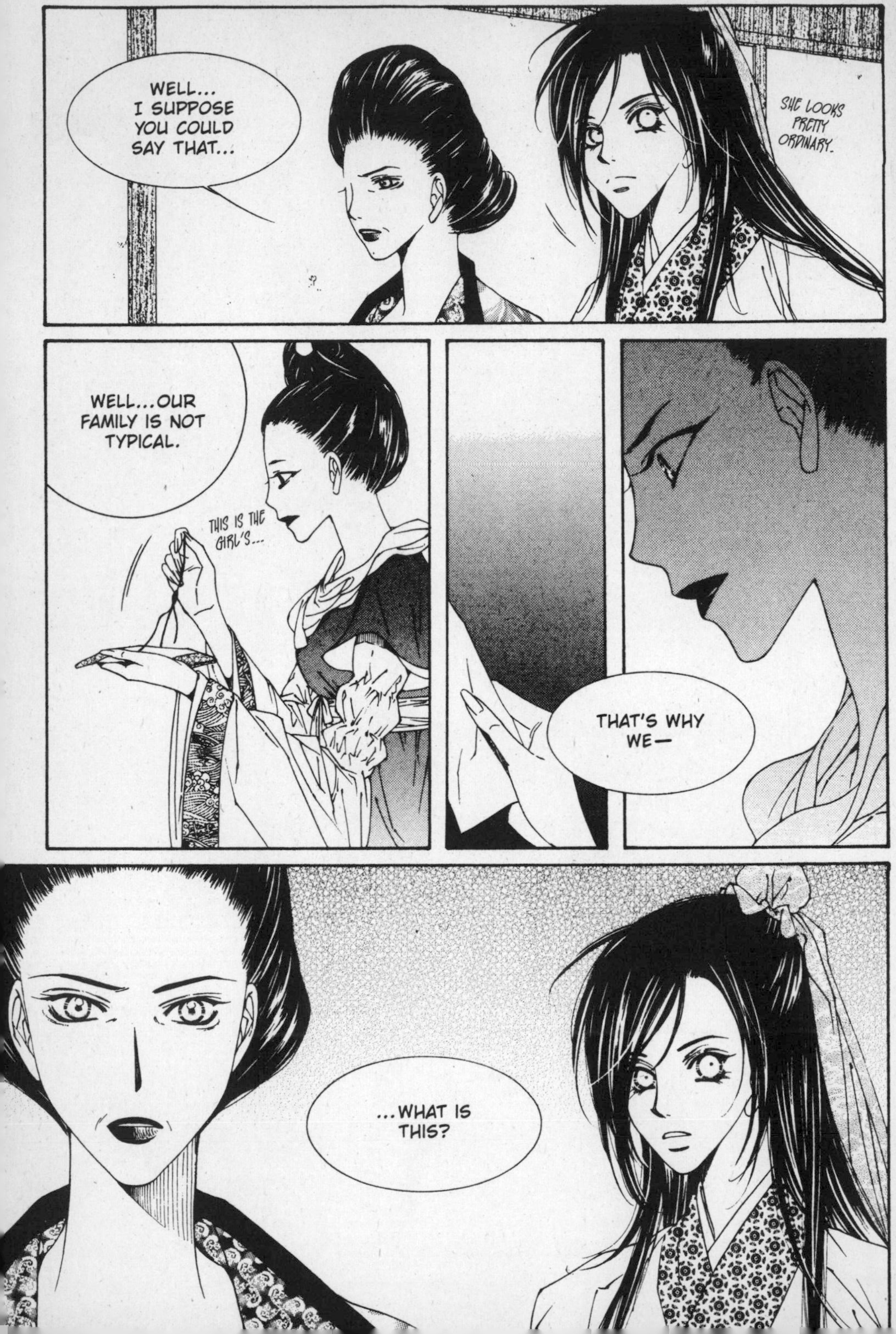
WELL... I SUPPOSE YOU COULD SAY THAT...
SHE LOOKS PRETTY ORDINARY.
WELL...OUR FAMILY IS NOT TYPICAL.
THIS IS THE GIRL'S...
THAT'S WHY WE—
...WHAT IS THIS?

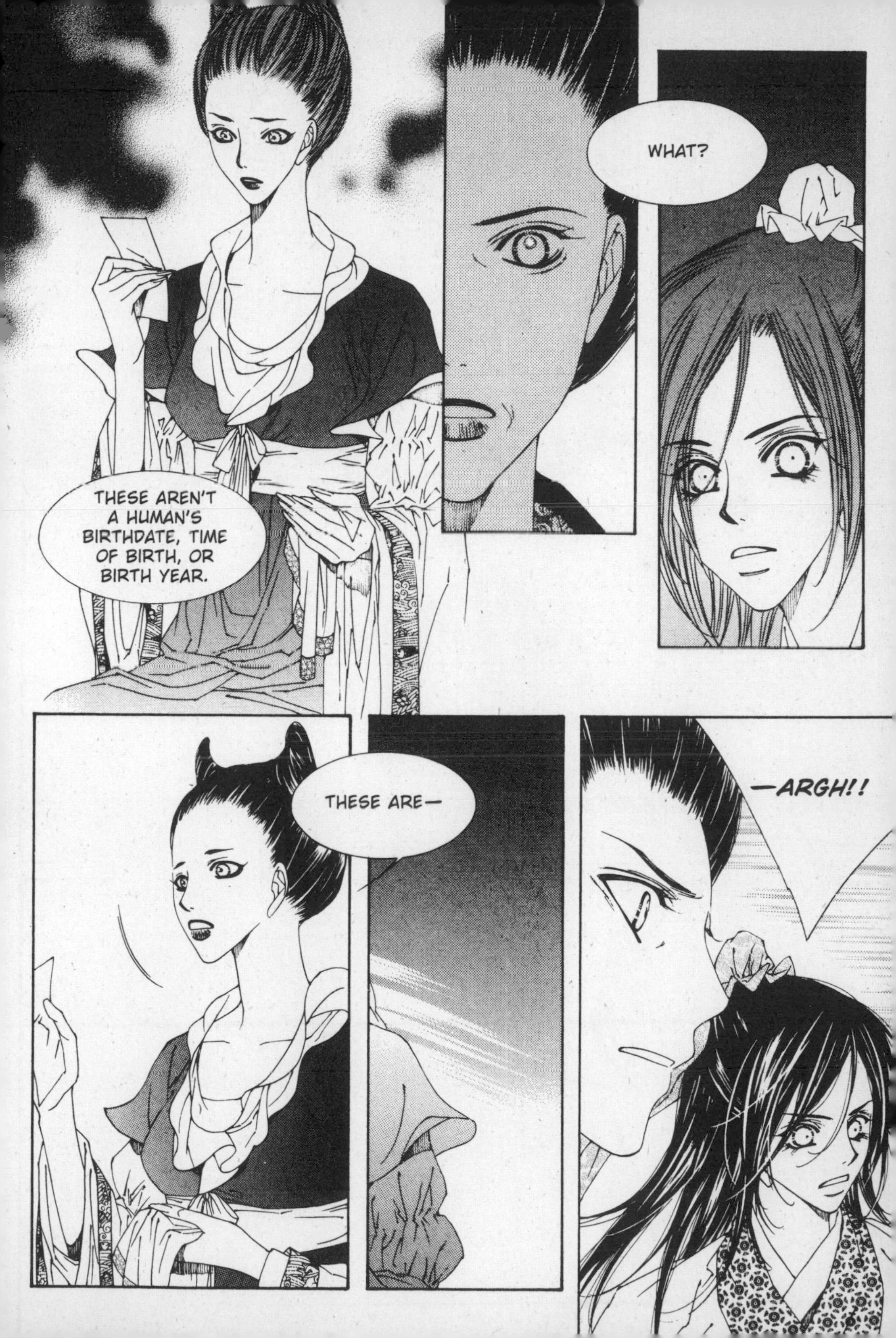
THESE AREN'T A HUMAN'S BIRTHDATE, TIME OF BIRTH, OR BIRTH YEAR.
WHAT?
THESE ARE—
—ARGH!!

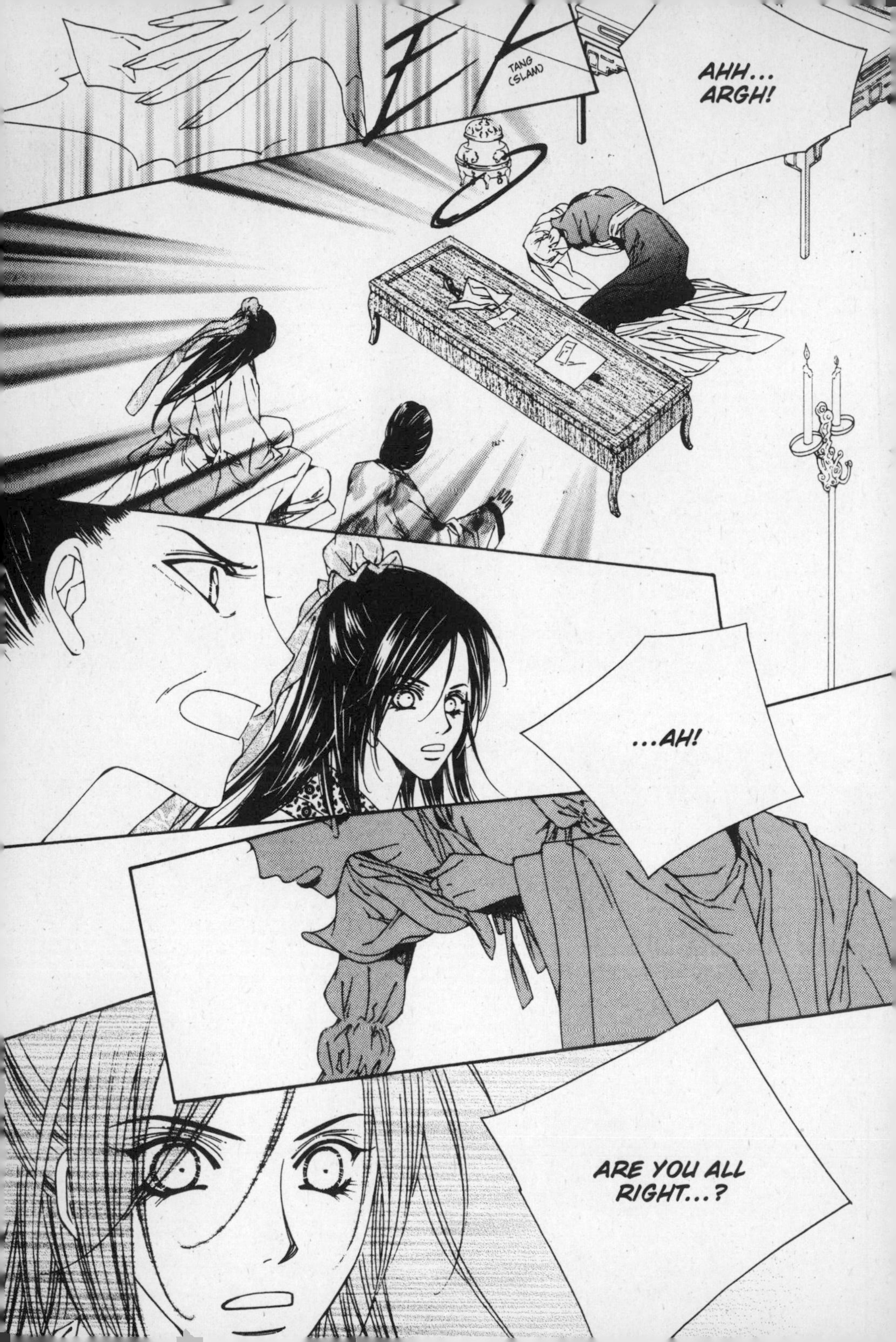
TANG (SLAM)
AHH... ARGH!
...AH!
ARE YOU ALL RIGHT...?

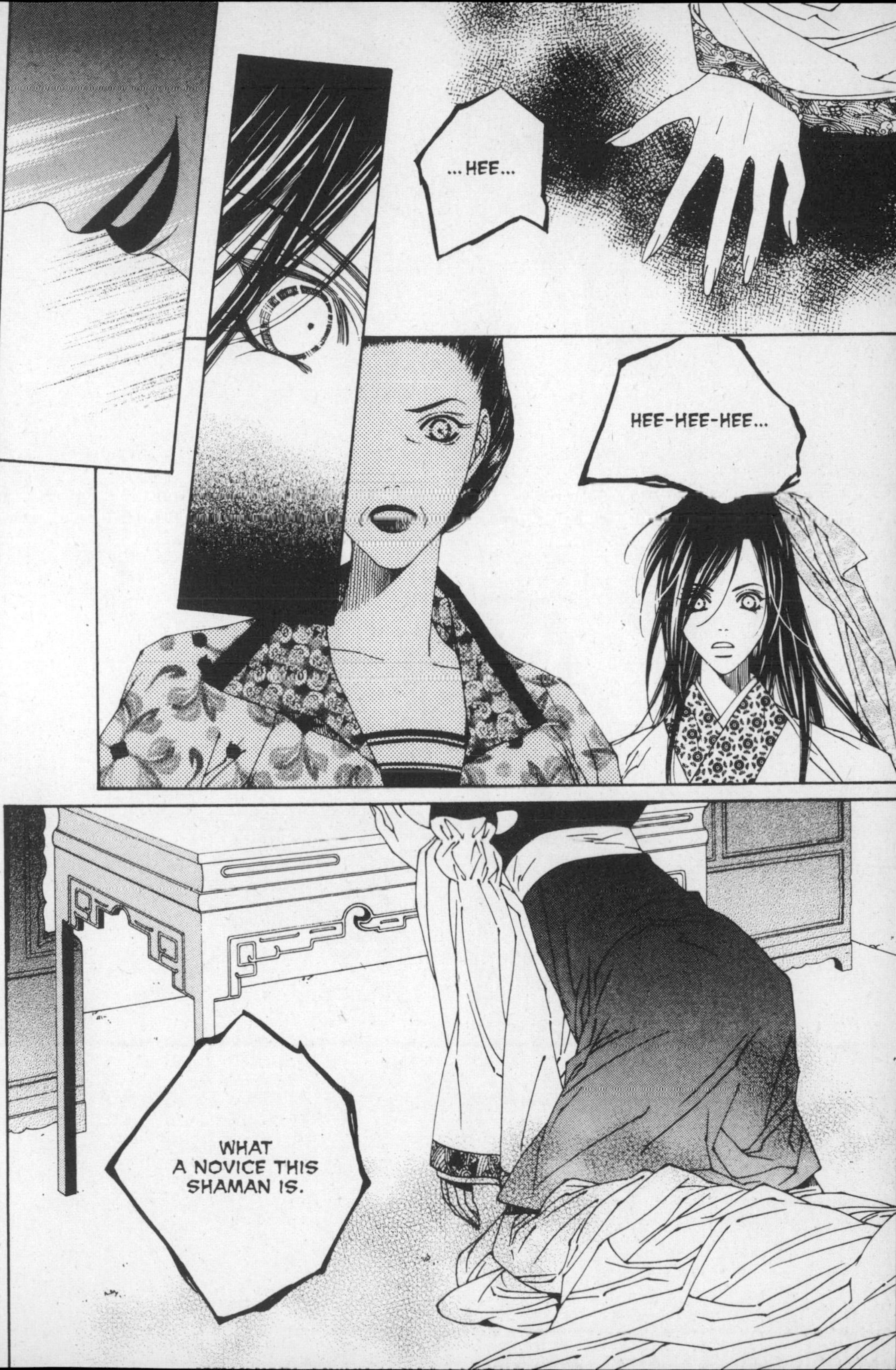
...HEE...
HEE-HEE-HEE...
WHAT A NOVICE THIS SHAMAN IS.

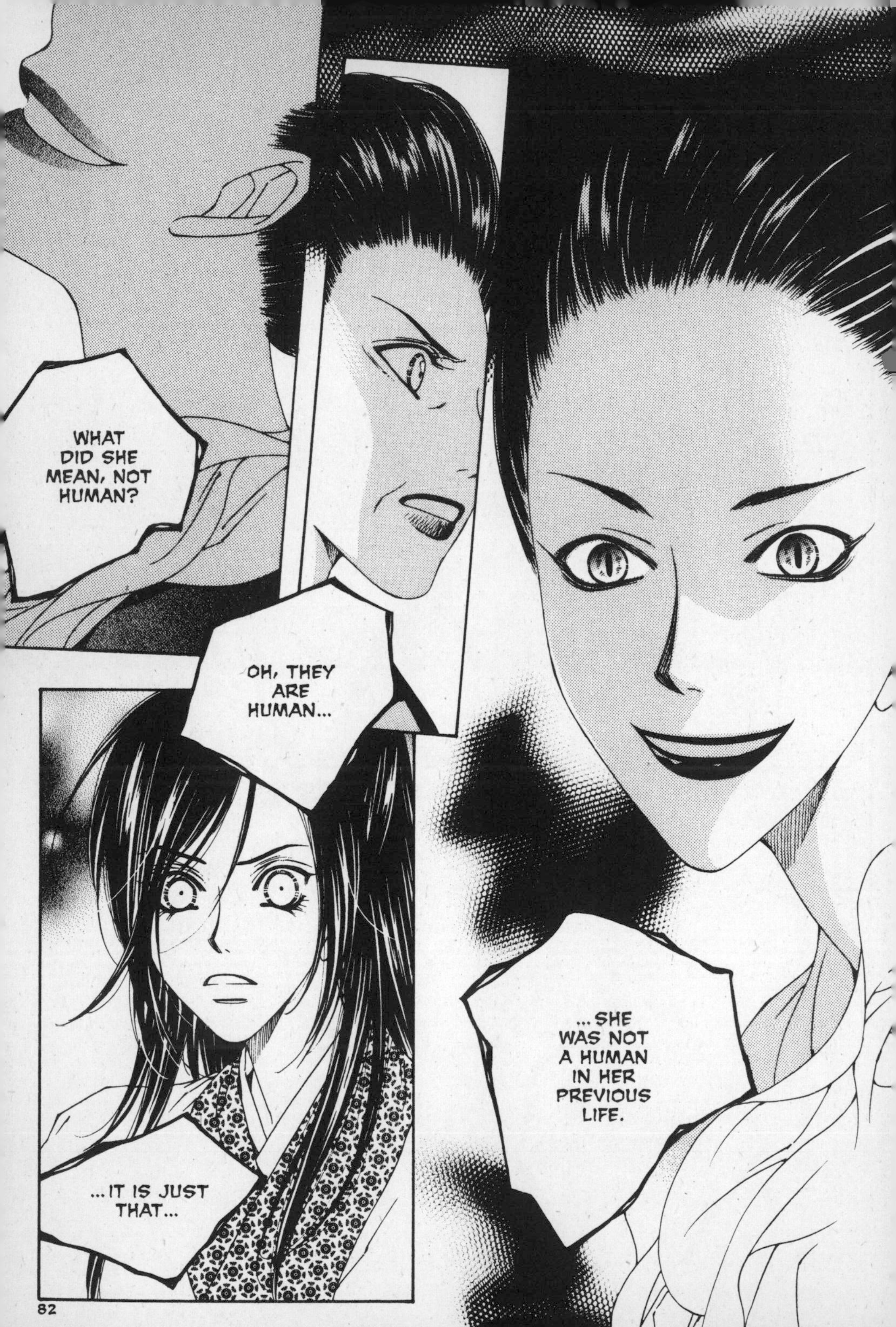
WHAT DID SHE MEAN, NOT HUMAN?
OH, THEY ARE HUMAN...
...IT IS JUST THAT...
...SHE WAS NOT A HUMAN IN HER PREVIOUS LIFE.

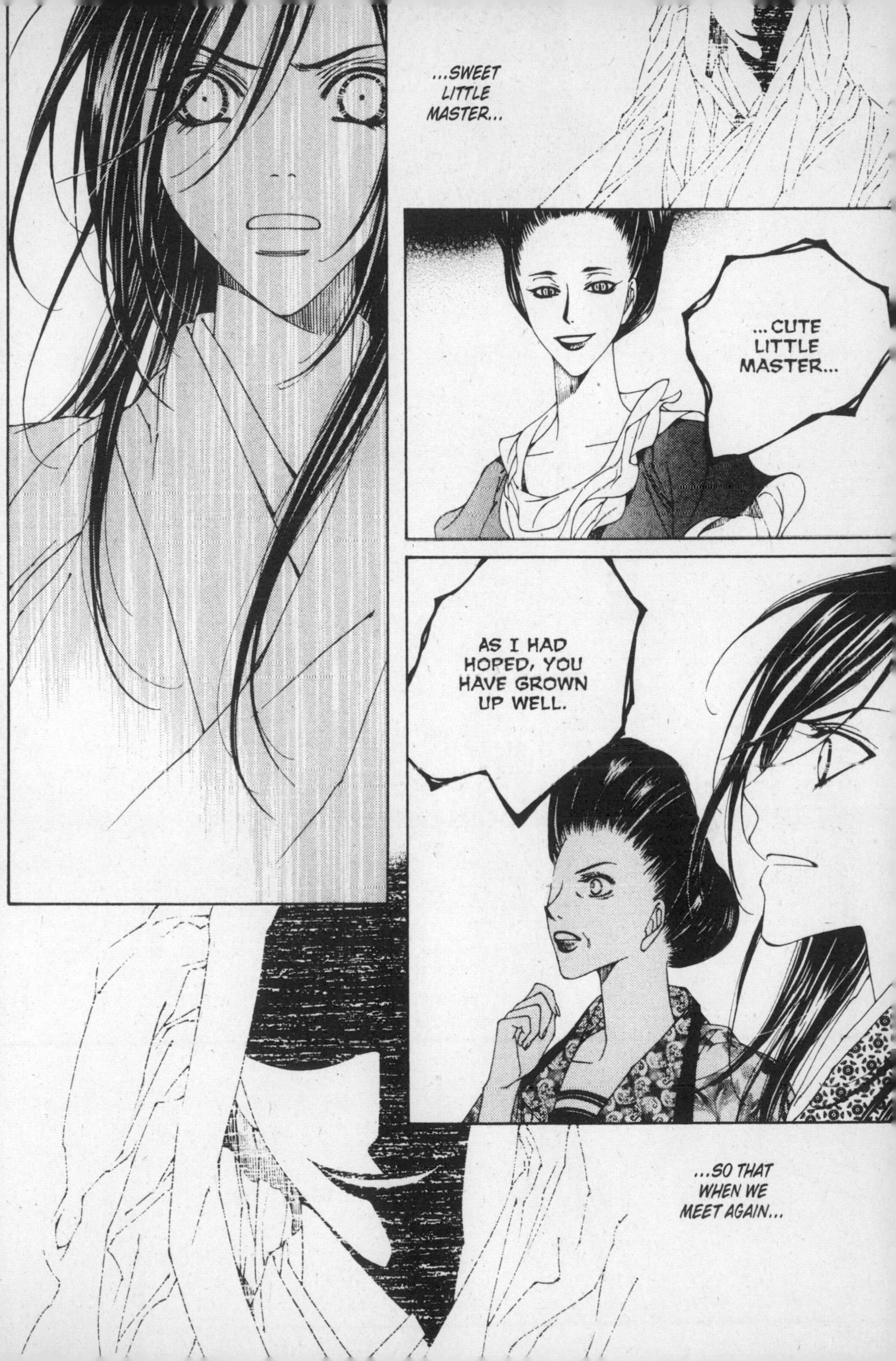
...SWEET LITTLE MASTER...
...CUTE LITTLE MASTER...
AS I HAD HOPED, YOU HAVE GROWN UP WELL.
...SO THAT WHEN WE MEET AGAIN...

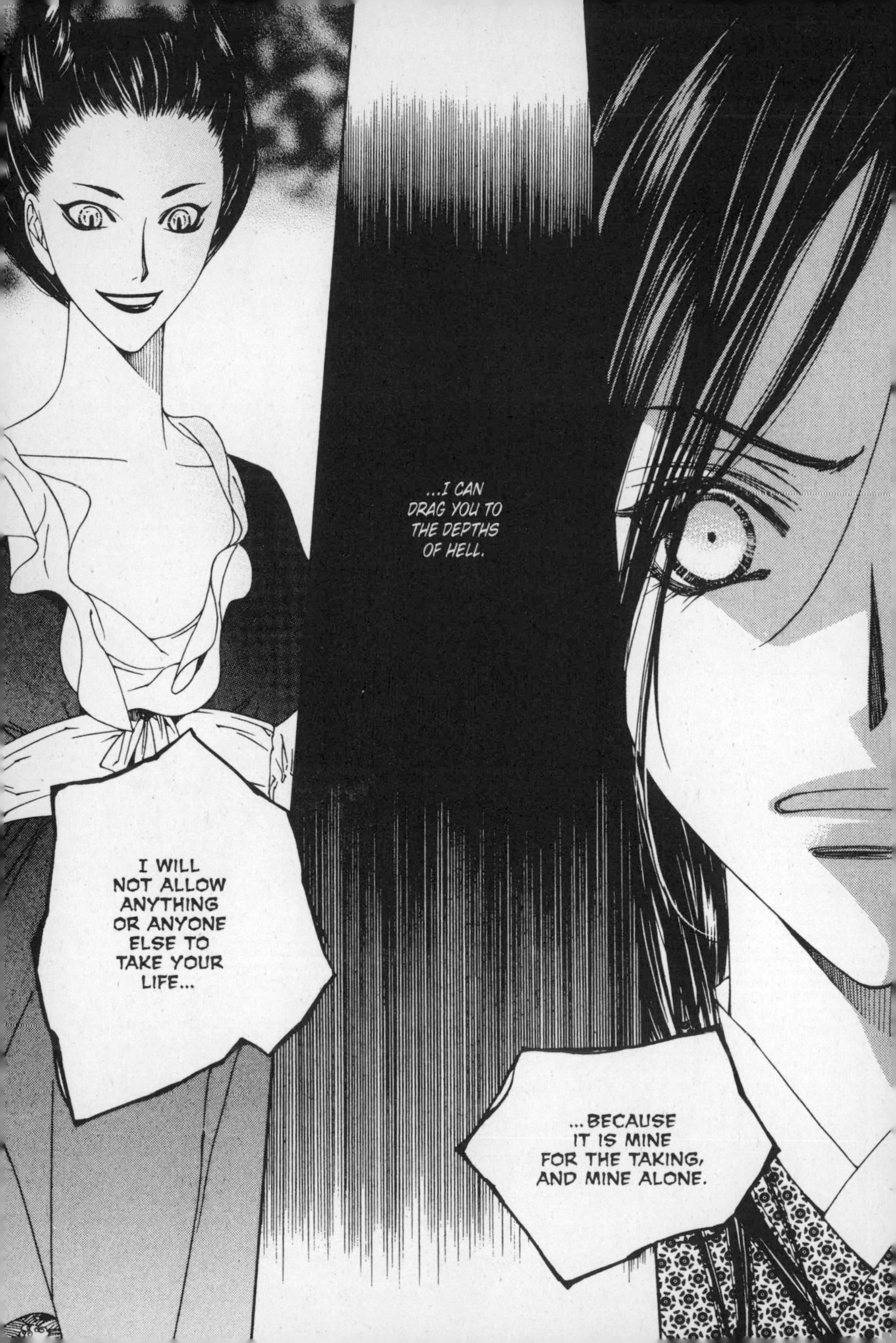
...I CAN DRAG YOU TO THE DEPTHS OF HELL.
I WILL NOT ALLOW ANYTHING OR ANYONE ELSE TO TAKE YOUR LIFE...
...BECAUSE IT IS MINE FOR THE TAKING, AND MINE ALONE.

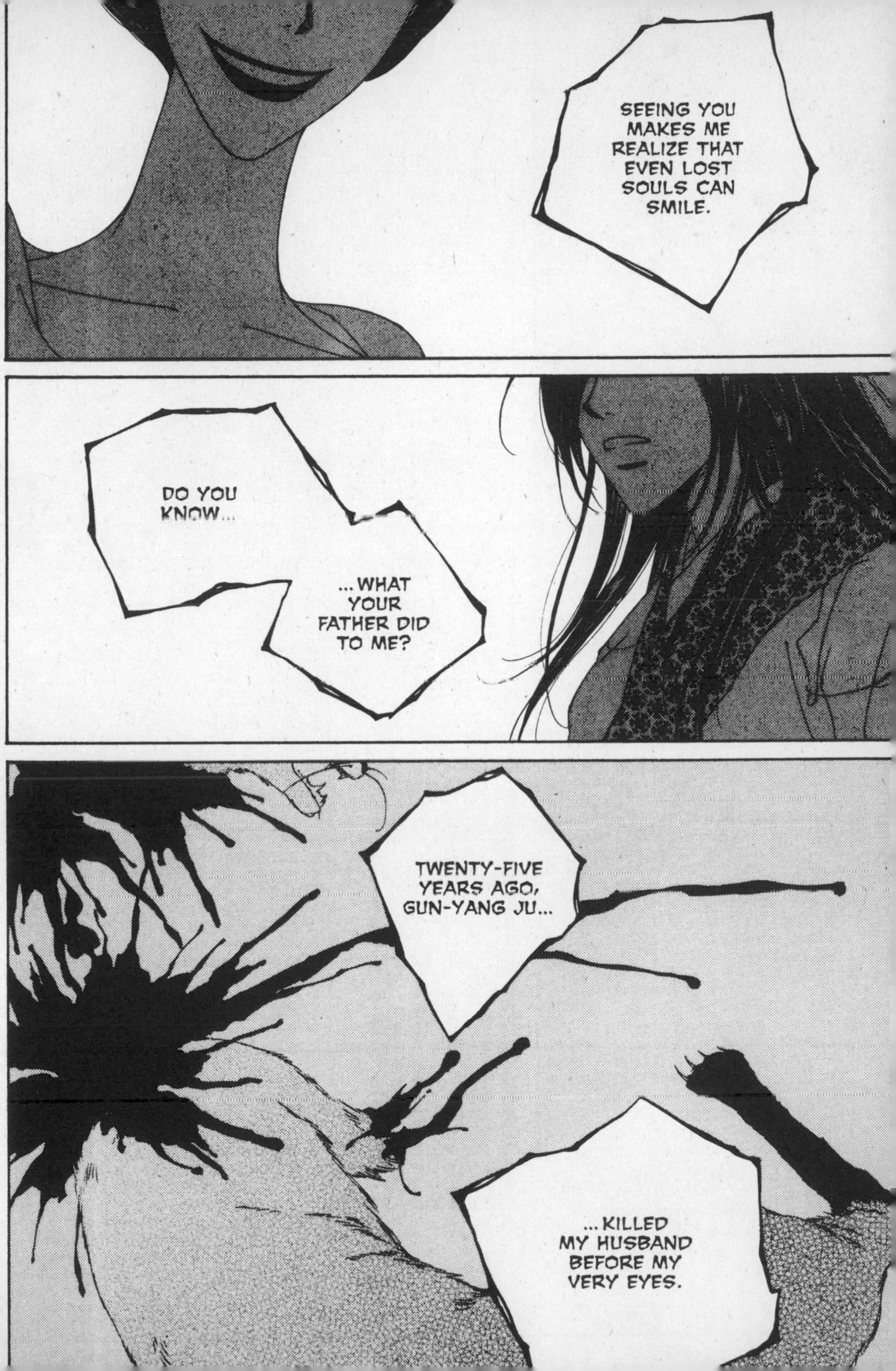
SEEING YOU MAKES ME REALIZE THAT EVEN LOST SOULS CAN SMILE.
DO YOU KNOW...
...WHAT YOUR FATHER DID TO ME?
TWENTY-FIVE YEARS AGO, GUN-YANG JU...
...KILLED MY HUSBAND BEFORE MY VERY EYES.

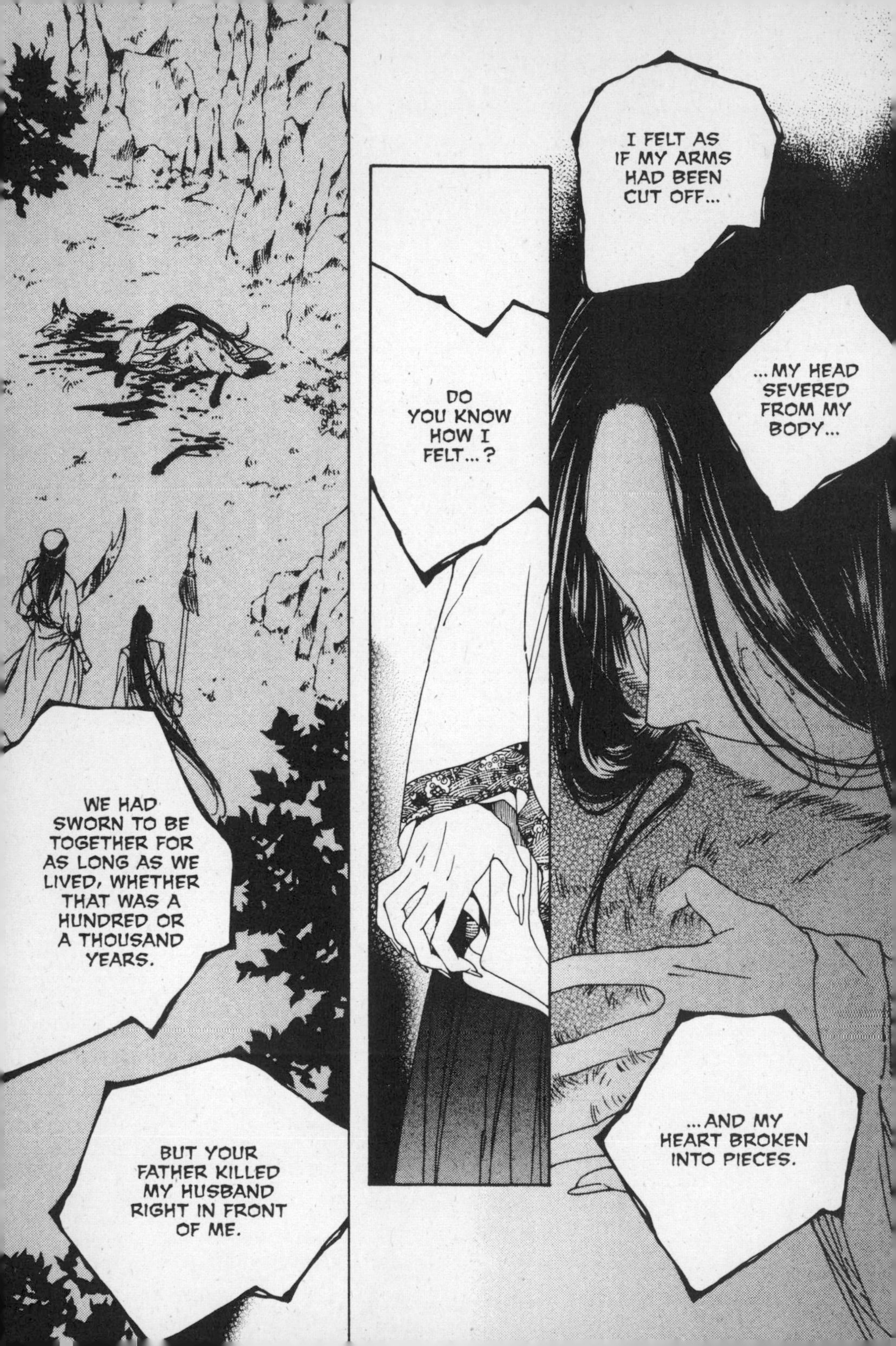
WE HAD SWORN TO BE TOGETHER FOR AS LONG AS WE LIVED, WHETHER THAT WAS A HUNDRED OR A THOUSAND YEARS.
BUT YOUR FATHER KILLED MY HUSBAND RIGHT IN FRONT OF ME.
DO YOU KNOW HOW I FELT...?
I FELT AS IF MY ARMS HAD BEEN CUT OFF...
...MY HEAD SEVERED FROM MY BODY...
...AND MY HEART BROKEN INTO PIECES.

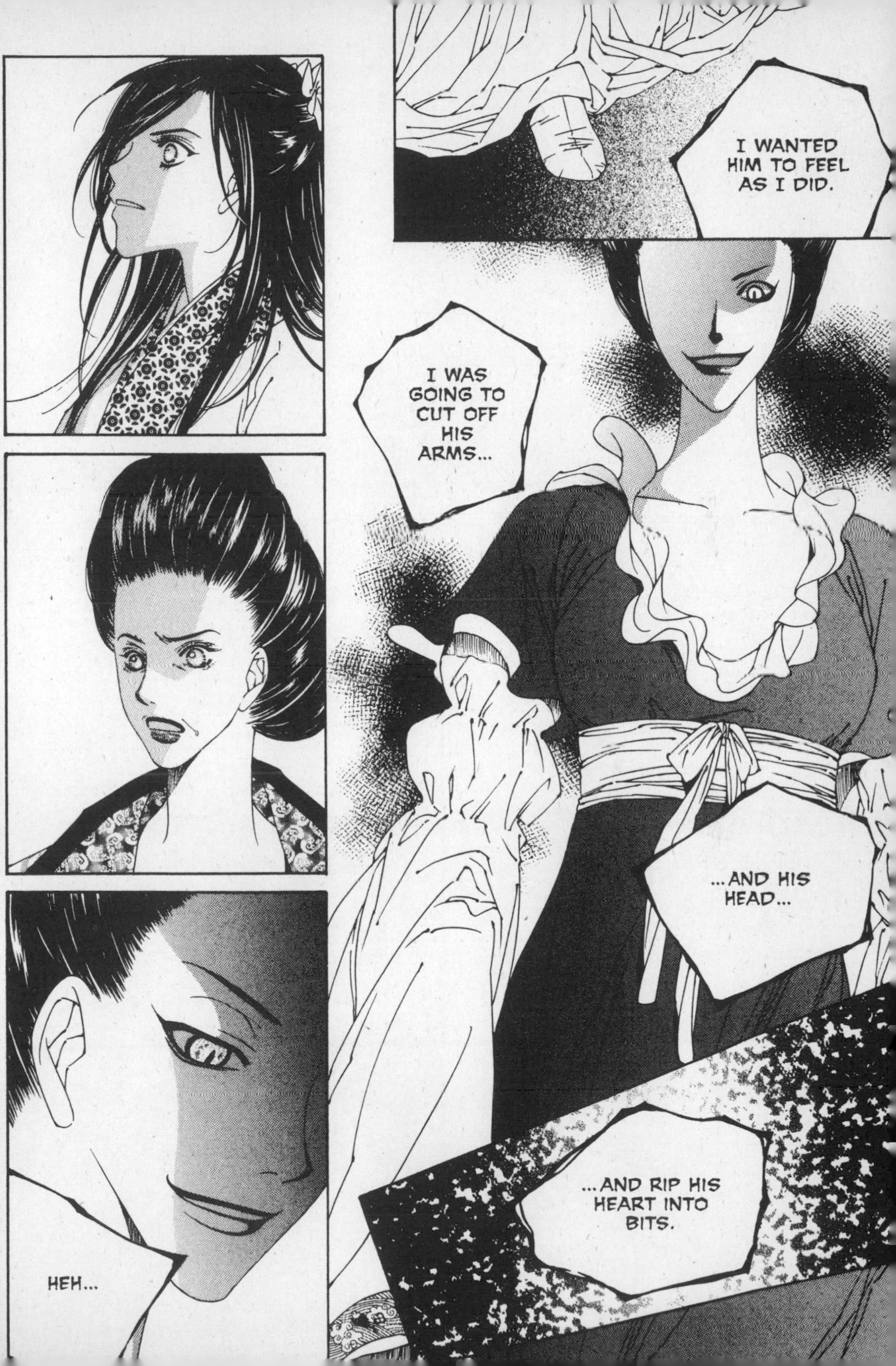
HEH...
I WANTED HIM TO FEEL AS I DID.
I WAS GOING TO CUT OFF HIS ARMS...
...AND HIS HEAD...
...AND RIP HIS HEART INTO BITS.

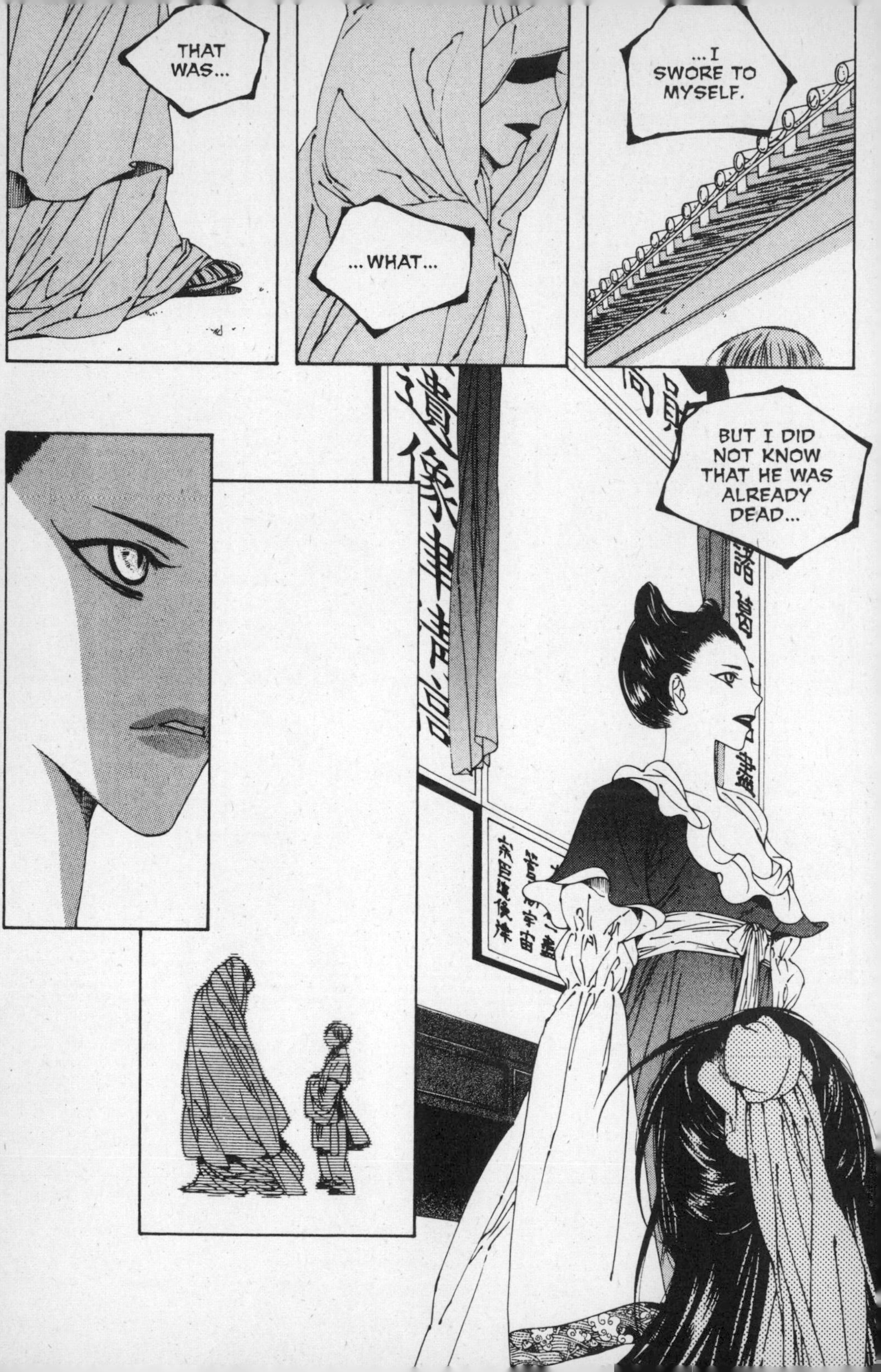
THAT WAS...
...WHAT...
...I SWORE TO MYSELF.
BUT I DID NOT KNOW THAT HE WAS ALREADY DEAD...

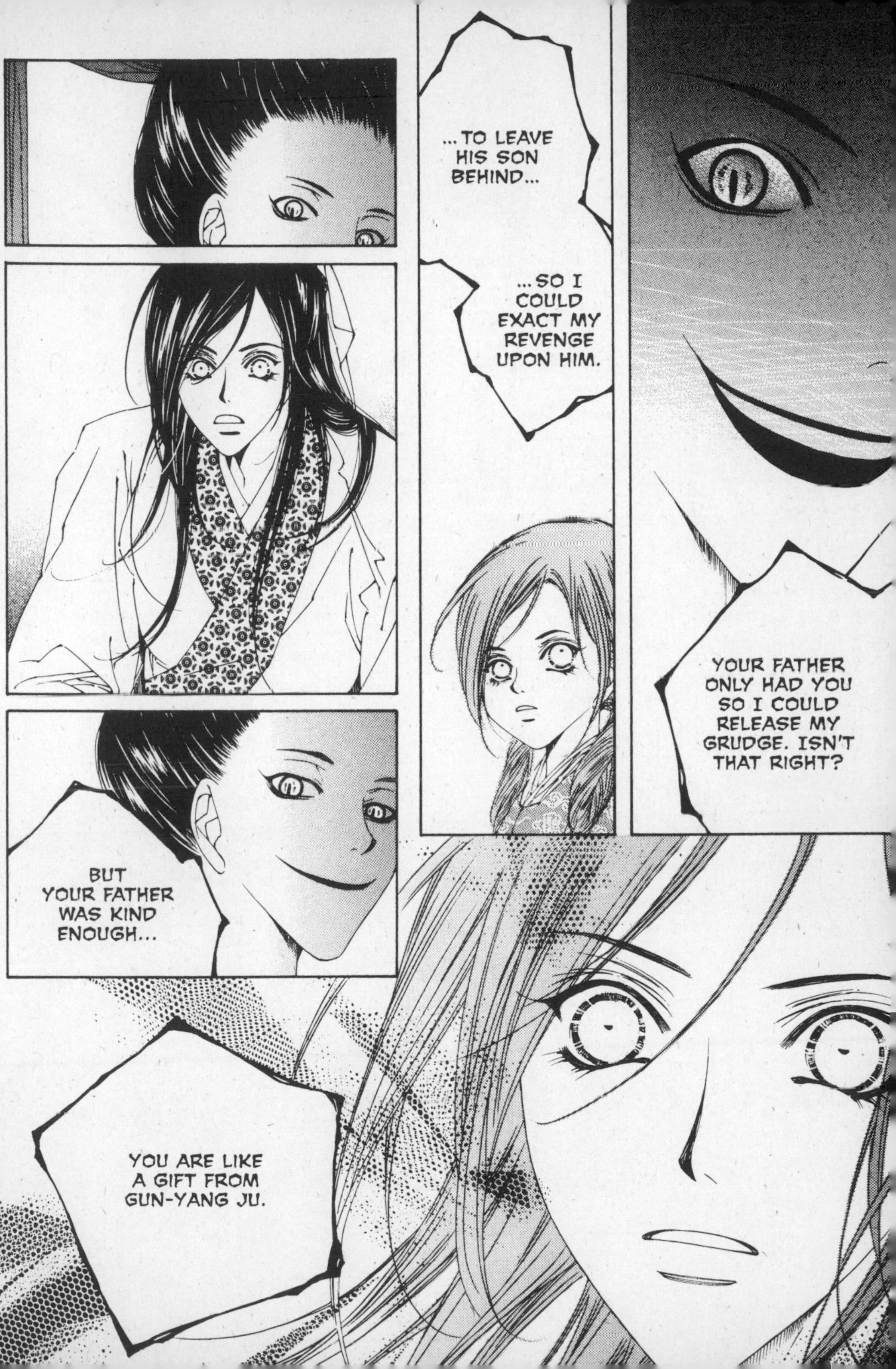
BUT YOUR FATHER WAS KIND ENOUGH...
...TO LEAVE HIS SON BEHIND...
...SO I COULD EXACT MY REVENGE UPON HIM.
YOUR FATHER ONLY HAD YOU SO I COULD RELEASE MY GRUDGE. ISN'T THAT RIGHT?
YOU ARE LIKE A GIFT FROM GUN-YANG JU.

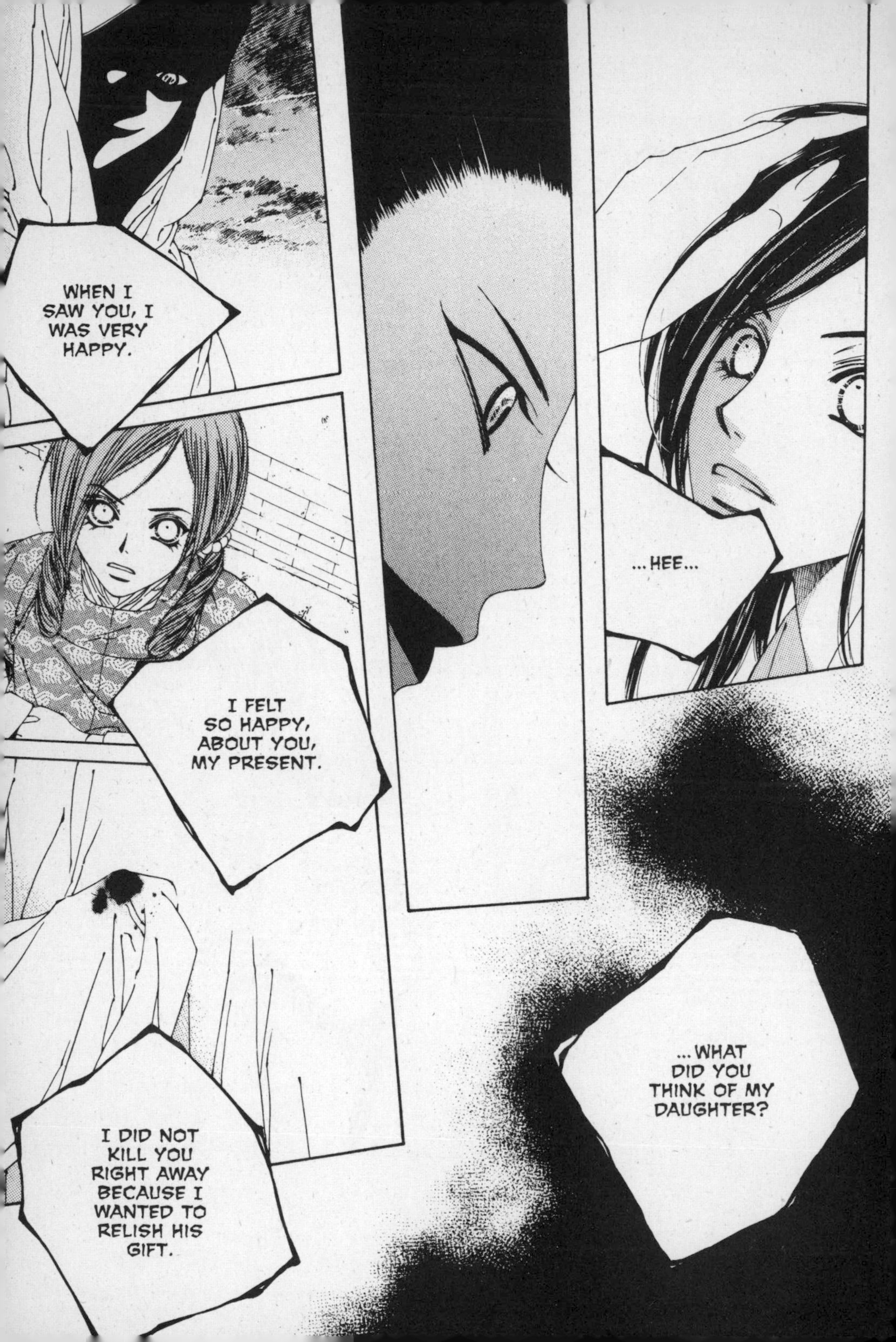
WHEN I SAW YOU, I WAS VERY HAPPY.
I FELT SO HAPPY, ABOUT YOU, MY PRESENT.
I DID NOT KILL YOU RIGHT AWAY BECAUSE I WANTED TO RELISH HIS GIFT.
...HEE...
...WHAT DID YOU THINK OF MY DAUGHTER?

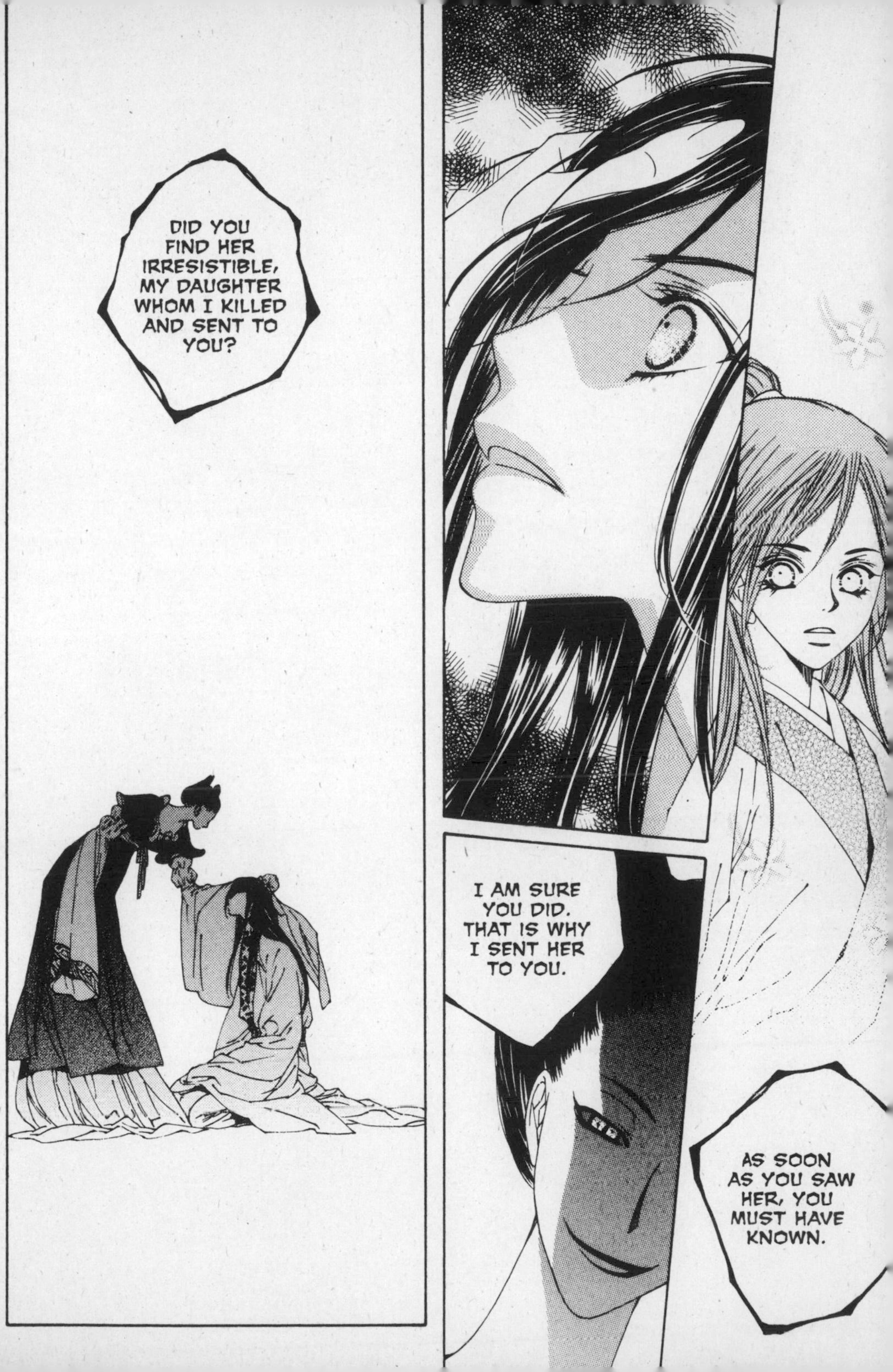
DID YOU FIND HER IRRESISTIBLE, MY DAUGHTER WHOM I KILLED AND SENT TO YOU?
I AM SURE YOU DID. THAT IS WHY I SENT HER TO YOU.
AS SOON AS YOU SAW HER, YOU MUST HAVE KNOWN.

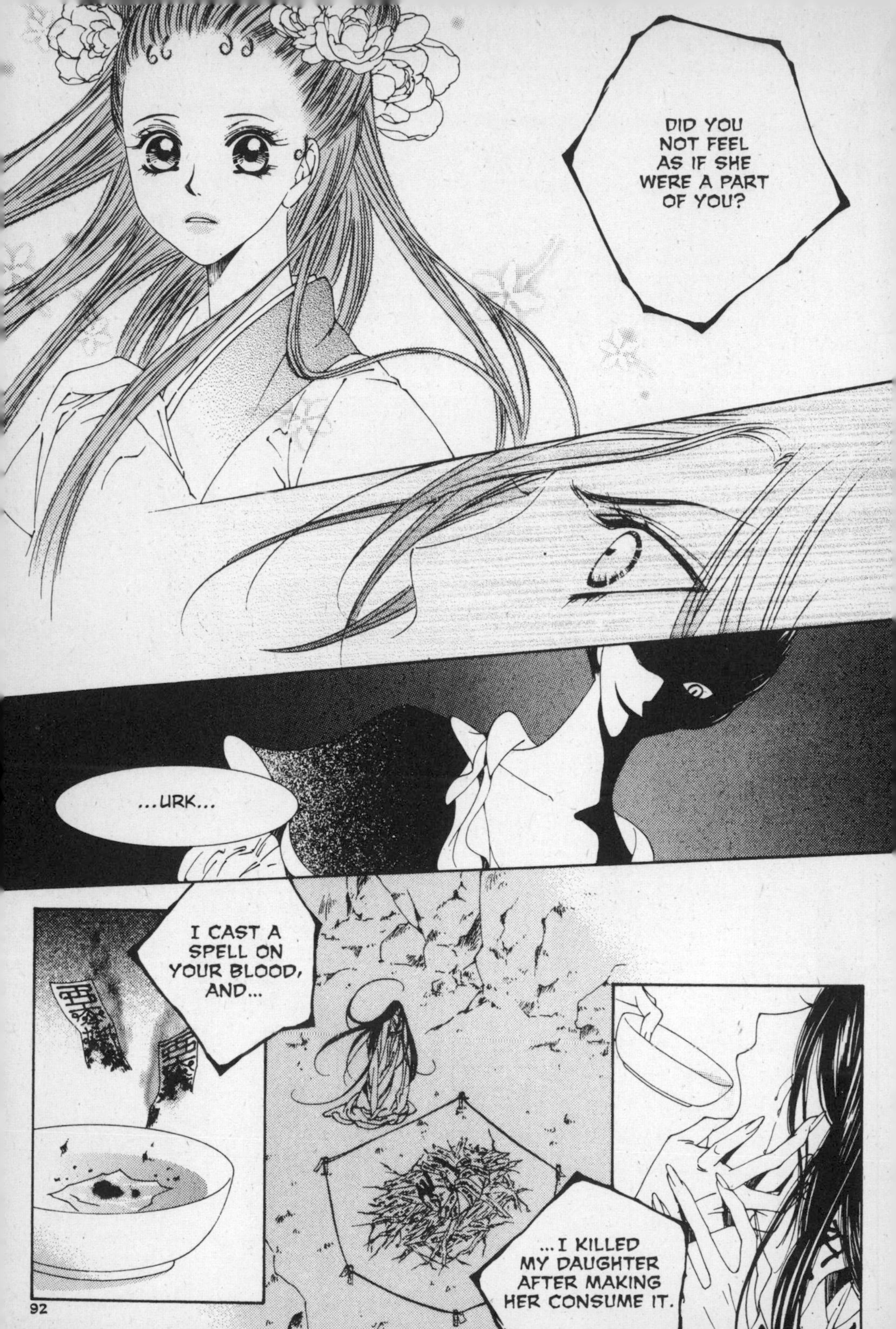
DID YOU NOT FEEL AS IF SHE WERE A PART OF YOU?
...URK...
I CAST A SPELL ON YOUR BLOOD, AND...
...I KILLED MY DAUGHTER AFTER MAKING HER CONSUME IT.

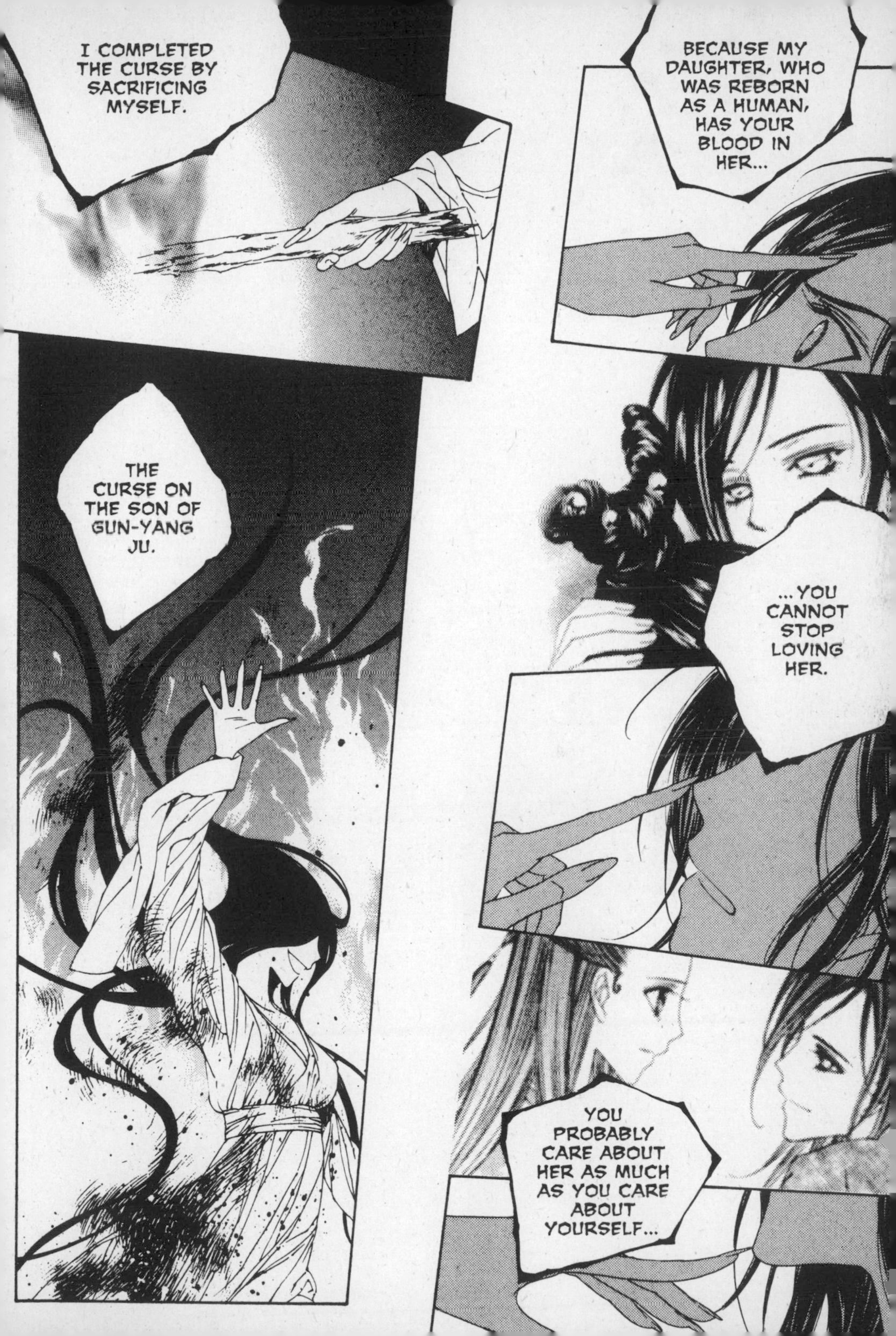
I COMPLETED THE CURSE BY SACRIFICING MYSELF.
THE CURSE ON THE SON OF GUN-YANG JU.
BECAUSE MY DAUGHTER, WHO WAS REBORN AS A HUMAN, HAS YOUR BLOOD IN HER...
...YOU CANNOT STOP LOVING HER.
YOU PROBABLY CARE ABOUT HER AS MUCH AS YOU CARE ABOUT YOURSELF...

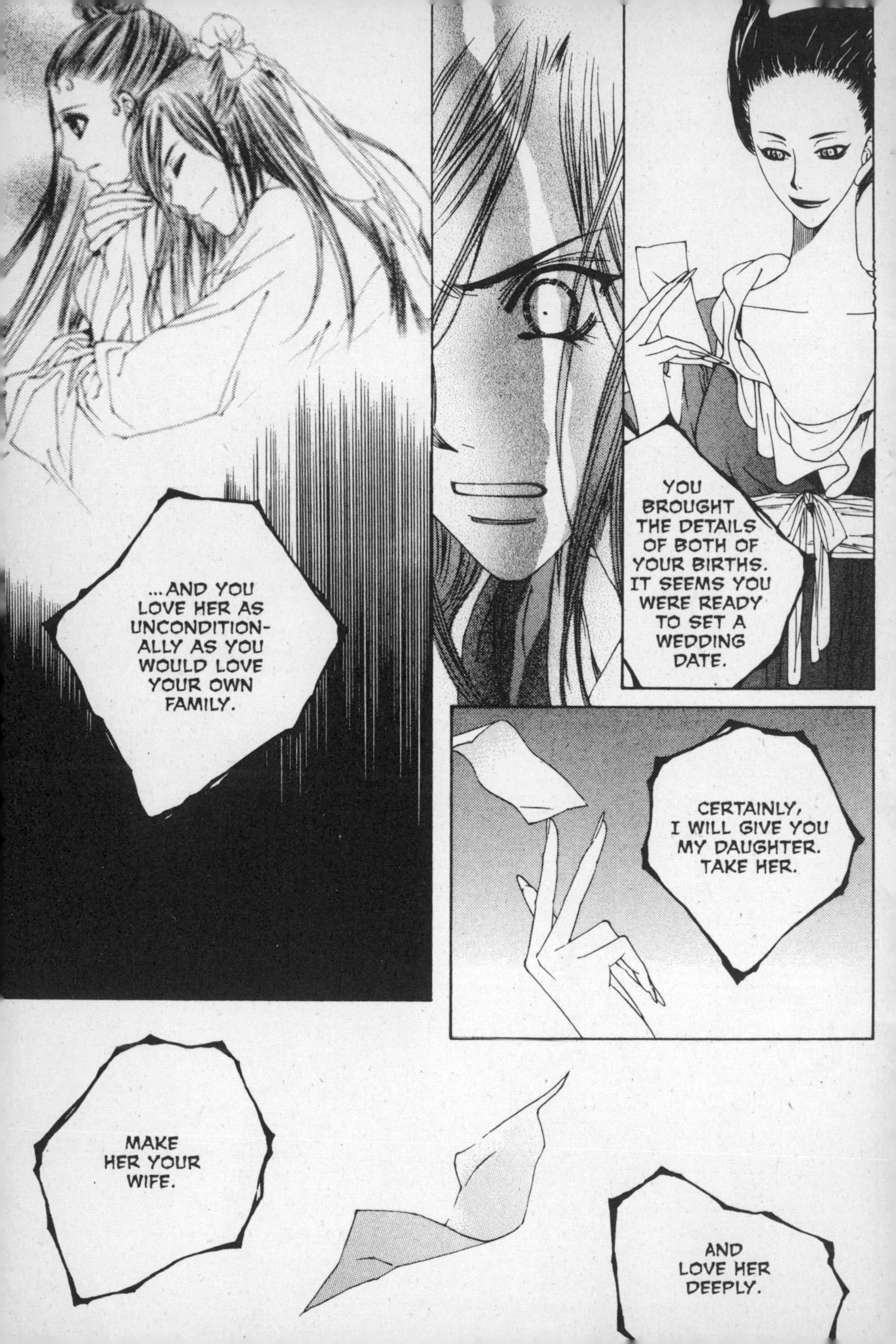
...AND YOU LOVE HER AS UNCONDITION-ALLY AS YOU WOULD LOVE YOUR OWN FAMILY.
YOU BROUGHT THE DETAILS OF BOTH OF YOUR BIRTHS. IT SEEMS YOU WERE READY TO SET A WEDDING DATE.
CERTAINLY, I WILL GIVE YOU MY DAUGHTER. TAKE HER.
MAKE HER YOUR WIFE.
AND LOVE HER DEEPLY.

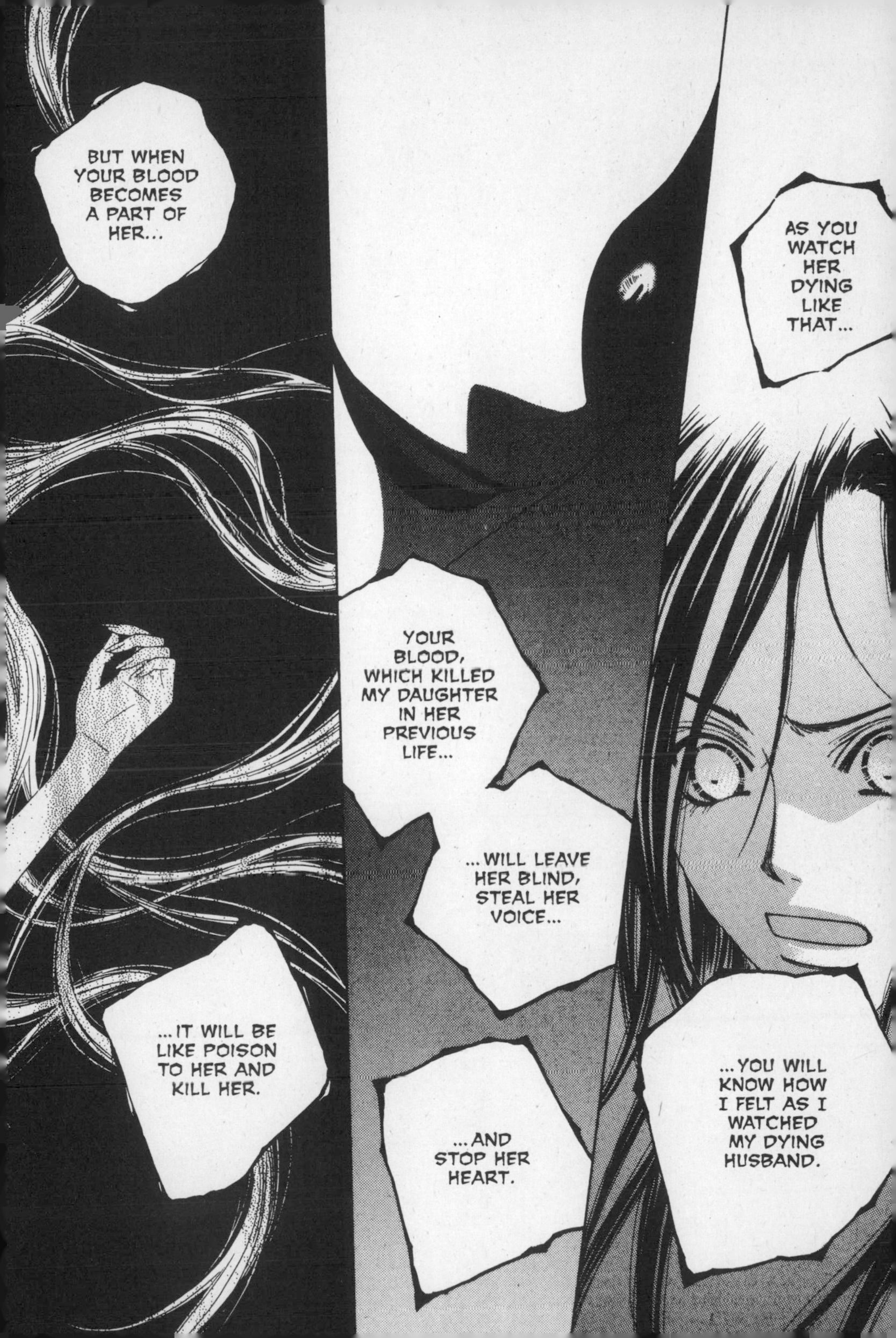
BUT WHEN YOUR BLOOD BECOMES A PART OF HER...
...IT WILL BE LIKE POISON TO HER AND KILL HER.
YOUR BLOOD, WHICH KILLED MY DAUGHTER IN HER PREVIOUS LIFE...
...WILL LEAVE HER BLIND, STEAL HER VOICE...
...AND STOP HER HEART.
AS YOU WATCH HER DYING LIKE THAT...
...YOU WILL KNOW HOW I FELT AS I WATCHED MY DYING HUSBAND.

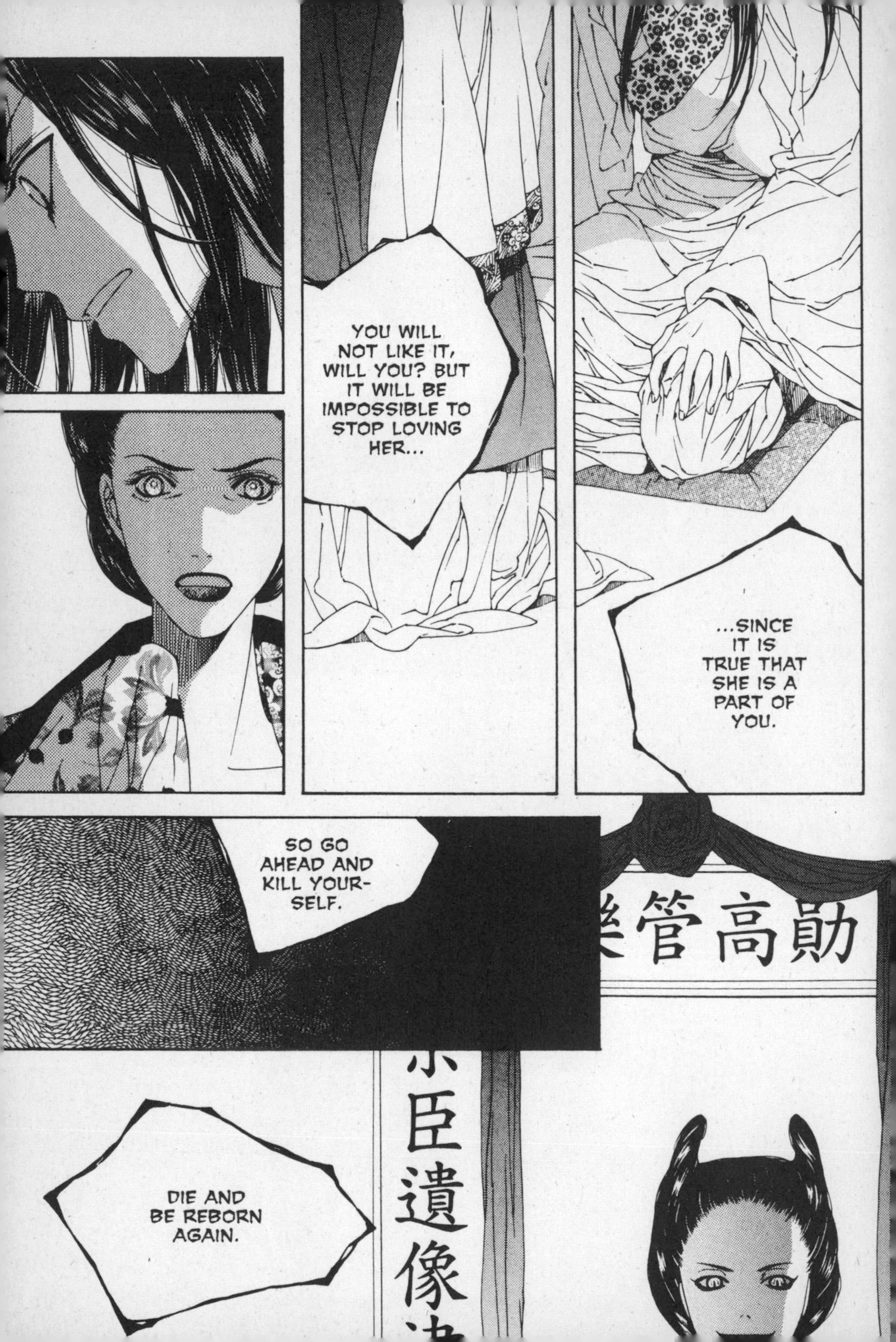
YOU WILL NOT LIKE IT, WILL YOU? BUT IT WILL BE IMPOSSIBLE TO STOP LOVING HER...
...SINCE IT IS TRUE THAT SHE IS A PART OF YOU.
SO GO AHEAD AND KILL YOUR-SELF.
勛高管
臣遺像
DIE AND BE REBORN AGAIN.

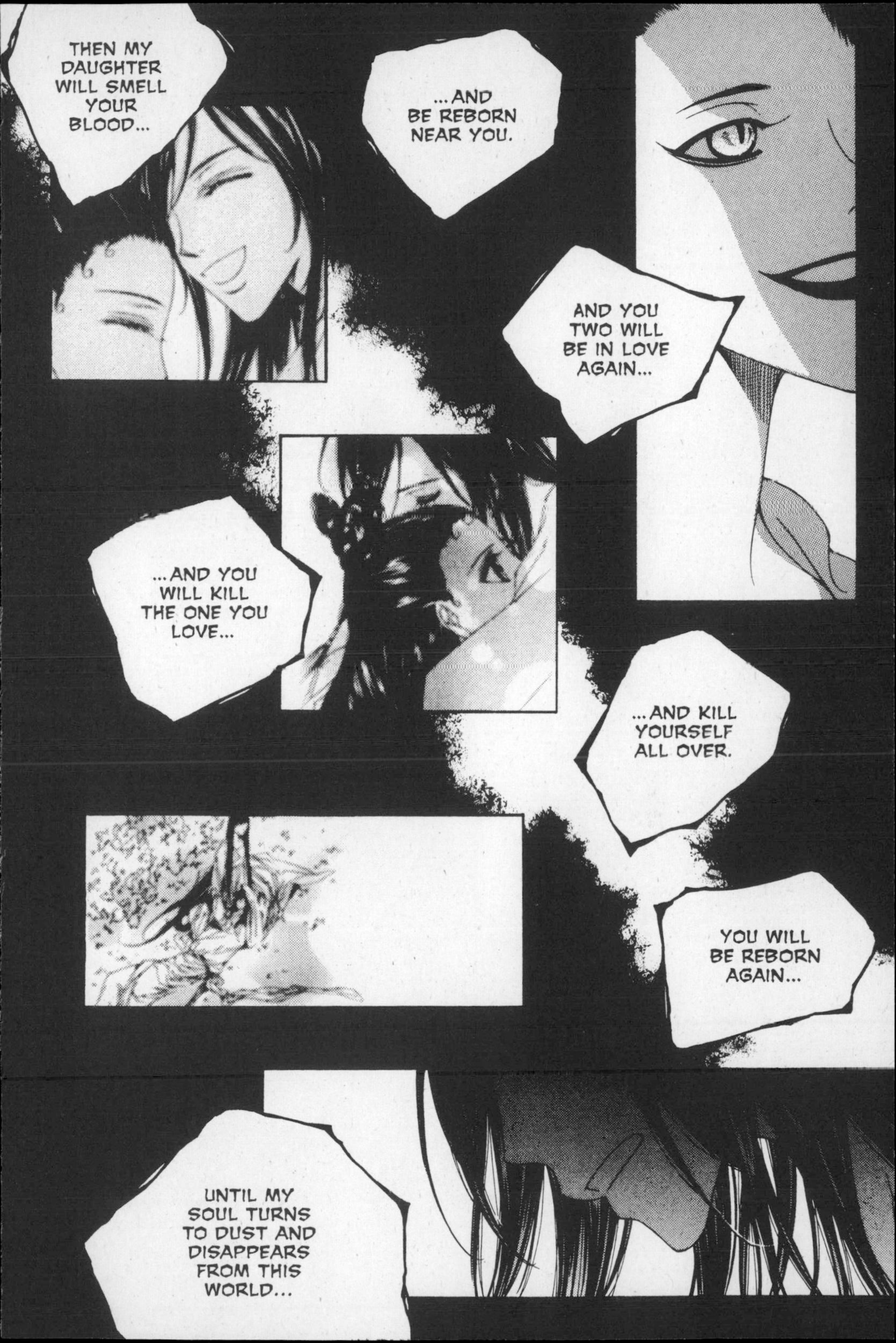
THEN MY DAUGHTER WILL SMELL YOUR BLOOD...
...AND BE REBORN NEAR YOU.
AND YOU TWO WILL BE IN LOVE AGAIN...
...AND YOU WILL KILL THE ONE YOU LOVE...
...AND KILL YOURSELF ALL OVER.
YOU WILL BE REBORN AGAIN...
UNTIL MY SOUL TURNS TO DUST AND DISAPPEARS FROM THIS WORLD...

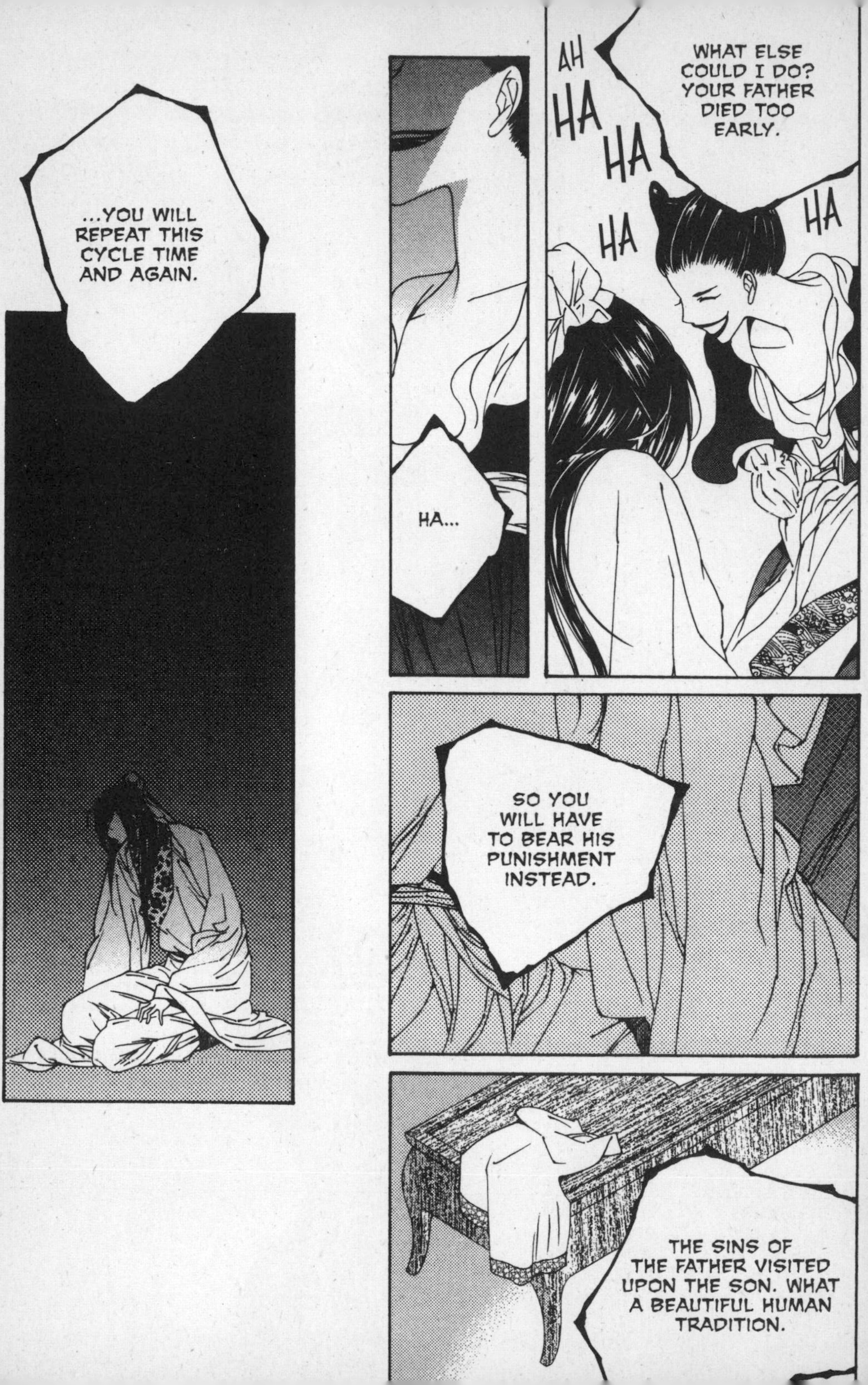
...YOU WILL REPEAT THIS CYCLE TIME AND AGAIN.
HA...
AH HA HA HA HA
WHAT ELSE COULD I DO? YOUR FATHER DIED TOO EARLY.
SO YOU WILL HAVE TO BEAR HIS PUNISHMENT INSTEAD.
THE SINS OF THE FATHER VISITED UPON THE SON. WHAT A BEAUTIFUL HUMAN TRADITION.

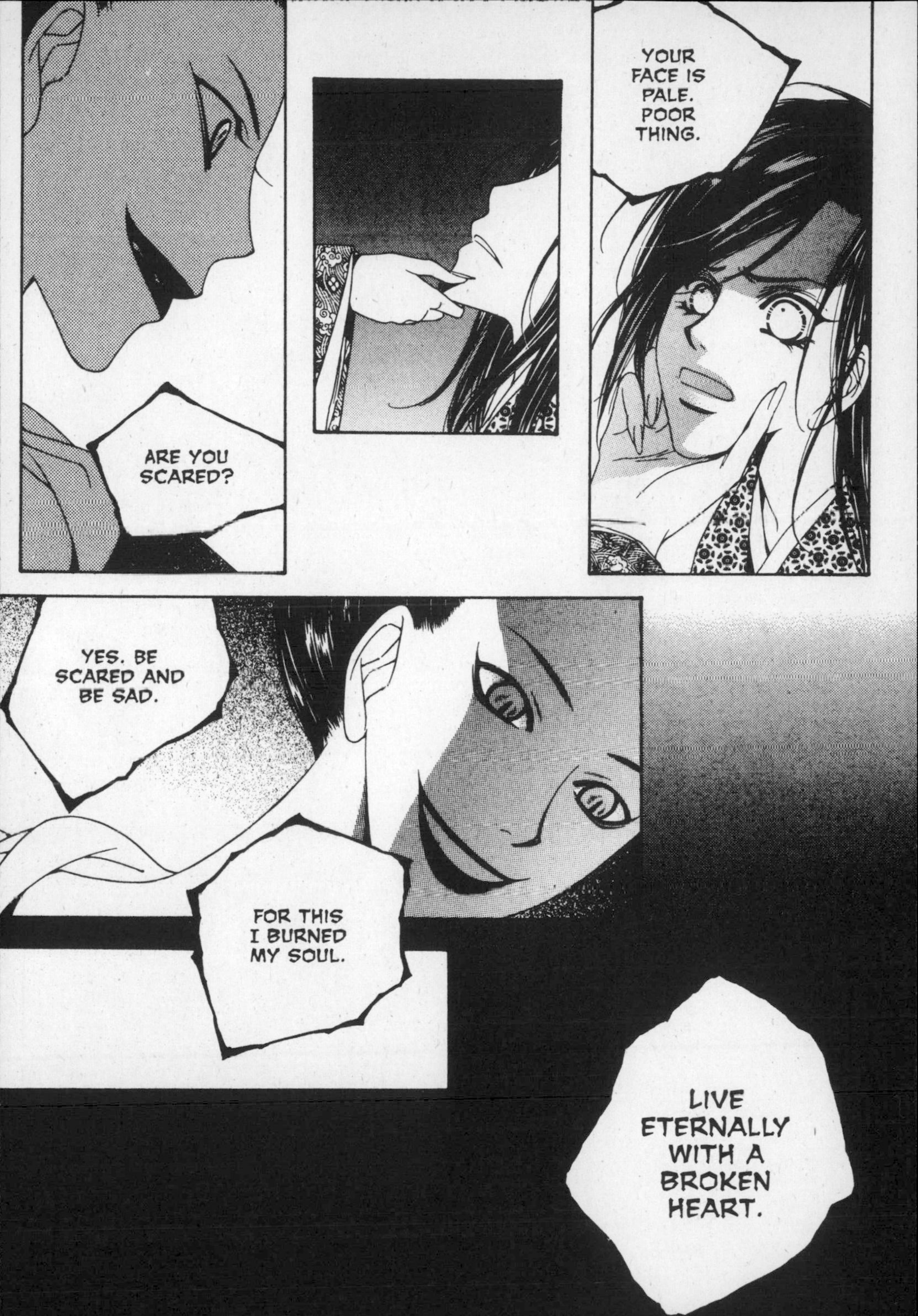
ARE YOU SCARED?
YOUR FACE IS PALE. POOR THING.
YES. BE SCARED AND BE SAD.
FOR THIS I BURNED MY SOUL.
LIVE ETERNALLY WITH A BROKEN HEART.

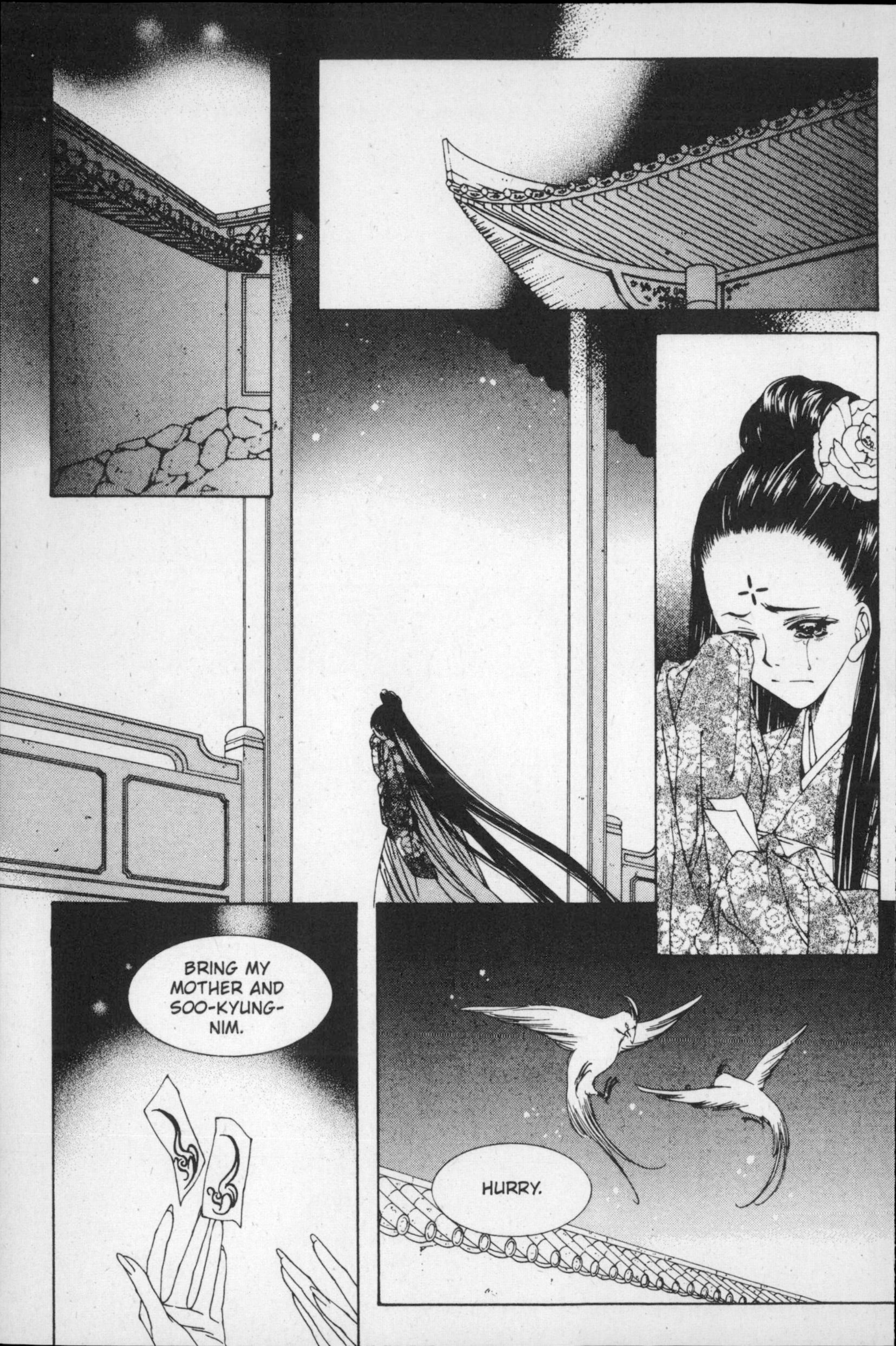
BRING MY MOTHER AND SOO-KYUNG-NIM.
HURRY.

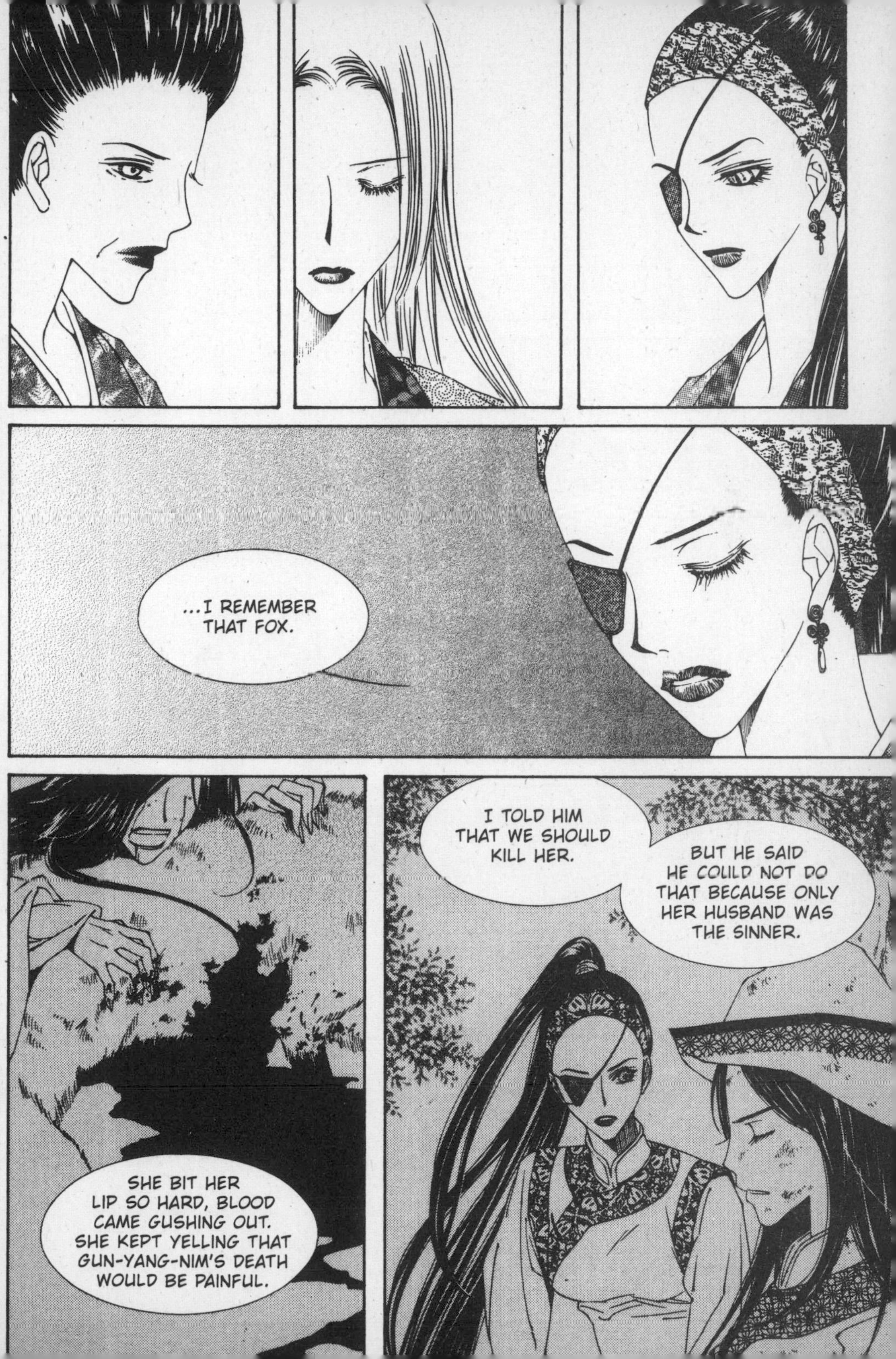
...I REMEMBER THAT FOX.
SHE BIT HER LIP SO HARD, BLOOD CAME GUSHING OUT. SHE KEPT YELLING THAT GUN-YANG-NIM'S DEATH WOULD BE PAINFUL.
I TOLD HIM THAT WE SHOULD KILL HER.
BUT HE SAID HE COULD NOT DO THAT BECAUSE ONLY HER HUSBAND WAS THE SINNER.

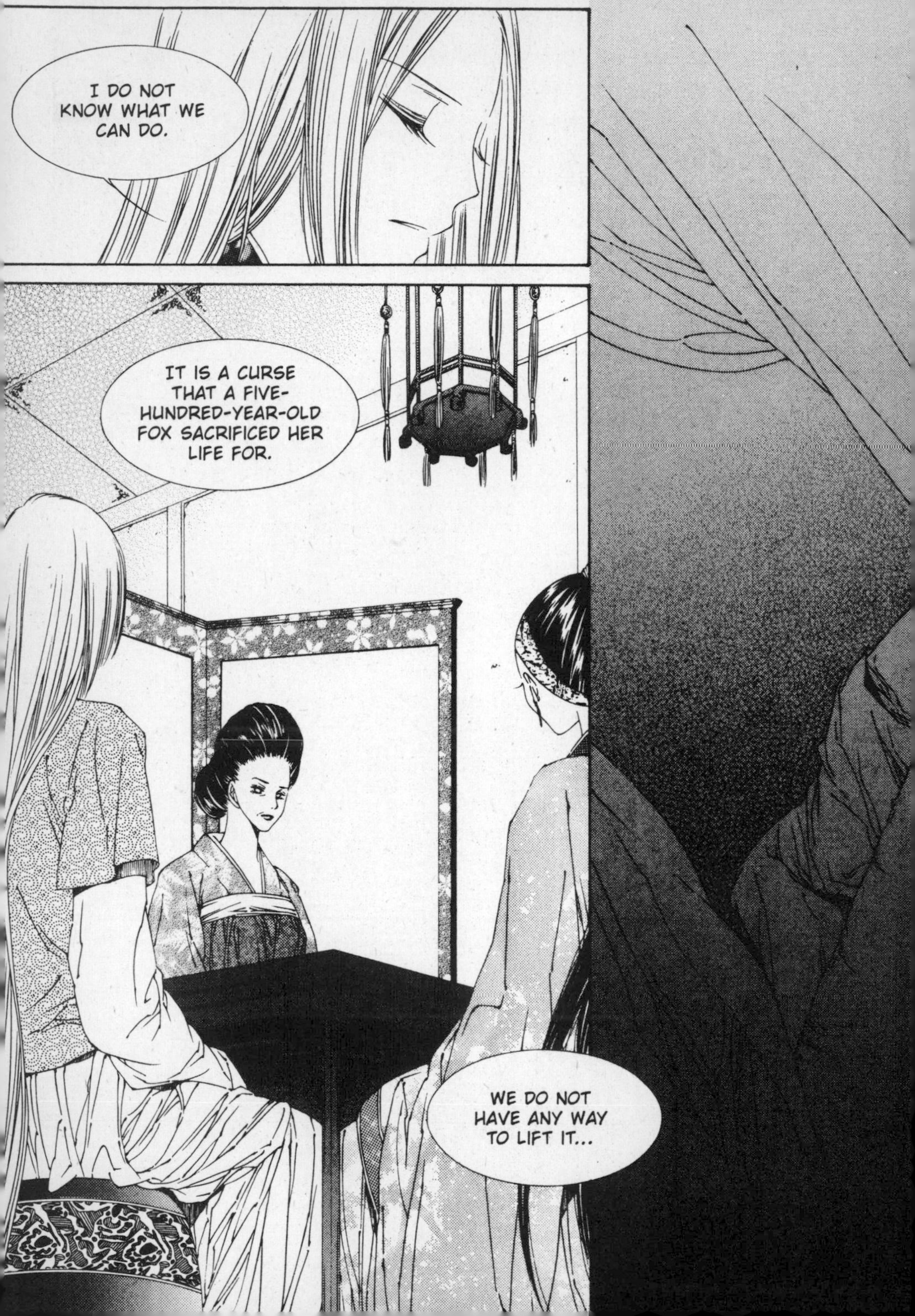

I DO NOT KNOW WHAT WE CAN DO.
IT IS A CURSE THAT A FIVE-HUNDRED-YEAR-OLD FOX SACRIFICED HER LIFE FOR.
WE DO NOT HAVE ANY WAY TO LIFT IT...

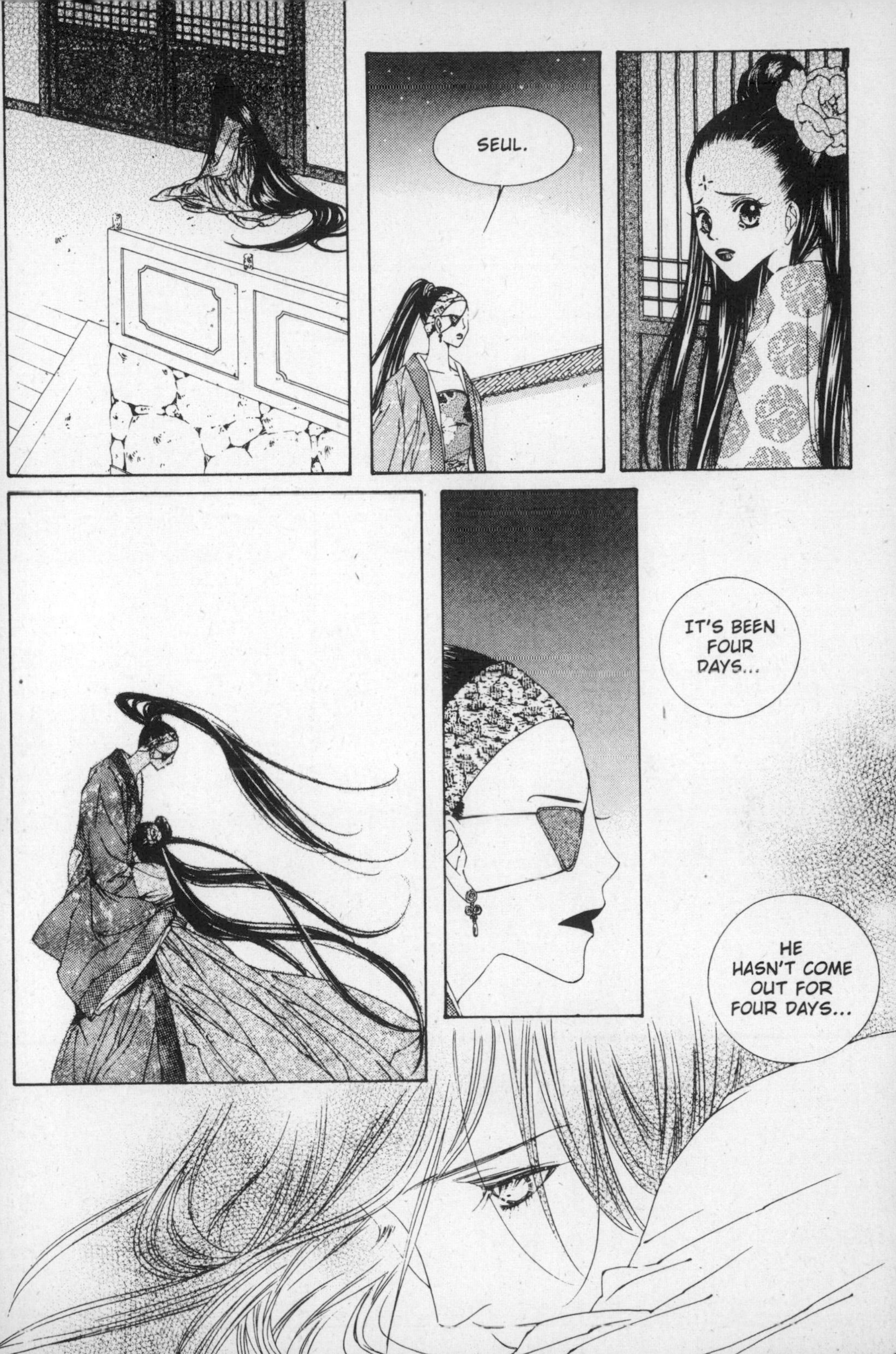
SEUL.
IT'S BEEN FOUR DAYS...
HE HASN'T COME OUT FOR FOUR DAYS...

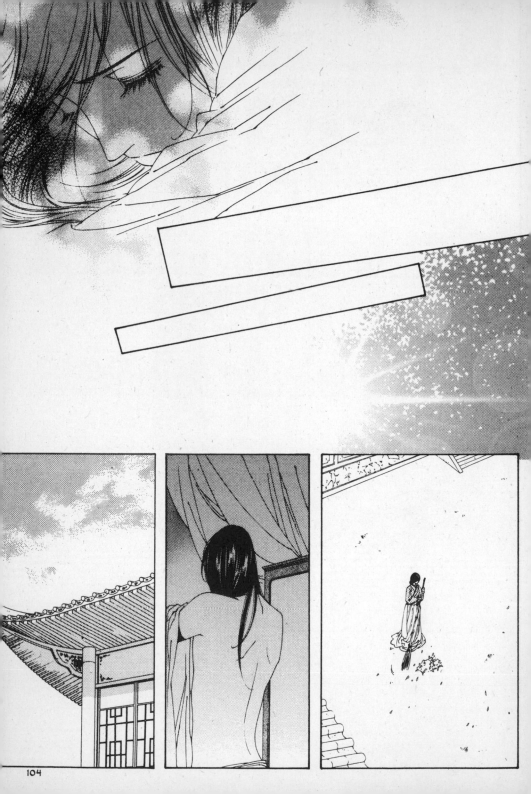

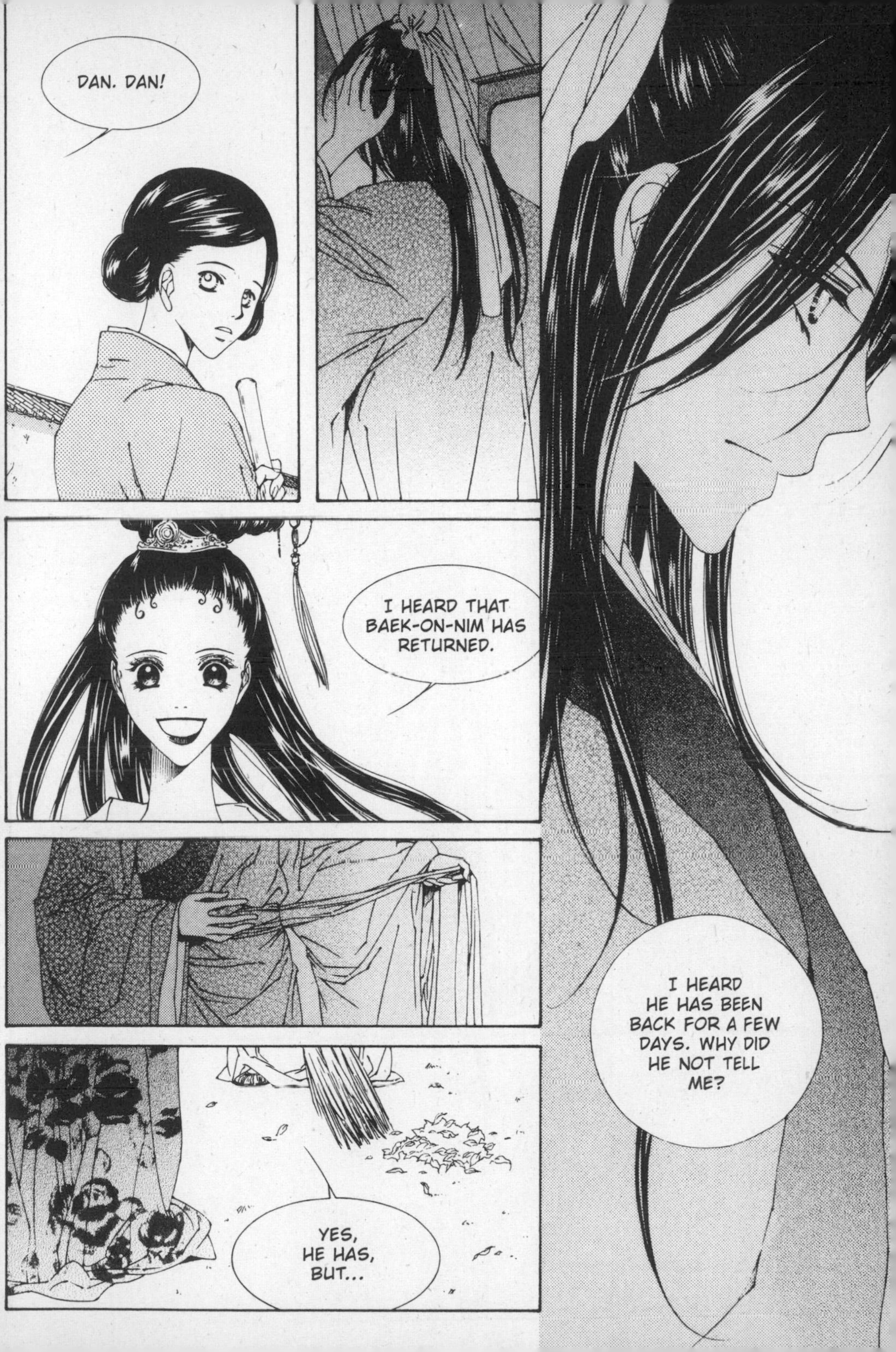
DAN. DAN!
I HEARD THAT BAEK-ON-NIM HAS RETURNED.
YES, HE HAS, BUT...
I HEARD HE HAS BEEN BACK FOR A FEW DAYS. WHY DID HE NOT TELL ME?

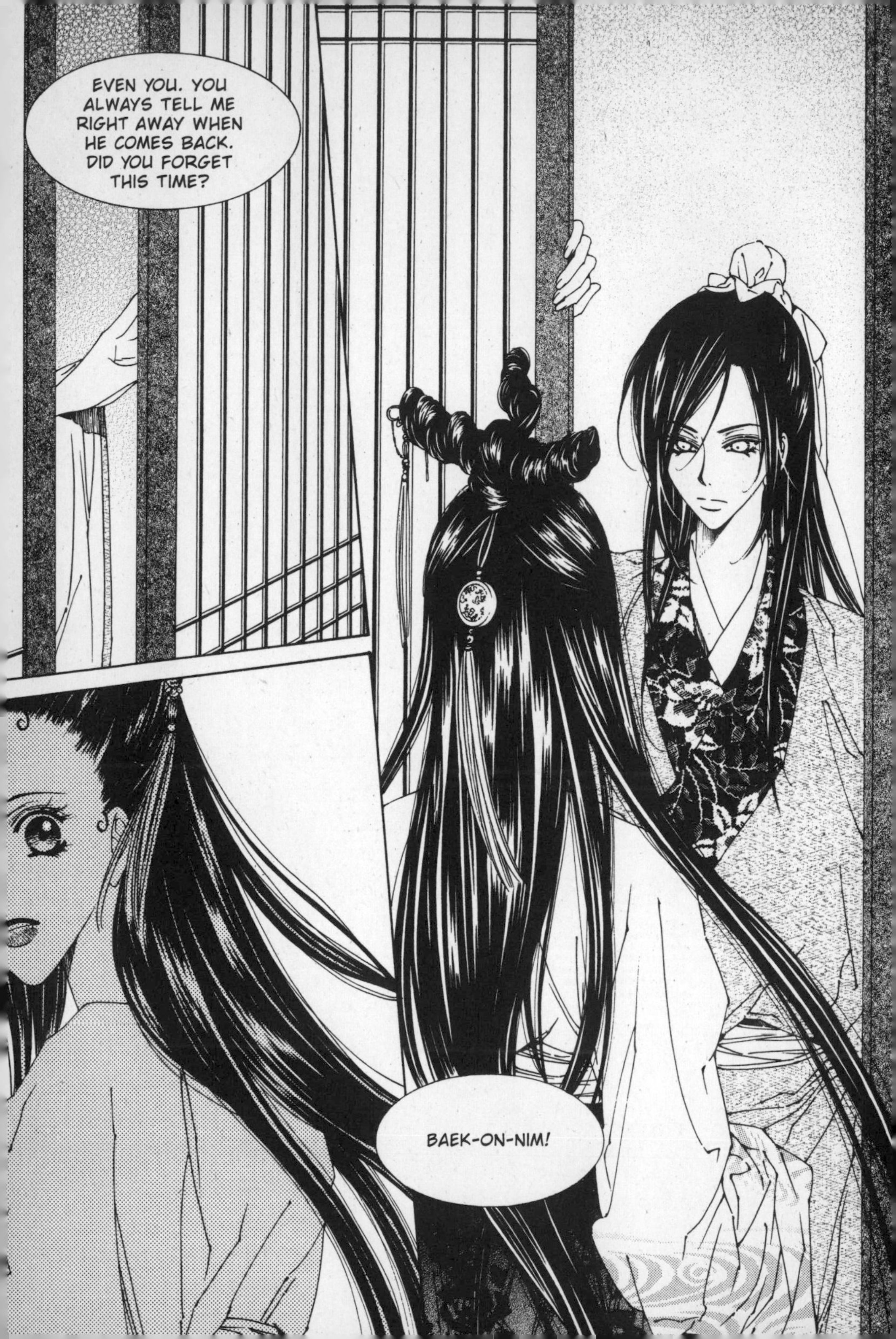
EVEN YOU. YOU ALWAYS TELL ME RIGHT AWAY WHEN HE COMES BACK. DID YOU FORGET THIS TIME?
BAEK-ON-NIM!

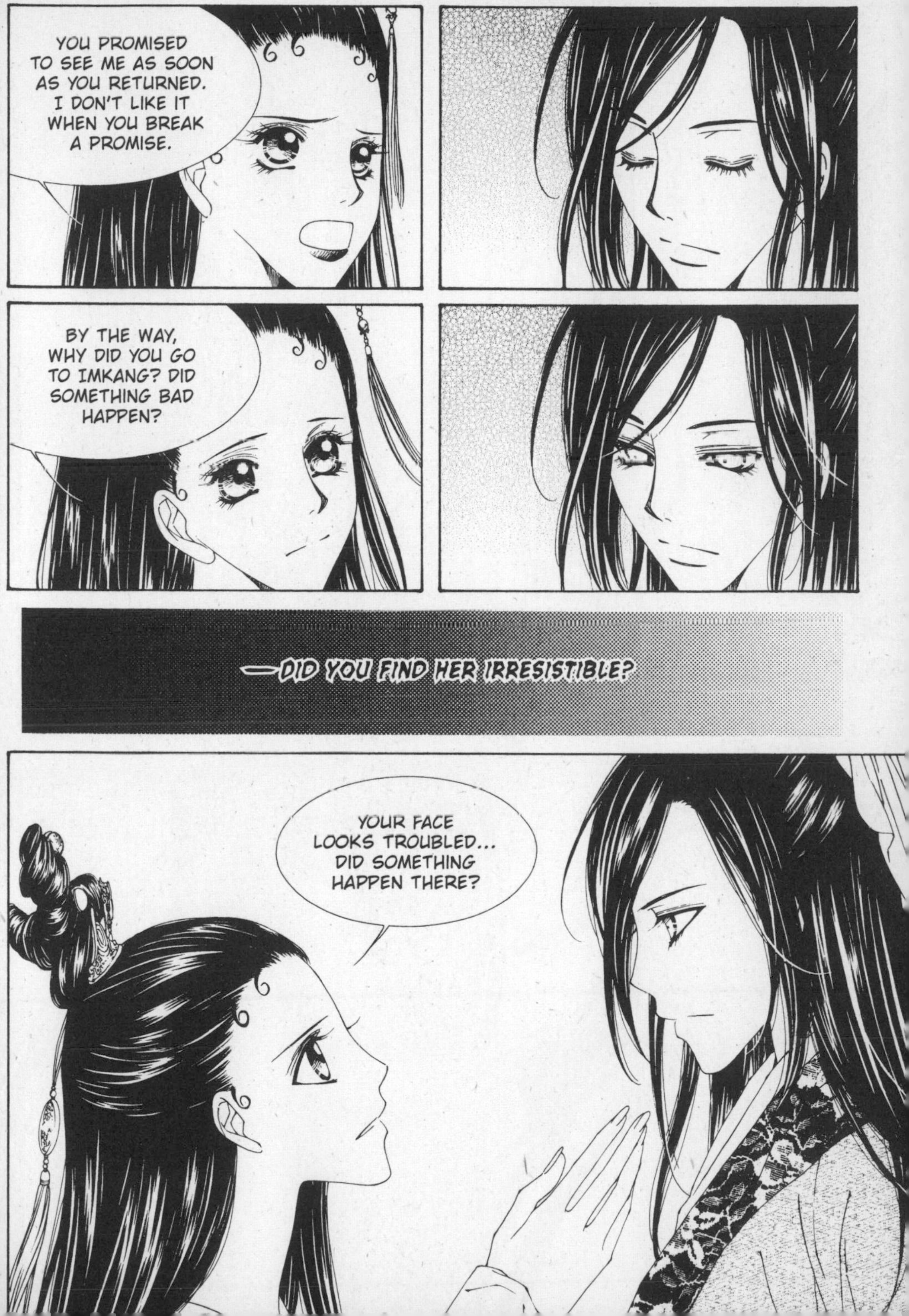
YOU PROMISED TO SEE ME AS SOON AS YOU RETURNED. I DON'T LIKE IT WHEN YOU BREAK A PROMISE.
BY THE WAY, WHY DID YOU GO TO IMKANG? DID SOMETHING BAD HAPPEN?
—DID YOU FIND HER IRRESISTIBLE?
YOUR FACE LOOKS TROUBLED... DID SOMETHING HAPPEN THERE?

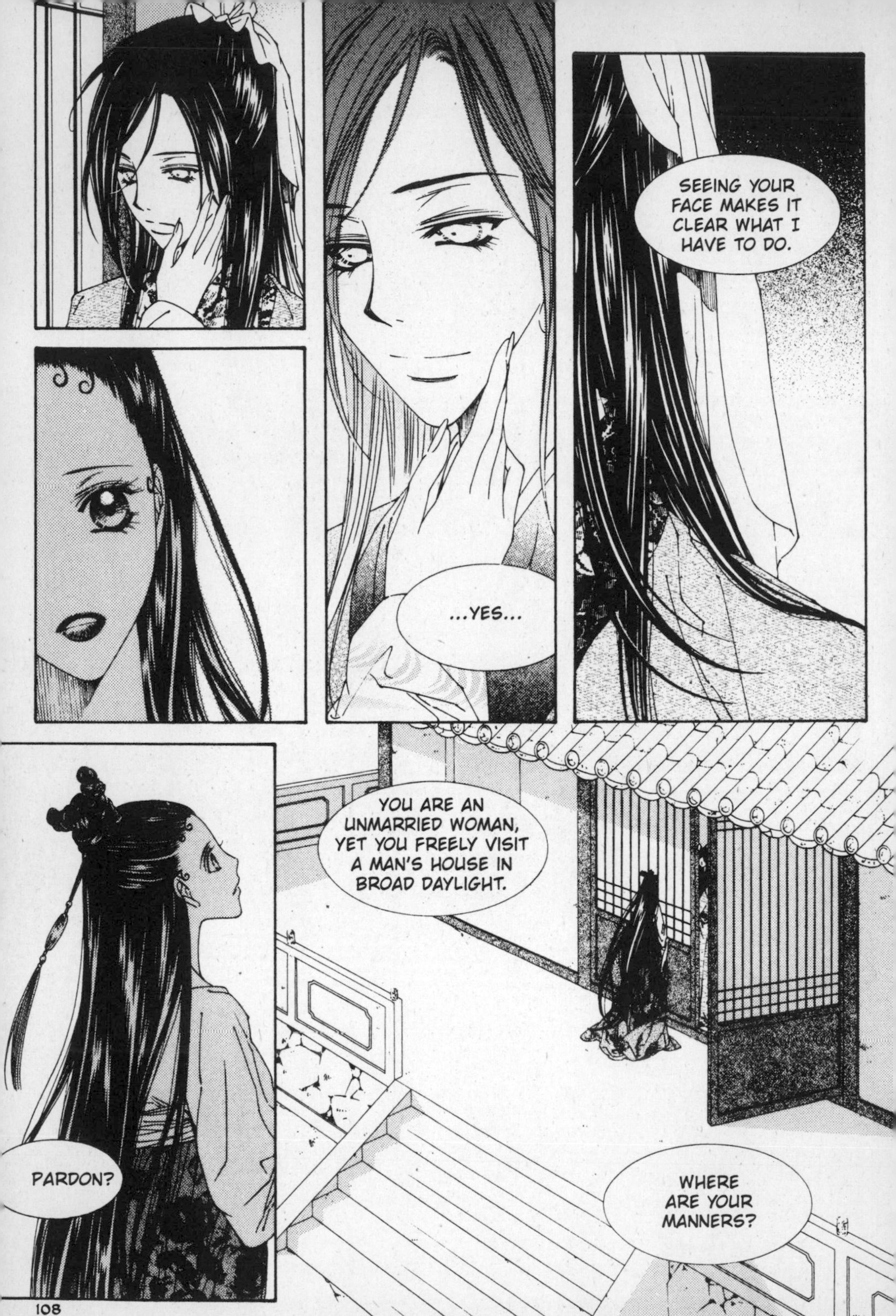
...YES...
SEEING YOUR FACE MAKES IT CLEAR WHAT I HAVE TO DO.
PARDON?
YOU ARE AN UNMARRIED WOMAN, YET YOU FREELY VISIT A MAN'S HOUSE IN BROAD DAYLIGHT.
WHERE ARE YOUR MANNERS?

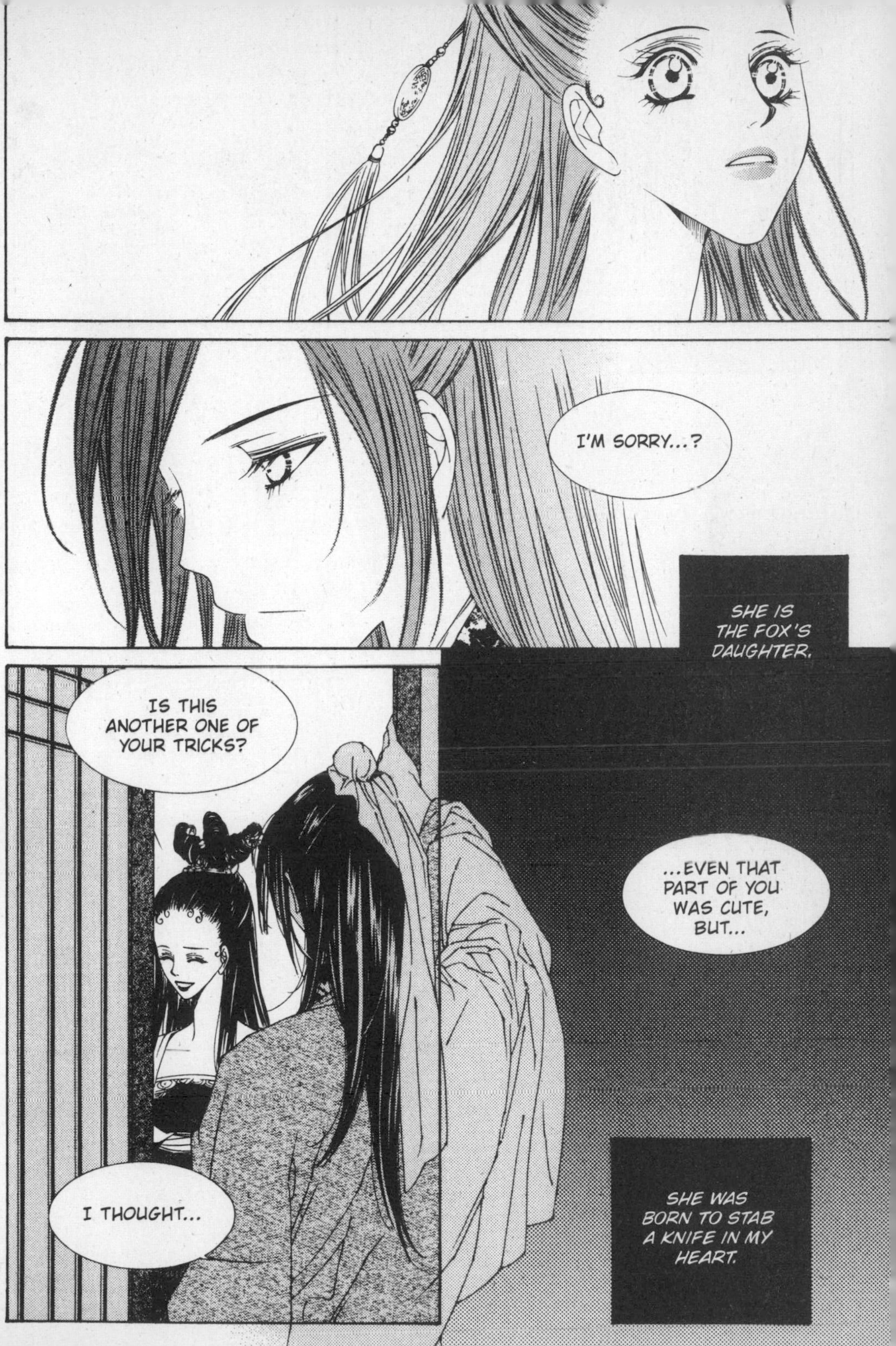
I'M SORRY...?
SHE IS THE FOX'S DAUGHTER.
IS THIS ANOTHER ONE OF YOUR TRICKS?
I THOUGHT...
...EVEN THAT PART OF YOU WAS CUTE, BUT...
SHE WAS BORN TO STAB A KNIFE IN MY HEART.

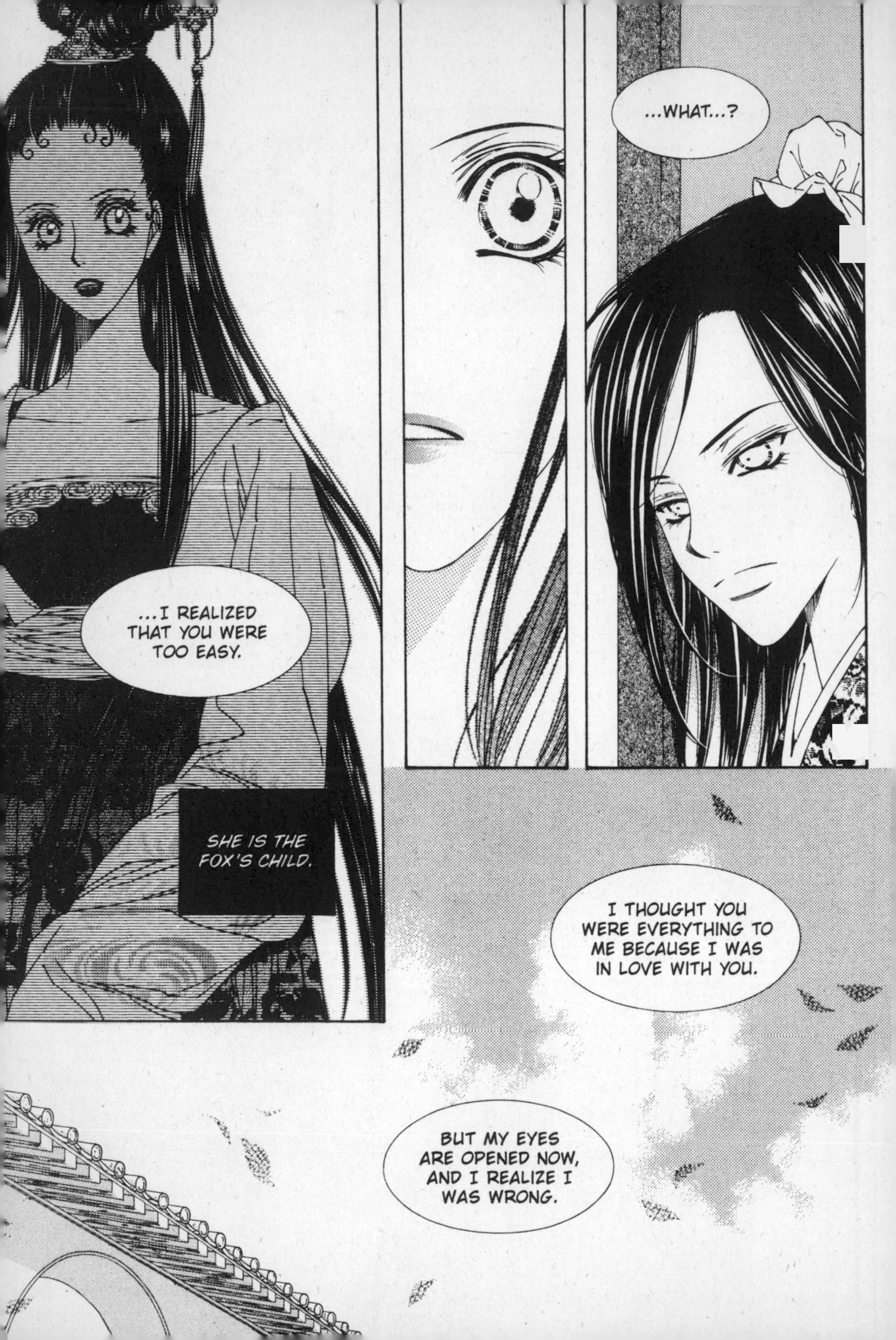
...I REALIZED THAT YOU WERE TOO EASY.
SHE IS THE FOX'S CHILD.
...WHAT...?
I THOUGHT YOU WERE EVERYTHING TO ME BECAUSE I WAS IN LOVE WITH YOU.
BUT MY EYES ARE OPENED NOW, AND I REALIZE I WAS WRONG.

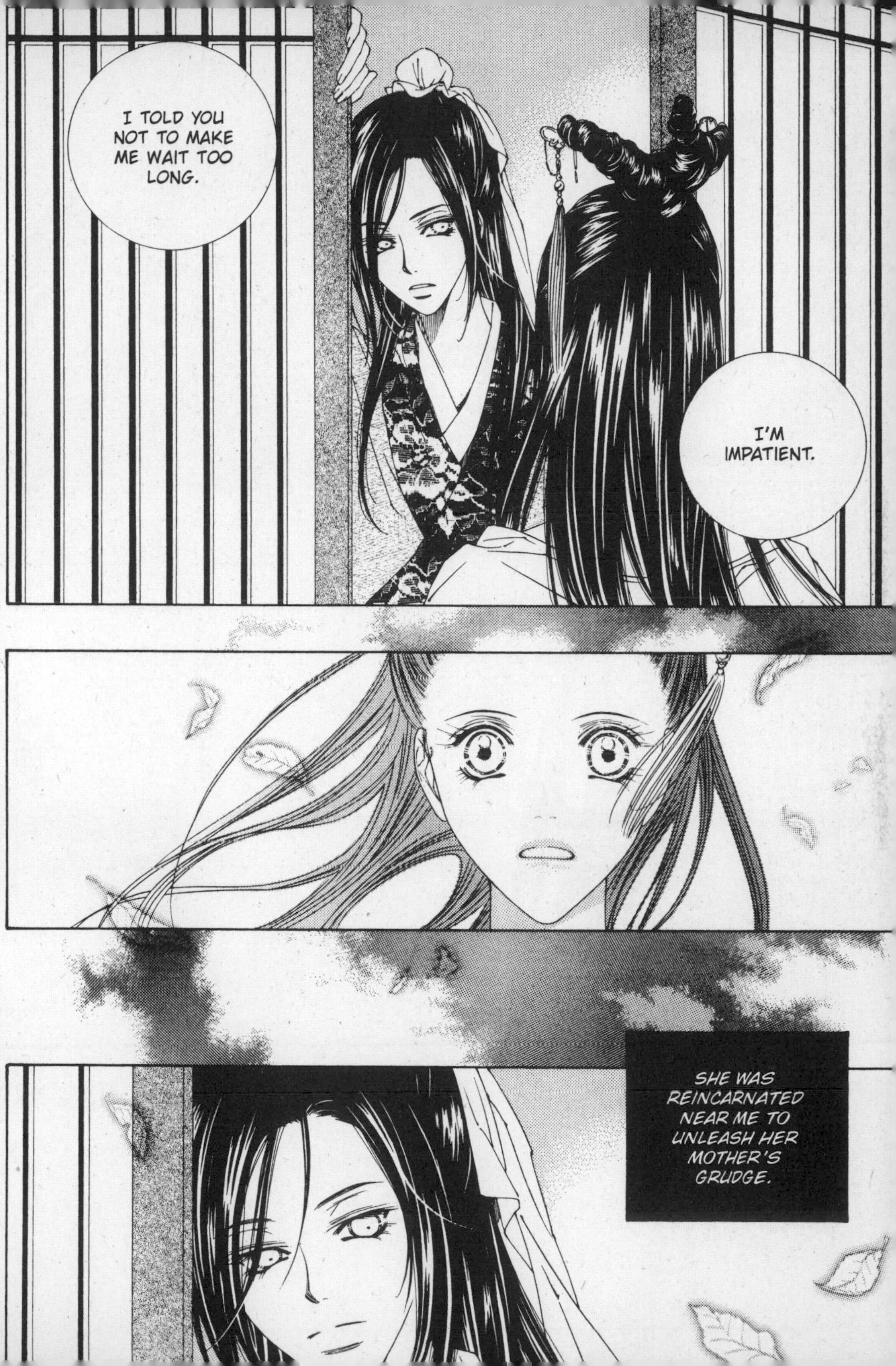
I TOLD YOU NOT TO MAKE ME WAIT TOO LONG.
I'M IMPATIENT.
SHE WAS REINCARNATED NEAR ME TO UNLEASH HER MOTHER'S GRUDGE.

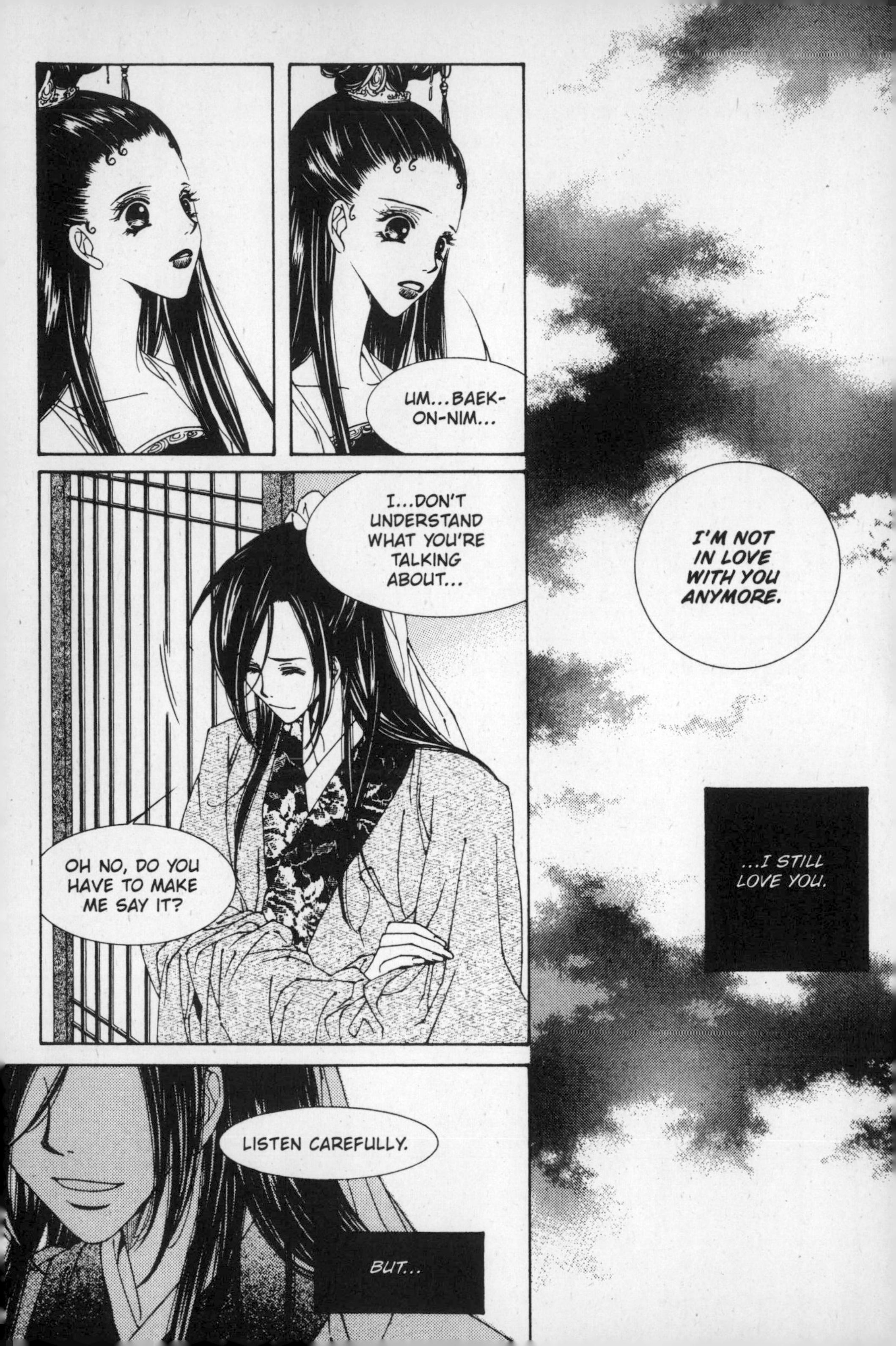
UM...BAEK-ON-NIM...
I...DON'T UNDERSTAND WHAT YOU'RE TALKING ABOUT...
OH NO, DO YOU HAVE TO MAKE ME SAY IT?
LISTEN CAREFULLY.
BUT...
I'M NOT IN LOVE WITH YOU ANYMORE.
...I STILL LOVE YOU.

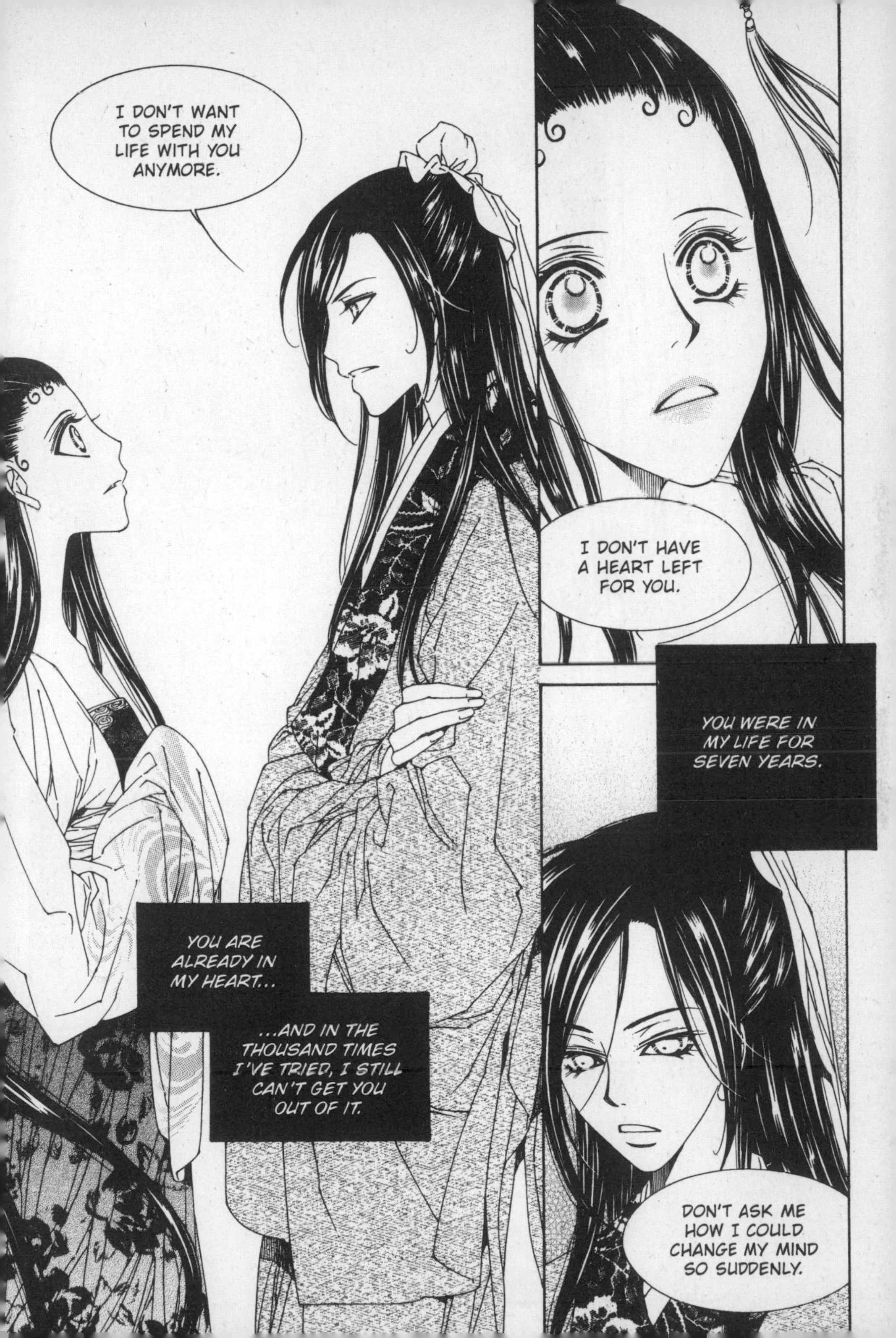
I DON'T WANT TO SPEND MY LIFE WITH YOU ANYMORE.
YOU ARE ALREADY IN MY HEART...
...AND IN THE THOUSAND TIMES I'VE TRIED, I STILL CAN'T GET YOU OUT OF IT.
I DON'T HAVE A HEART LEFT FOR YOU.
YOU WERE IN MY LIFE FOR SEVEN YEARS.
DON'T ASK ME HOW I COULD CHANGE MY MIND SO SUDDENLY.

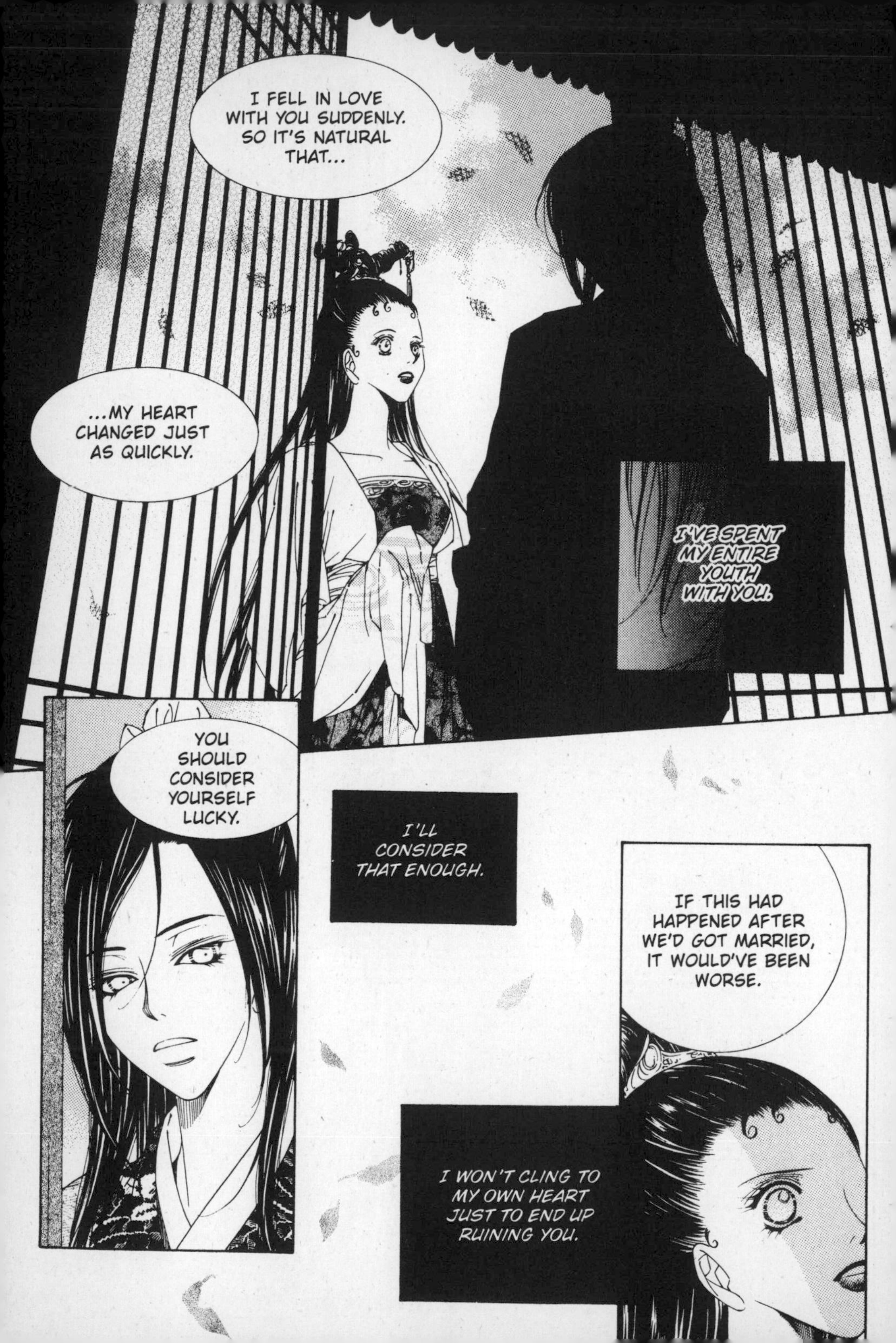
I FELL IN LOVE WITH YOU SUDDENLY. SO IT'S NATURAL THAT...
...MY HEART CHANGED JUST AS QUICKLY.
I'VE SPENT MY ENTIRE YOUTH WITH YOU.
YOU SHOULD CONSIDER YOURSELF LUCKY.
I'LL CONSIDER THAT ENOUGH.
IF THIS HAD HAPPENED AFTER WE'D GOT MARRIED, IT WOULD'VE BEEN WORSE.
I WON'T CLING TO MY OWN HEART JUST TO END UP RUINING YOU.

NEXT TIME YOU MEET ANOTHER MAN...

OR HE'LL FIND FAULT WITH YOU.

...MIND YOUR MANNERS.

SO YOU FORGET ABOUT ME.

THIS HEART THAT I CANNOT SURRENDER...

...I'LL HIDE AS IF IT VANISHED.

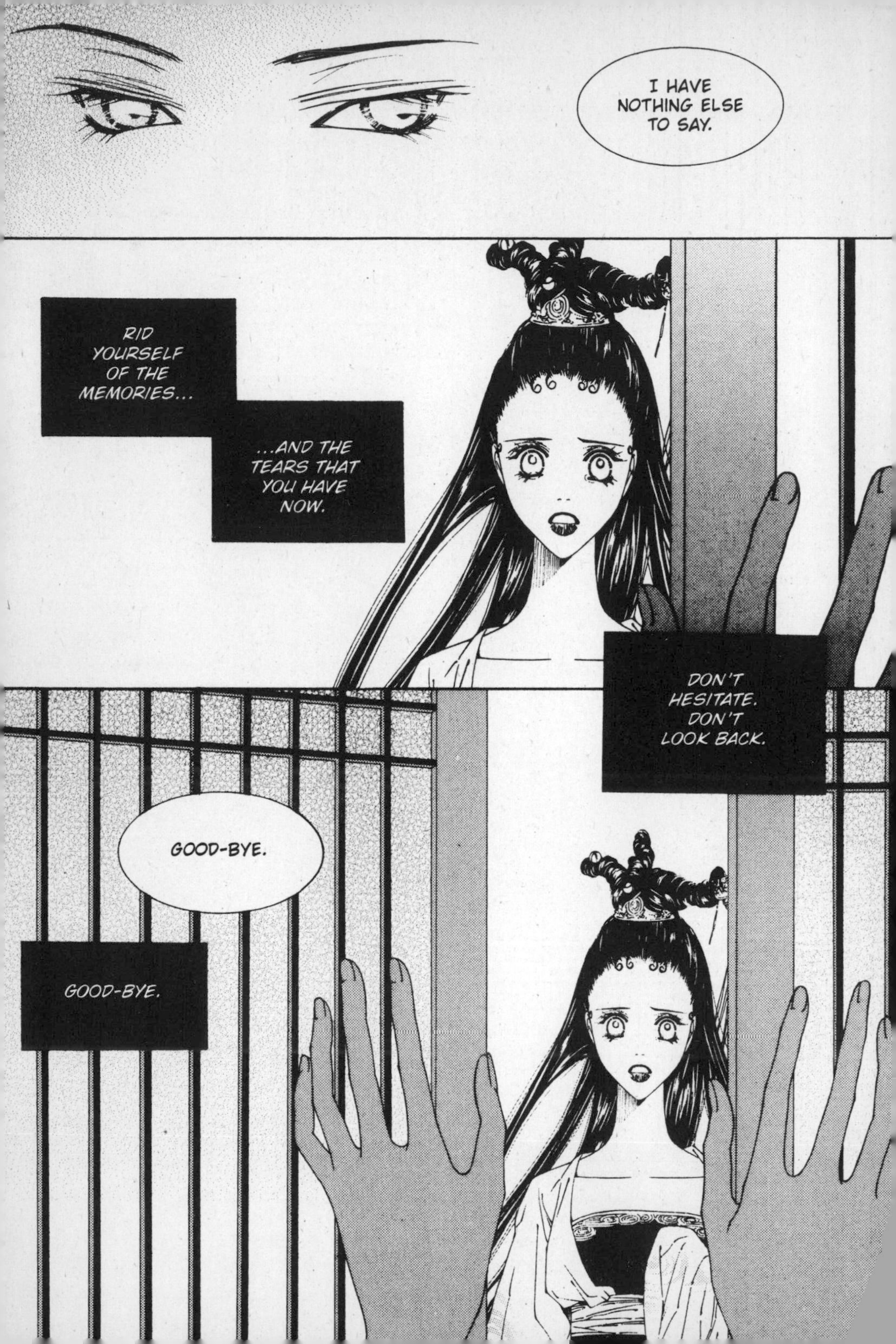
I HAVE NOTHING ELSE TO SAY.
RID YOURSELF OF THE MEMORIES...
...AND THE TEARS THAT YOU HAVE NOW.
DON'T HESITATE. DON'T LOOK BACK.
GOOD-BYE.
GOOD-BYE.

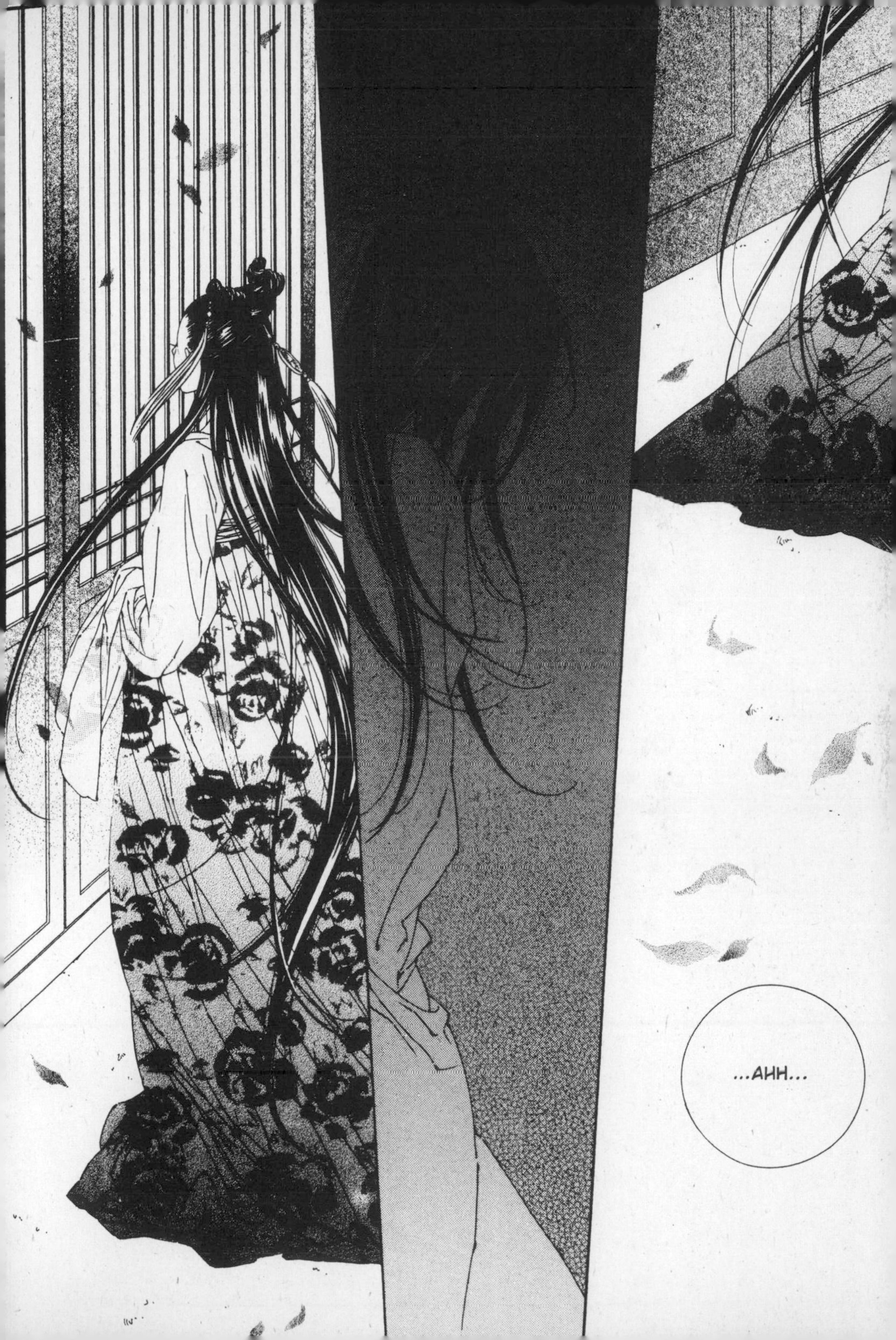
...AHH...

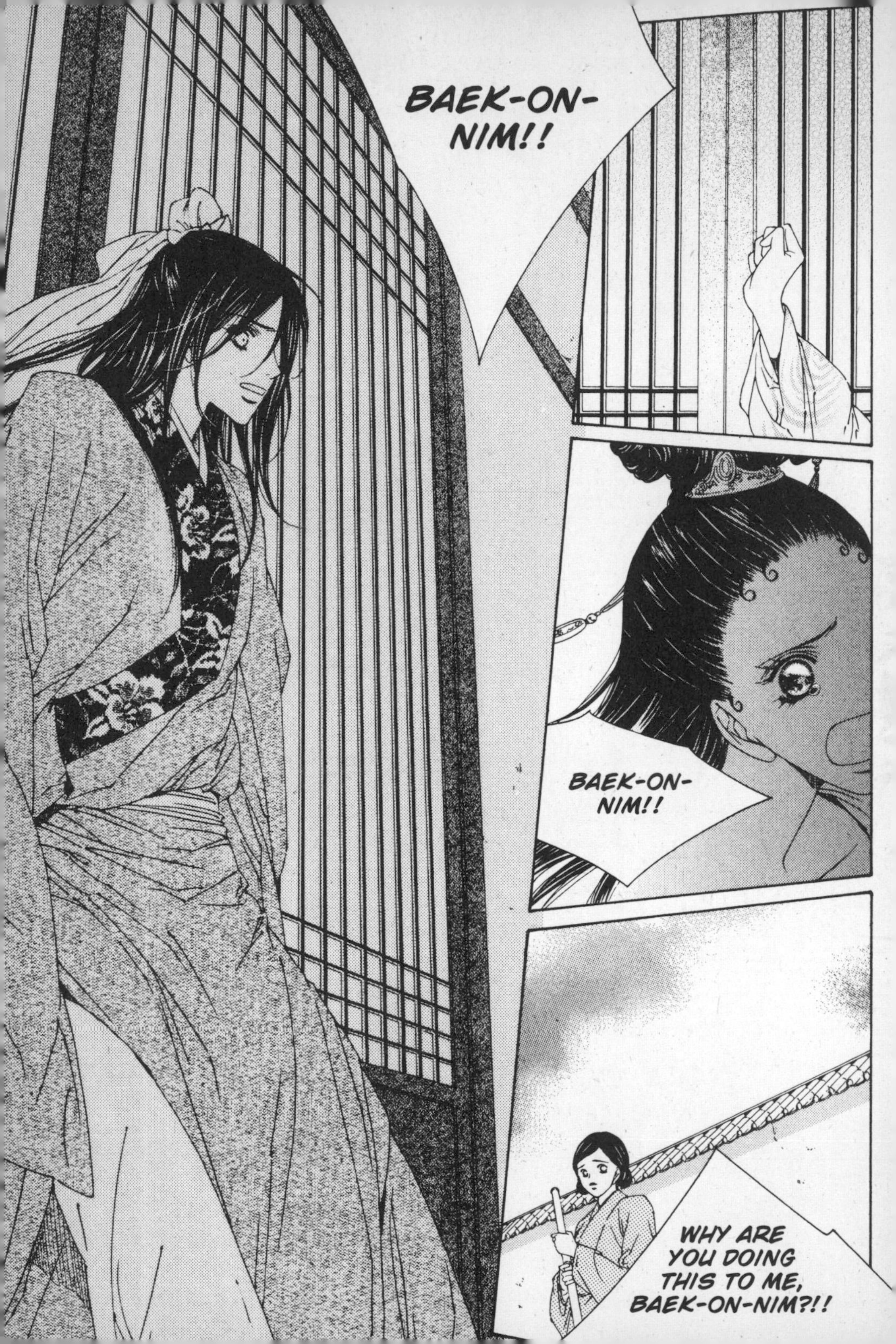
BAEK-ON-
NIM!!
BAEK-ON-
NIM!!
WHY ARE
YOU DOING
THIS TO ME,
BAEK-ON-NIM?!!

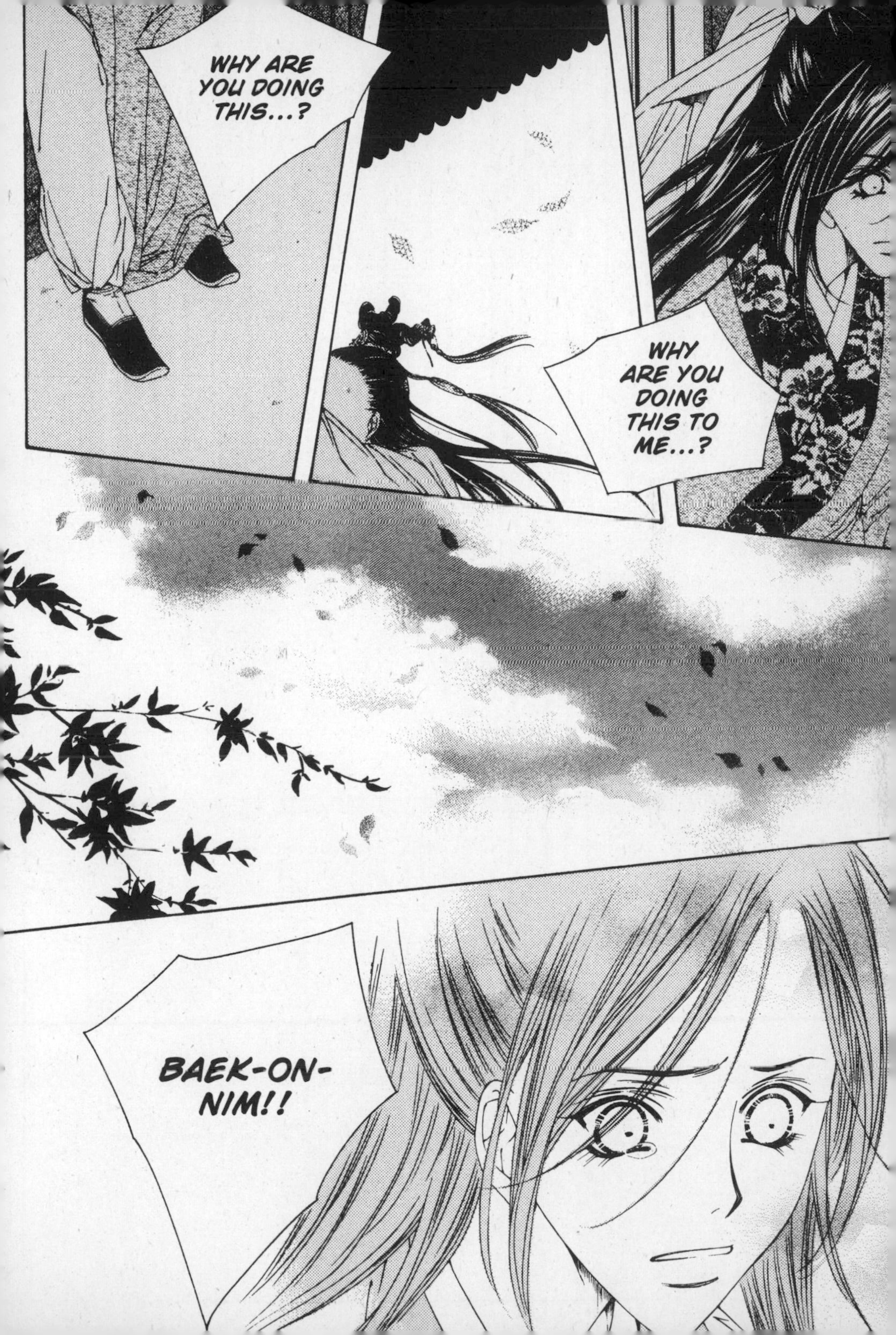
WHY ARE YOU DOING THIS...?
WHY ARE YOU DOING THIS TO ME...?
BAEK-ON-NIM!!

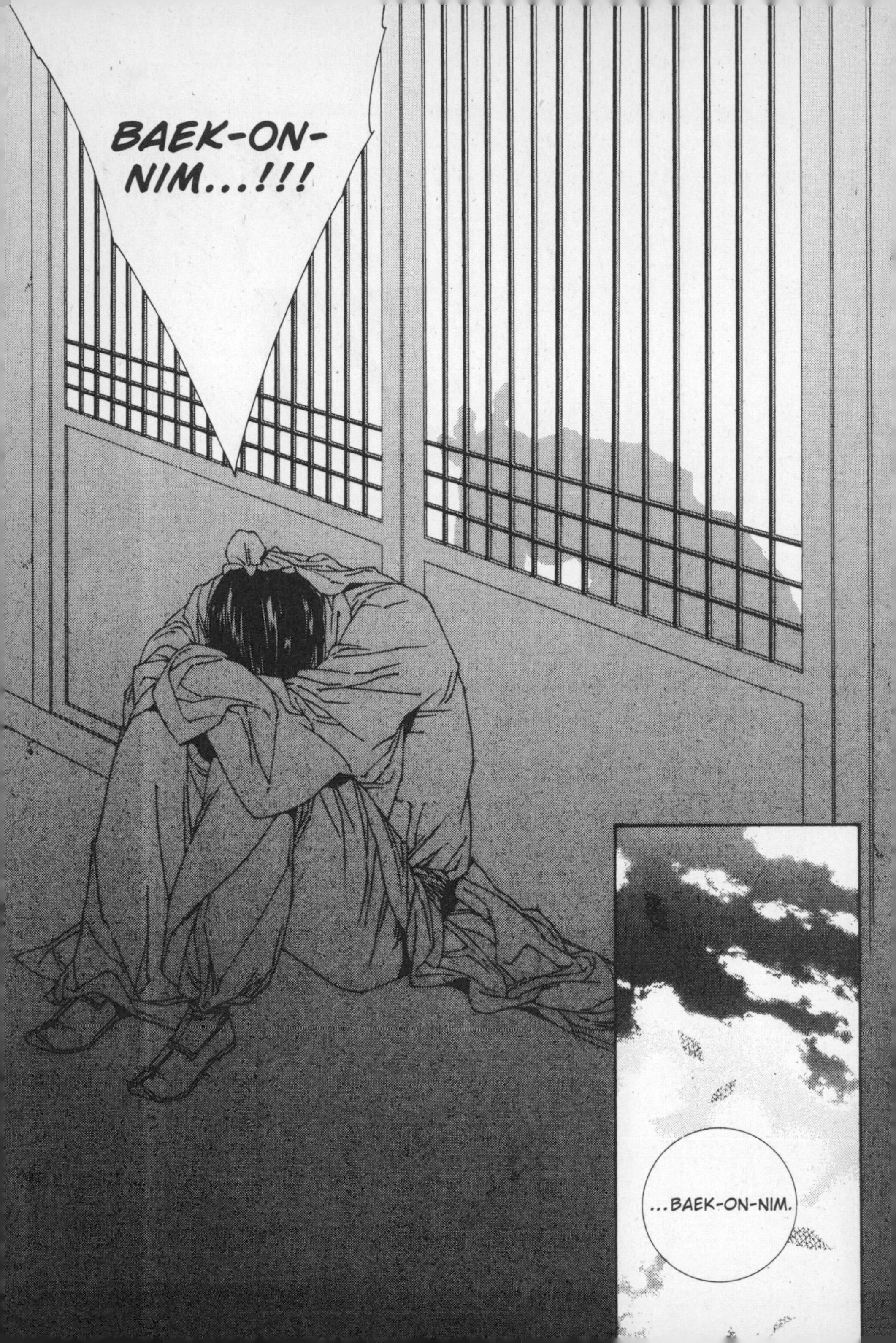
BAEK-ON-NIM...!!!
...BAEK-ON-NIM.

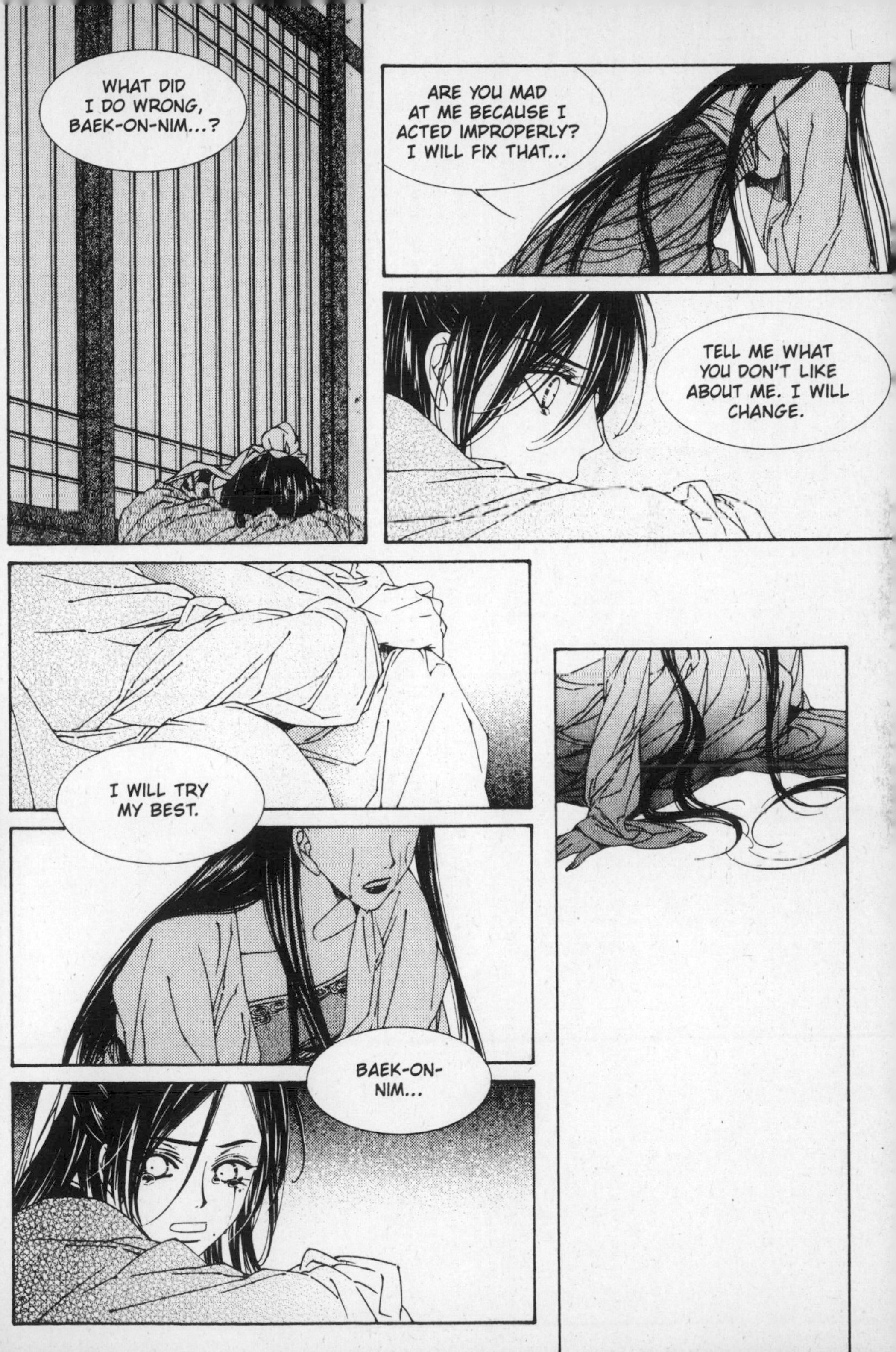
WHAT DID I DO WRONG, BAEK-ON-NIM...?
ARE YOU MAD AT ME BECAUSE I ACTED IMPROPERLY? I WILL FIX THAT...
TELL ME WHAT YOU DON'T LIKE ABOUT ME. I WILL CHANGE.
I WILL TRY MY BEST.
BAEK-ON-NIM...

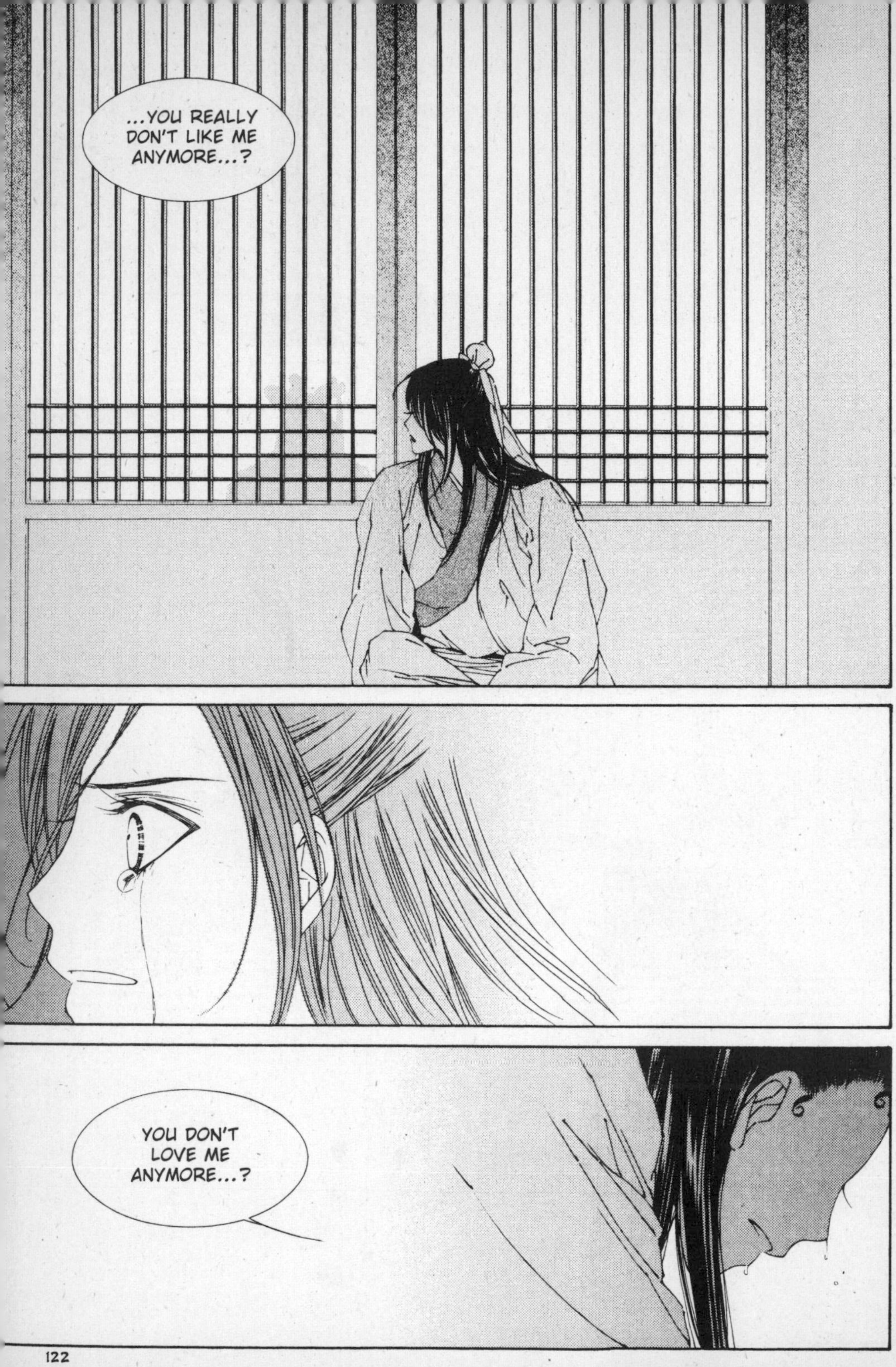
...YOU REALLY DON'T LIKE ME ANYMORE...?
YOU DON'T LOVE ME ANYMORE...?

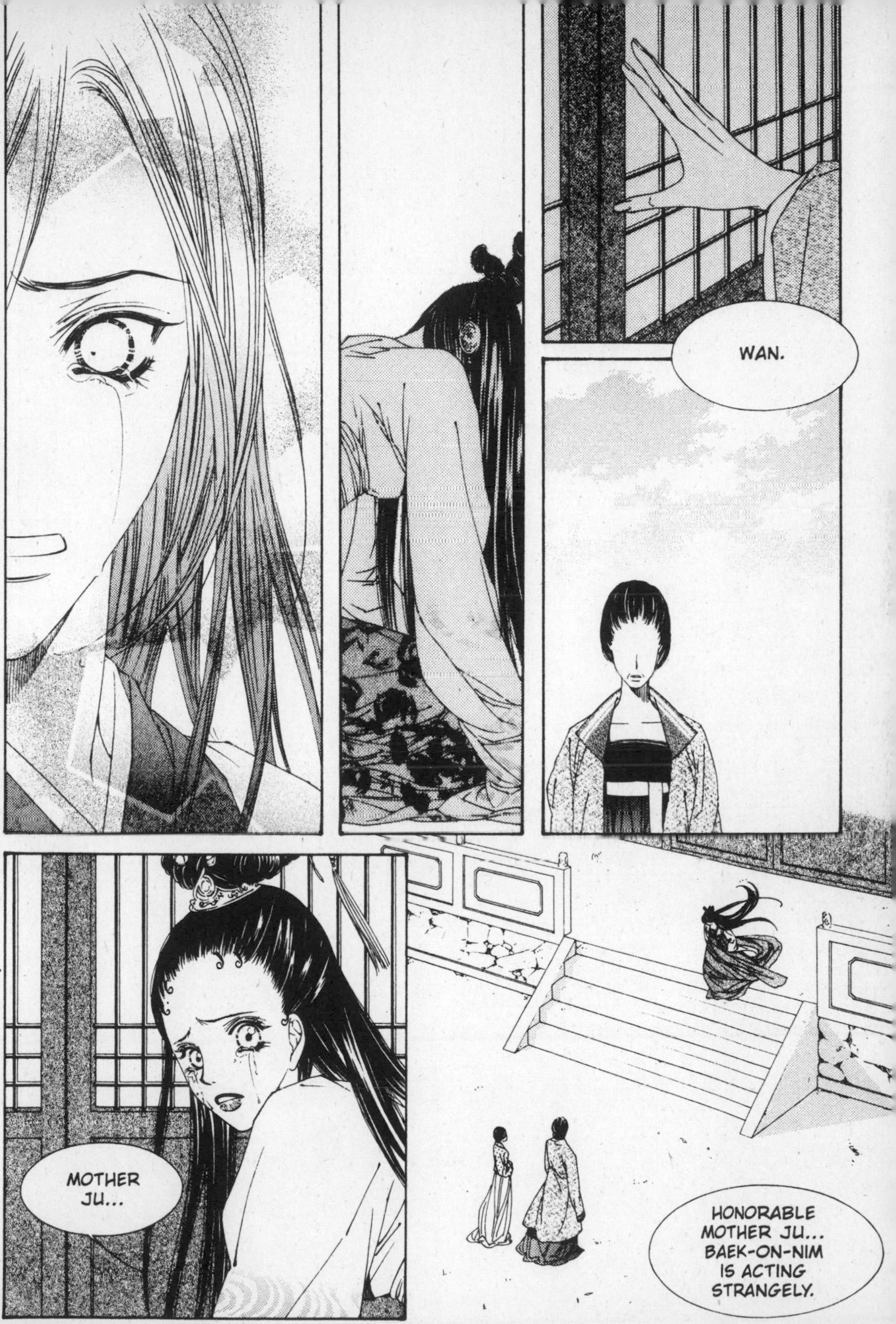
WAN.
MOTHER JU...
HONORABLE MOTHER JU... BAEK-ON-NIM IS ACTING STRANGELY.

BAEK-ON-NIM SAID—

...WAN.

...YOU SHOULD LEAVE.

...WHEN THE TIME IS RIGHT...I WILL TRY TO EXPLAIN. SO, TILL THEN...

...YOU SHOULD GO HOME.

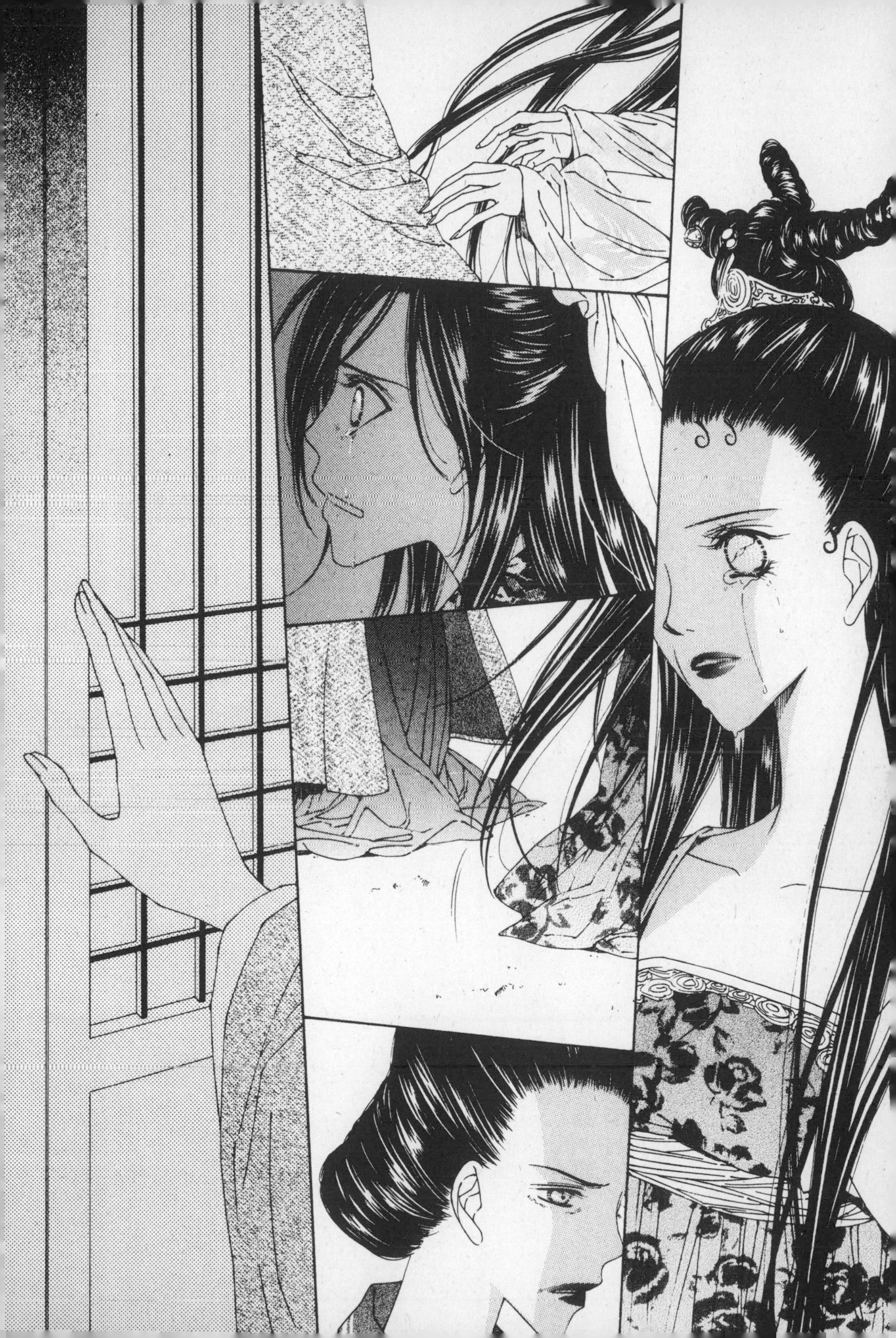

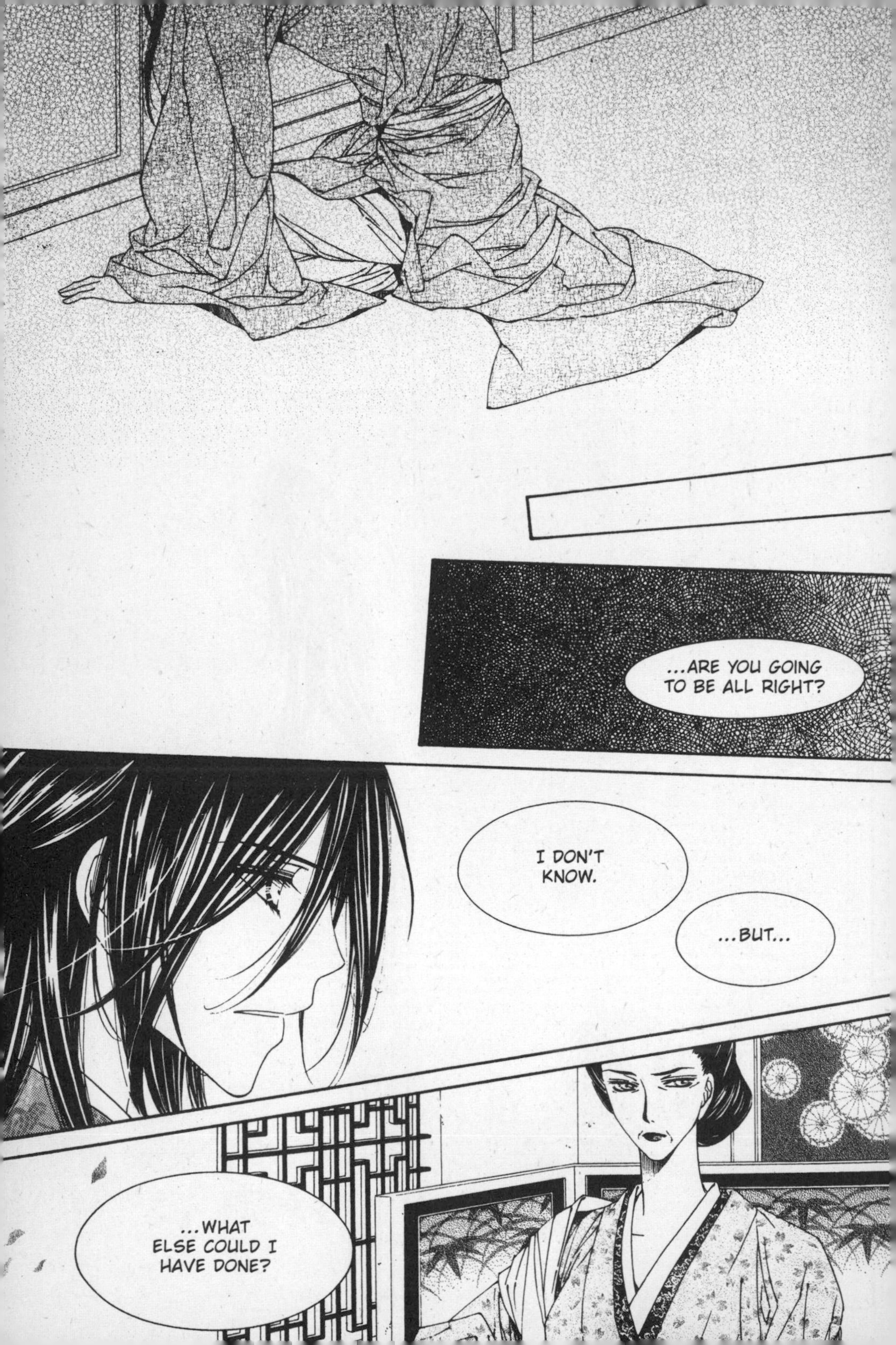
...ARE YOU GOING TO BE ALL RIGHT?
I DON'T KNOW.
...BUT...
...WHAT ELSE COULD I HAVE DONE?

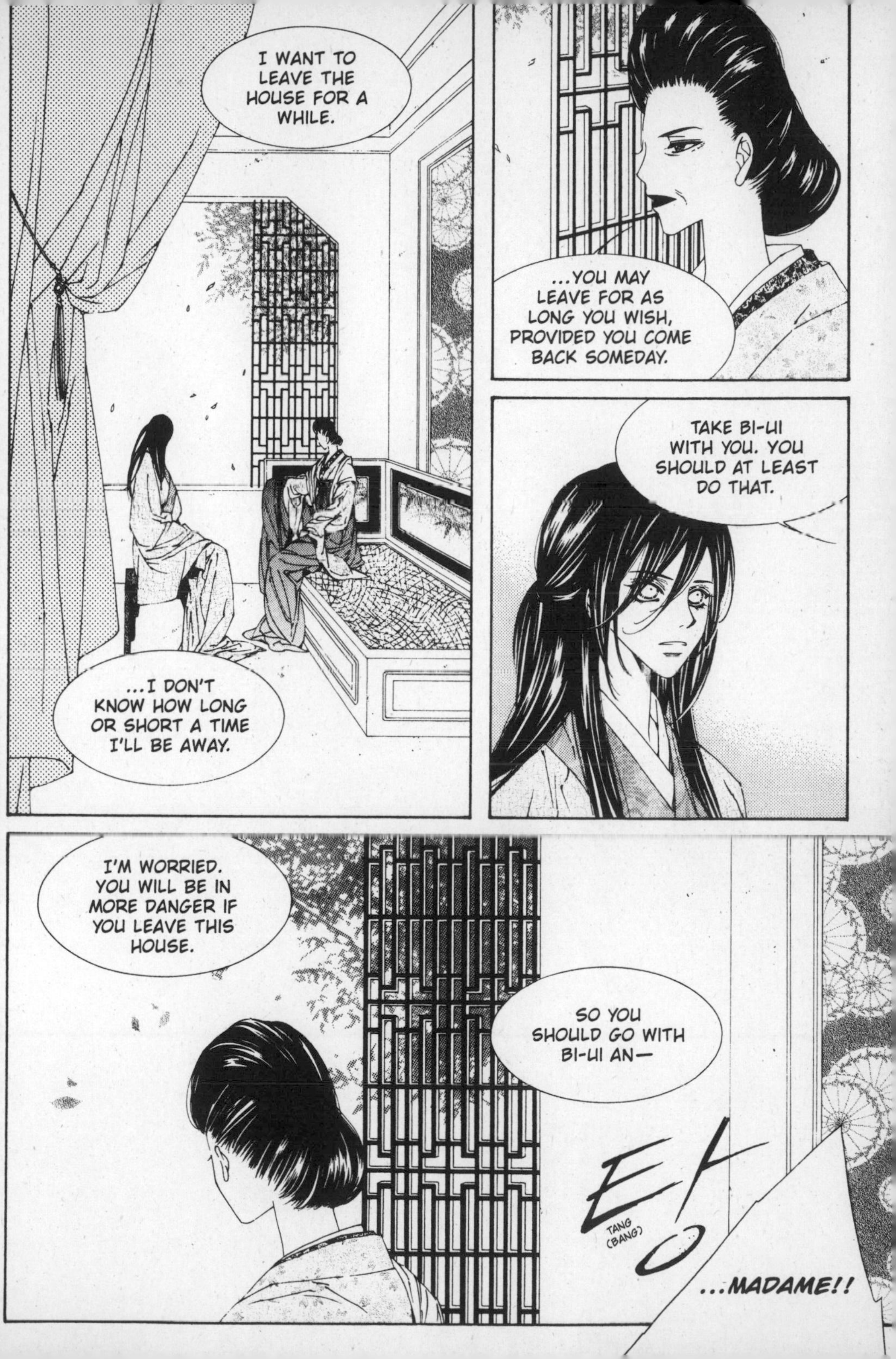
I WANT TO LEAVE THE HOUSE FOR A WHILE.
...I DON'T KNOW HOW LONG OR SHORT A TIME I'LL BE AWAY.
...YOU MAY LEAVE FOR AS LONG YOU WISH, PROVIDED YOU COME BACK SOMEDAY.
TAKE BI-UI WITH YOU. YOU SHOULD AT LEAST DO THAT.
I'M WORRIED. YOU WILL BE IN MORE DANGER IF YOU LEAVE THIS HOUSE.
SO YOU SHOULD GO WITH BI-UI AN—
TANG (BANG)
...MADAME!!

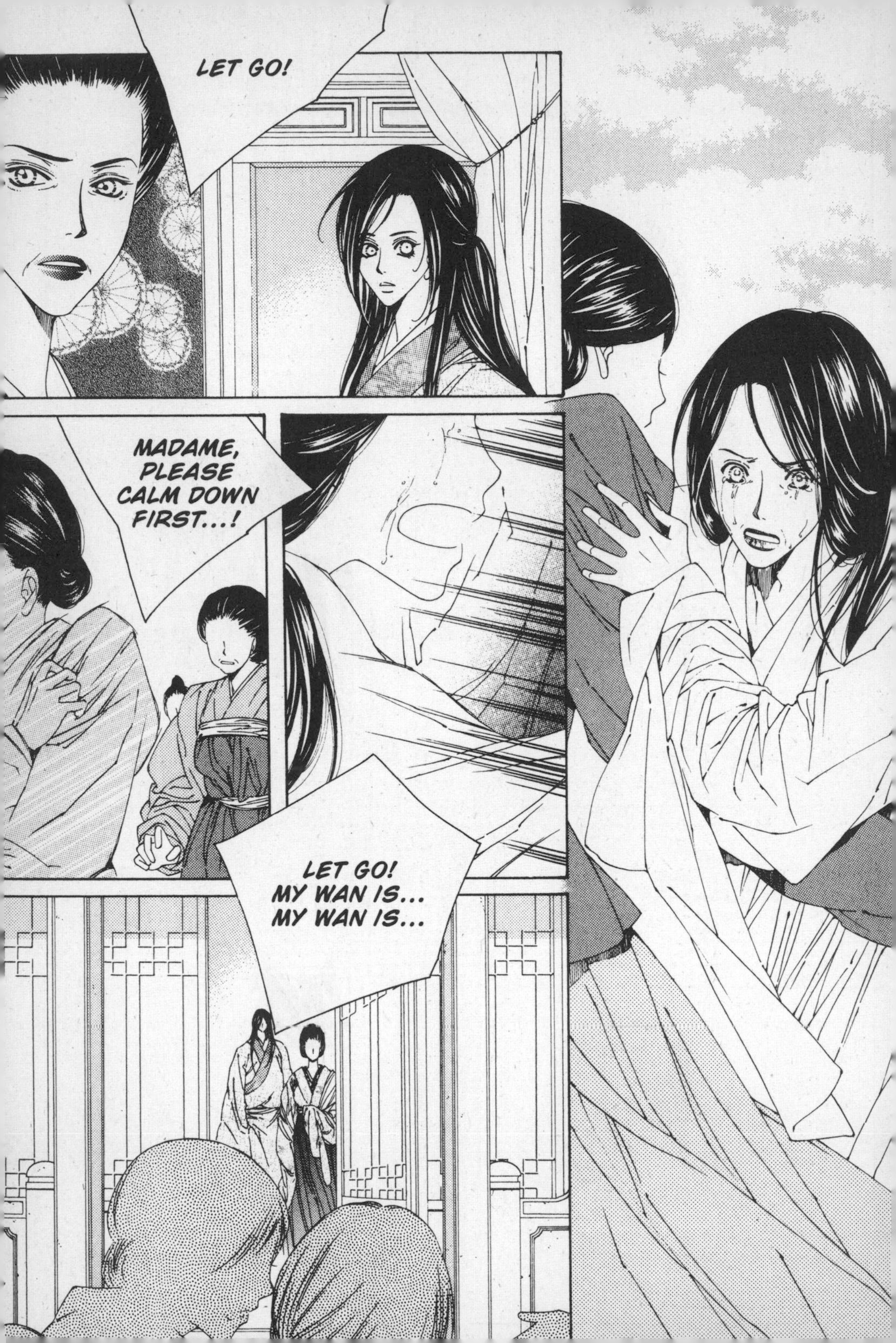
LET GO!
MADAME, PLEASE CALM DOWN FIRST...!
LET GO! MY WAN IS... MY WAN IS...

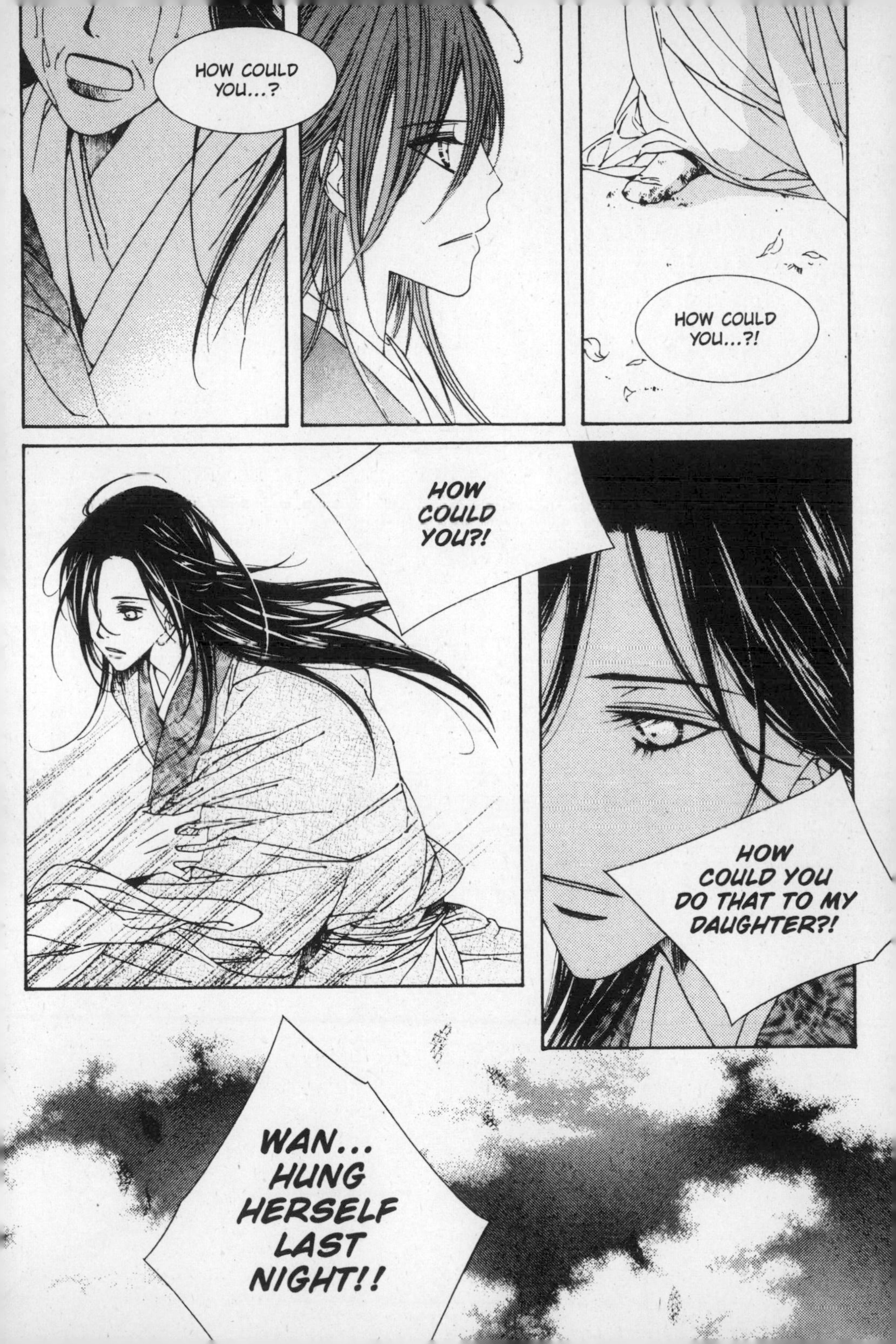
HOW COULD YOU...?
HOW COULD YOU...?!
HOW COULD YOU?!
HOW COULD YOU DO THAT TO MY DAUGHTER?!
WAN... HUNG HERSELF LAST NIGHT!!

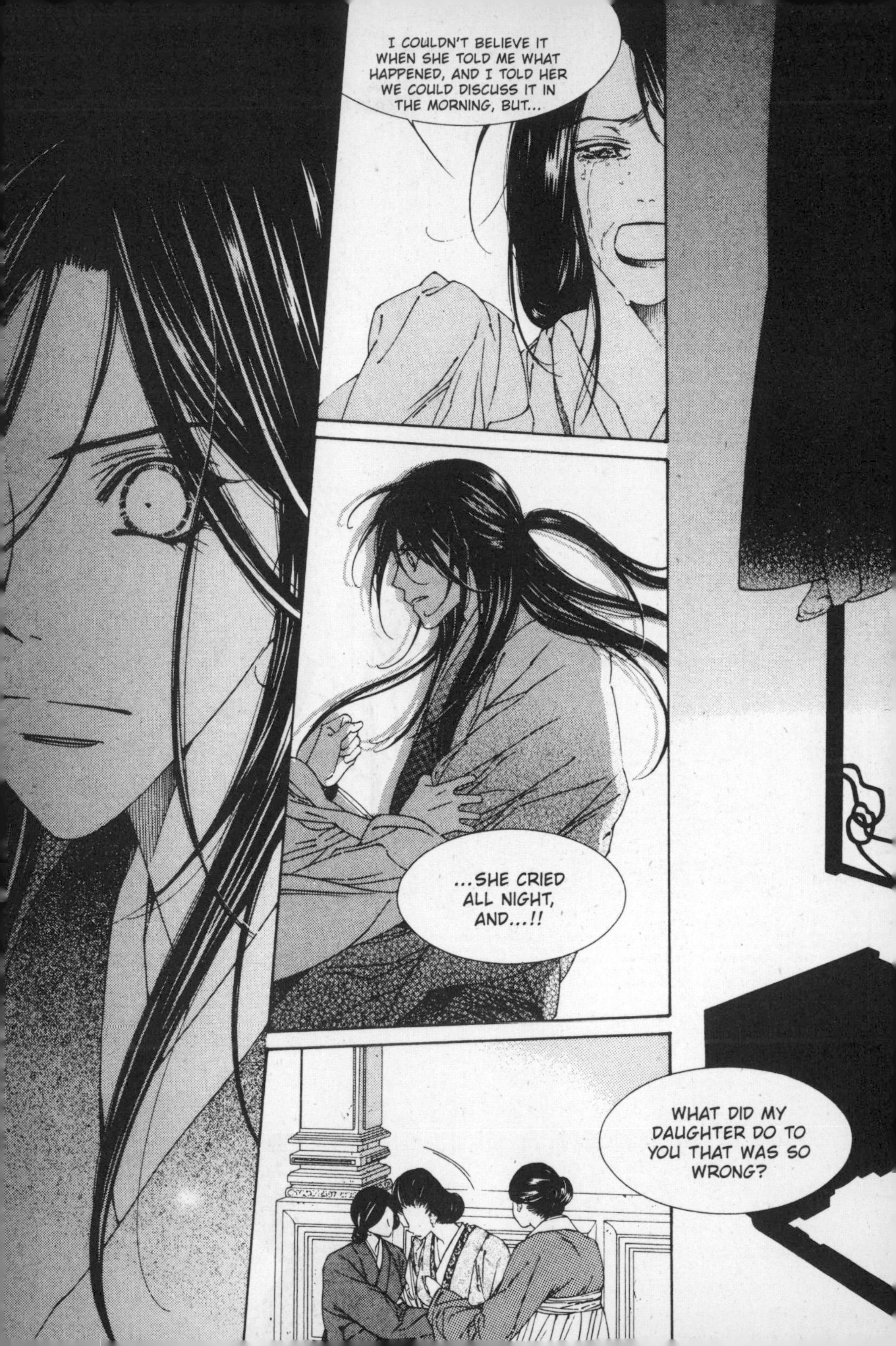
I COULDN'T BELIEVE IT WHEN SHE TOLD ME WHAT HAPPENED, AND I TOLD HER WE COULD DISCUSS IT IN THE MORNING, BUT...
...SHE CRIED ALL NIGHT, AND...!!
WHAT DID MY DAUGHTER DO TO YOU THAT WAS SO WRONG?

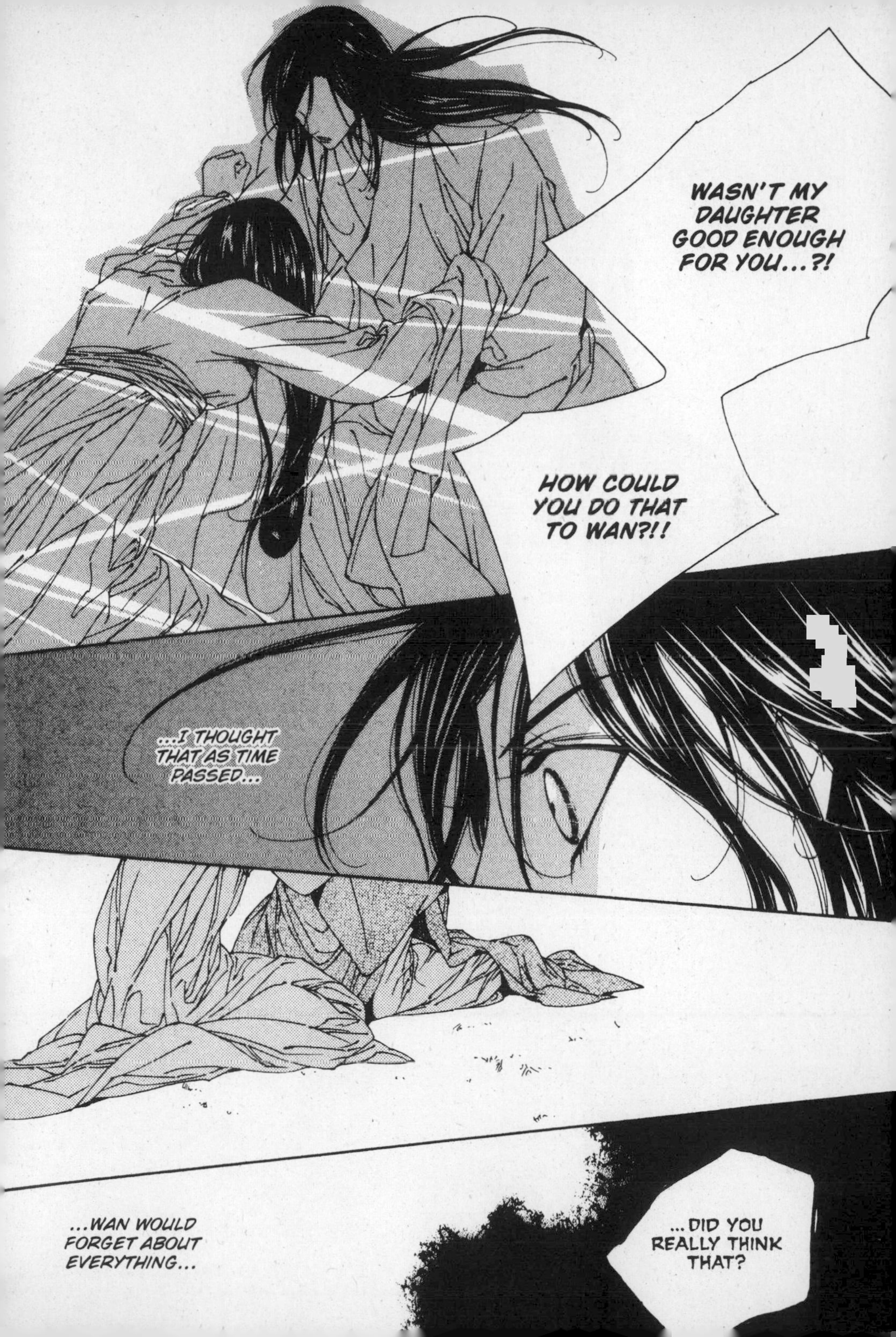

WASN'T MY DAUGHTER GOOD ENOUGH FOR YOU...?!
HOW COULD YOU DO THAT TO WAN?!!
...I THOUGHT THAT AS TIME PASSED...
...WAN WOULD FORGET ABOUT EVERYTHING...
...DID YOU REALLY THINK THAT?

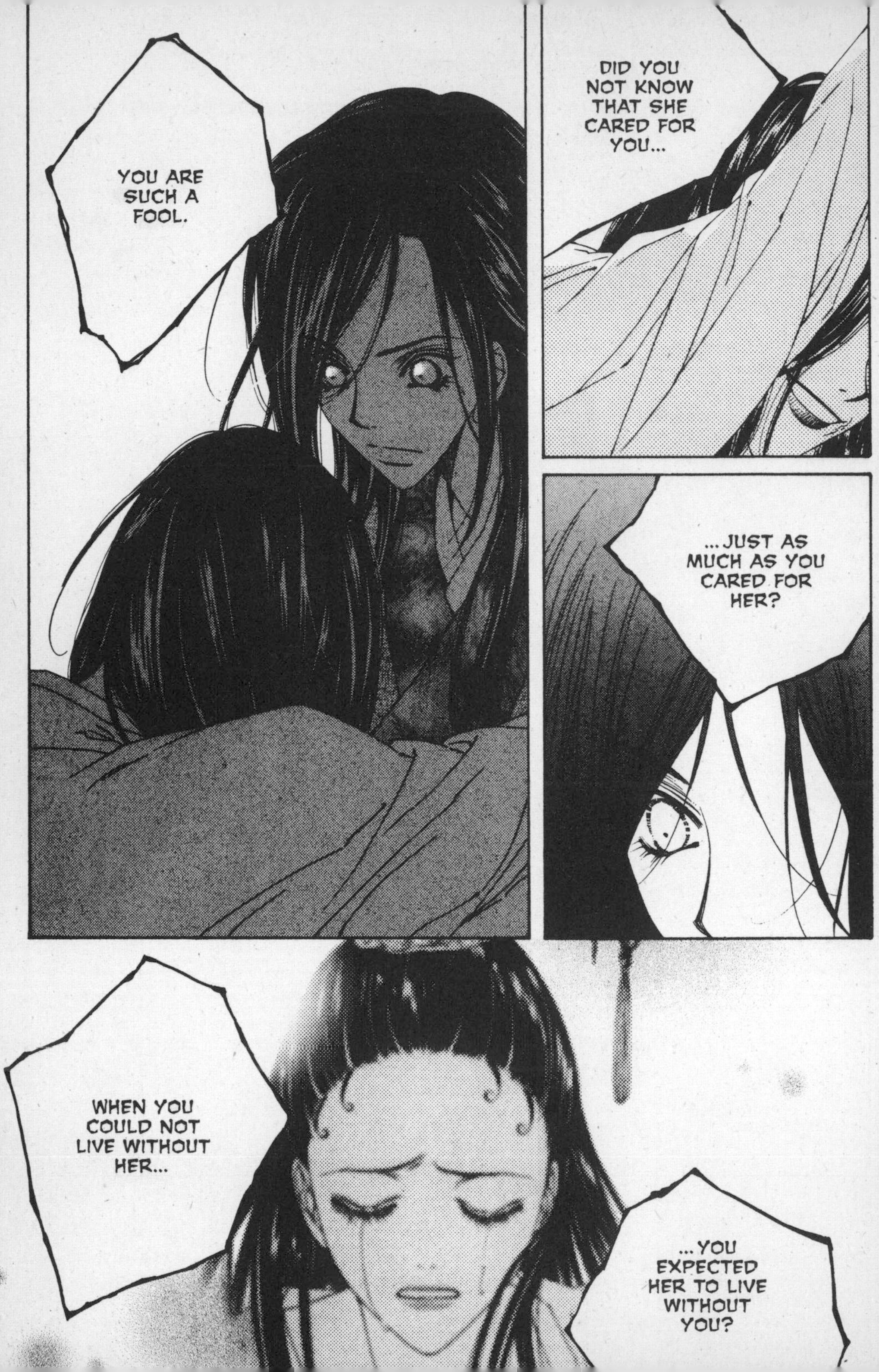
YOU ARE SUCH A FOOL.
DID YOU NOT KNOW THAT SHE CARED FOR YOU...
...JUST AS MUCH AS YOU CARED FOR HER?
WHEN YOU COULD NOT LIVE WITHOUT HER...
...YOU EXPECTED HER TO LIVE WITHOUT YOU?

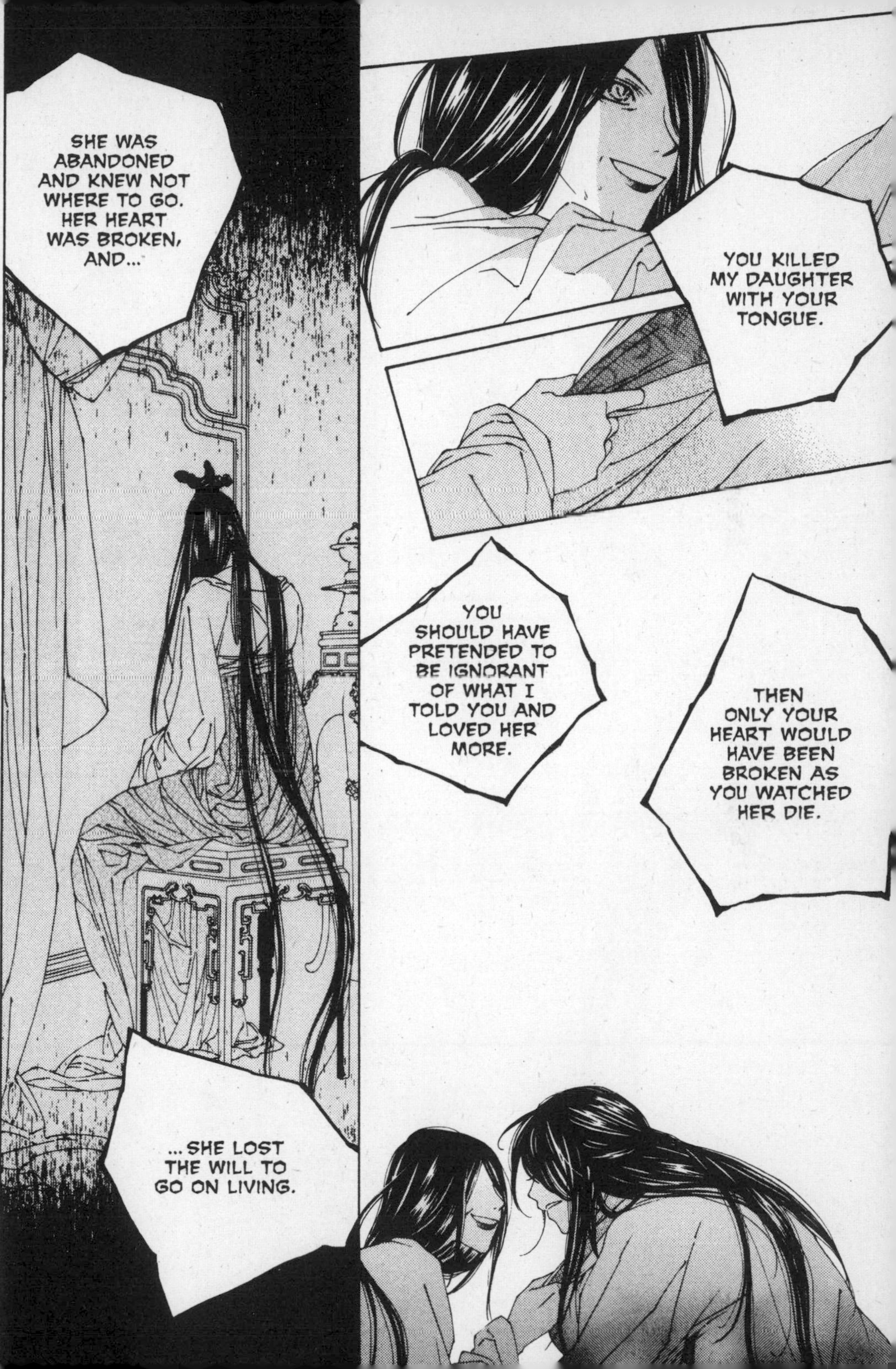
SHE WAS ABANDONED AND KNEW NOT WHERE TO GO. HER HEART WAS BROKEN, AND...
...SHE LOST THE WILL TO GO ON LIVING.
YOU KILLED MY DAUGHTER WITH YOUR TONGUE.
YOU SHOULD HAVE PRETENDED TO BE IGNORANT OF WHAT I TOLD YOU AND LOVED HER MORE.
THEN ONLY YOUR HEART WOULD HAVE BEEN BROKEN AS YOU WATCHED HER DIE.

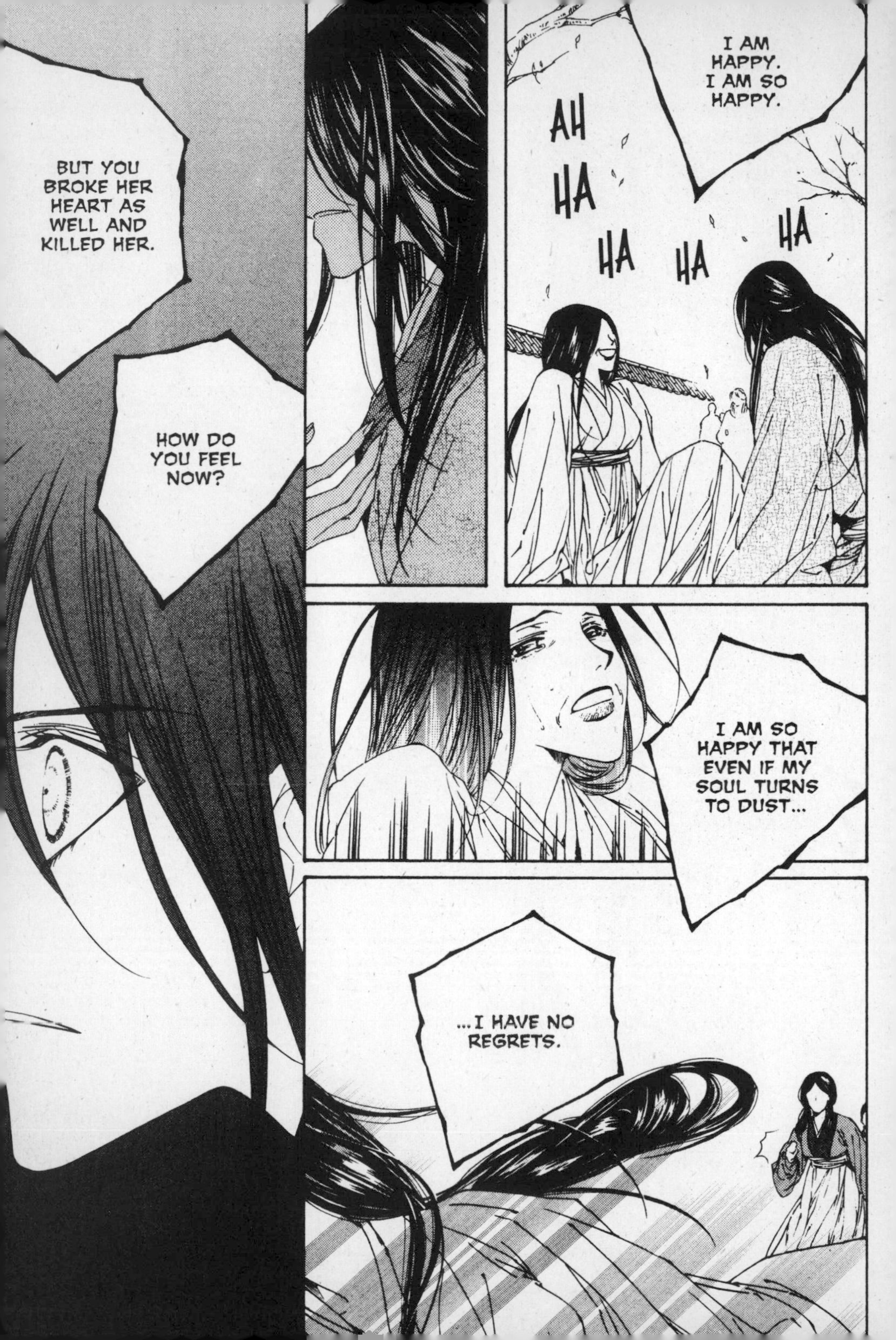
BUT YOU BROKE HER HEART AS WELL AND KILLED HER.
HOW DO YOU FEEL NOW?
I AM HAPPY. I AM SO HAPPY.
AH HA HA HA HA
I AM SO HAPPY THAT EVEN IF MY SOUL TURNS TO DUST...
...I HAVE NO REGRETS.

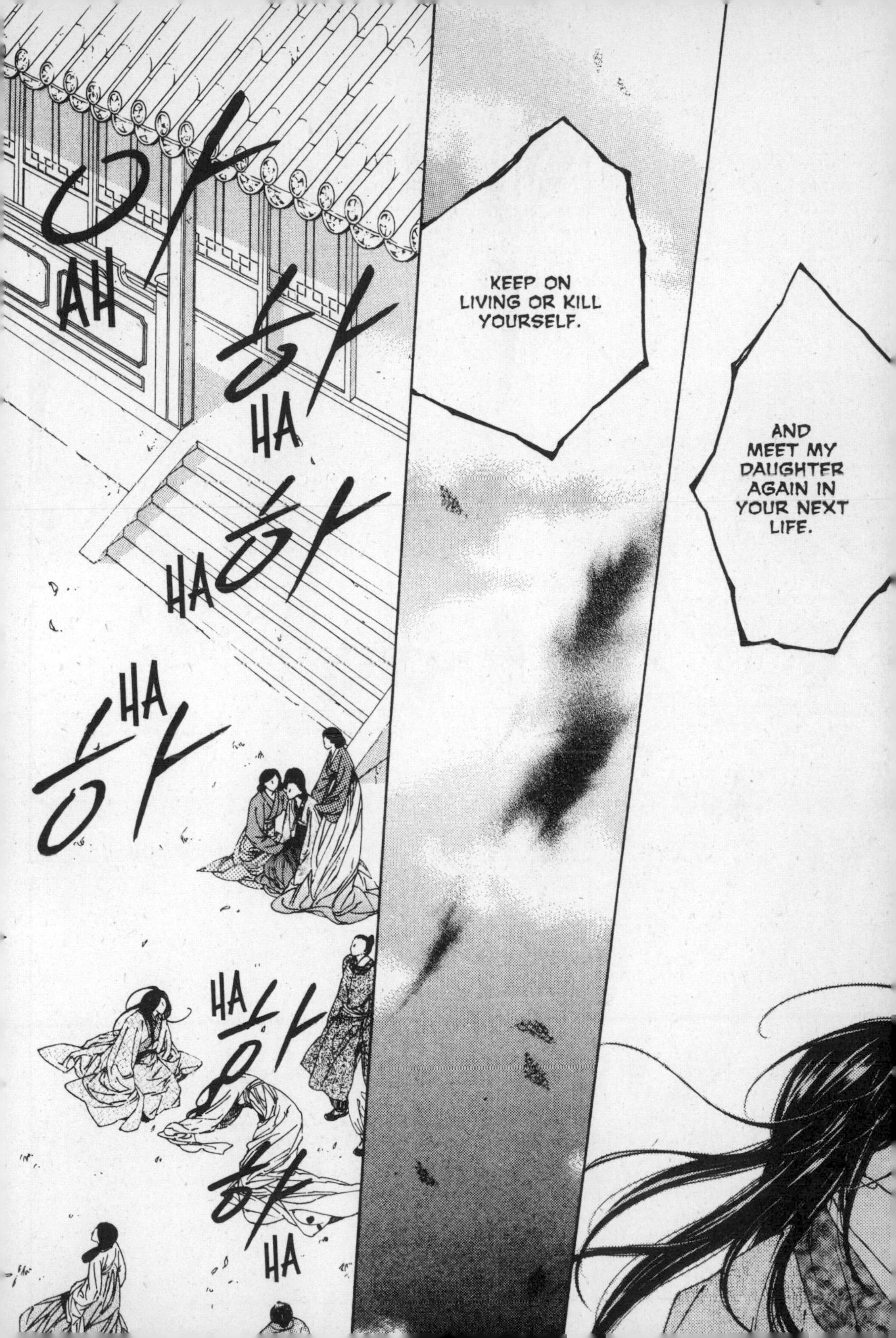

아
AH
하
HA
하
HA
HA
하
HA
하
하
HA
KEEP ON LIVING OR KILL YOURSELF.
AND MEET MY DAUGHTER AGAIN IN YOUR NEXT LIFE.

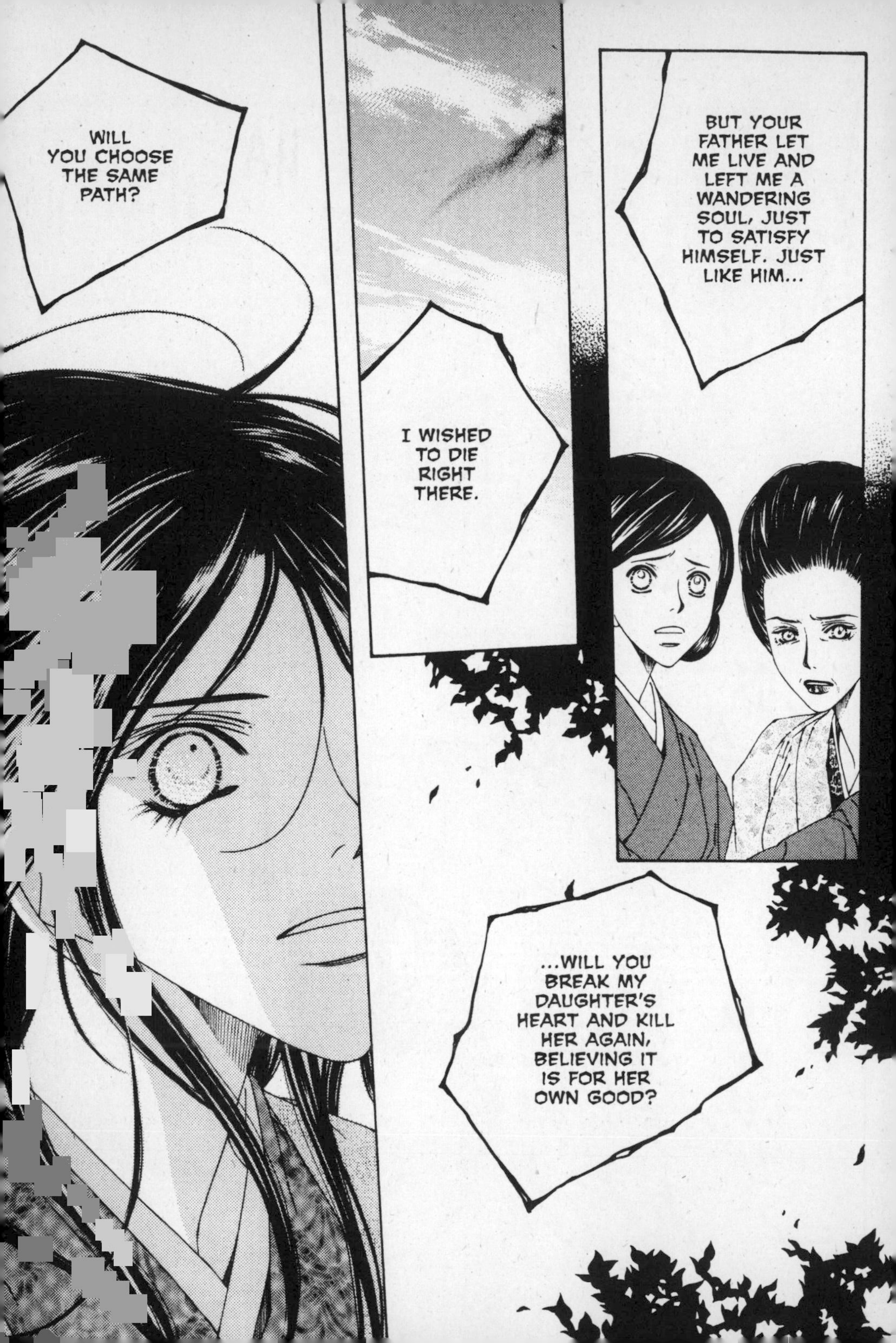
WILL YOU CHOOSE THE SAME PATH?
I WISHED TO DIE RIGHT THERE.
BUT YOUR FATHER LET ME LIVE AND LEFT ME A WANDERING SOUL, JUST TO SATISFY HIMSELF. JUST LIKE HIM...
...WILL YOU BREAK MY DAUGHTER'S HEART AND KILL HER AGAIN, BELIEVING IT IS FOR HER OWN GOOD?

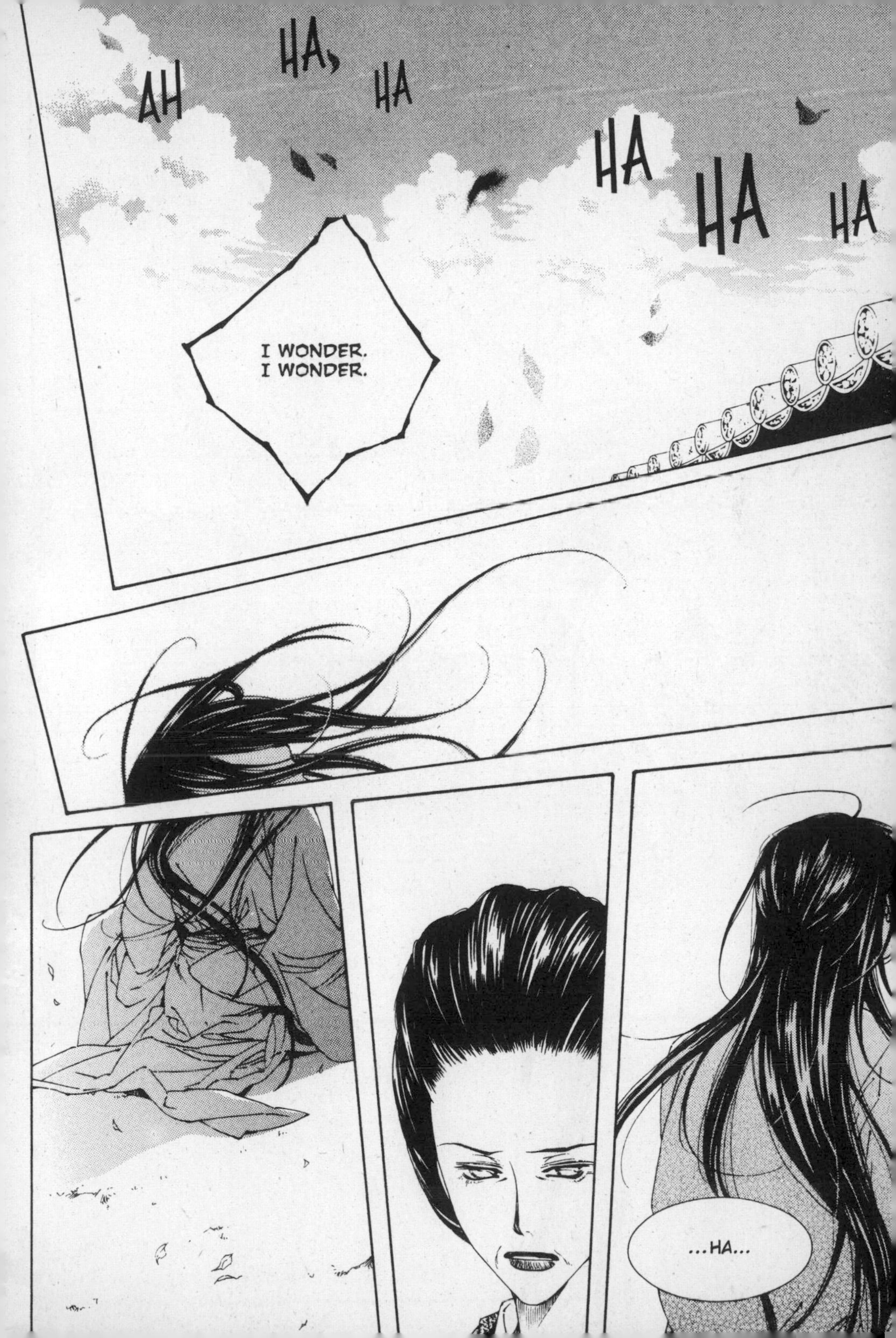
AH
HA, HA
HA
HA
HA
I WONDER.
I WONDER.
...HA...

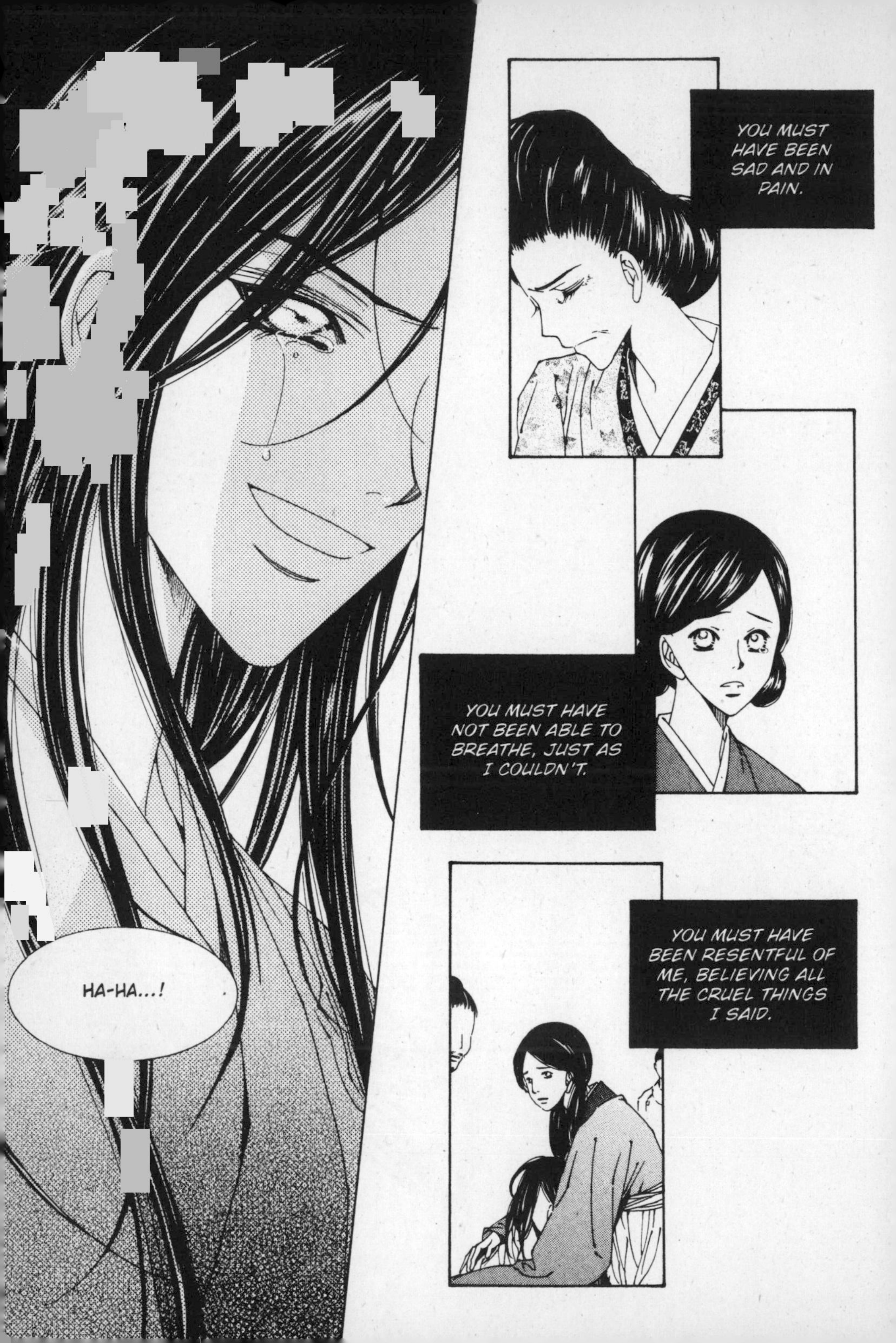
HA-HA...!
YOU MUST HAVE BEEN SAD AND IN PAIN.
YOU MUST HAVE NOT BEEN ABLE TO BREATHE, JUST AS I COULDN'T.
YOU MUST HAVE BEEN RESENTFUL OF ME, BELIEVING ALL THE CRUEL THINGS I SAID.

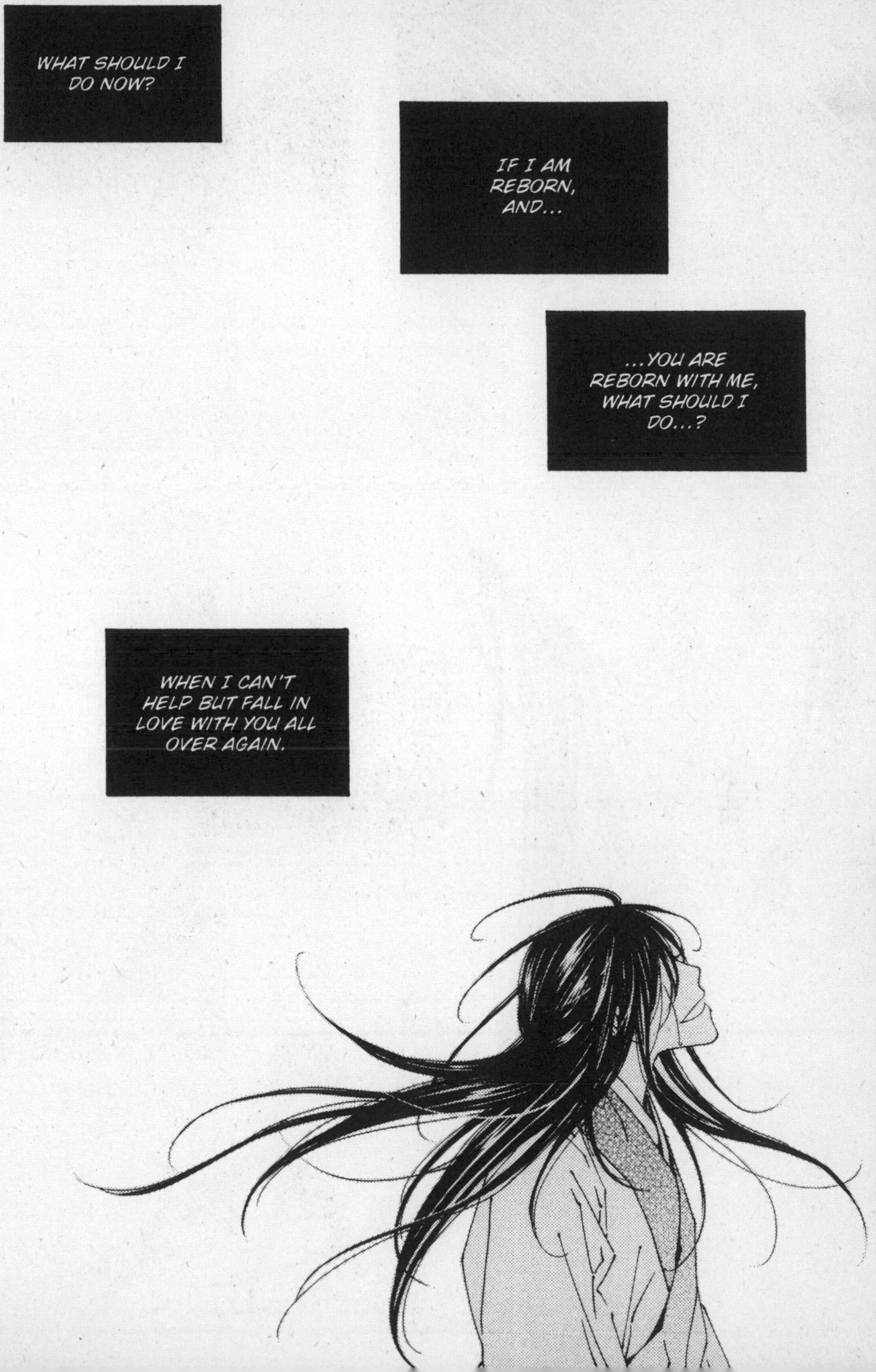
WHAT SHOULD I DO NOW?
IF I AM REBORN, AND...
...YOU ARE REBORN WITH ME, WHAT SHOULD I DO...?
WHEN I CAN'T HELP BUT FALL IN LOVE WITH YOU ALL OVER AGAIN.

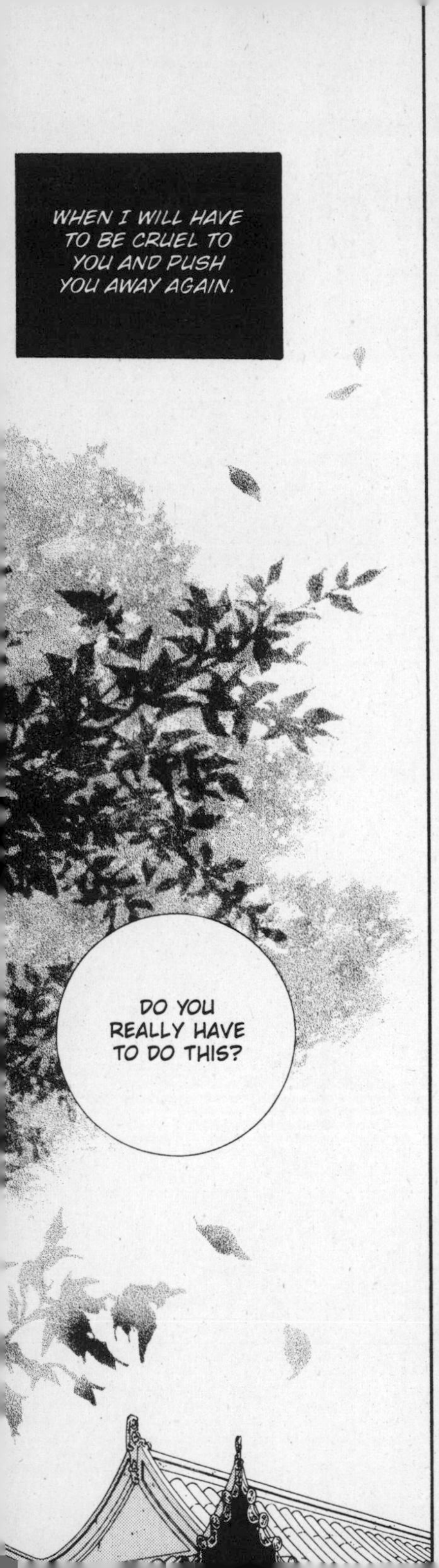
WHEN I WILL HAVE TO BE CRUEL TO YOU AND PUSH YOU AWAY AGAIN.
DO YOU REALLY HAVE TO DO THIS?

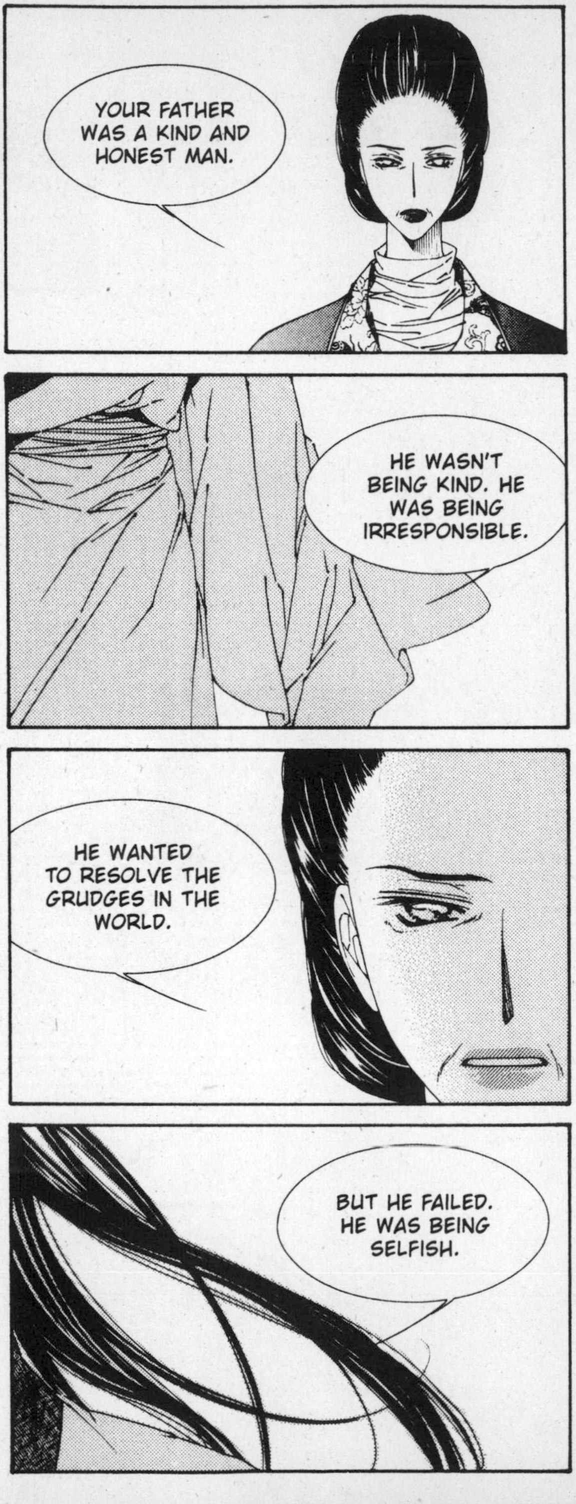
YOUR FATHER WAS A KIND AND HONEST MAN.
HE WASN'T BEING KIND. HE WAS BEING IRRESPONSIBLE.
HE WANTED TO RESOLVE THE GRUDGES IN THE WORLD.
BUT HE FAILED. HE WAS BEING SELFISH.

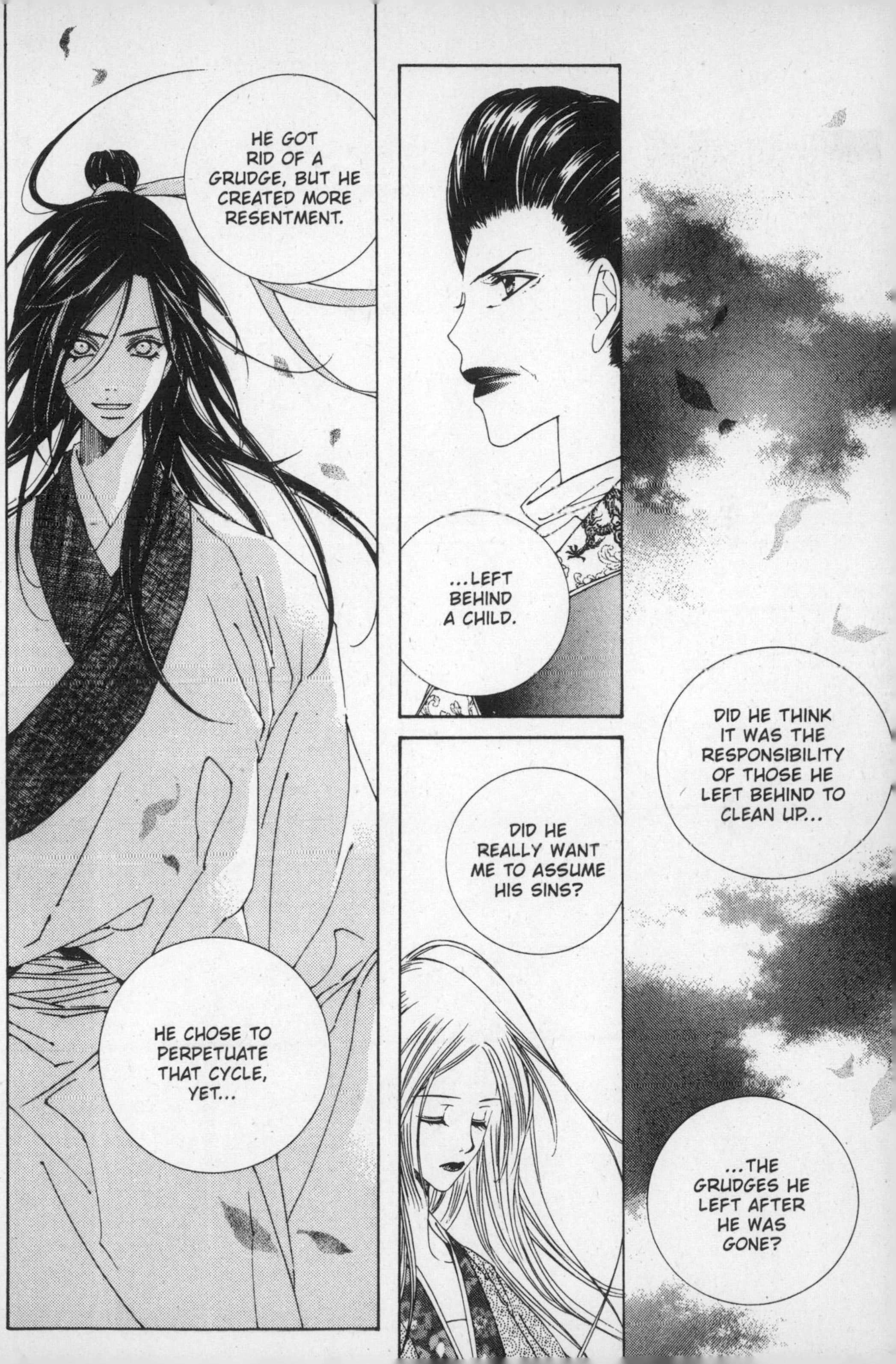
HE GOT RID OF A GRUDGE, BUT HE CREATED MORE RESENTMENT.
HE CHOSE TO PERPETUATE THAT CYCLE, YET...
...LEFT BEHIND A CHILD.
DID HE REALLY WANT ME TO ASSUME HIS SINS?
DID HE THINK IT WAS THE RESPONSIBILITY OF THOSE HE LEFT BEHIND TO CLEAN UP...
...THE GRUDGES HE LEFT AFTER HE WAS GONE?

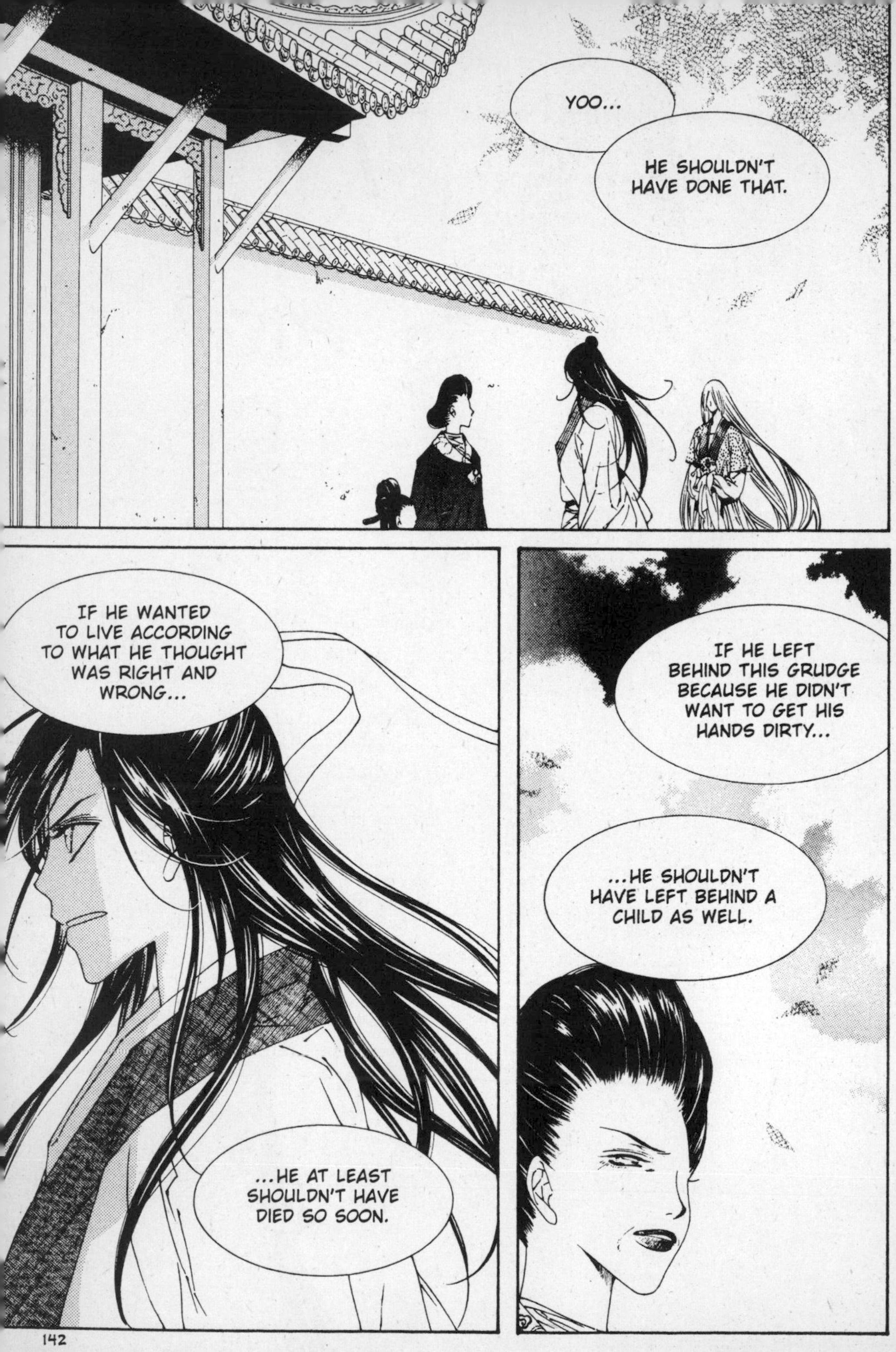
YOO...
HE SHOULDN'T HAVE DONE THAT.
IF HE WANTED TO LIVE ACCORDING TO WHAT HE THOUGHT WAS RIGHT AND WRONG...
...HE AT LEAST SHOULDN'T HAVE DIED SO SOON.
IF HE LEFT BEHIND THIS GRUDGE BECAUSE HE DIDN'T WANT TO GET HIS HANDS DIRTY...
...HE SHOULDN'T HAVE LEFT BEHIND A CHILD AS WELL.

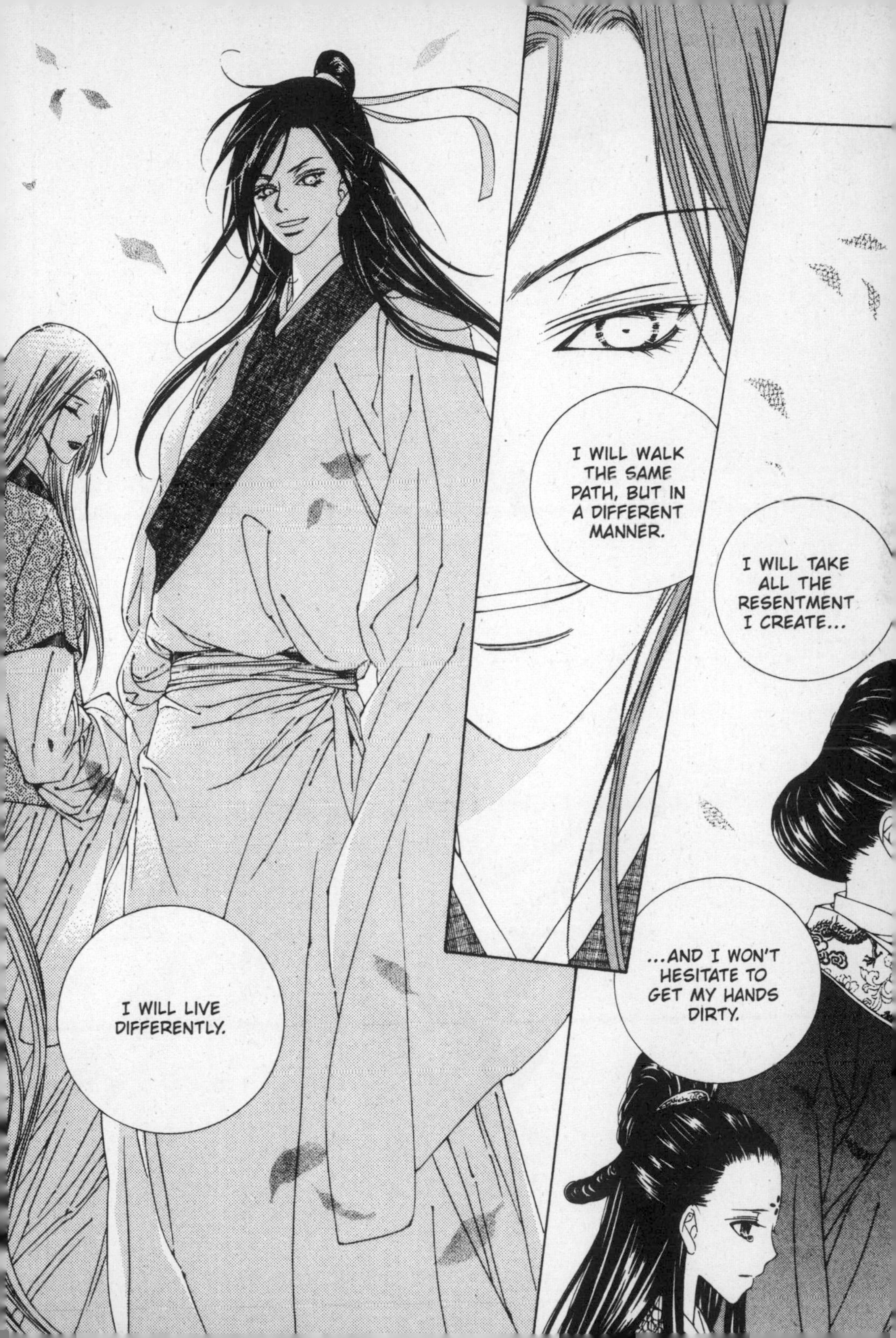
I WILL LIVE DIFFERENTLY.
I WILL WALK THE SAME PATH, BUT IN A DIFFERENT MANNER.
I WILL TAKE ALL THE RESENTMENT I CREATE...
...AND I WON'T HESITATE TO GET MY HANDS DIRTY.

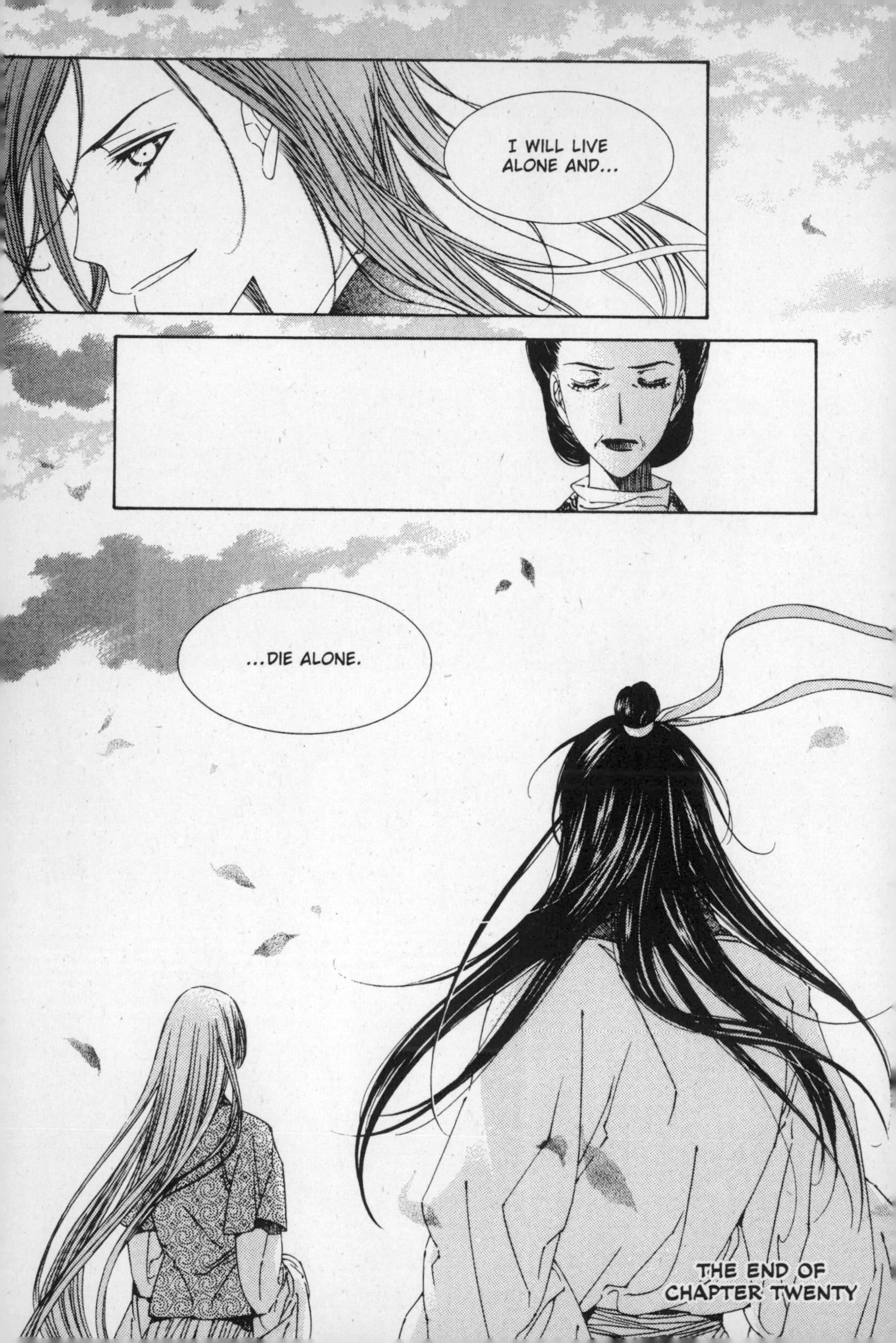
I WILL LIVE ALONE AND...
...DIE ALONE.
THE END OF CHAPTER TWENTY

TIME
AND
AGAIN

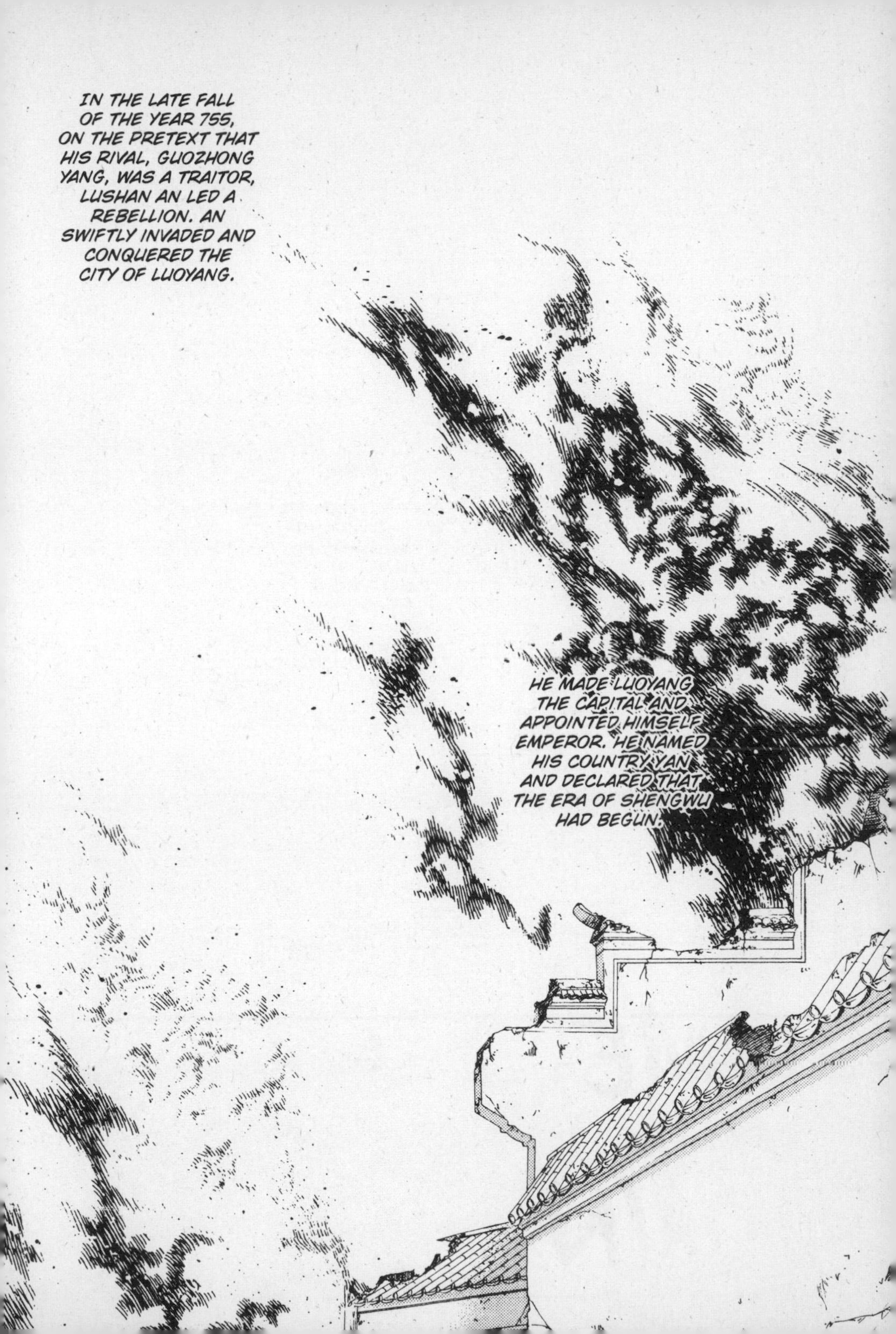
IN THE LATE FALL OF THE YEAR 755, ON THE PRETEXT THAT HIS RIVAL, GUOZHONG YANG, WAS A TRAITOR, LUSHAN AN LED A REBELLION. AN SWIFTLY INVADED AND CONQUERED THE CITY OF LUOYANG.
HE MADE LUOYANG THE CAPITAL AND APPOINTED HIMSELF EMPEROR. HE NAMED HIS COUNTRY YAN AND DECLARED THAT THE ERA OF SHENGWU HAD BEGUN.

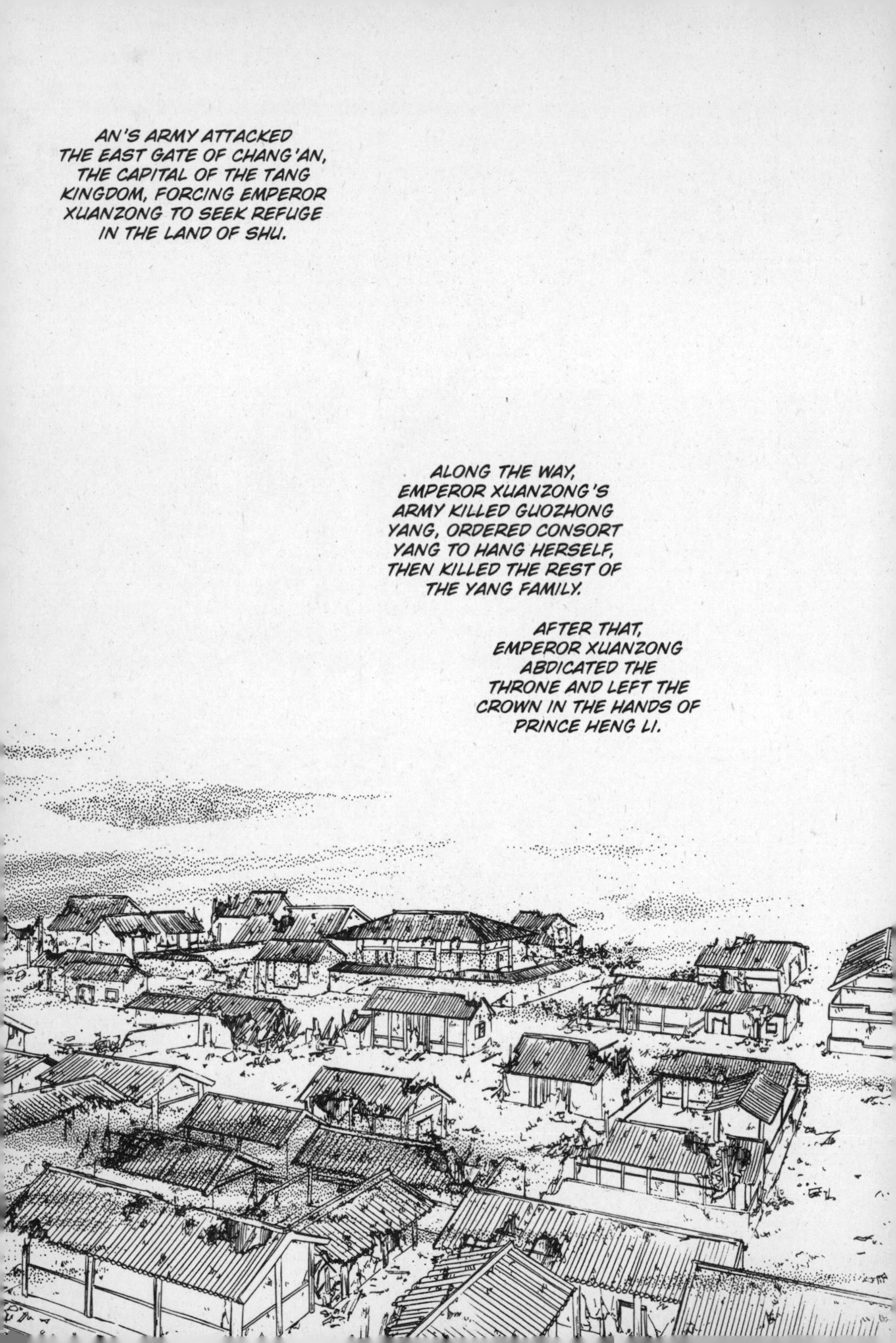
AN'S ARMY ATTACKED THE EAST GATE OF CHANG'AN, THE CAPITAL OF THE TANG KINGDOM, FORCING EMPEROR XUANZONG TO SEEK REFUGE IN THE LAND OF SHU.
ALONG THE WAY, EMPEROR XUANZONG'S ARMY KILLED GUOZHONG YANG, ORDERED CONSORT YANG TO HANG HERSELF, THEN KILLED THE REST OF THE YANG FAMILY.
AFTER THAT, EMPEROR XUANZONG ABDICATED THE THRONE AND LEFT THE CROWN IN THE HANDS OF PRINCE HENG LI.

THE STREETS WERE FILLED WITH PANIC AND DISARRAY, AND THE RIVERS RAN RED WITH BLOOD. THE SOUND OF WEEPING WAS UNENDING AS THE LIGHT OF BURNING HOUSES RAGED. IT WAS EIGHT YEARS BEFORE THE CHAOS SUBSIDED, AND THE GREAT TANG DYNASTY SLOWLY DECLINED OVER THE NEXT ONE HUNDRED AND FIFTY YEARS.

FINAL CHAPTER
THE END OF THE SKY

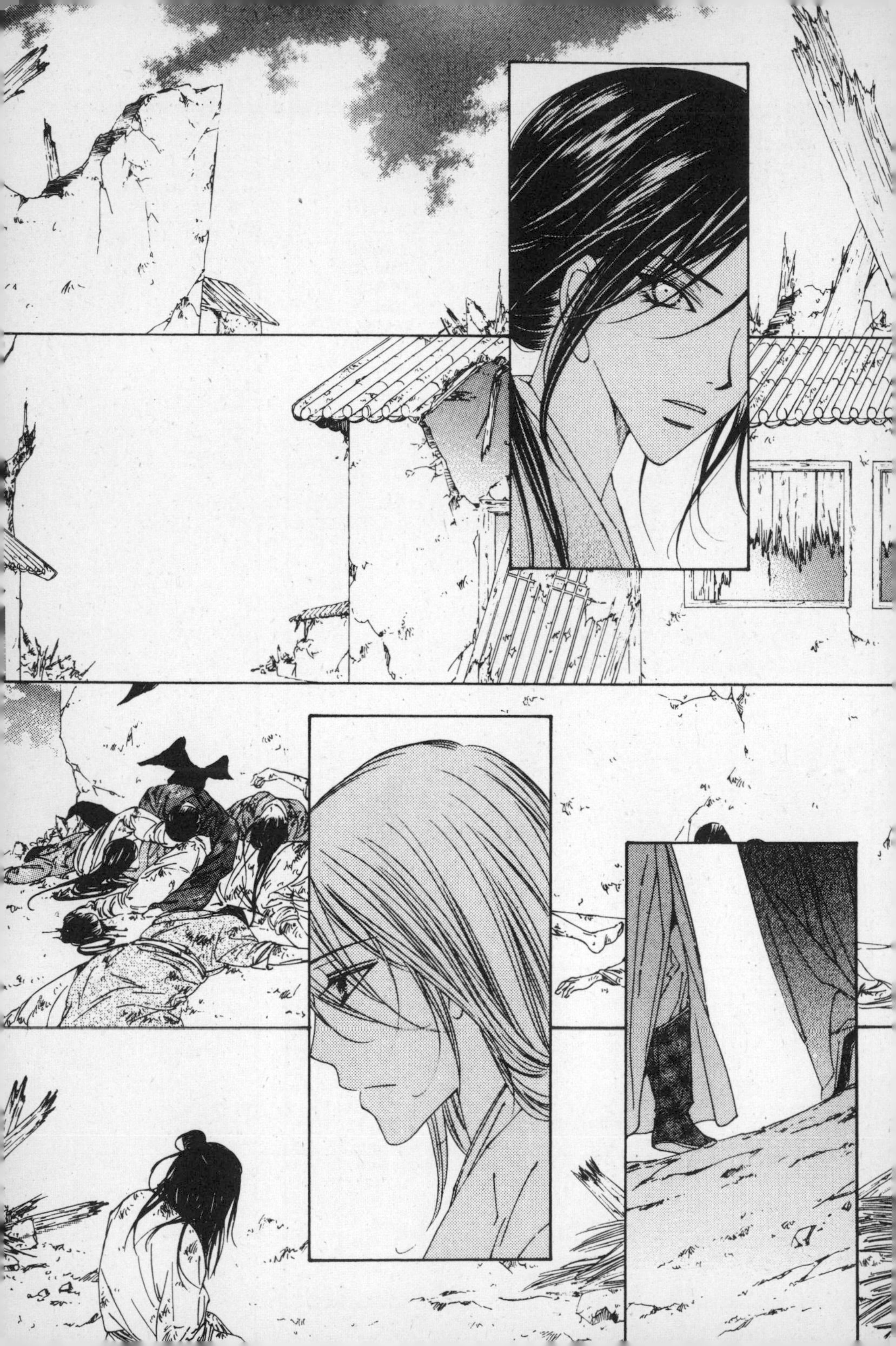

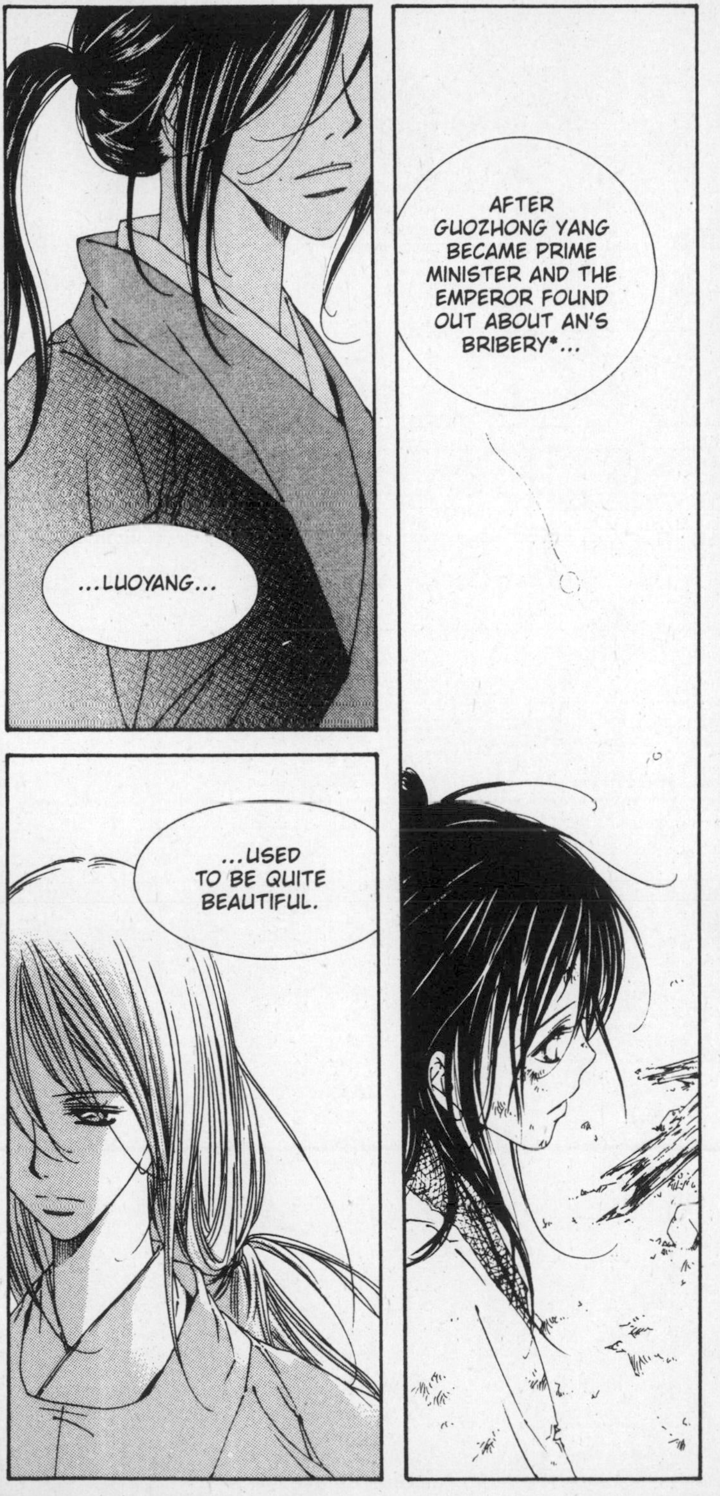
...LUOYANG...
...USED TO BE QUITE BEAUTIFUL.
AFTER GUOZHONG YANG BECAME PRIME MINISTER AND THE EMPEROR FOUND OUT ABOUT AN'S BRIBERY*...
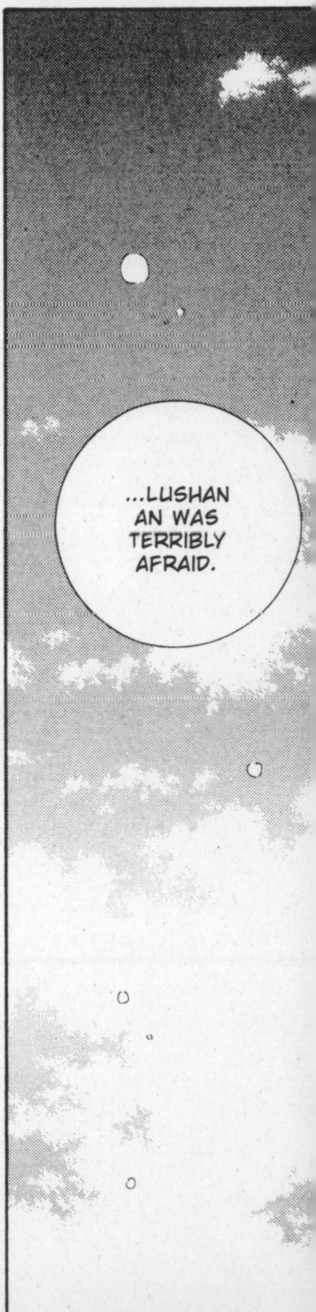
...LUSHAN AN WAS TERRIBLY AFRAID.

*EMPEROR XUANZONG TRUSTED LUSHAN AN AGAINST THE ADVICE OF THE CROWN PRINCE AND GUOZHONG YANG. WHEN THE EMPEROR SENT EUNUCH QIULIN FU TO CHECK ON LUSHAN AN, HE WAS BRIBED BY AN TO GIVE A GOOD REPORT. WHEN EMPEROR XUANZONG HEARD ABOUT THIS, HE BEGAN TO DOUBT AN'S LOYALTY.

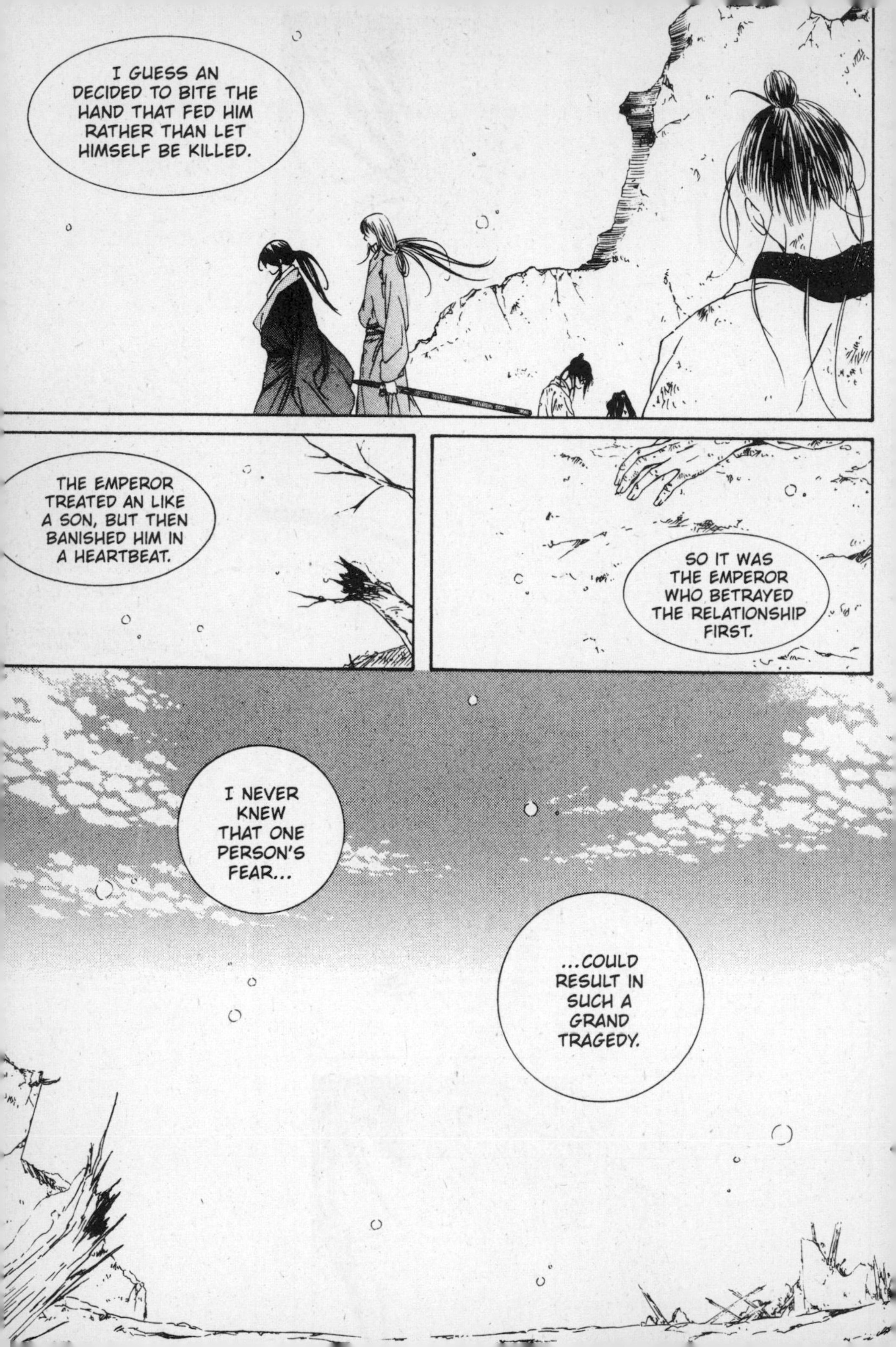
I GUESS AN DECIDED TO BITE THE HAND THAT FED HIM RATHER THAN LET HIMSELF BE KILLED.
THE EMPEROR TREATED AN LIKE A SON, BUT THEN BANISHED HIM IN A HEARTBEAT.
SO IT WAS THE EMPEROR WHO BETRAYED THE RELATIONSHIP FIRST.
I NEVER KNEW THAT ONE PERSON'S FEAR...
...COULD RESULT IN SUCH A GRAND TRAGEDY.

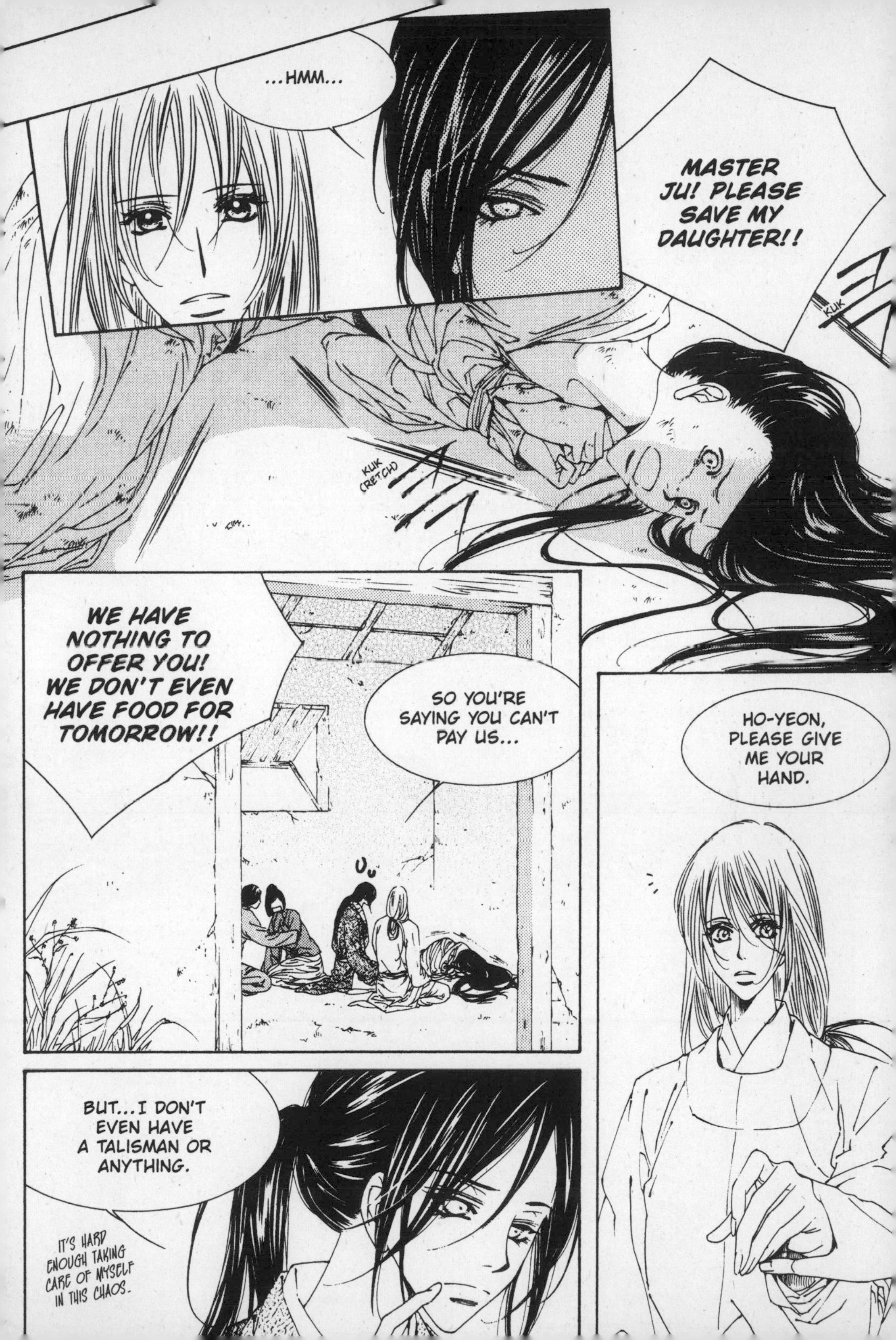
...HMM...
MASTER JU! PLEASE SAVE MY DAUGHTER!!
KUK
KUK (RETCH)
WE HAVE NOTHING TO OFFER YOU! WE DON'T EVEN HAVE FOOD FOR TOMORROW!!
SO YOU'RE SAYING YOU CAN'T PAY US...
HO-YEON, PLEASE GIVE ME YOUR HAND.
BUT...I DON'T EVEN HAVE A TALISMAN OR ANYTHING.
IT'S HARD ENOUGH TAKING CARE OF MYSELF IN THIS CHAOS.

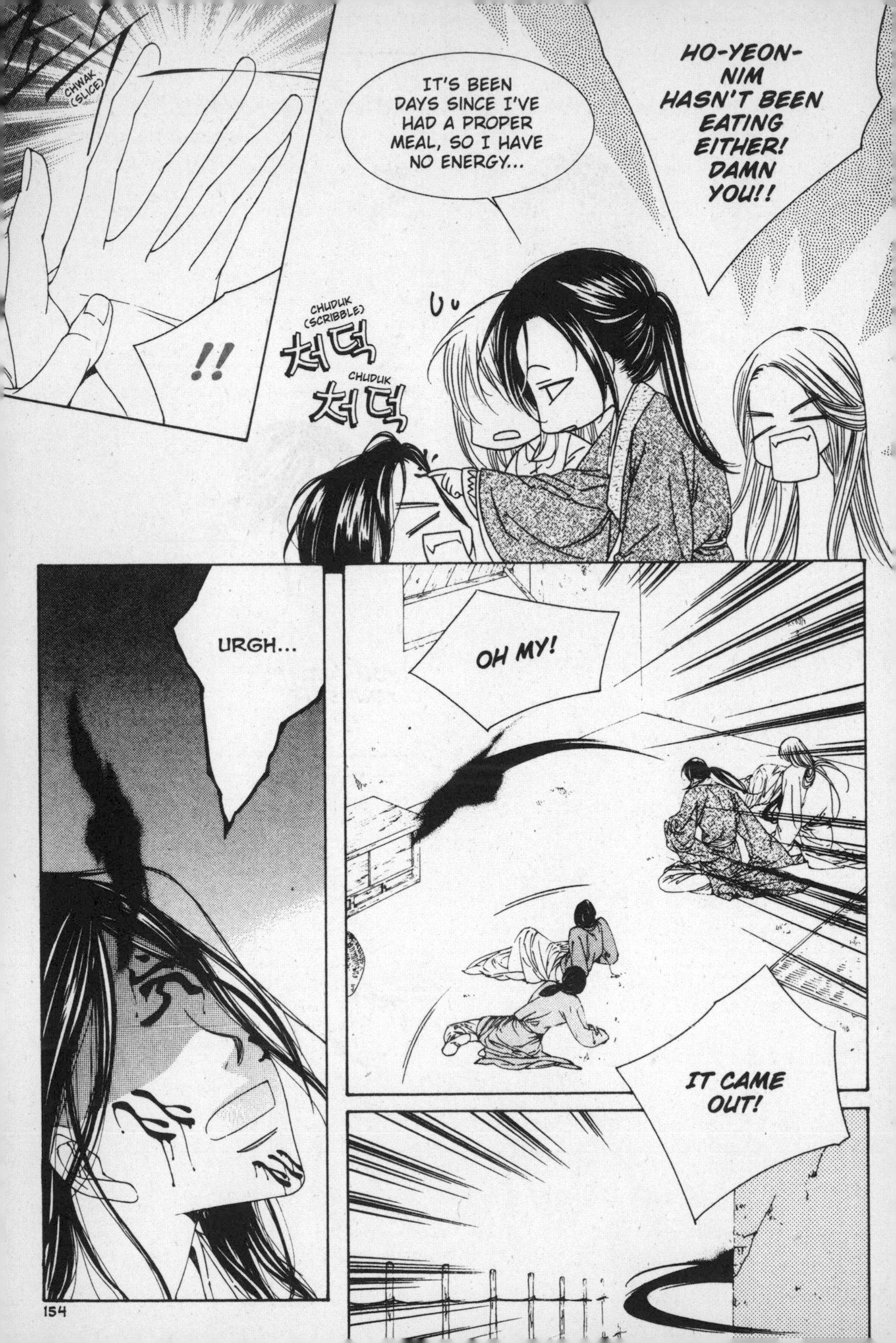
CHWAK (SLICE)
IT'S BEEN DAYS SINCE I'VE HAD A PROPER MEAL, SO I HAVE NO ENERGY...
HO-YEON-NIM HASN'T BEEN EATING EITHER! DAMN YOU!!
!!
CHUDUK (SCRIBBLE)
처덕
CHUDUK
처덕
URGH...
OH MY!
IT CAME OUT!

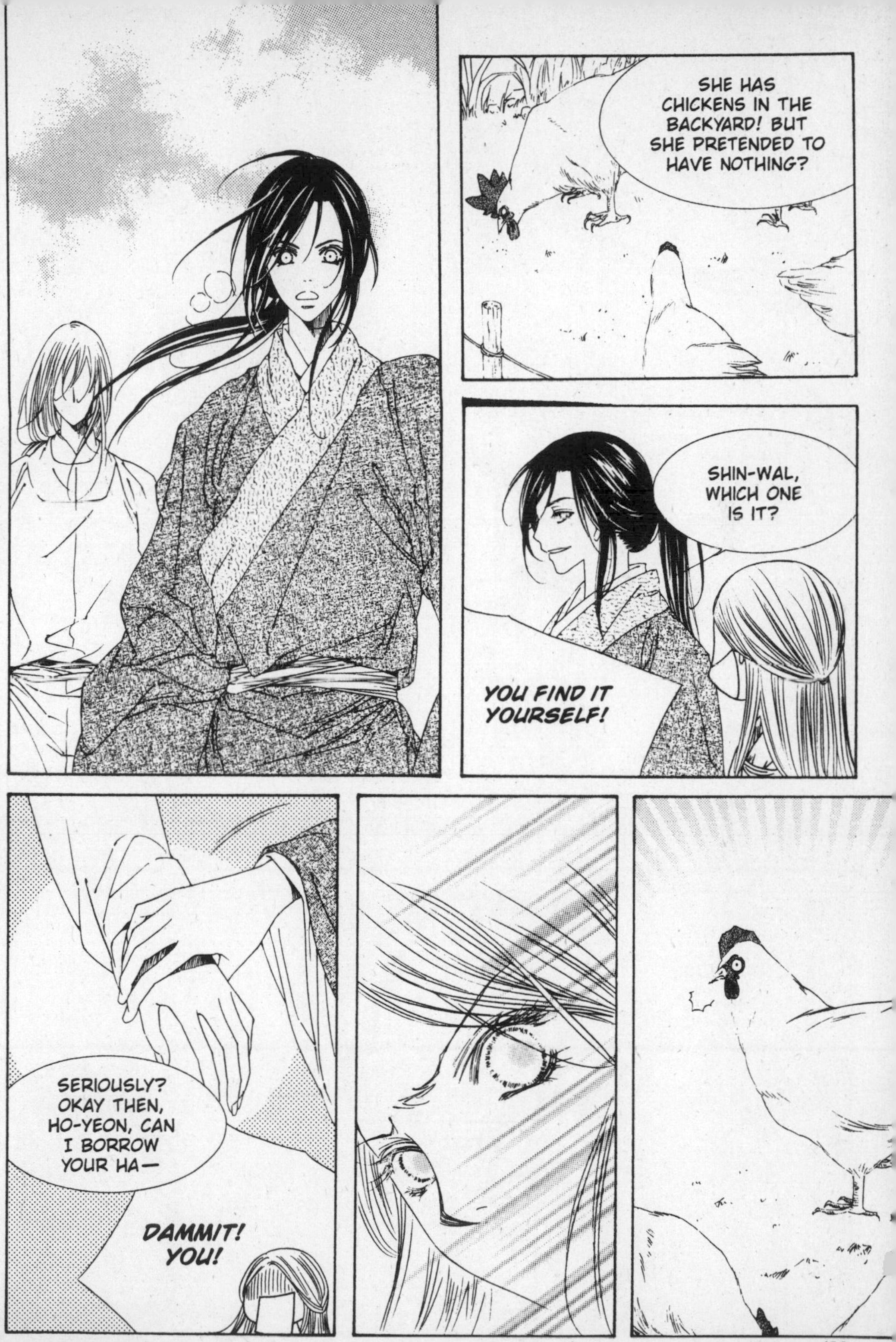
SHE HAS CHICKENS IN THE BACKYARD! BUT SHE PRETENDED TO HAVE NOTHING?
SHIN-WAL, WHICH ONE IS IT?
YOU FIND IT YOURSELF!
SERIOUSLY? OKAY THEN, HO-YEON, CAN I BORROW YOUR HA—
DAMMIT! YOU!

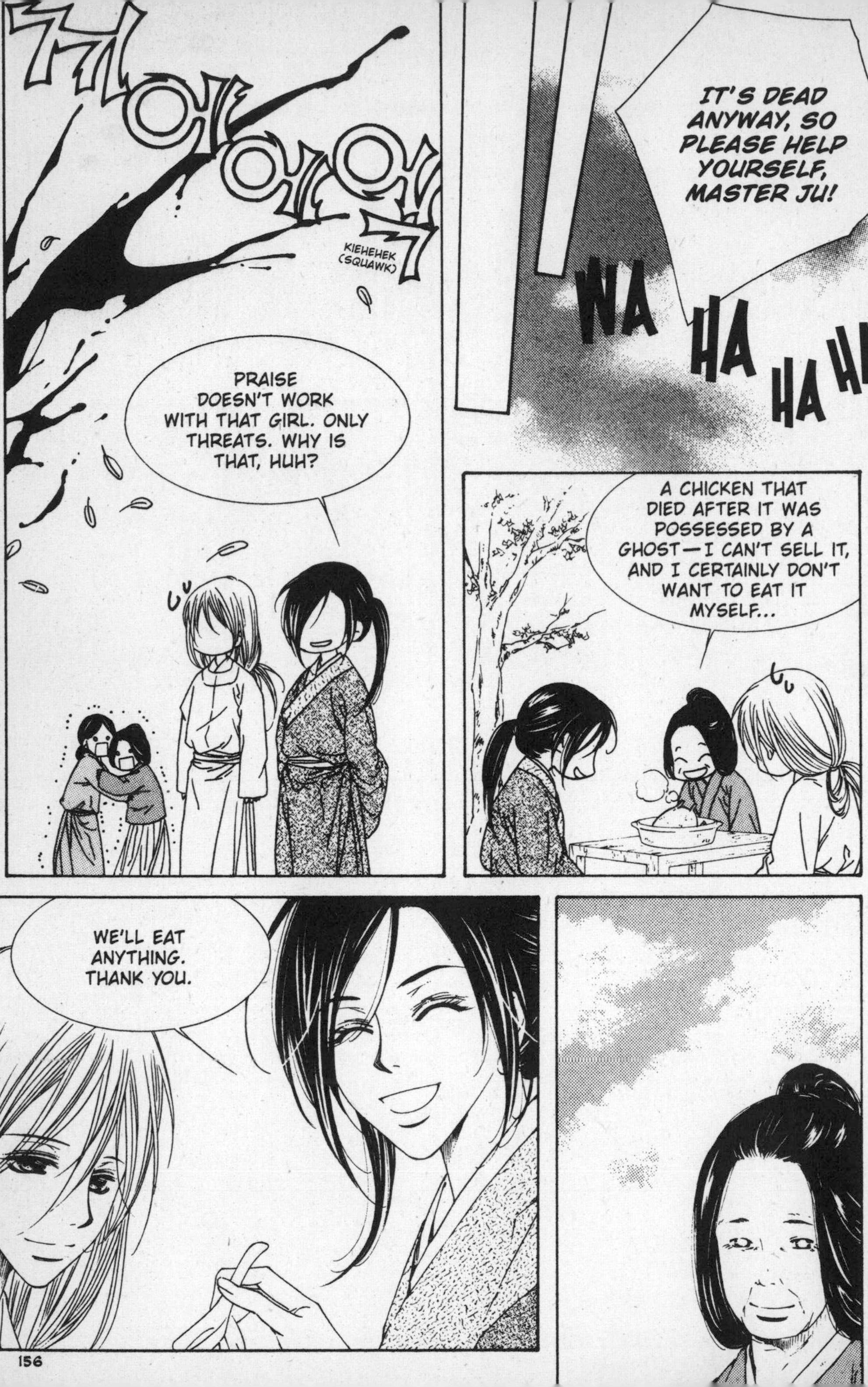
KIEHEHEK (SQUAWK)
PRAISE DOESN'T WORK WITH THAT GIRL. ONLY THREATS. WHY IS THAT, HUH?
IT'S DEAD ANYWAY, SO PLEASE HELP YOURSELF, MASTER JU!
WA HA HA HA HA
A CHICKEN THAT DIED AFTER IT WAS POSSESSED BY A GHOST—I CAN'T SELL IT, AND I CERTAINLY DON'T WANT TO EAT IT MYSELF...
WE'LL EAT ANYTHING. THANK YOU.

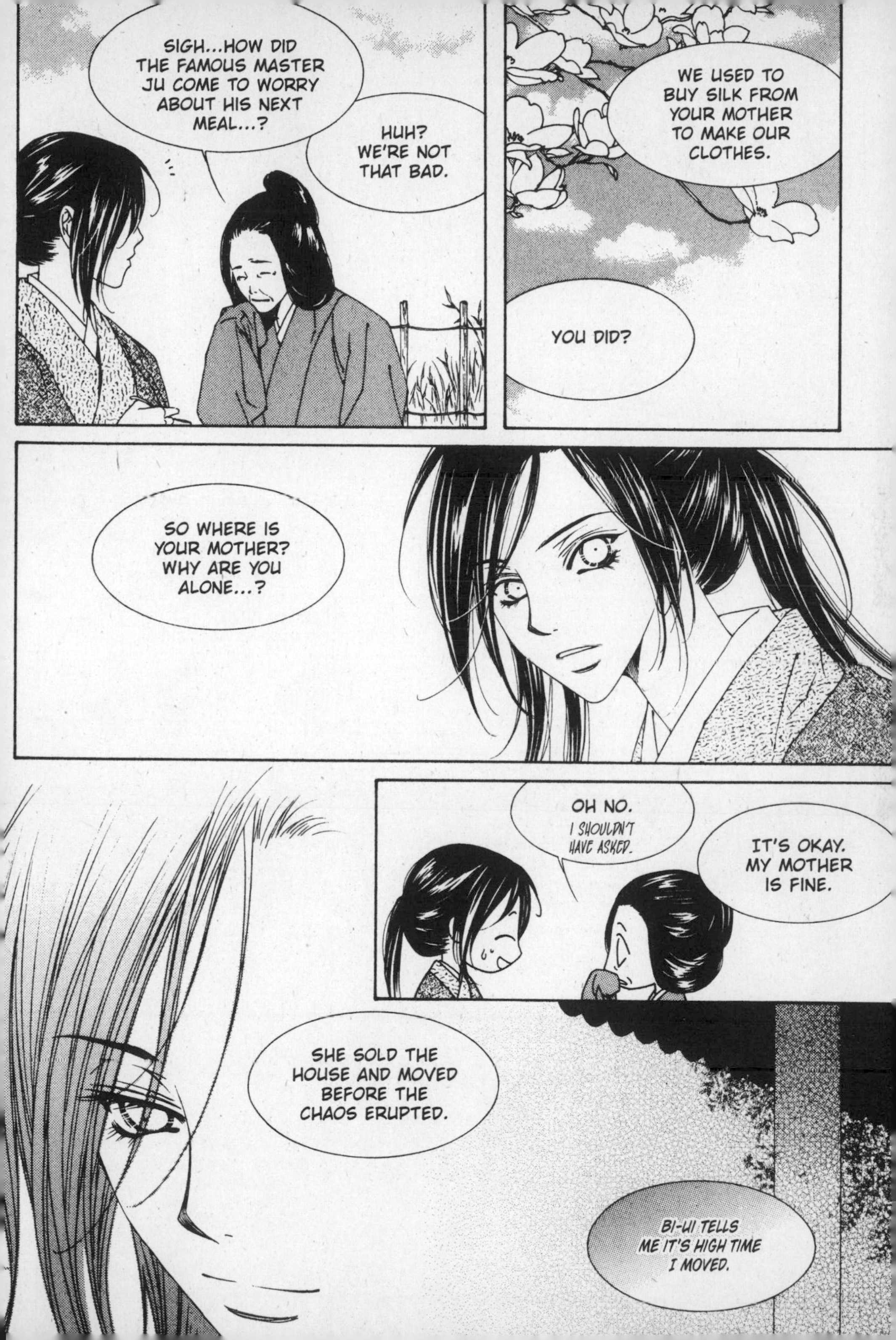
SIGH...HOW DID THE FAMOUS MASTER JU COME TO WORRY ABOUT HIS NEXT MEAL...?
HUH? WE'RE NOT THAT BAD.
WE USED TO BUY SILK FROM YOUR MOTHER TO MAKE OUR CLOTHES.
YOU DID?
SO WHERE IS YOUR MOTHER? WHY ARE YOU ALONE...?
OH NO. I SHOULDN'T HAVE ASKED.
IT'S OKAY. MY MOTHER IS FINE.
SHE SOLD THE HOUSE AND MOVED BEFORE THE CHAOS ERUPTED.
BI-UI TELLS ME IT'S HIGH TIME I MOVED.

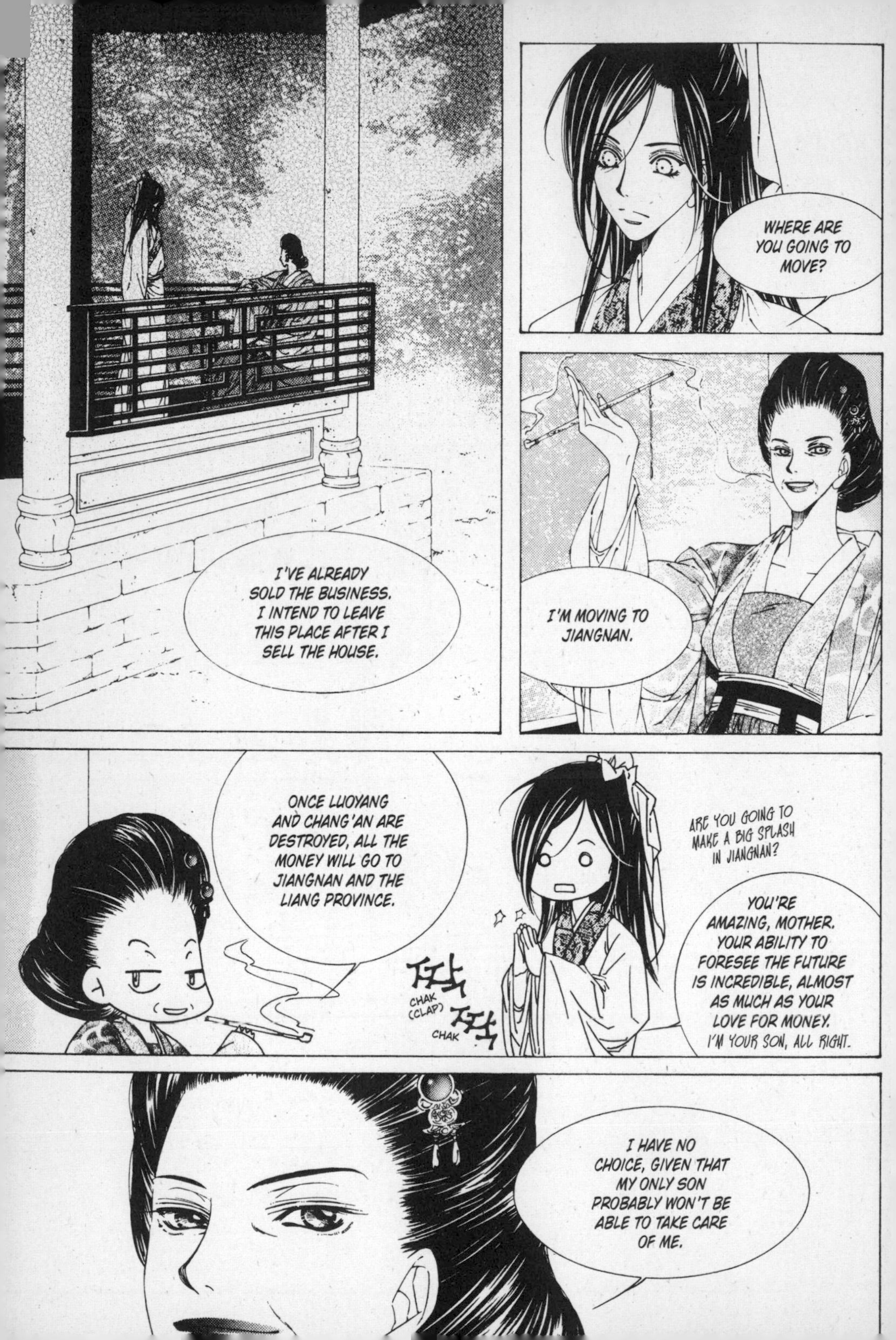
I'VE ALREADY SOLD THE BUSINESS. I INTEND TO LEAVE THIS PLACE AFTER I SELL THE HOUSE.
WHERE ARE YOU GOING TO MOVE?
I'M MOVING TO JIANGNAN.
ONCE LUOYANG AND CHANG'AN ARE DESTROYED, ALL THE MONEY WILL GO TO JIANGNAN AND THE LIANG PROVINCE.
CHAK (CLAP)
CHAK
ARE YOU GOING TO MAKE A BIG SPLASH IN JIANGNAN?
YOU'RE AMAZING, MOTHER. YOUR ABILITY TO FORESEE THE FUTURE IS INCREDIBLE, ALMOST AS MUCH AS YOUR LOVE FOR MONEY.
I'M YOUR SON, ALL RIGHT.
I HAVE NO CHOICE, GIVEN THAT MY ONLY SON PROBABLY WON'T BE ABLE TO TAKE CARE OF ME.

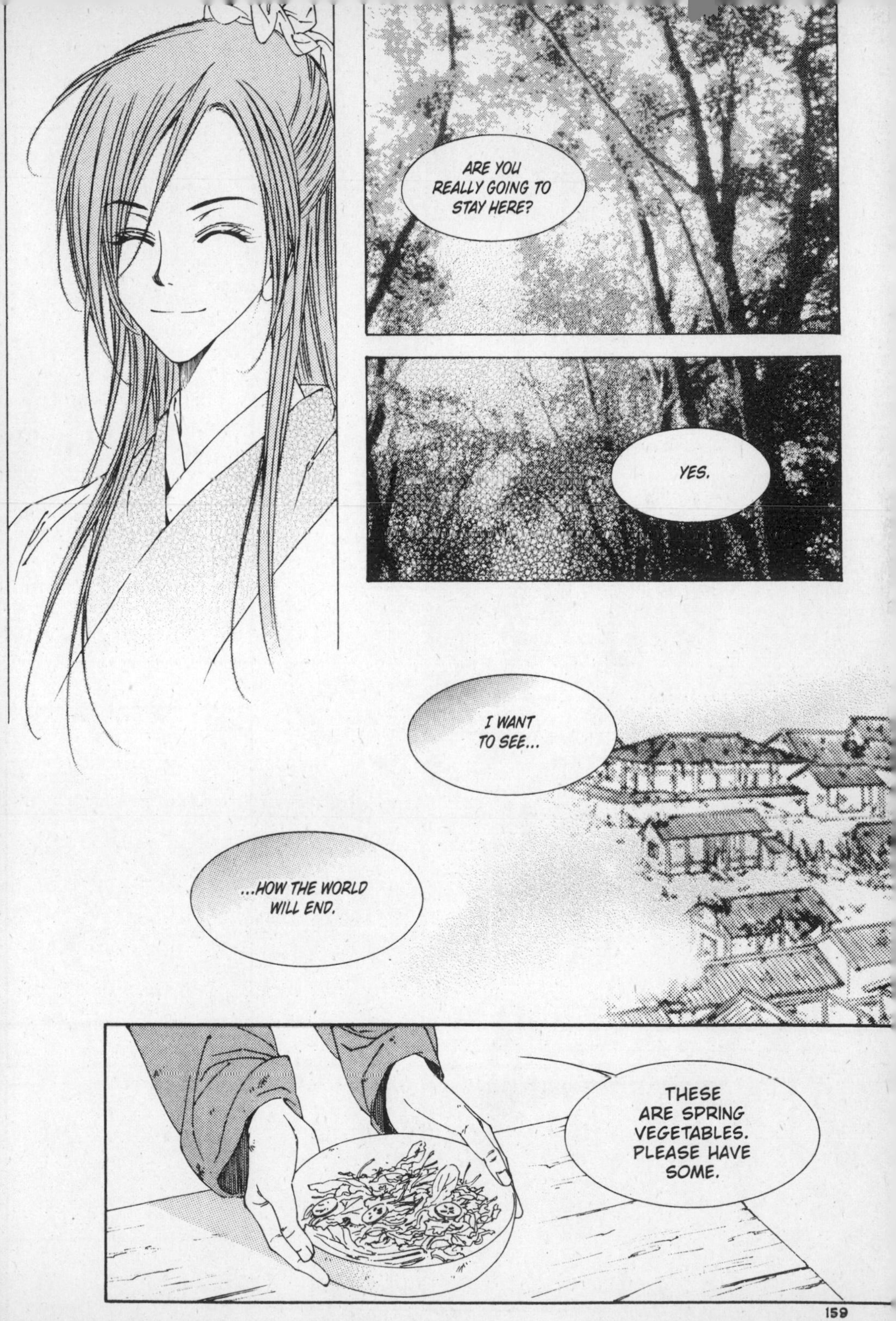
ARE YOU REALLY GOING TO STAY HERE?
YES.
I WANT TO SEE...
...HOW THE WORLD WILL END.
THESE ARE SPRING VEGETABLES. PLEASE HAVE SOME.

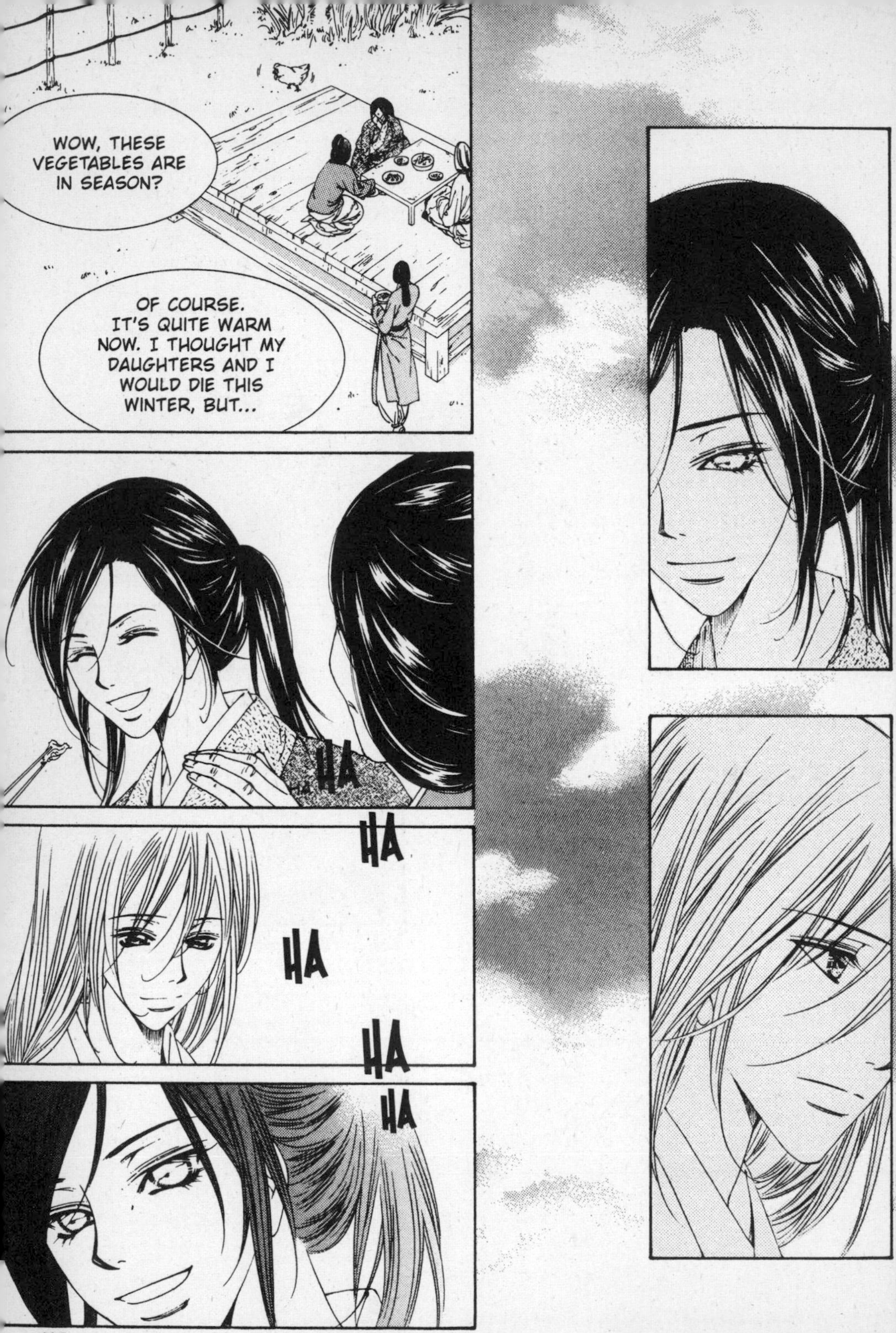
WOW, THESE VEGETABLES ARE IN SEASON?
OF COURSE. IT'S QUITE WARM NOW. I THOUGHT MY DAUGHTERS AND I WOULD DIE THIS WINTER, BUT...
HA HA
HA
HA
HA
HA

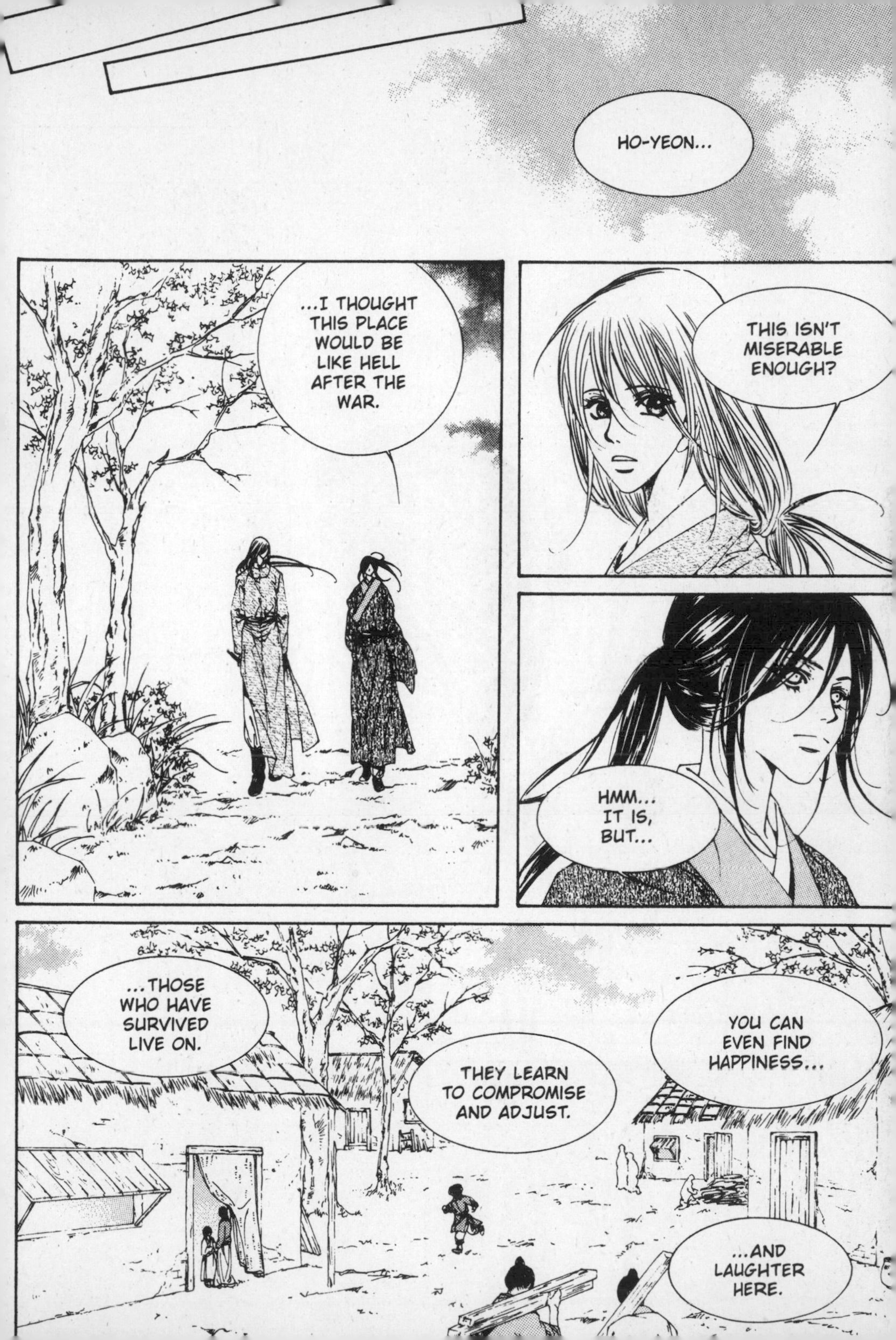
HO-YEON...
...I THOUGHT THIS PLACE WOULD BE LIKE HELL AFTER THE WAR.
THIS ISN'T MISERABLE ENOUGH?
HMM... IT IS, BUT...
...THOSE WHO HAVE SURVIVED LIVE ON.
THEY LEARN TO COMPROMISE AND ADJUST.
YOU CAN EVEN FIND HAPPINESS...
...AND LAUGHTER HERE.

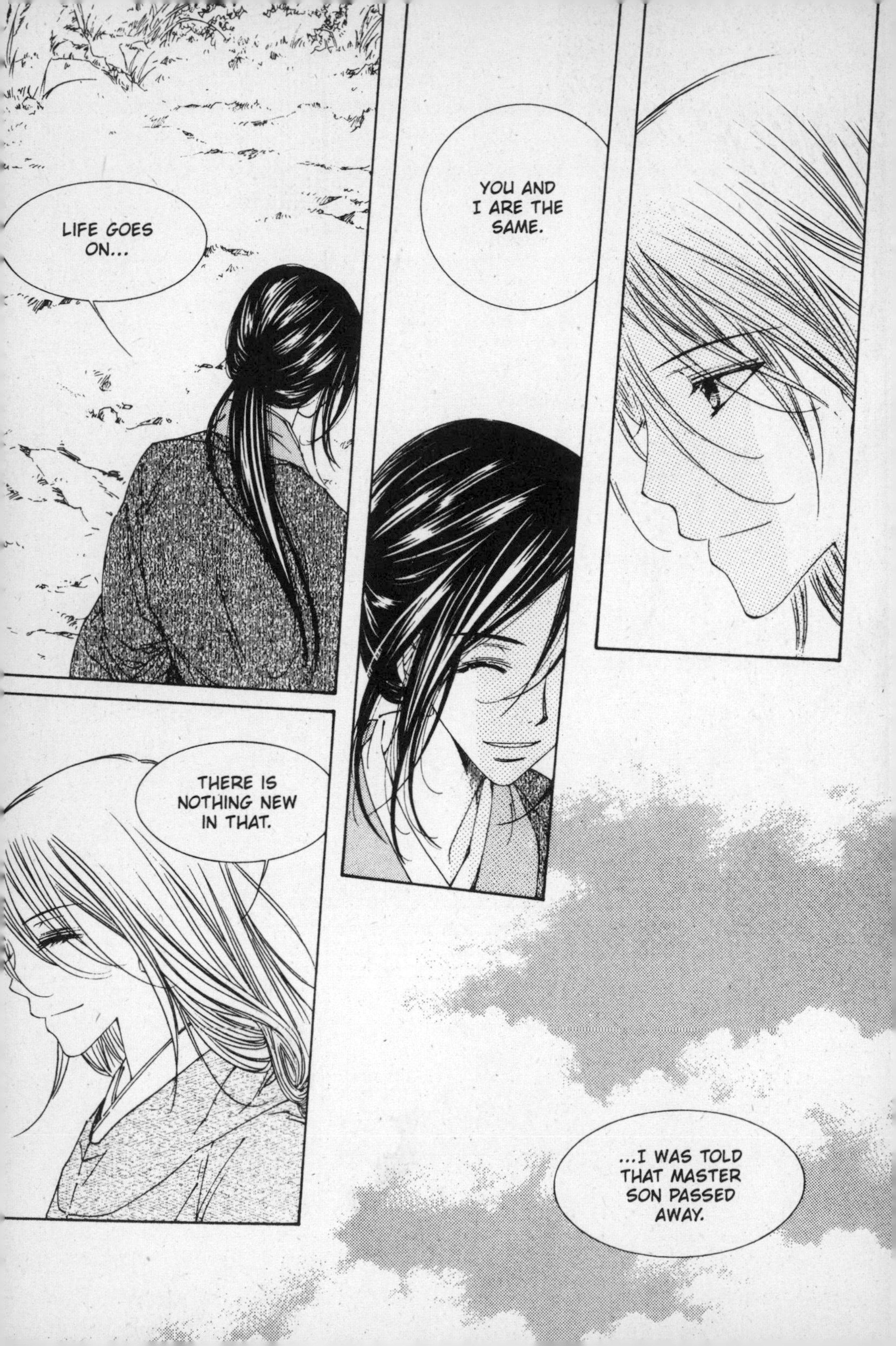
LIFE GOES ON...
YOU AND I ARE THE SAME.
THERE IS NOTHING NEW IN THAT.
...I WAS TOLD THAT MASTER SON PASSED AWAY.

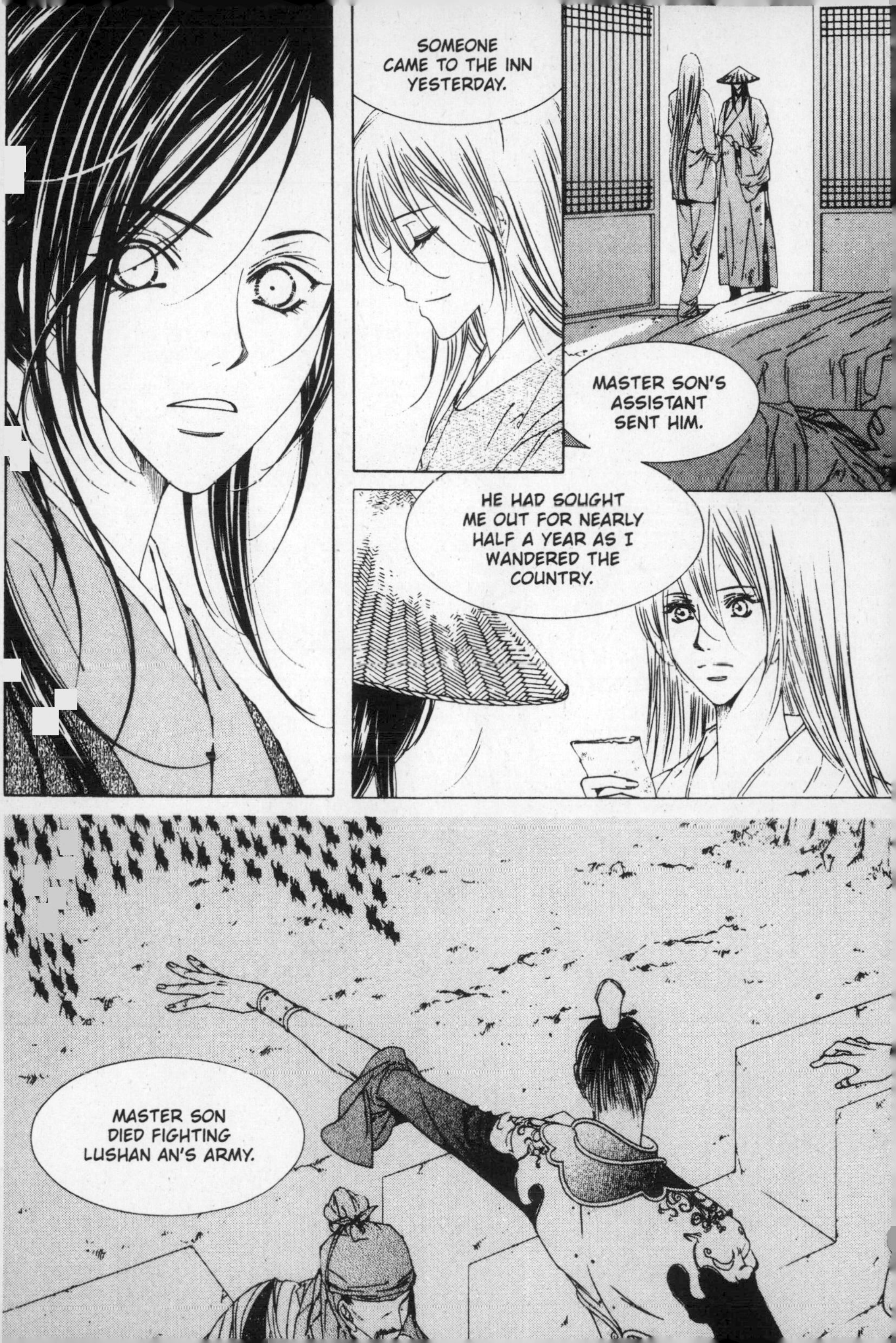
SOMEONE CAME TO THE INN YESTERDAY.
MASTER SON'S ASSISTANT SENT HIM.
HE HAD SOUGHT ME OUT FOR NEARLY HALF A YEAR AS I WANDERED THE COUNTRY.
MASTER SON DIED FIGHTING LUSHAN AN'S ARMY.

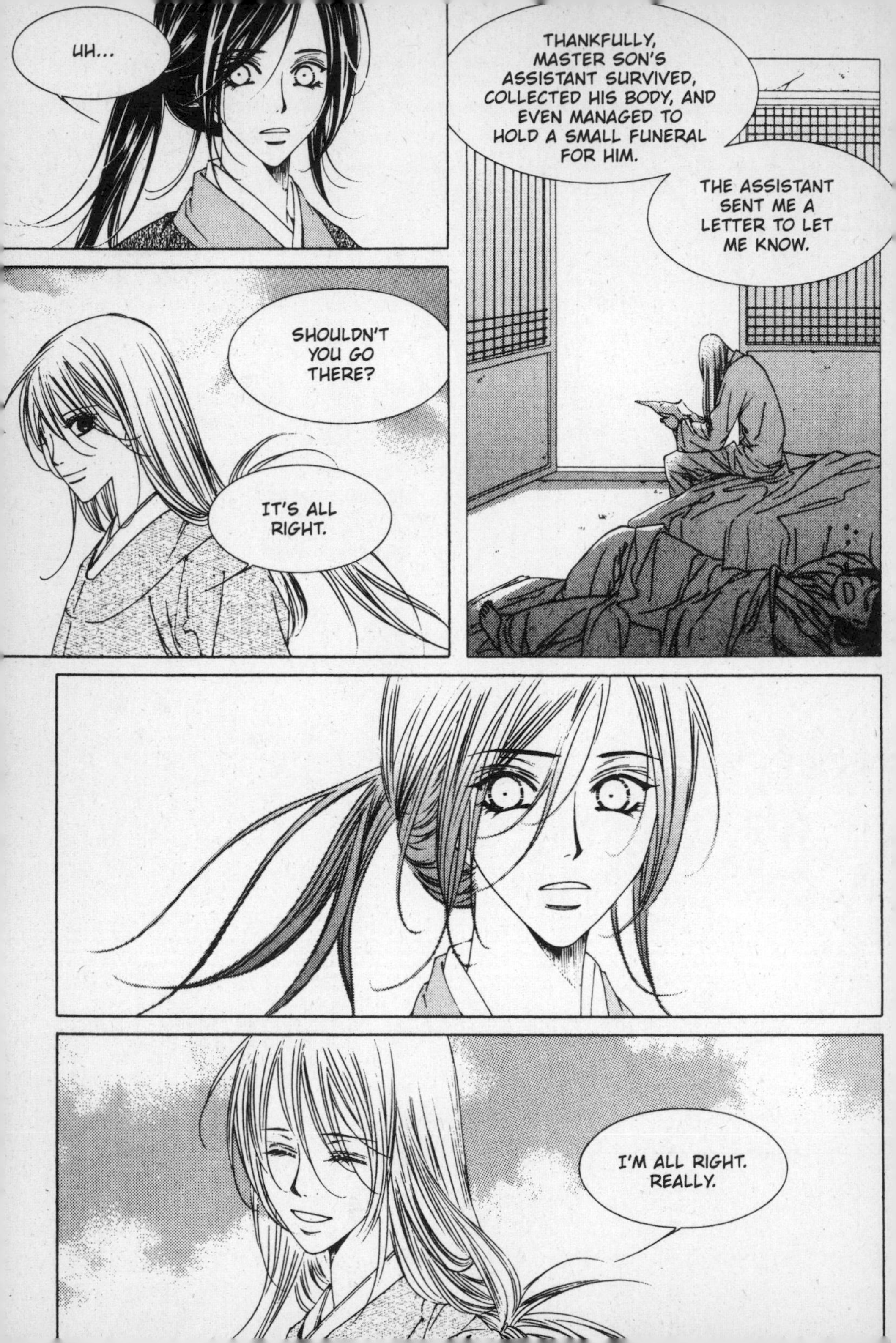
UH...
THANKFULLY, MASTER SON'S ASSISTANT SURVIVED, COLLECTED HIS BODY, AND EVEN MANAGED TO HOLD A SMALL FUNERAL FOR HIM.
THE ASSISTANT SENT ME A LETTER TO LET ME KNOW.
SHOULDN'T YOU GO THERE?
IT'S ALL RIGHT.
I'M ALL RIGHT. REALLY.

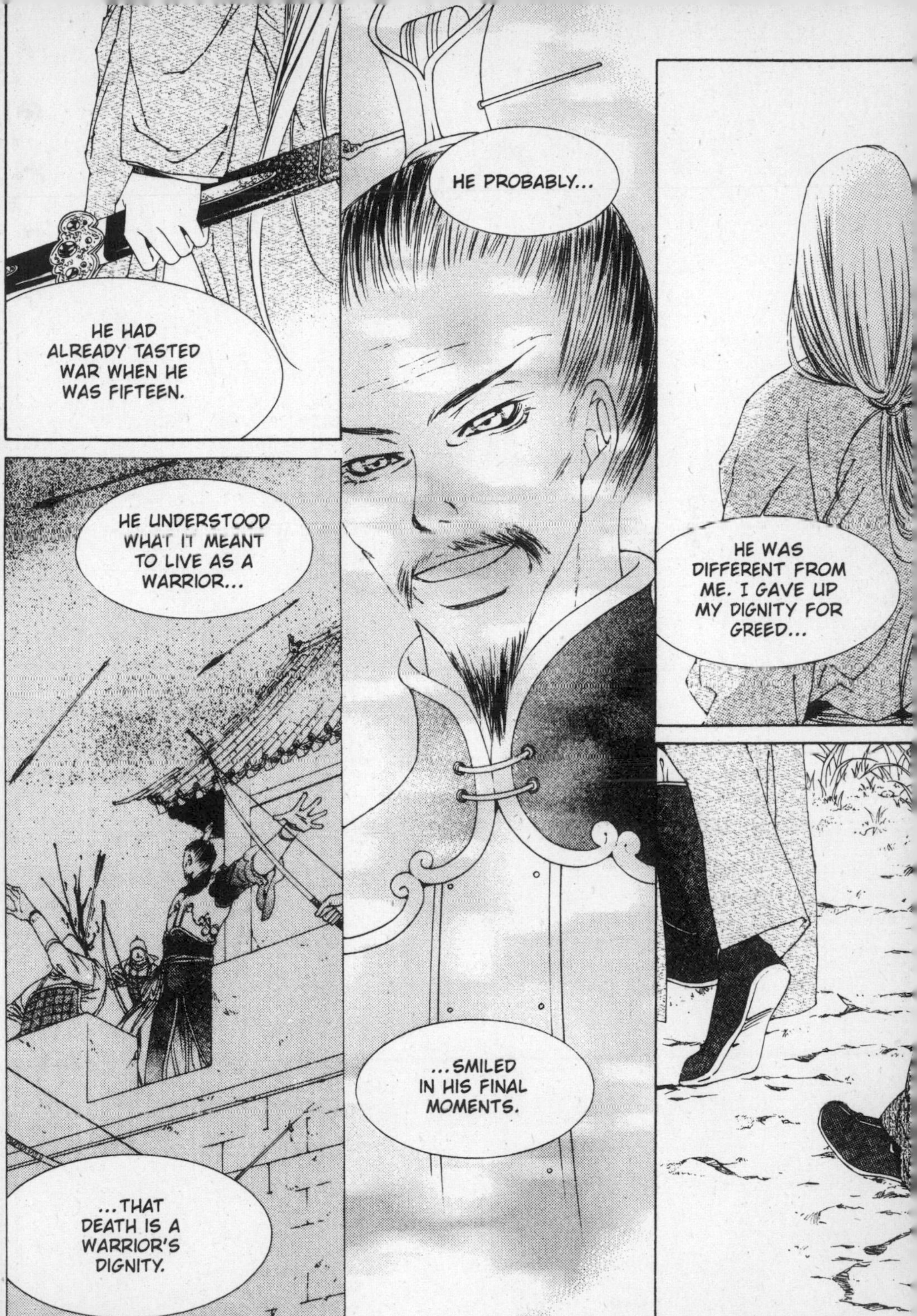
HE HAD ALREADY TASTED WAR WHEN HE WAS FIFTEEN.
HE UNDERSTOOD WHAT IT MEANT TO LIVE AS A WARRIOR...
...THAT DEATH IS A WARRIOR'S DIGNITY.
HE PROBABLY...
...SMILED IN HIS FINAL MOMENTS.
HE WAS DIFFERENT FROM ME. I GAVE UP MY DIGNITY FOR GREED...

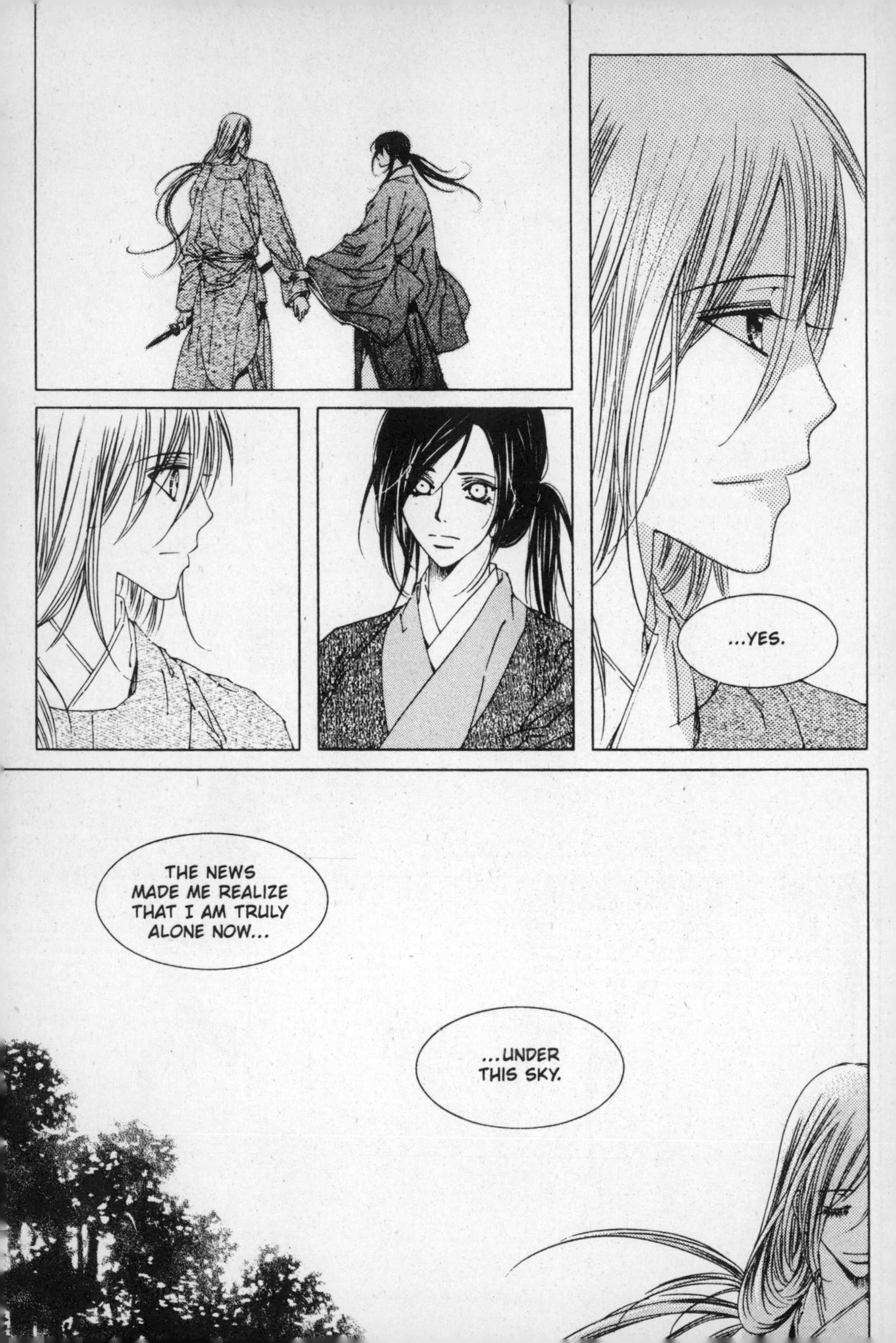
...YES.
THE NEWS MADE ME REALIZE THAT I AM TRULY ALONE NOW...
...UNDER THIS SKY.

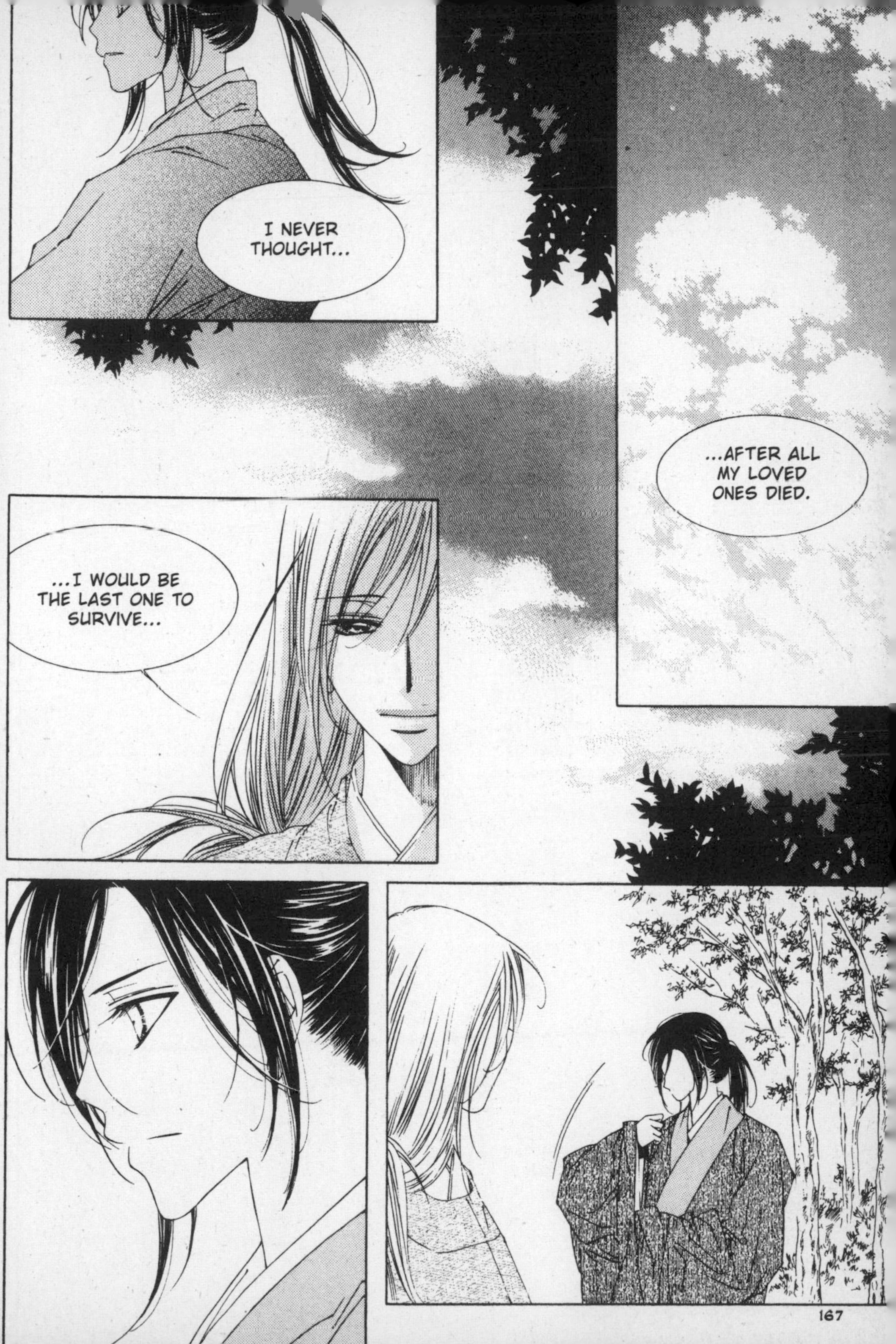
I NEVER THOUGHT...
...AFTER ALL MY LOVED ONES DIED.
...I WOULD BE THE LAST ONE TO SURVIVE...

WHAT'S THIS?

IT'S BEEF JERKY I STOLE FROM THE RESTAURANT YESTERDAY.

CAN'T YOU TELL?

WHY DID YOU DO THAT?

BECAUSE THE OWNER MADE ME ANGRY. SHE REUSED FOOD LEFT BEHIND BY OTHER CUSTOMERS.

I KNEW YOU'D NAG ME ALL DAY IF YOU FOUND OUT, SO I WAS GOING TO EAT IT BY MYSELF. BUT I'LL SHARE. HERE.

YOU STILL HAVE HIGH DEMANDS DESPITE THE CHAOTIC STATE OF THE WORLD...

THIS IS A MATTER OF PRINCIPLE. NO MATTER WHAT'S GOING ON IN THE WORLD, YOU MUST HAVE SOME PRINCIPLES. DON'T YOU KNOW THAT?

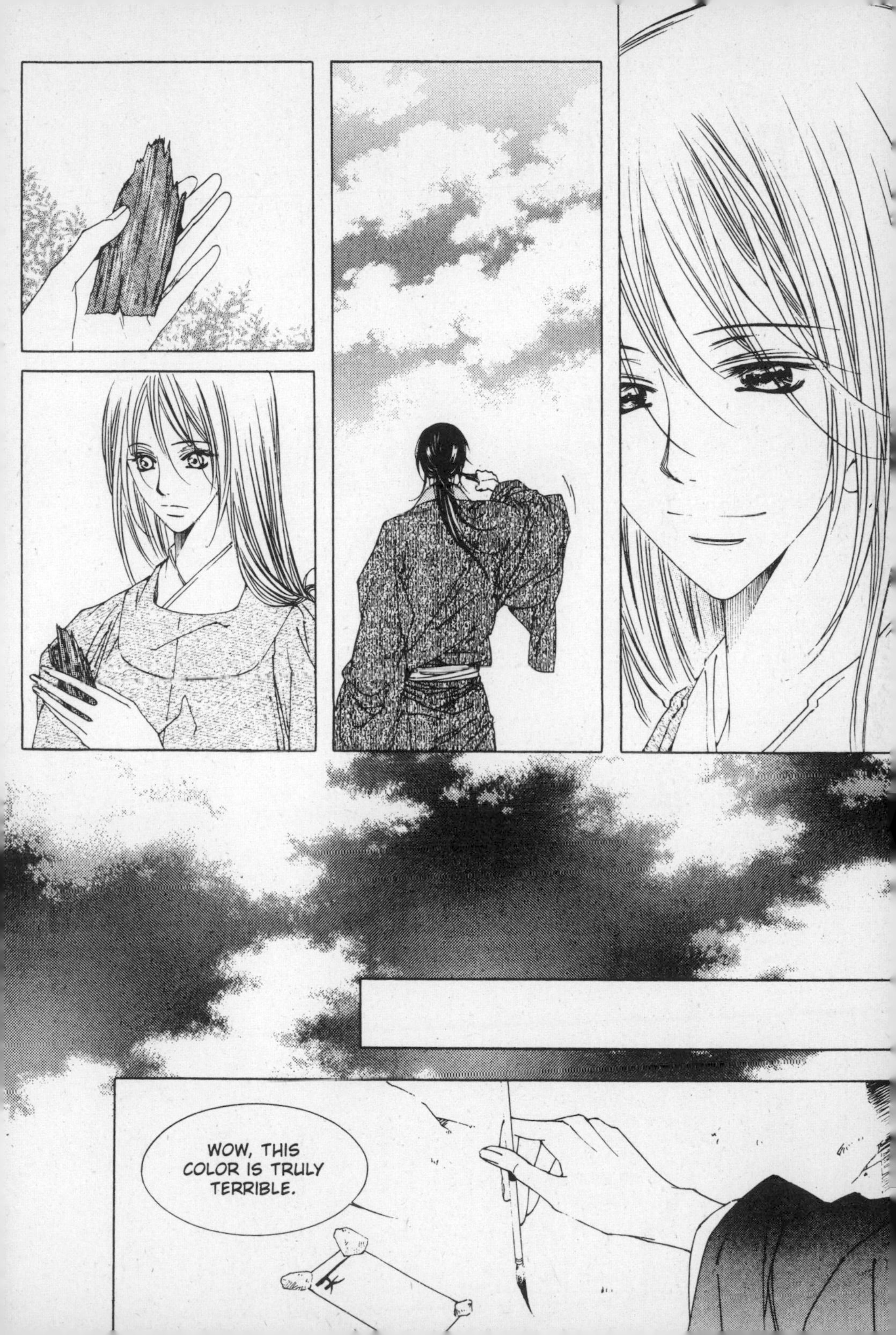
WOW, THIS COLOR IS TRULY TERRIBLE.

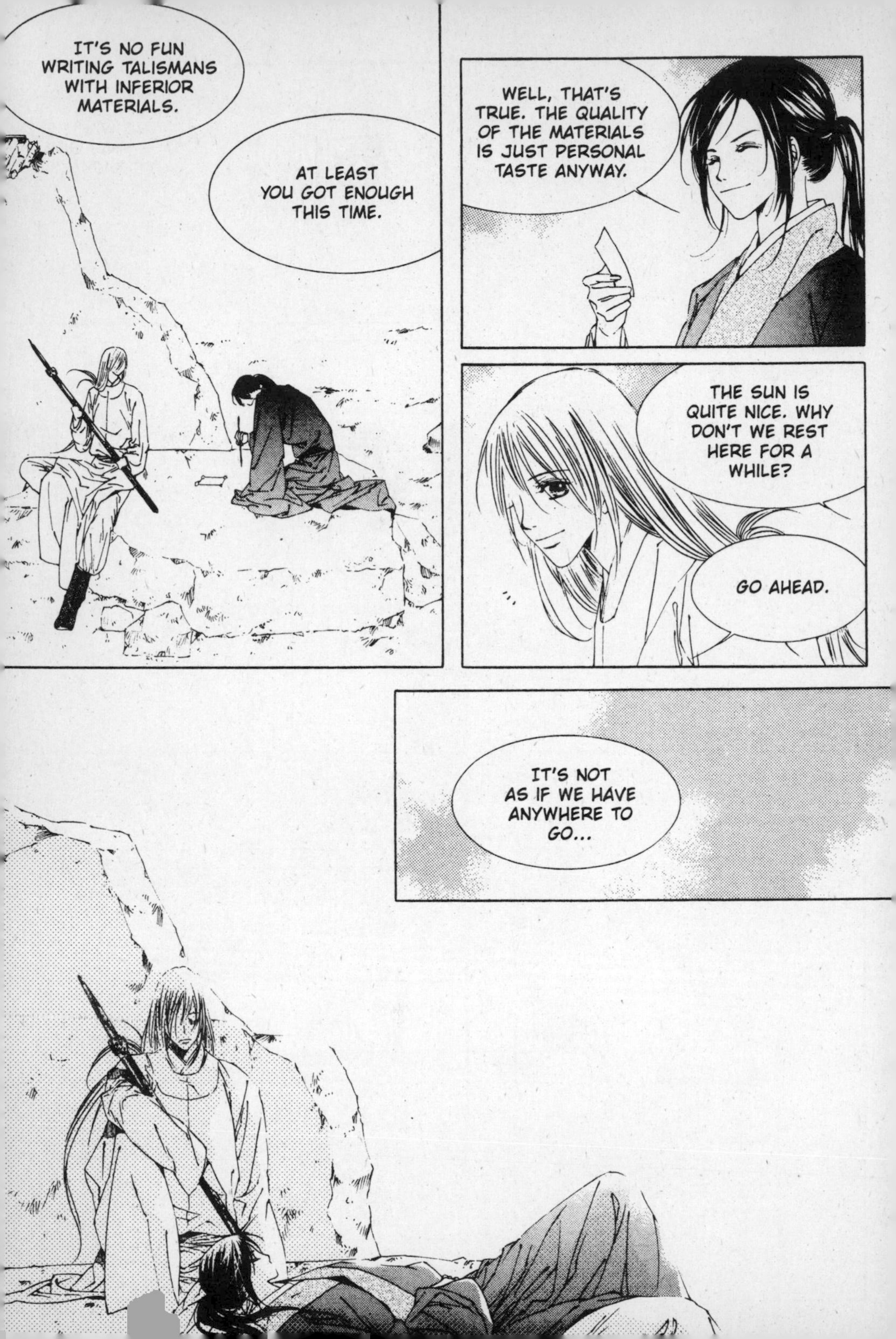
IT'S NO FUN WRITING TALISMANS WITH INFERIOR MATERIALS.
AT LEAST YOU GOT ENOUGH THIS TIME.
WELL, THAT'S TRUE. THE QUALITY OF THE MATERIALS IS JUST PERSONAL TASTE ANYWAY.
THE SUN IS QUITE NICE. WHY DON'T WE REST HERE FOR A WHILE?
...
GO AHEAD.
IT'S NOT AS IF WE HAVE ANYWHERE TO GO...

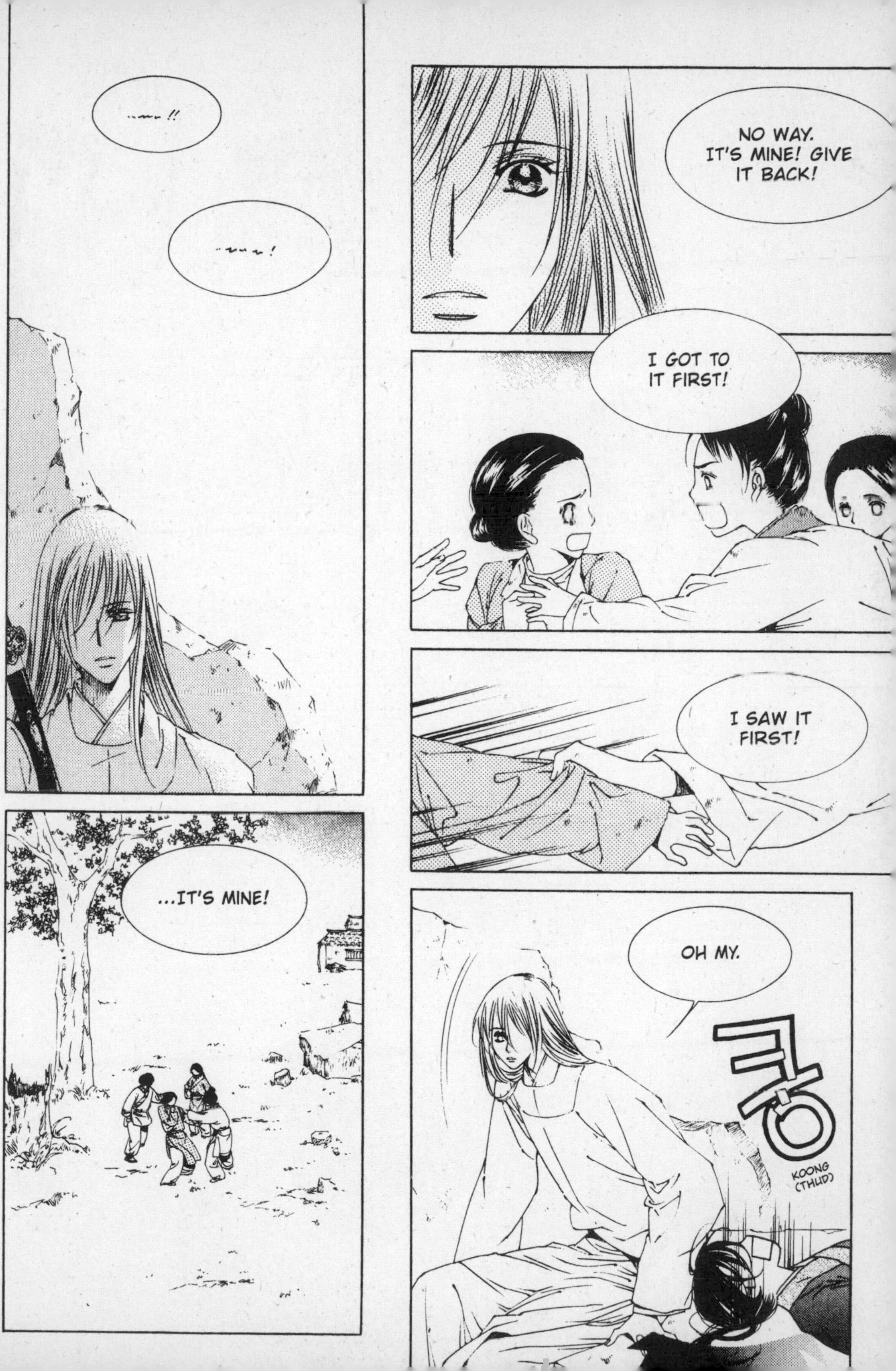
...IT'S MINE!
NO WAY. IT'S MINE! GIVE IT BACK!
I GOT TO IT FIRST!
I SAW IT FIRST!
OH MY.
KOONG (THUD)

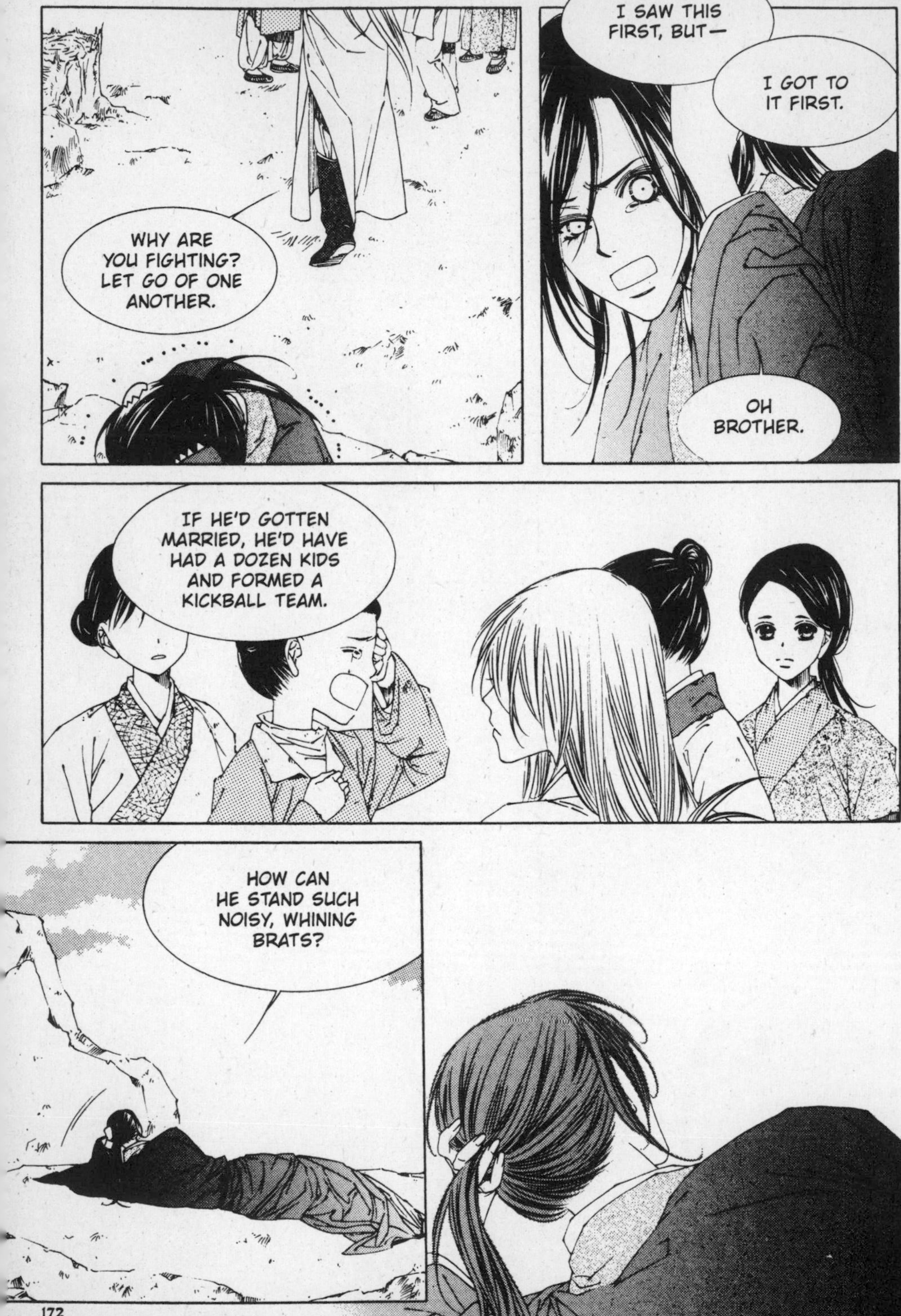
WHY ARE YOU FIGHTING? LET GO OF ONE ANOTHER.
I SAW THIS FIRST, BUT—
I GOT TO IT FIRST.
OH BROTHER.
IF HE'D GOTTEN MARRIED, HE'D HAVE HAD A DOZEN KIDS AND FORMED A KICKBALL TEAM.
HOW CAN HE STAND SUCH NOISY, WHINING BRATS?

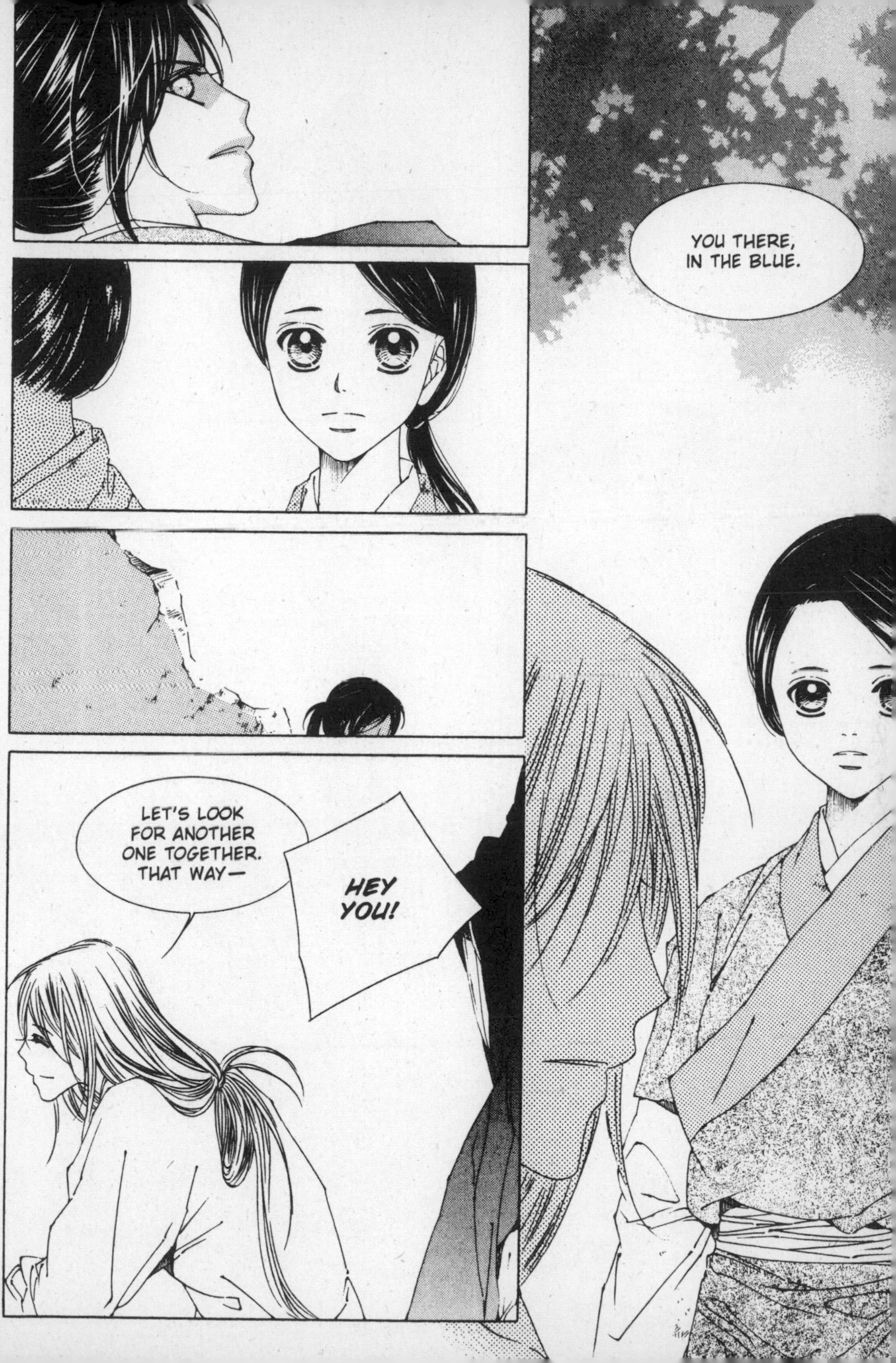
LET'S LOOK FOR ANOTHER ONE TOGETHER. THAT WAY—
HEY YOU!
YOU THERE, IN THE BLUE.

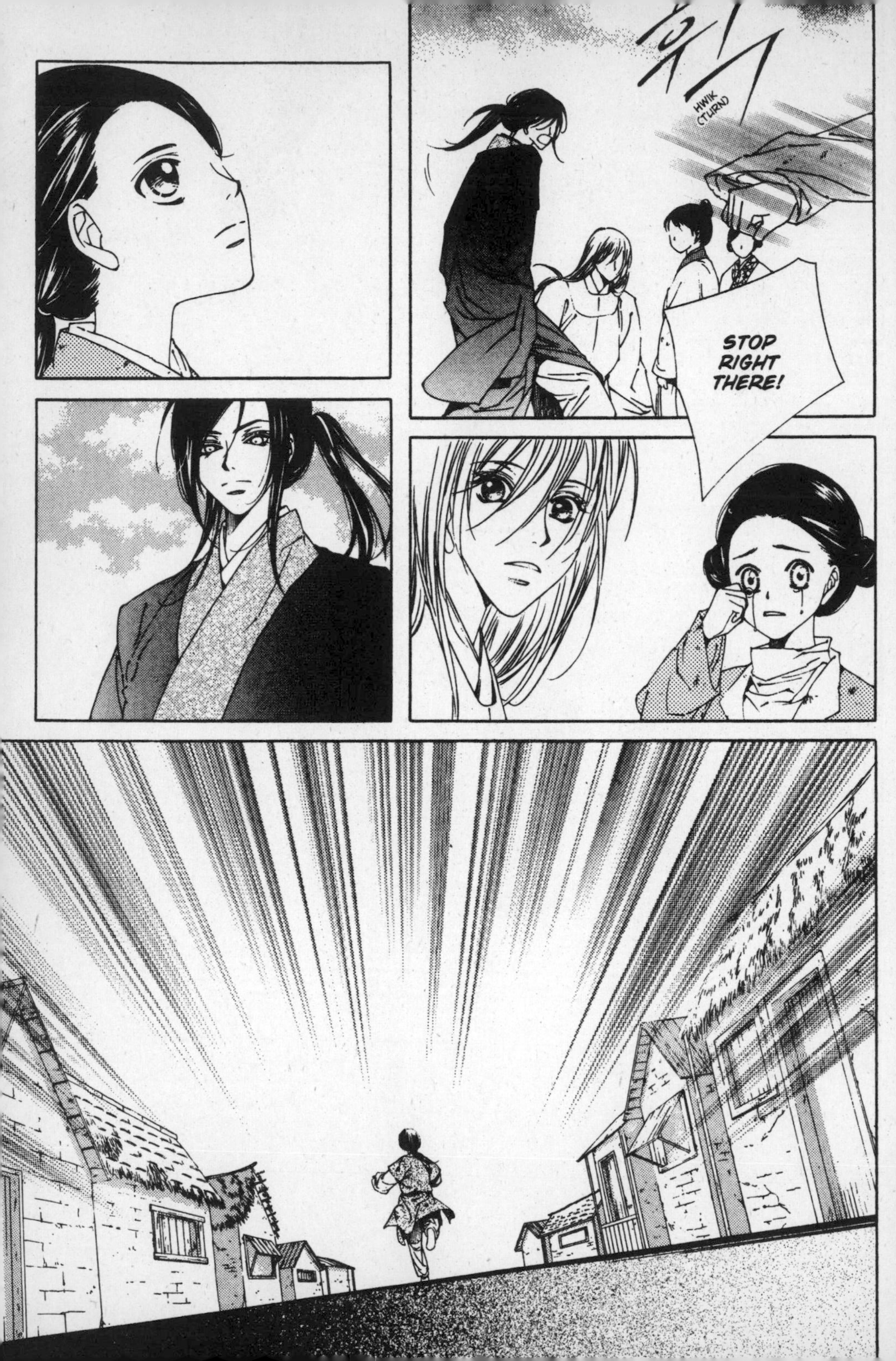
HWIK (TURN)
STOP RIGHT THERE!

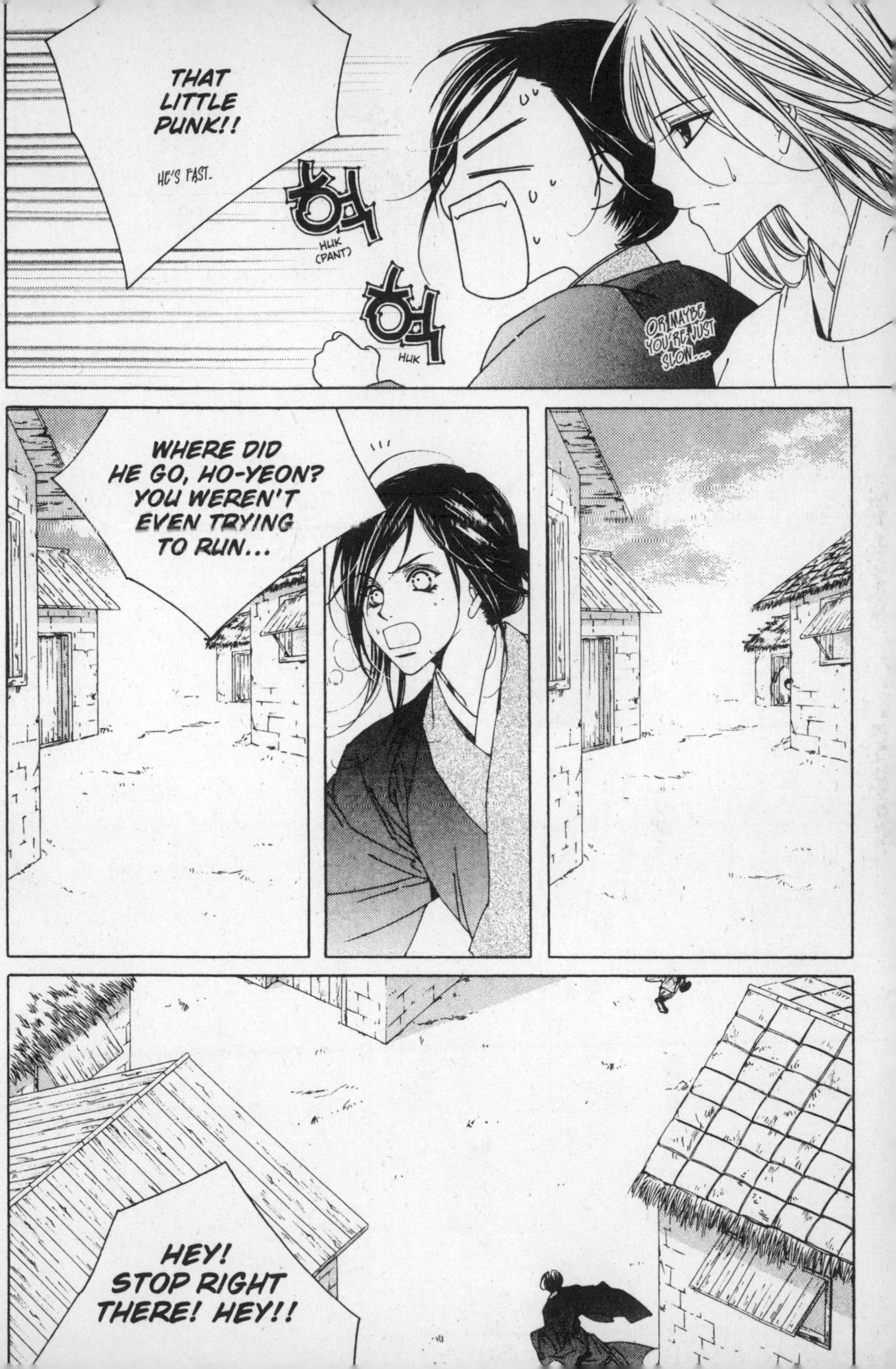
THAT LITTLE PUNK!!
HE'S FAST.
HUK (PANT)
HUK
OR MAYBE YOU'RE JUST SLOW...
WHERE DID HE GO, HO-YEON? YOU WEREN'T EVEN TRYING TO RUN...
HEY! STOP RIGHT THERE! HEY!!

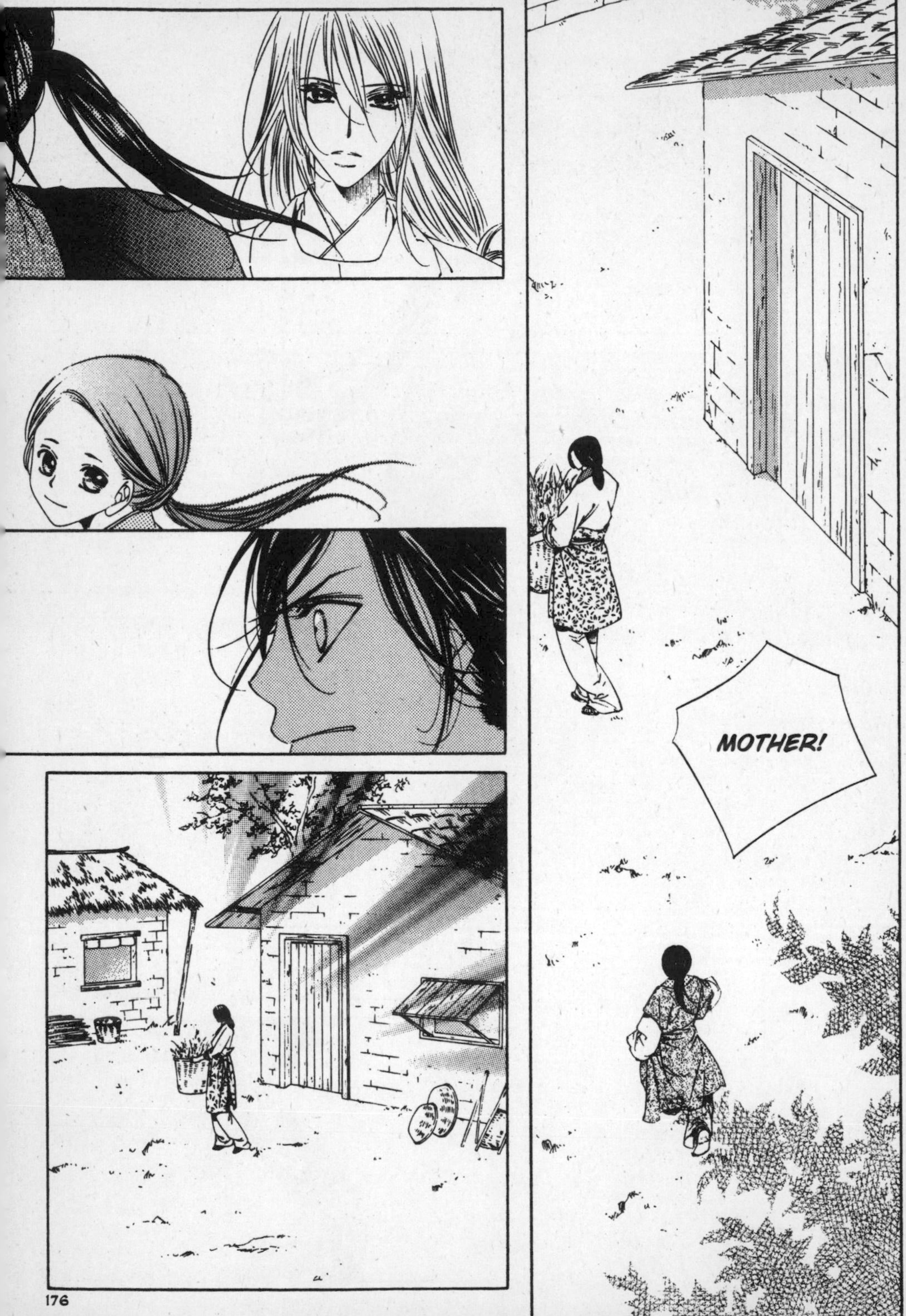
MOTHER!

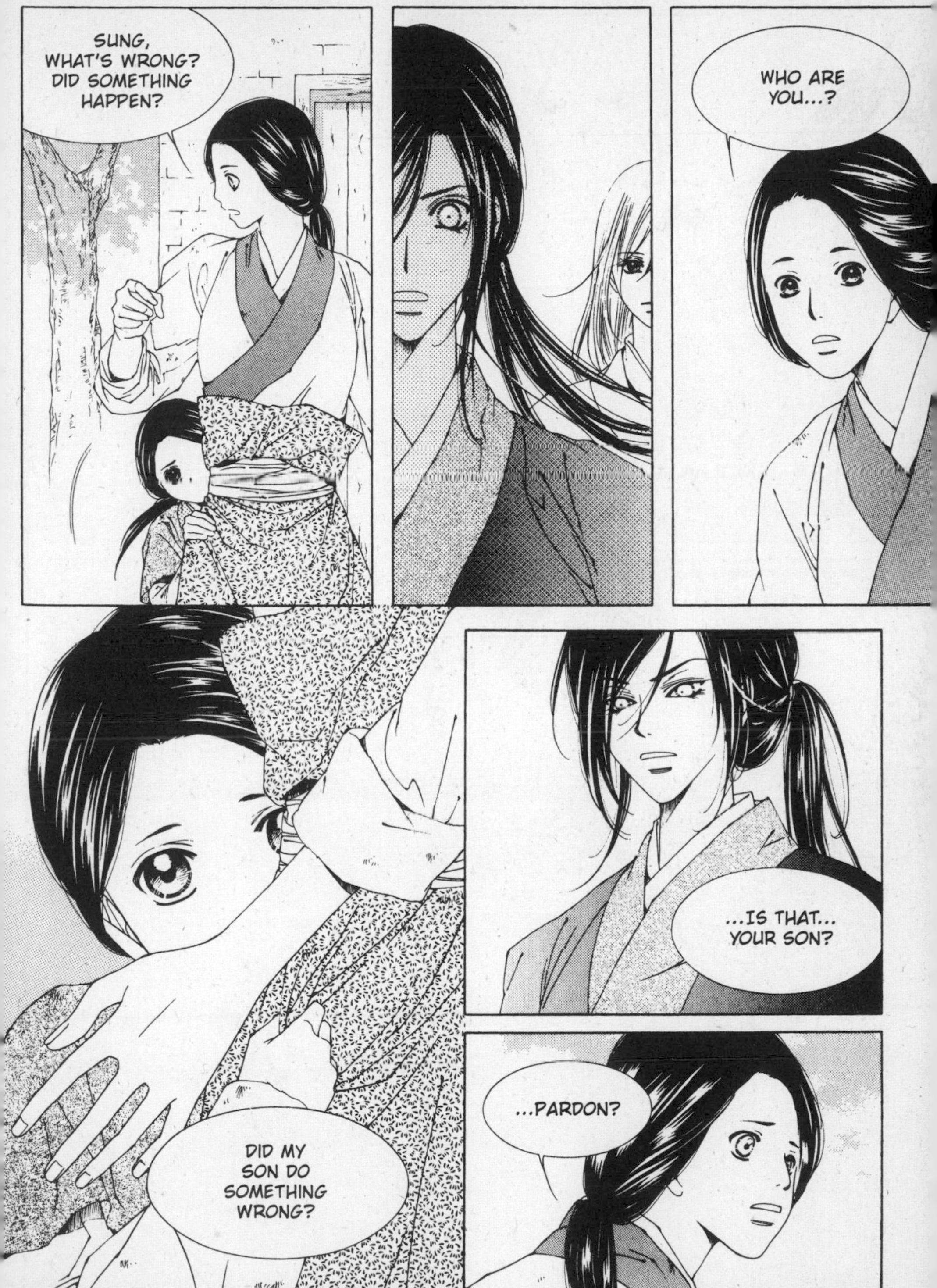
SUNG, WHAT'S WRONG? DID SOMETHING HAPPEN?
WHO ARE YOU...?
DID MY SON DO SOMETHING WRONG?
...IS THAT... YOUR SON?
...PARDON?

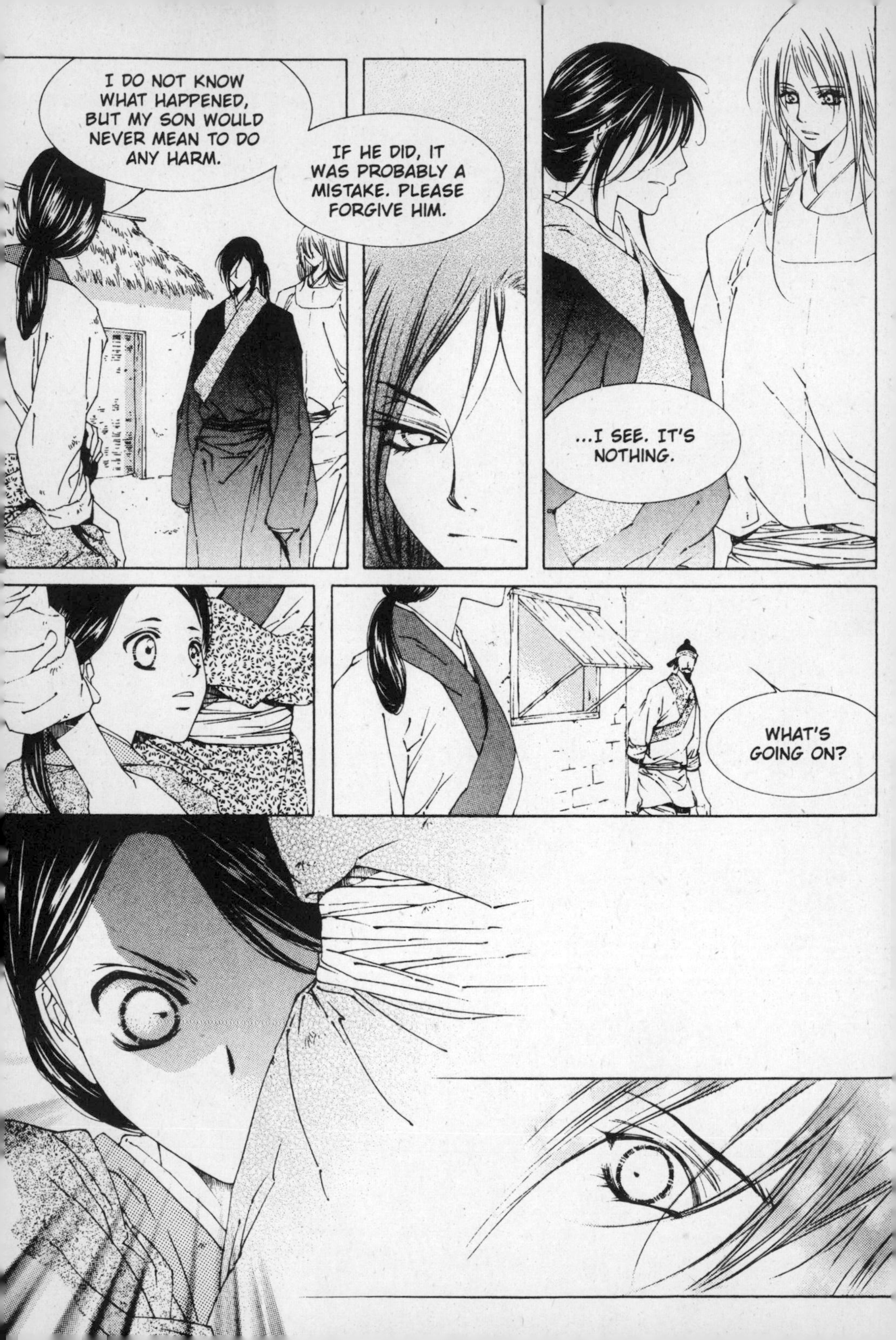
I DO NOT KNOW WHAT HAPPENED, BUT MY SON WOULD NEVER MEAN TO DO ANY HARM.
IF HE DID, IT WAS PROBABLY A MISTAKE. PLEASE FORGIVE HIM.
...I SEE. IT'S NOTHING.
WHAT'S GOING ON?

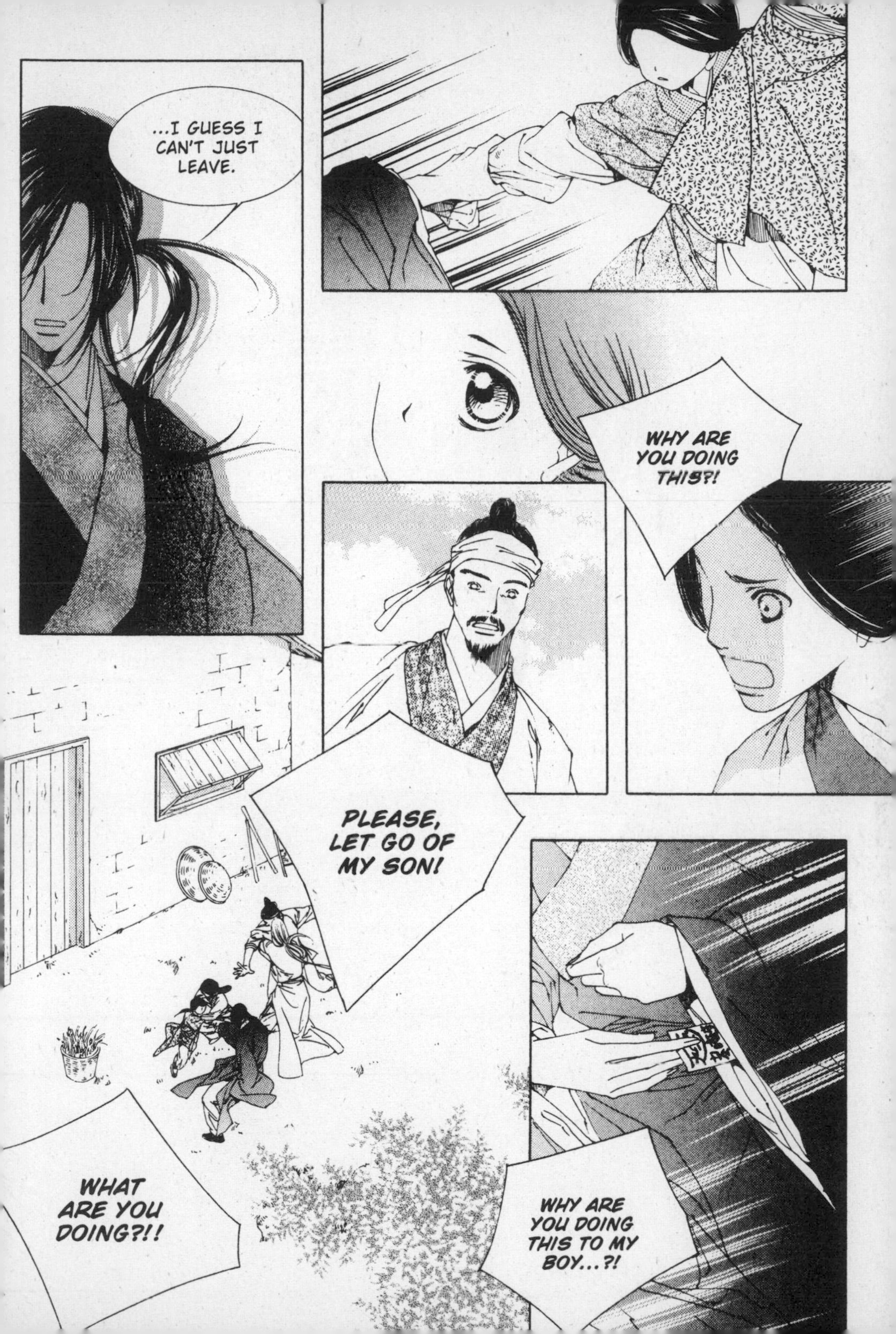
...I GUESS I CAN'T JUST LEAVE.
WHY ARE YOU DOING THIS?!
PLEASE, LET GO OF MY SON!
WHAT ARE YOU DOING?!!
WHY ARE YOU DOING THIS TO MY BOY...?!

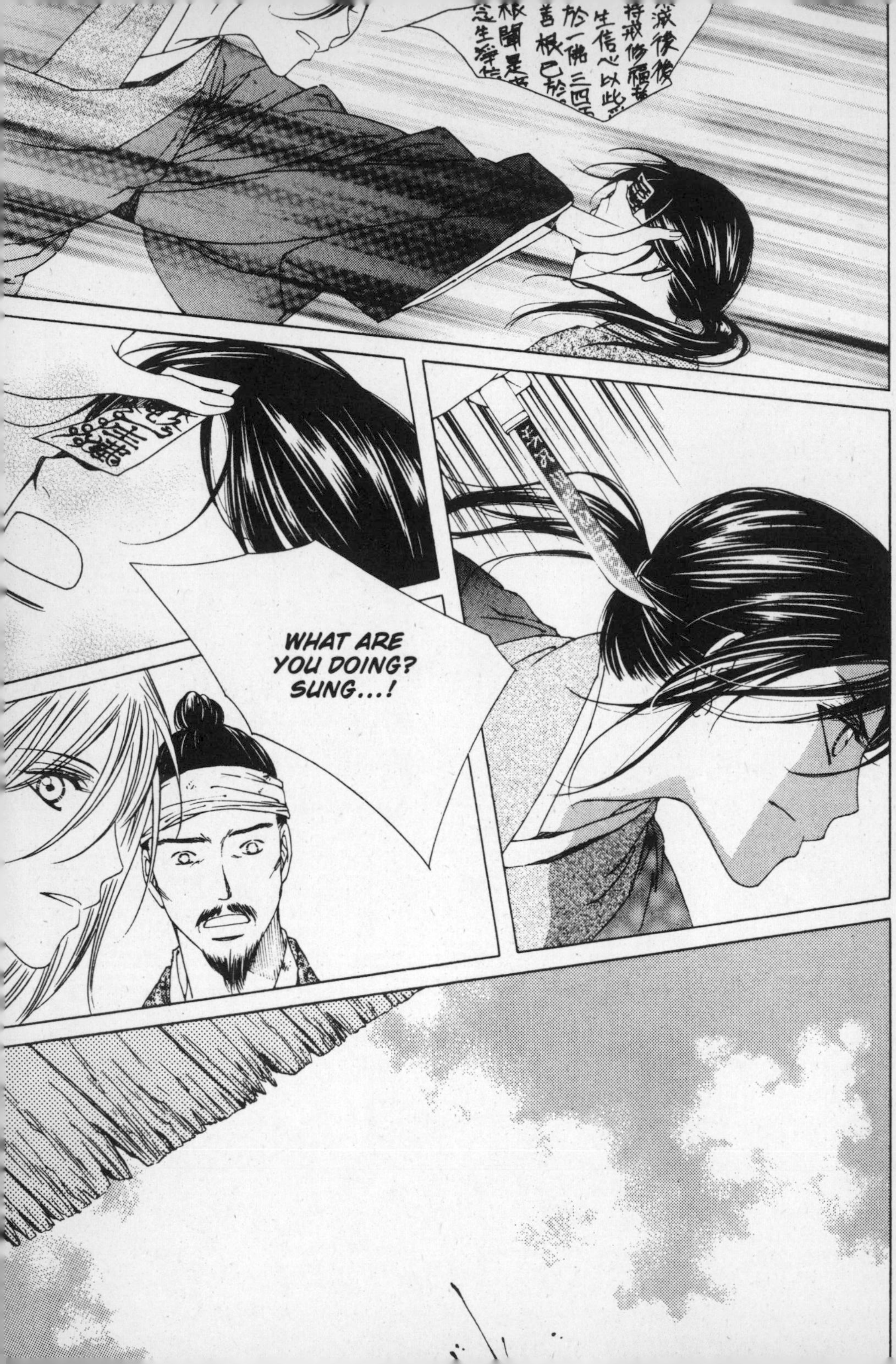
WHAT ARE YOU DOING? SUNG...!

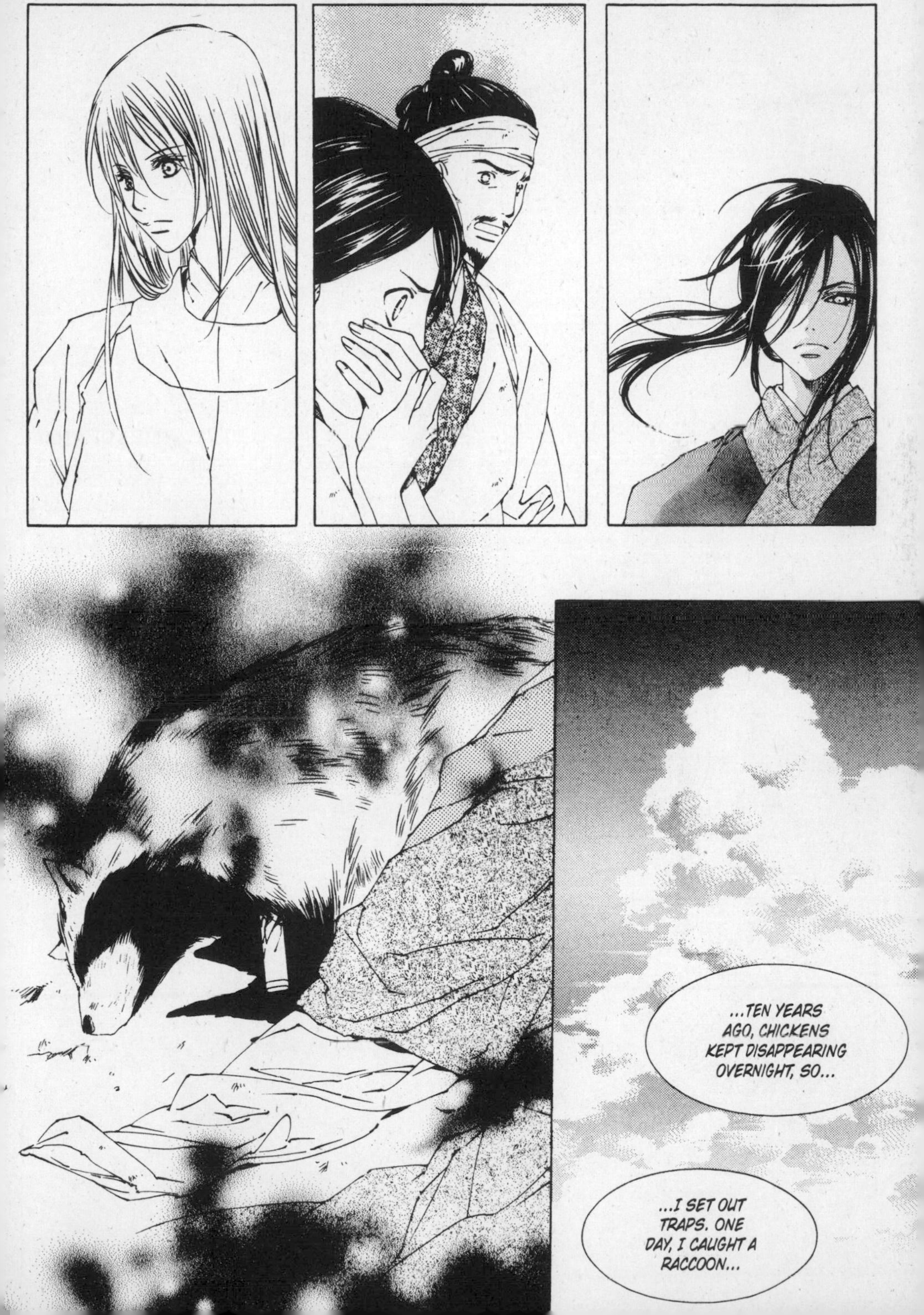
...TEN YEARS AGO, CHICKENS KEPT DISAPPEARING OVERNIGHT, SO...
...I SET OUT TRAPS. ONE DAY, I CAUGHT A RACCOON...

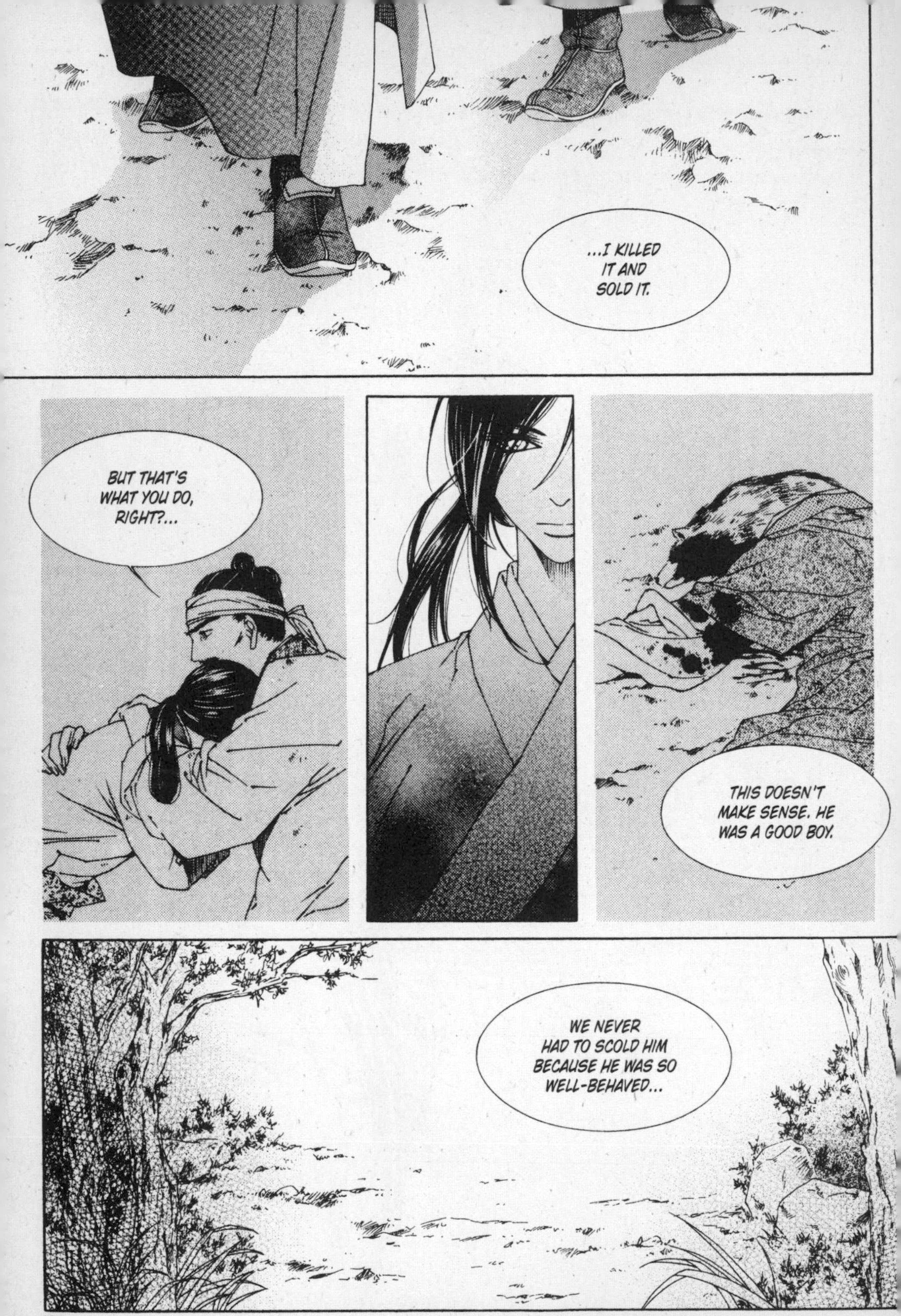

...I KILLED IT AND SOLD IT.
BUT THAT'S WHAT YOU DO, RIGHT?...
THIS DOESN'T MAKE SENSE. HE WAS A GOOD BOY.
WE NEVER HAD TO SCOLD HIM BECAUSE HE WAS SO WELL-BEHAVED...

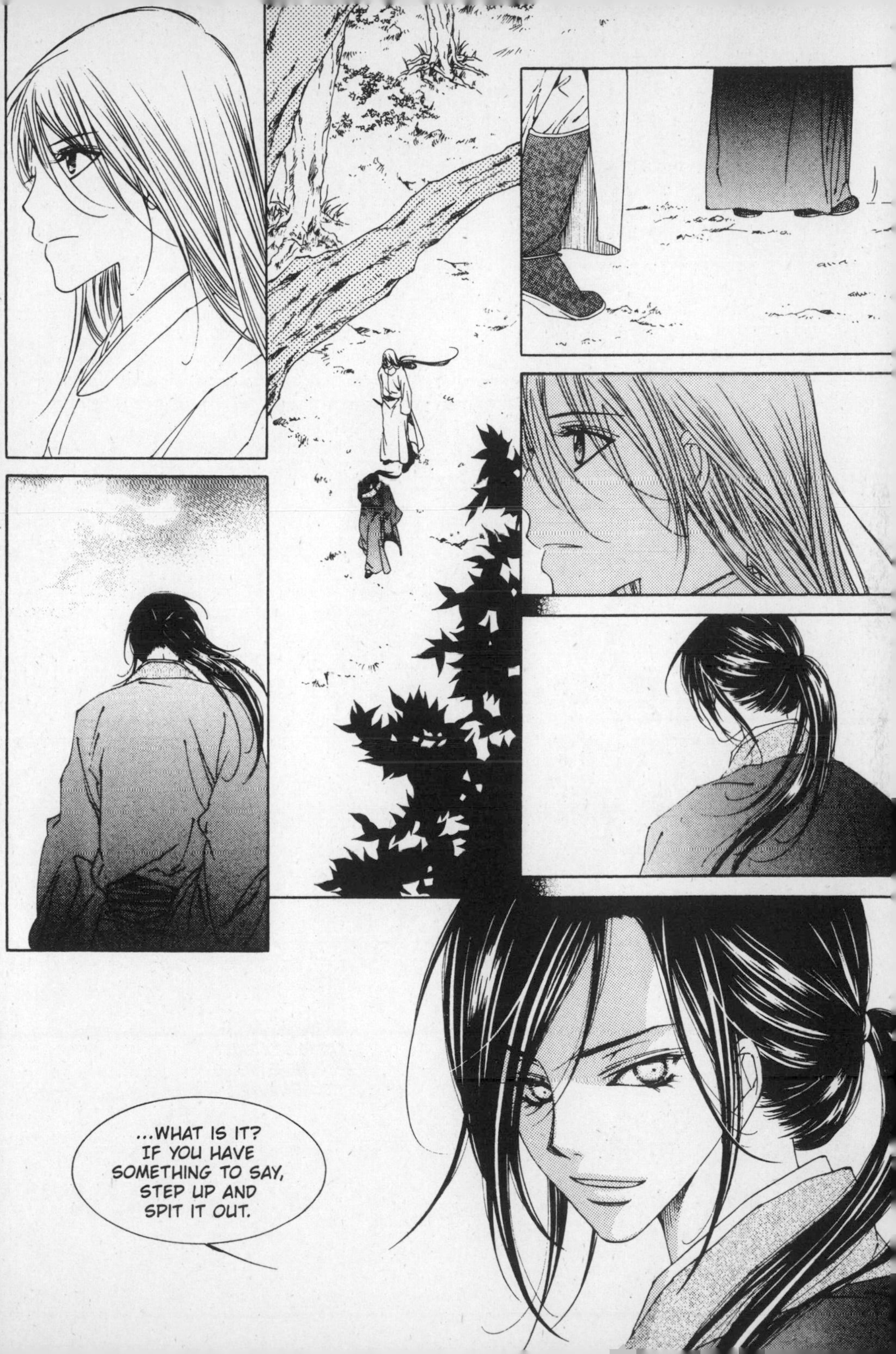
...WHAT IS IT? IF YOU HAVE SOMETHING TO SAY, STEP UP AND SPIT IT OUT.

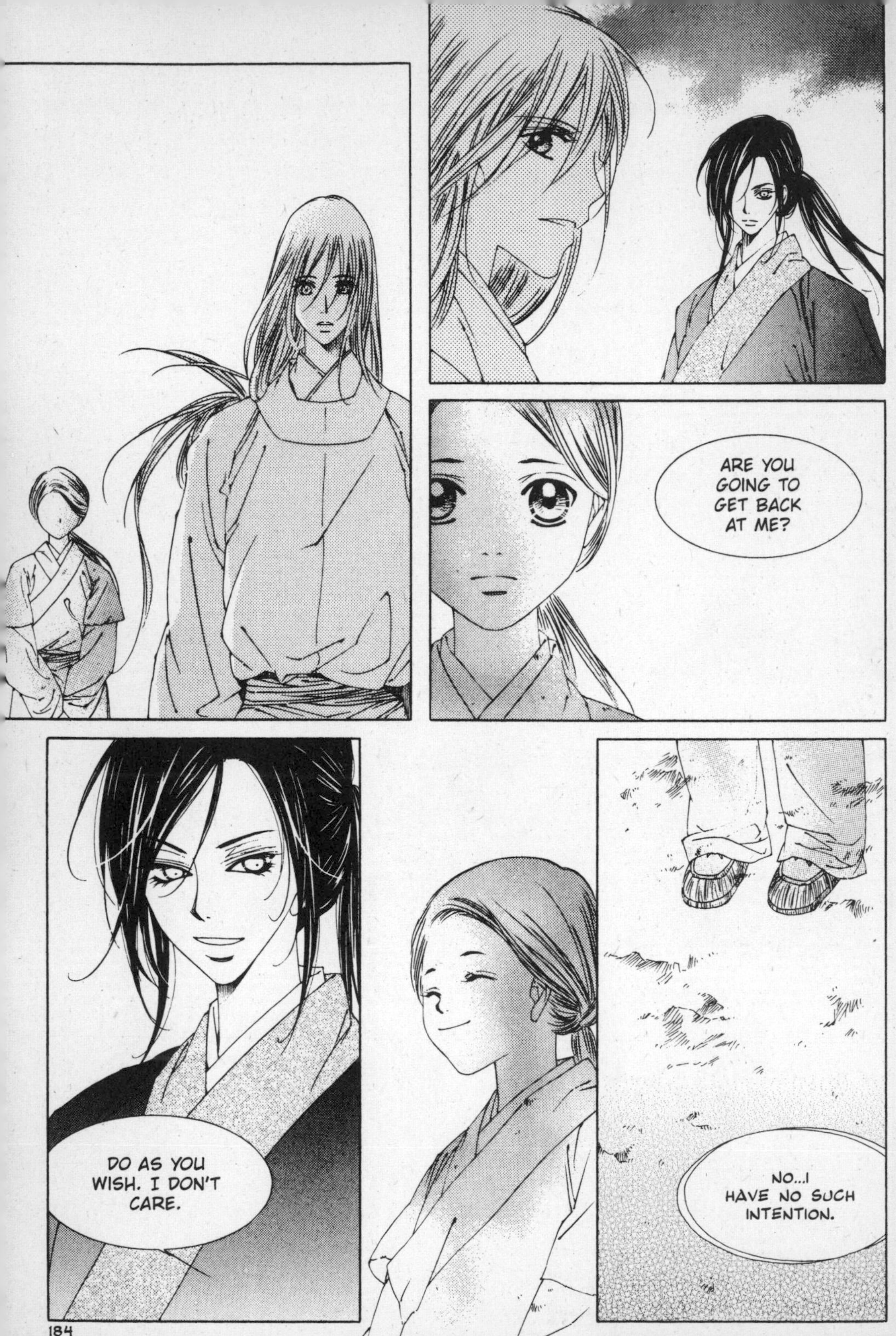
ARE YOU GOING TO GET BACK AT ME?
DO AS YOU WISH. I DON'T CARE.
NO...I HAVE NO SUCH INTENTION.

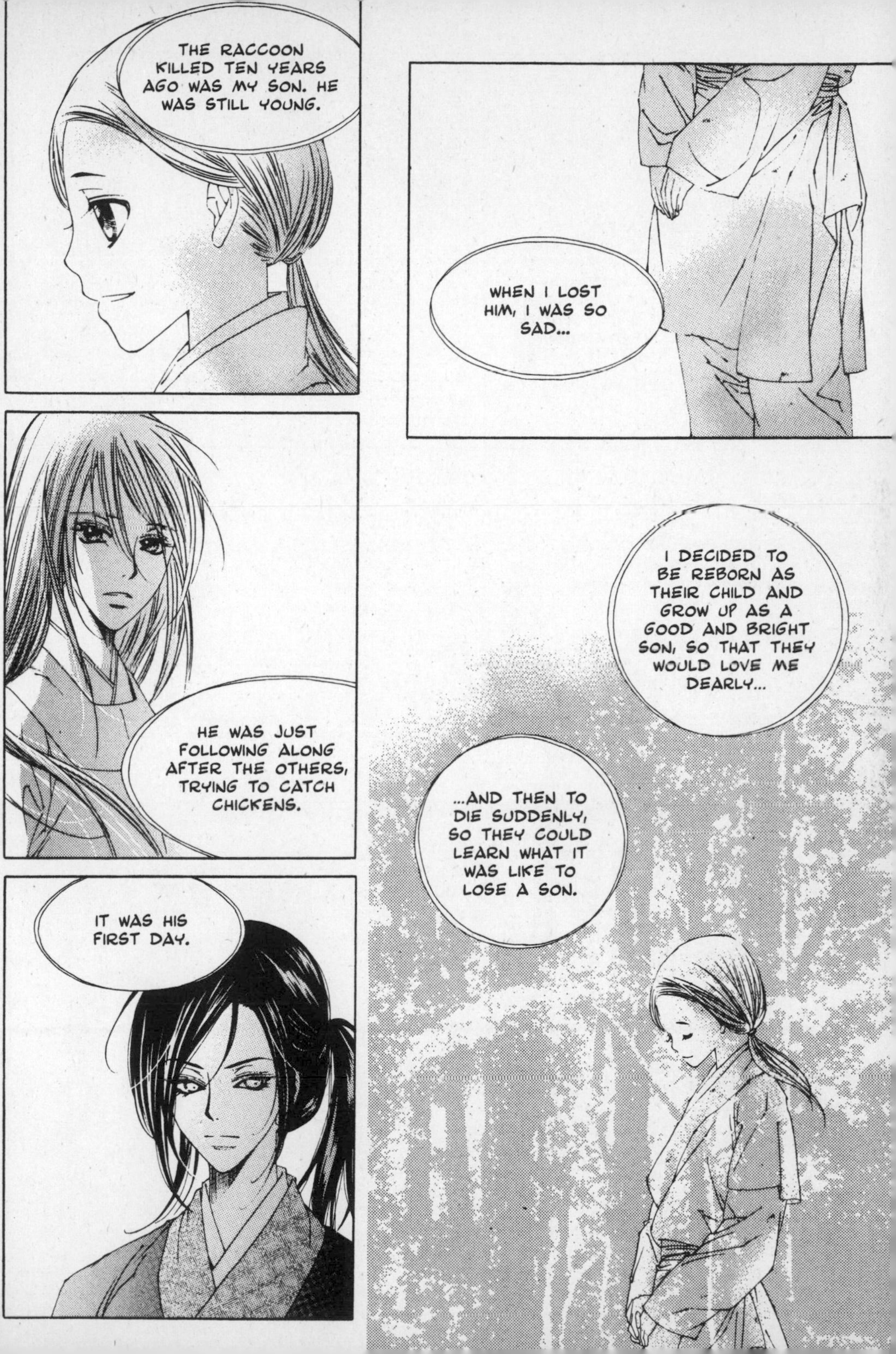
THE RACCOON KILLED TEN YEARS AGO WAS MY SON. HE WAS STILL YOUNG.
WHEN I LOST HIM, I WAS SO SAD...
HE WAS JUST FOLLOWING ALONG AFTER THE OTHERS, TRYING TO CATCH CHICKENS.
IT WAS HIS FIRST DAY.
I DECIDED TO BE REBORN AS THEIR CHILD AND GROW UP AS A GOOD AND BRIGHT SON, SO THAT THEY WOULD LOVE ME DEARLY...
...AND THEN TO DIE SUDDENLY, SO THEY COULD LEARN WHAT IT WAS LIKE TO LOSE A SON.

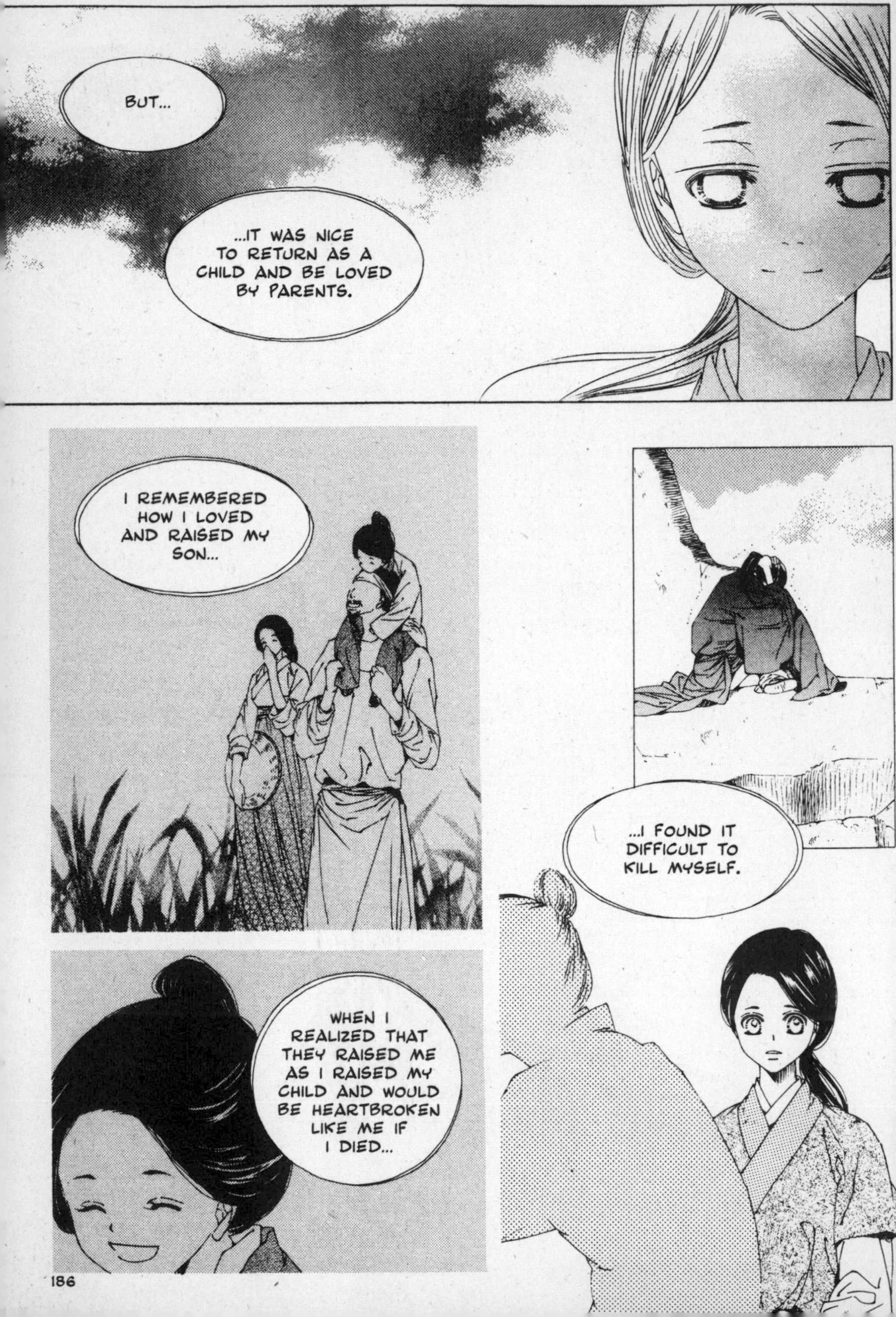
BUT...
...IT WAS NICE TO RETURN AS A CHILD AND BE LOVED BY PARENTS.
I REMEMBERED HOW I LOVED AND RAISED MY SON...
WHEN I REALIZED THAT THEY RAISED ME AS I RAISED MY CHILD AND WOULD BE HEARTBROKEN LIKE ME IF I DIED...
...I FOUND IT DIFFICULT TO KILL MYSELF.

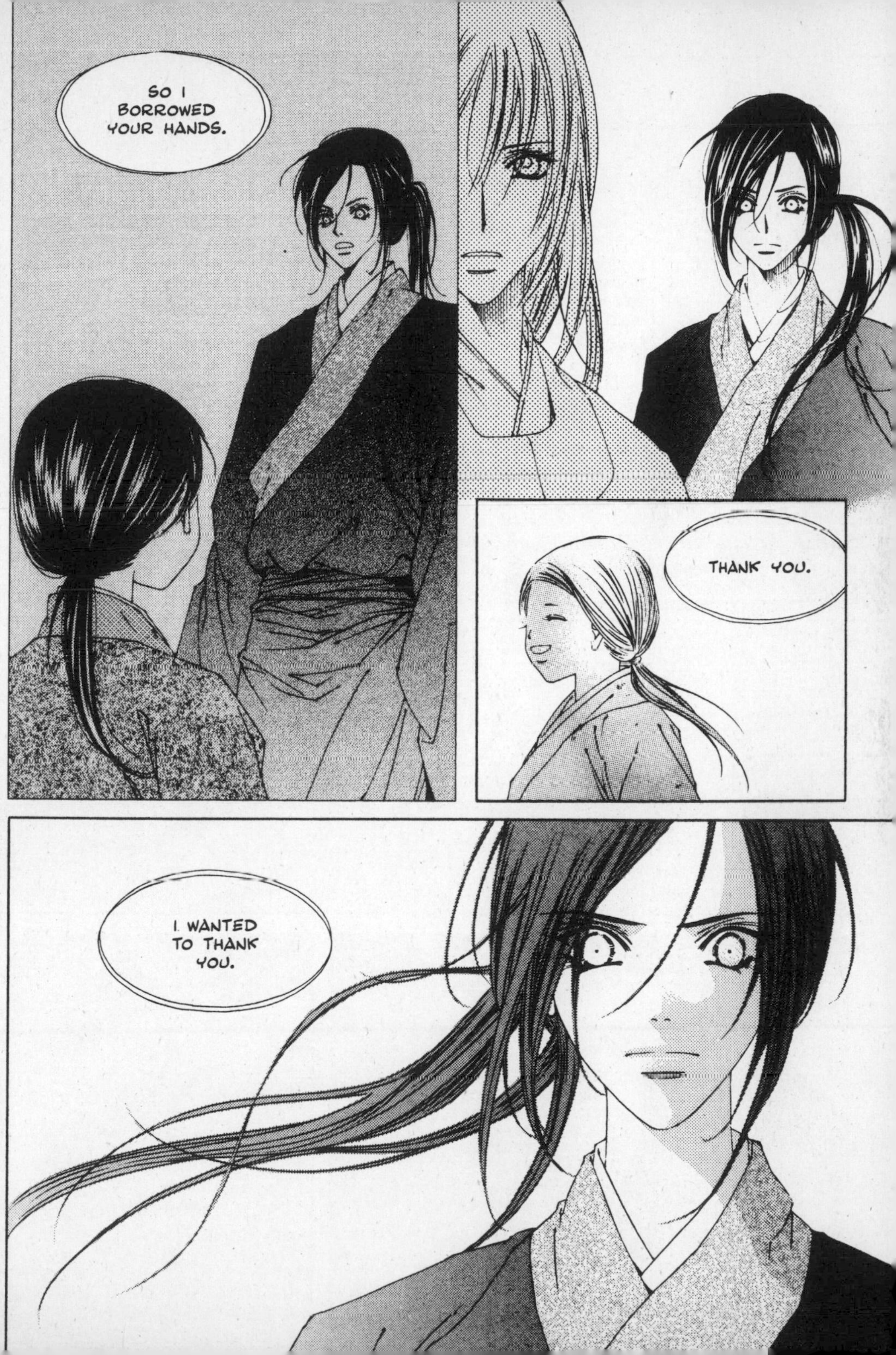
SO I BORROWED YOUR HANDS.
THANK YOU.
I WANTED TO THANK YOU.

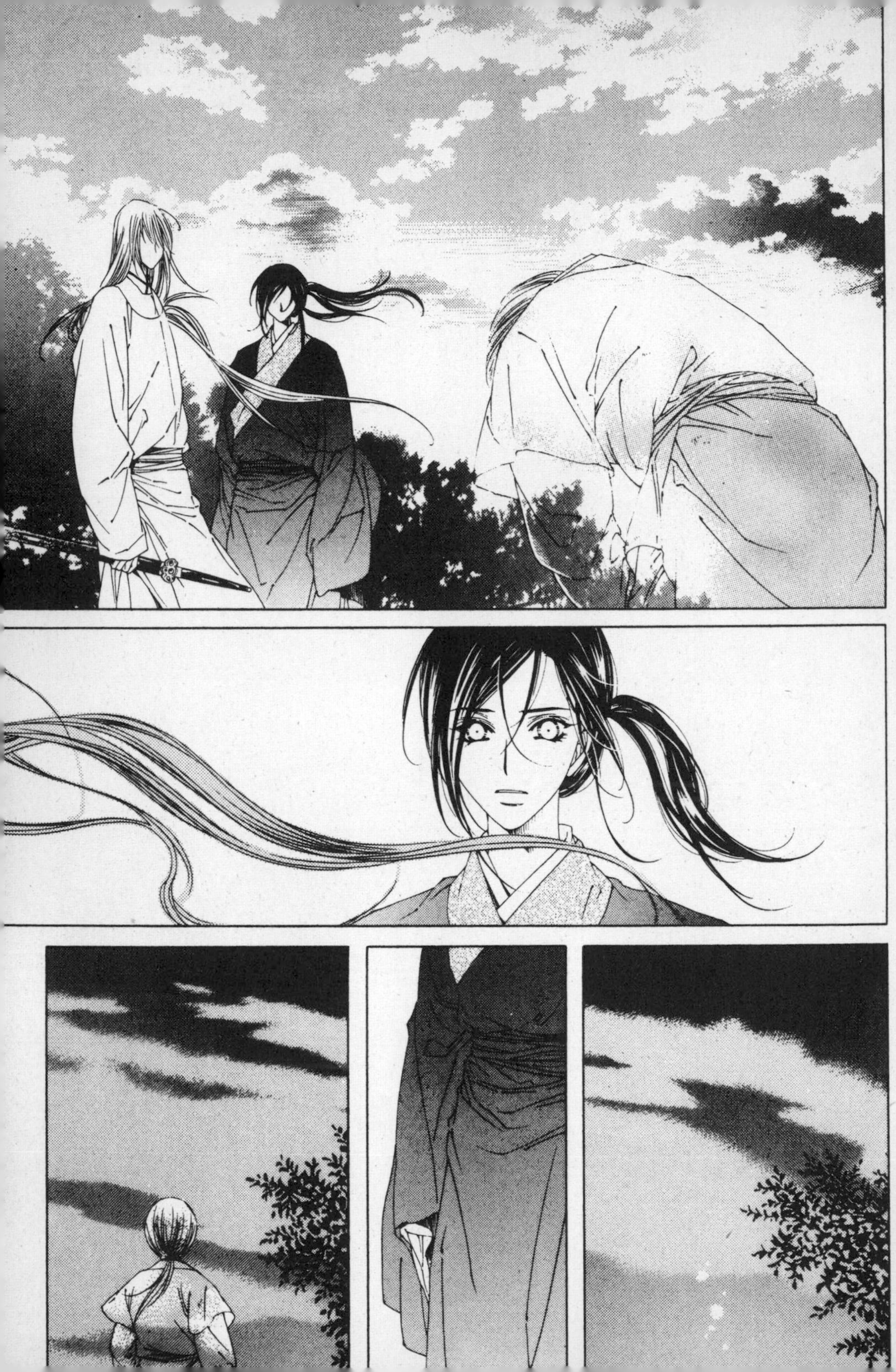

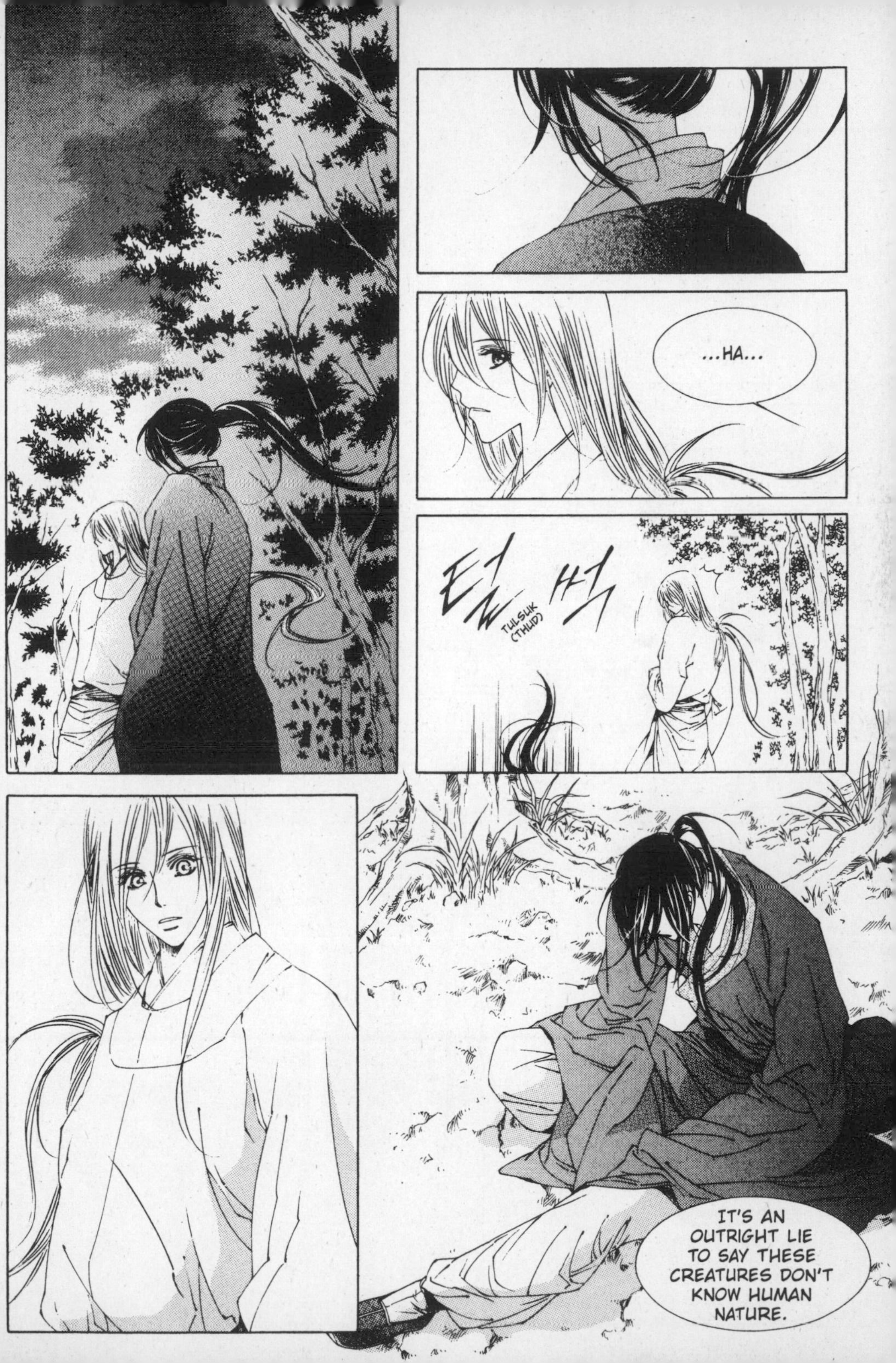
...HA...
털썩
TULSUK (THUD)
IT'S AN OUTRIGHT LIE TO SAY THESE CREATURES DON'T KNOW HUMAN NATURE.

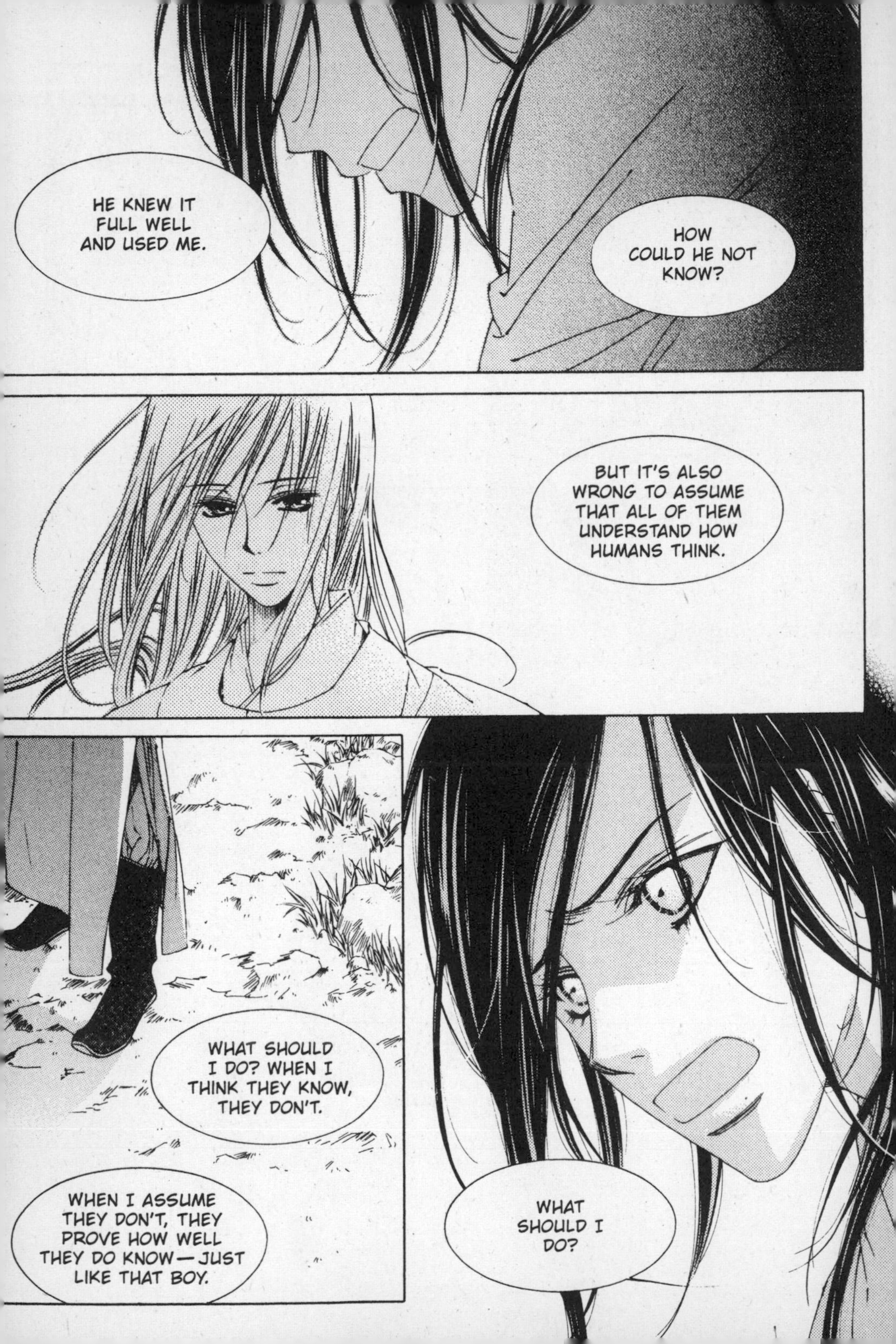
HE KNEW IT FULL WELL AND USED ME.
HOW COULD HE NOT KNOW?
BUT IT'S ALSO WRONG TO ASSUME THAT ALL OF THEM UNDERSTAND HOW HUMANS THINK.
WHAT SHOULD I DO? WHEN I THINK THEY KNOW, THEY DON'T.
WHEN I ASSUME THEY DON'T, THEY PROVE HOW WELL THEY DO KNOW—JUST LIKE THAT BOY.
WHAT SHOULD I DO?

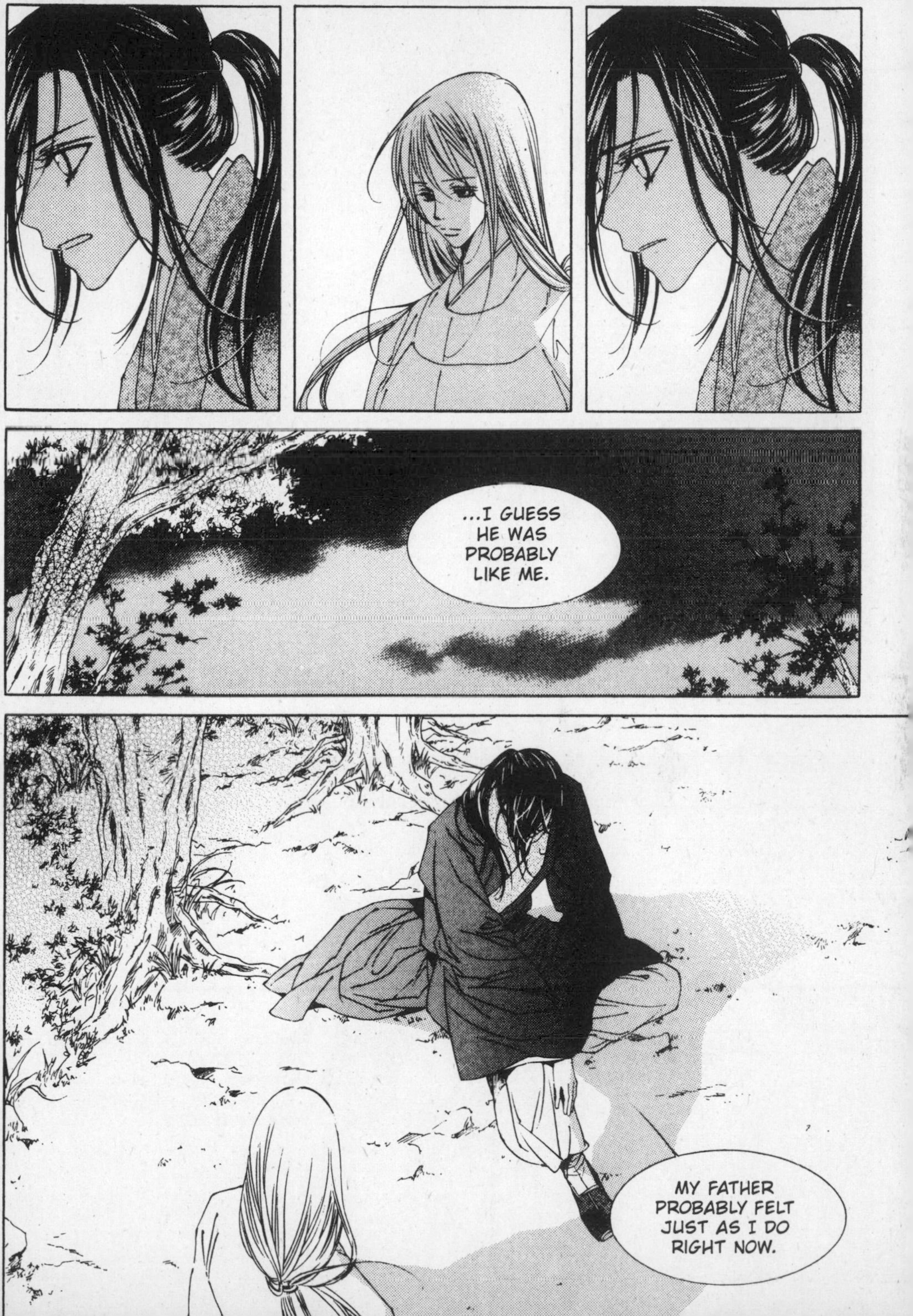

...I GUESS HE WAS PROBABLY LIKE ME.
MY FATHER PROBABLY FELT JUST AS I DO RIGHT NOW.

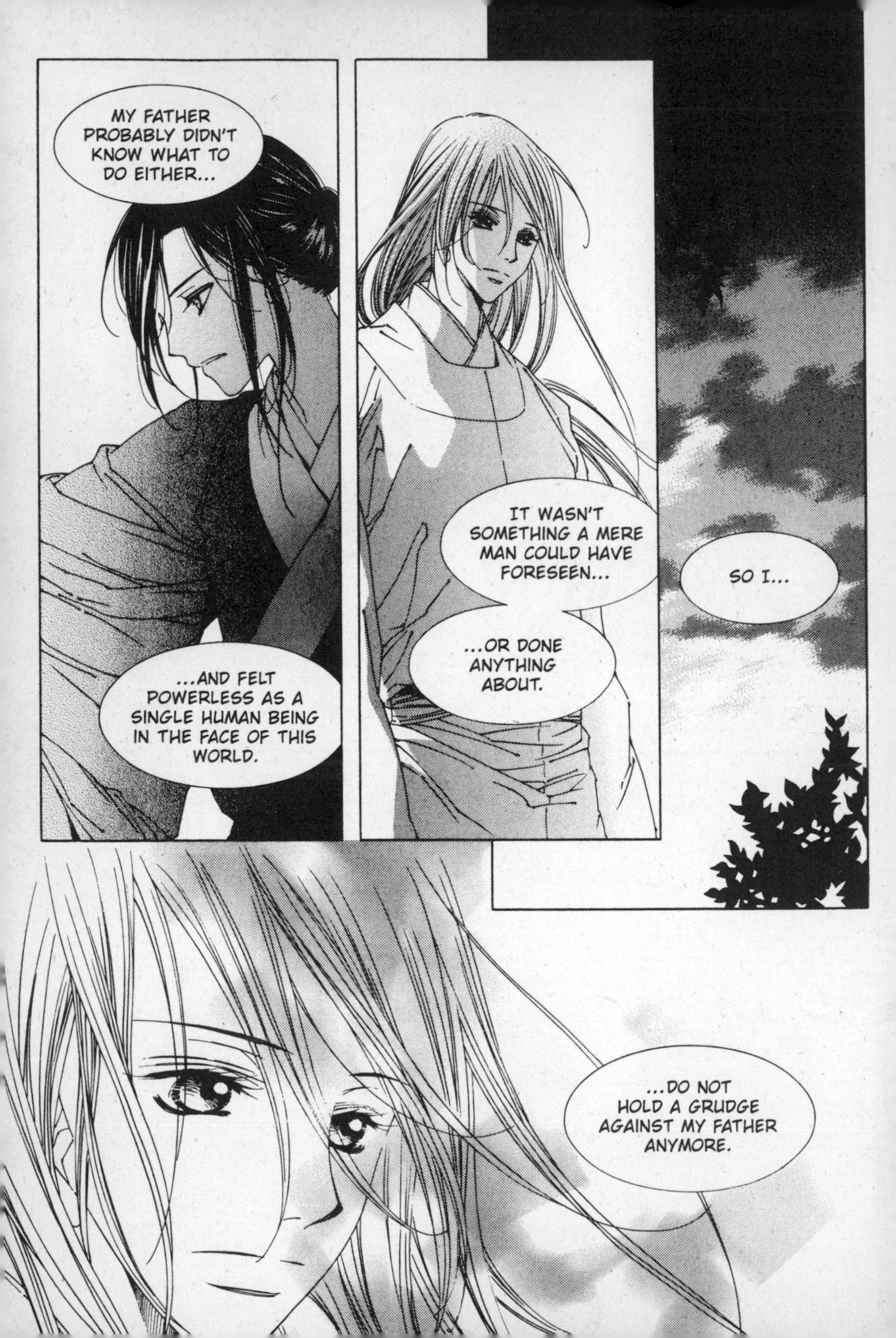
MY FATHER PROBABLY DIDN'T KNOW WHAT TO DO EITHER...
...AND FELT POWERLESS AS A SINGLE HUMAN BEING IN THE FACE OF THIS WORLD.
IT WASN'T SOMETHING A MERE MAN COULD HAVE FORESEEN...
...OR DONE ANYTHING ABOUT.
SO I...
...DO NOT HOLD A GRUDGE AGAINST MY FATHER ANYMORE.

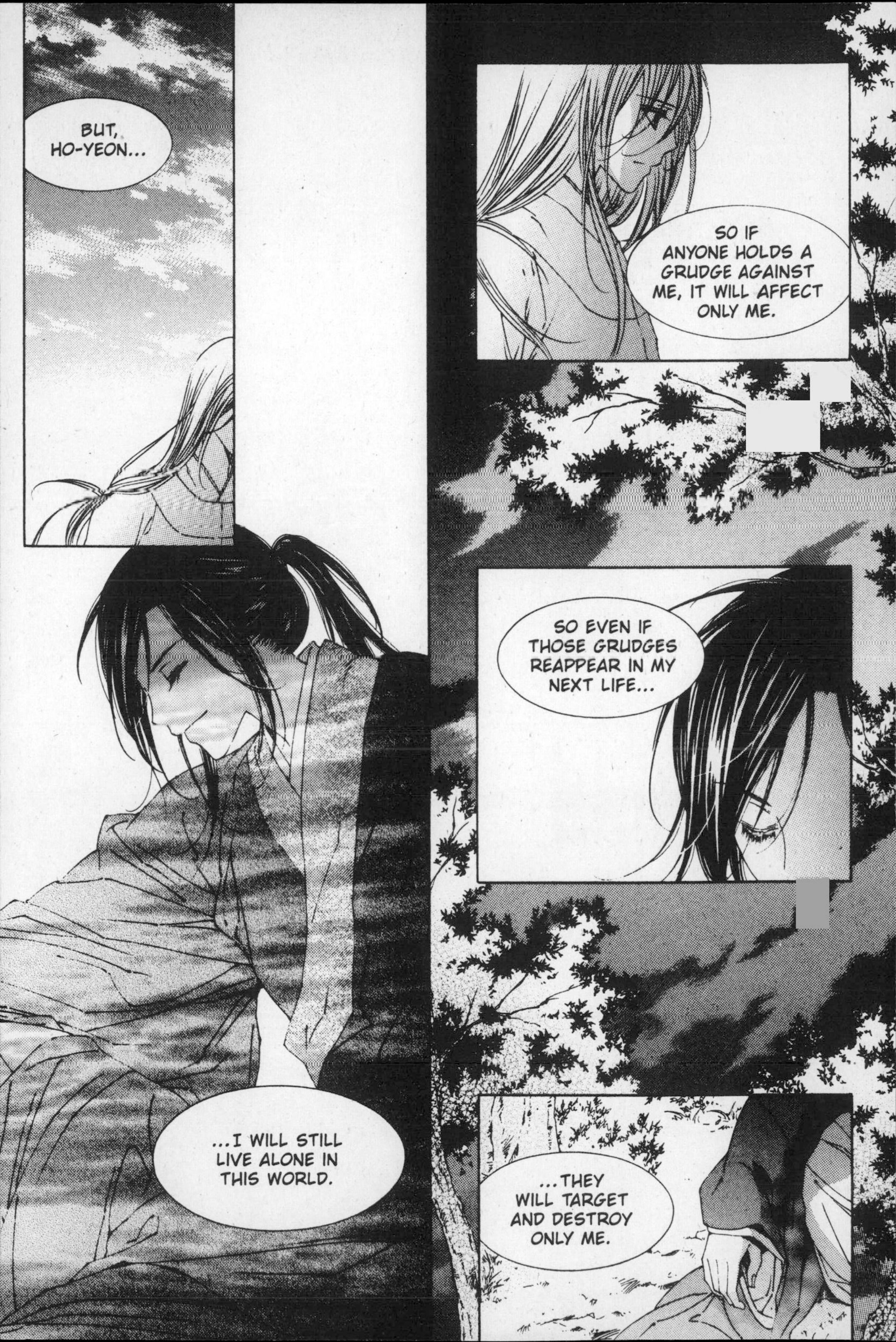
BUT, HO-YEON...
...I WILL STILL LIVE ALONE IN THIS WORLD.
SO IF ANYONE HOLDS A GRUDGE AGAINST ME, IT WILL AFFECT ONLY ME.
SO EVEN IF THOSE GRUDGES REAPPEAR IN MY NEXT LIFE...
...THEY WILL TARGET AND DESTROY ONLY ME.

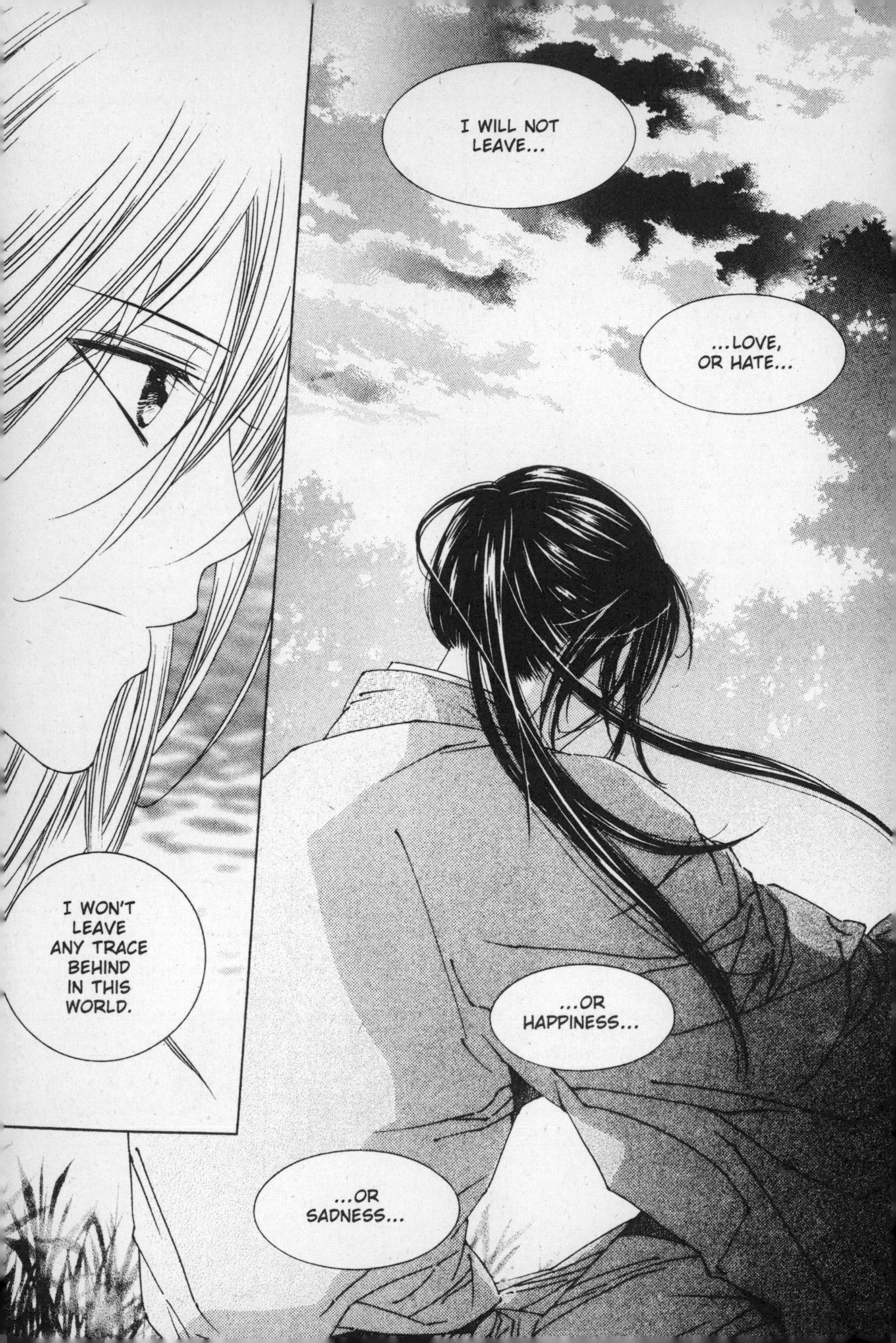
I WON'T LEAVE ANY TRACE BEHIND IN THIS WORLD.
I WILL NOT LEAVE...
...LOVE, OR HATE...
...OR HAPPINESS...
...OR SADNESS...

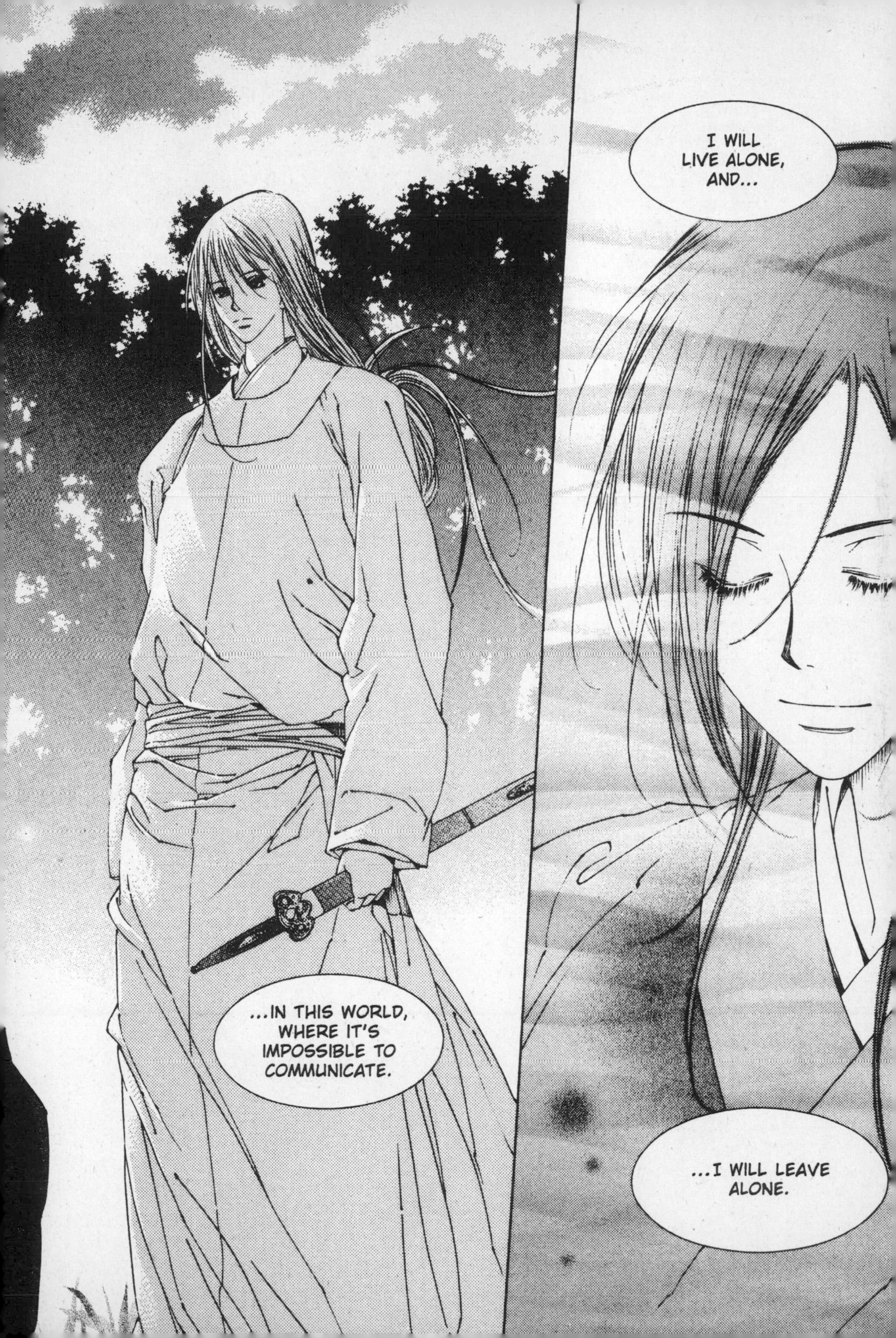
...IN THIS WORLD, WHERE IT'S IMPOSSIBLE TO COMMUNICATE.
I WILL LIVE ALONE, AND...
...I WILL LEAVE ALONE.

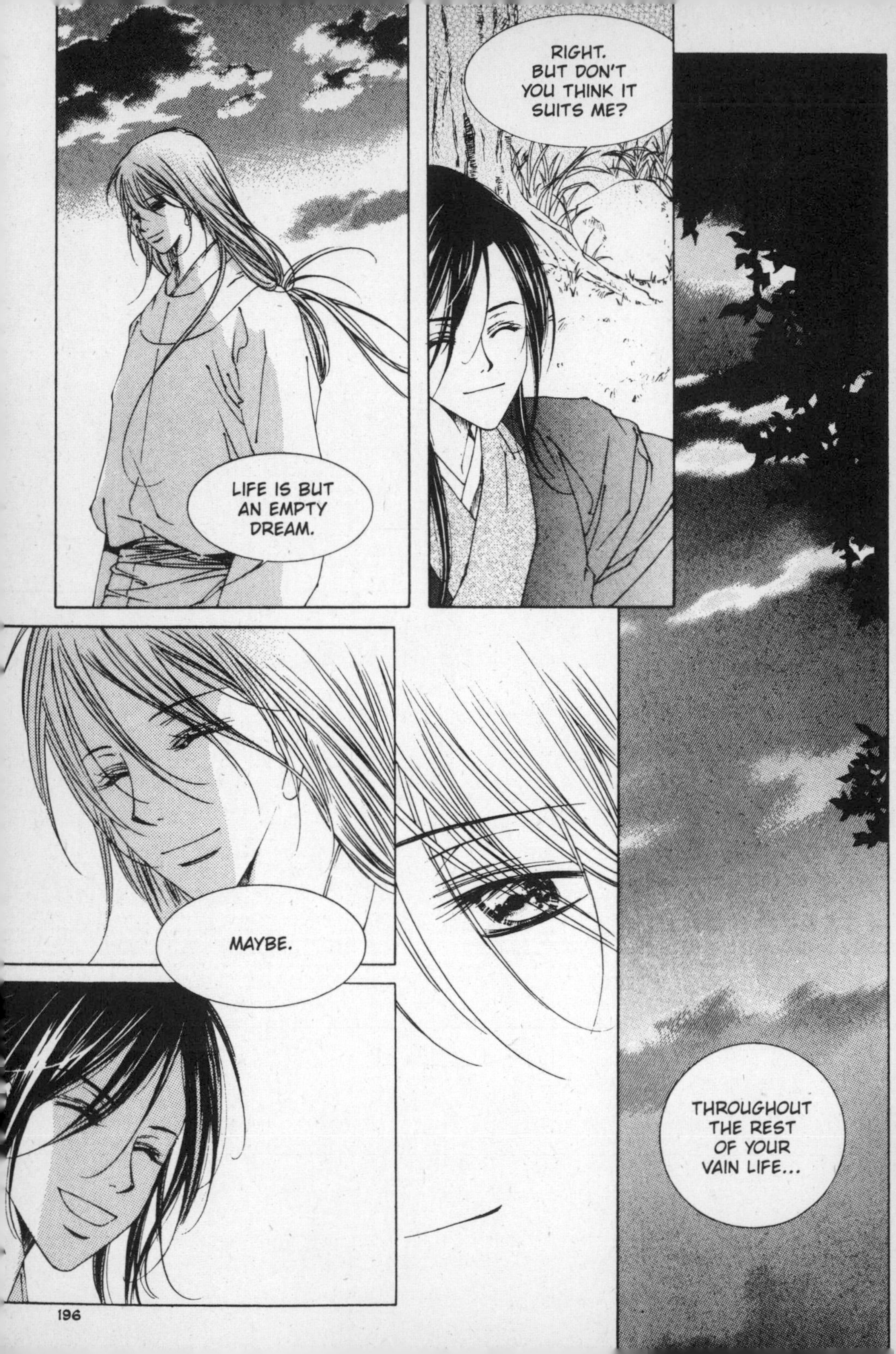
LIFE IS BUT AN EMPTY DREAM.
RIGHT. BUT DON'T YOU THINK IT SUITS ME?
MAYBE.
THROUGHOUT THE REST OF YOUR VAIN LIFE...

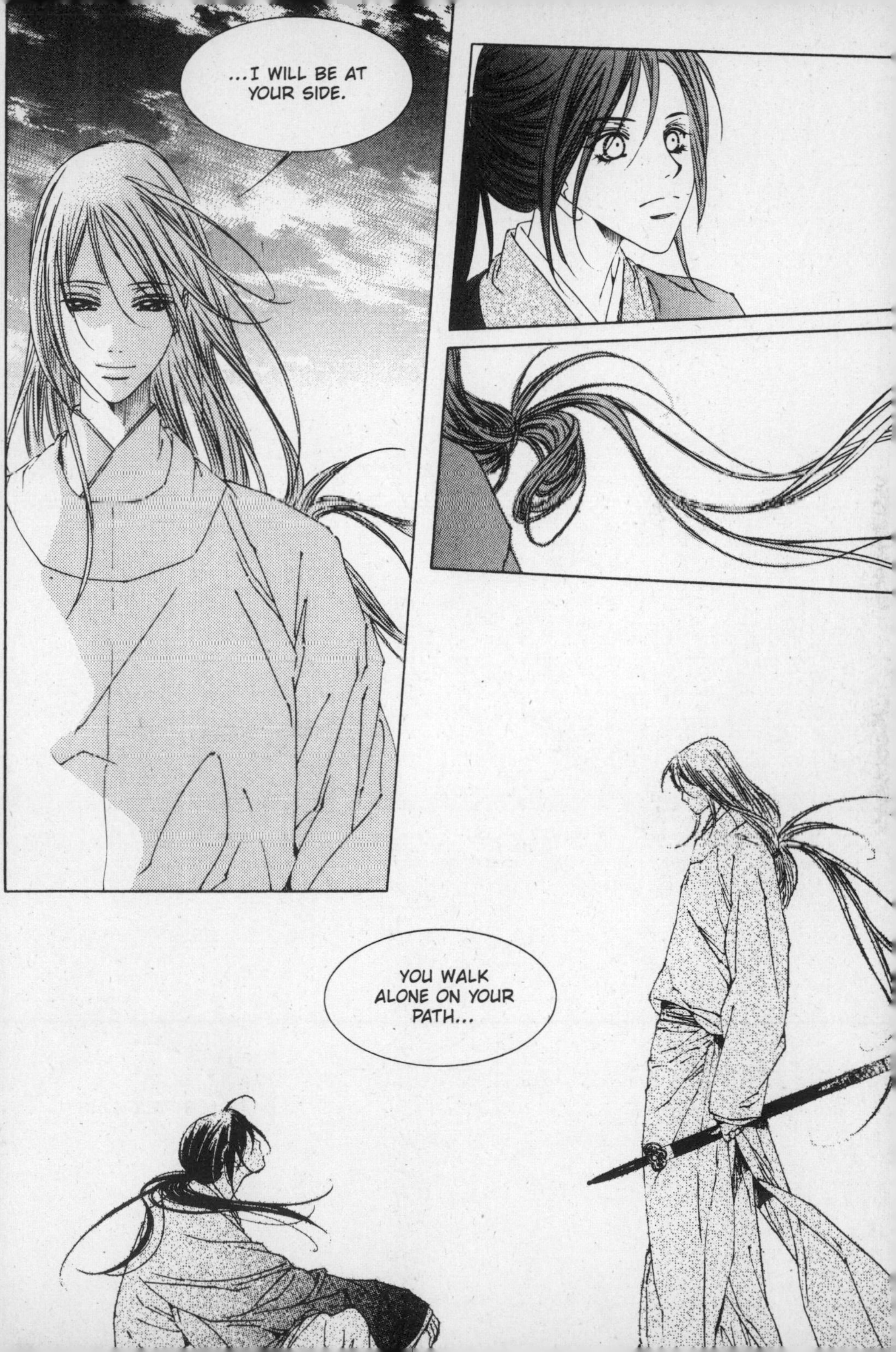
...I WILL BE AT YOUR SIDE.
YOU WALK ALONE ON YOUR PATH...

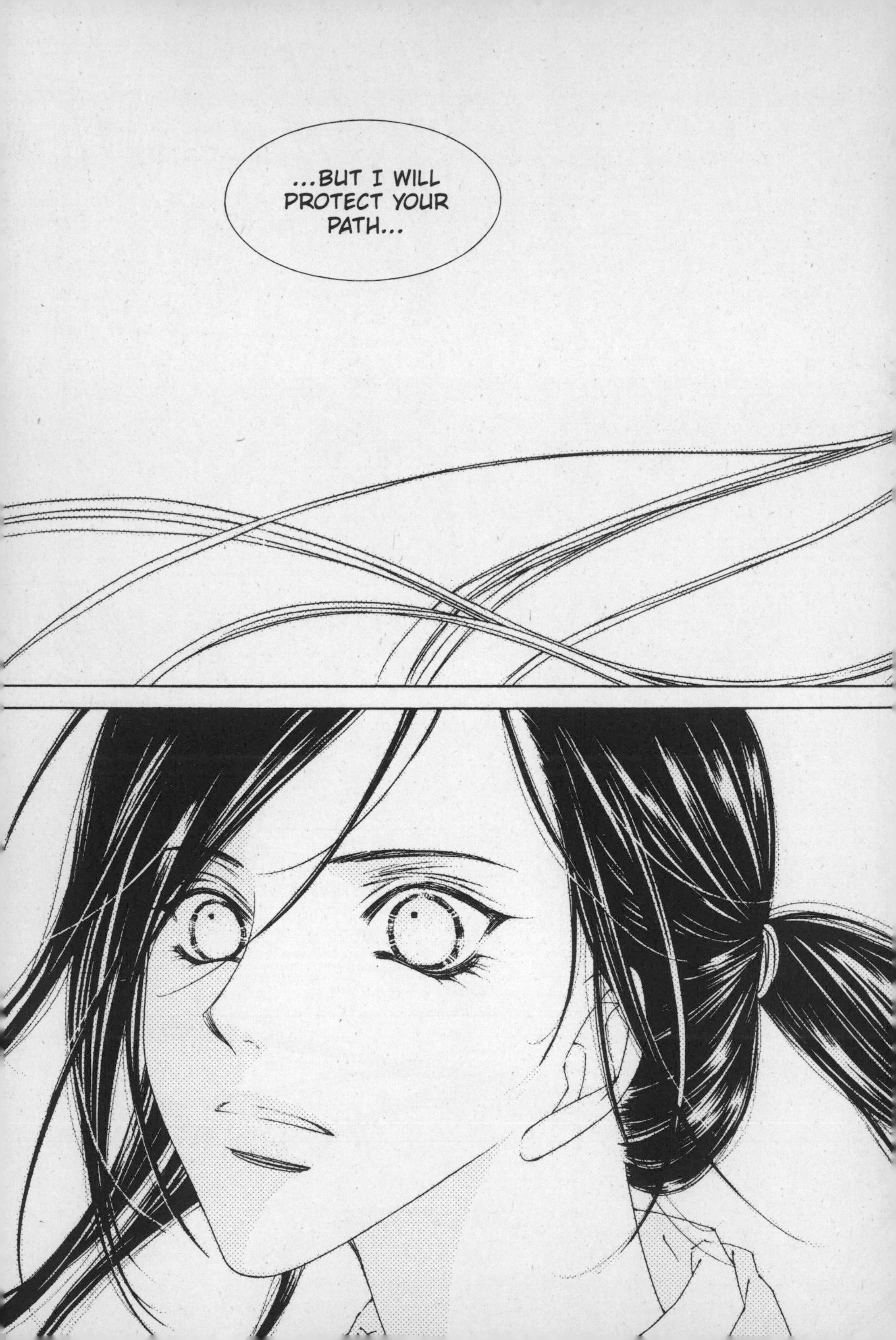
...BUT I WILL PROTECT YOUR PATH...

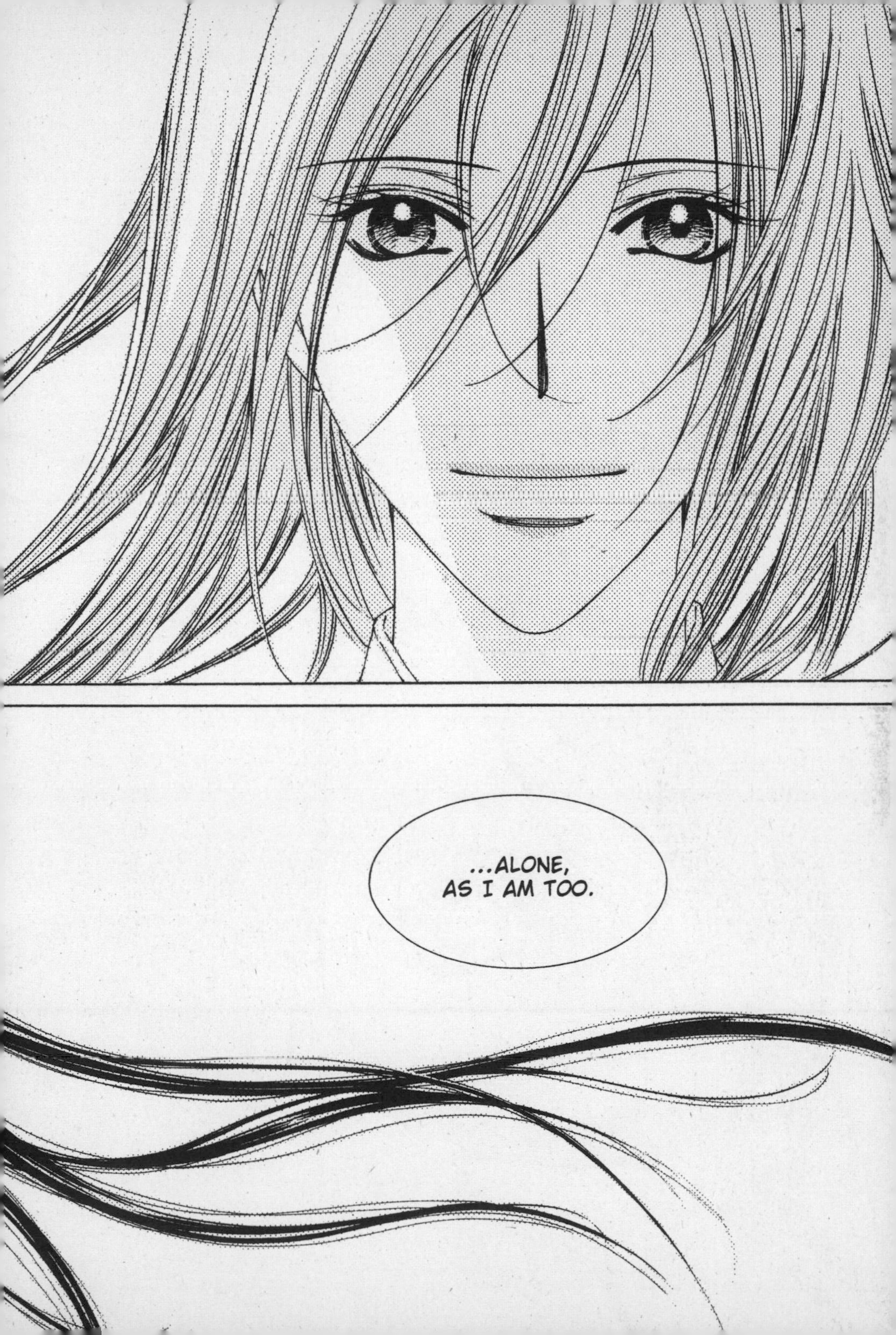
...ALONE, AS I AM TOO.

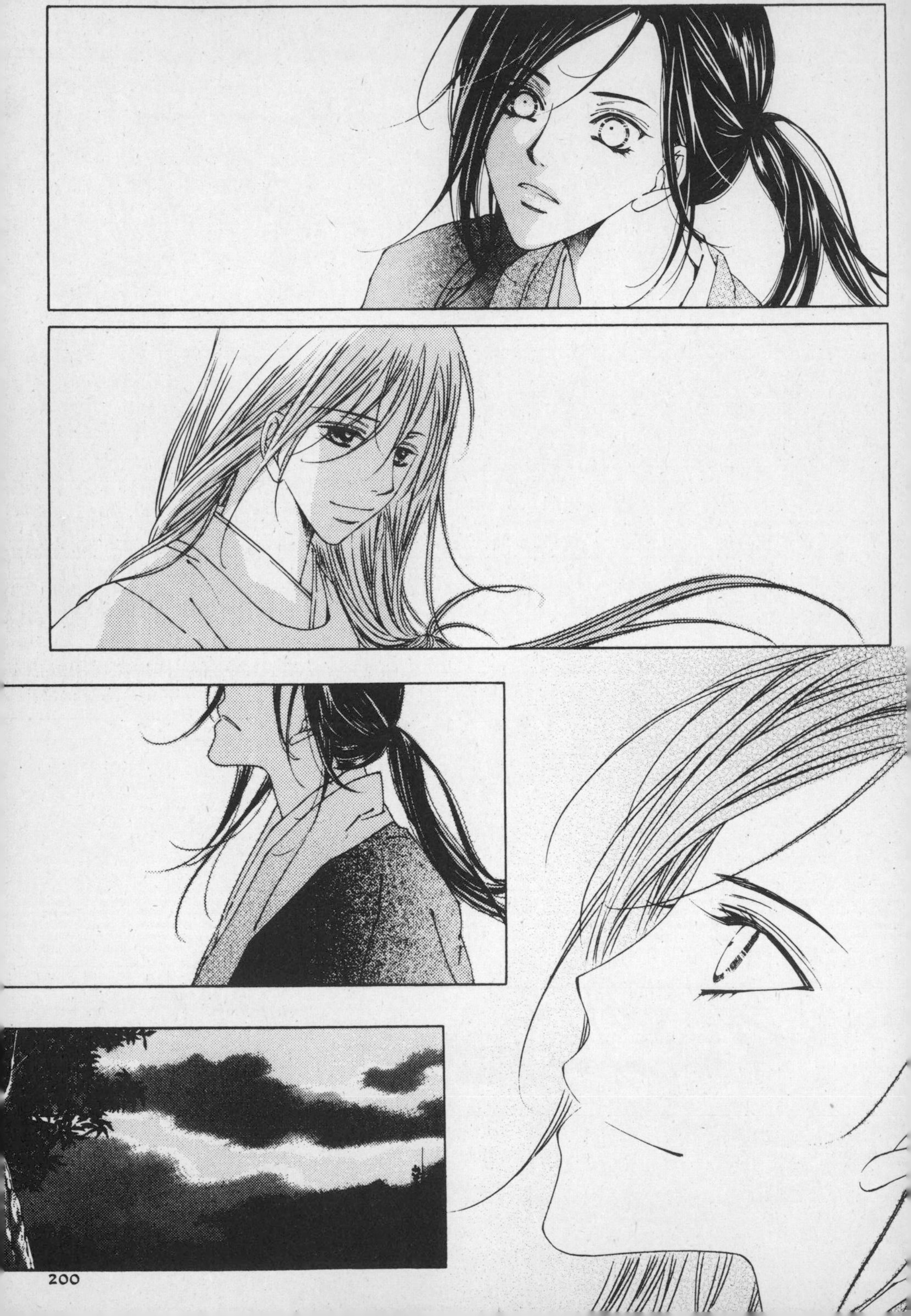

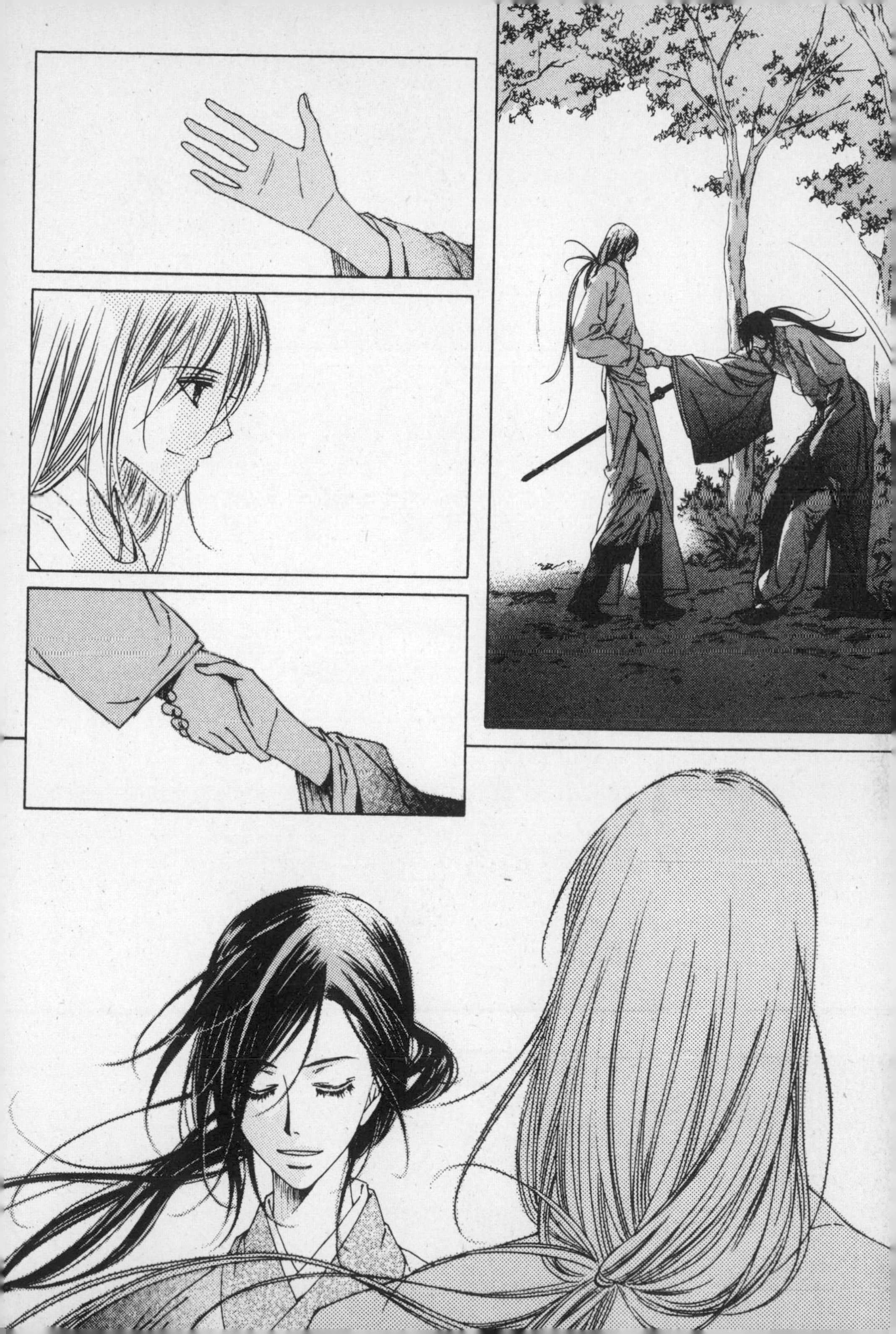

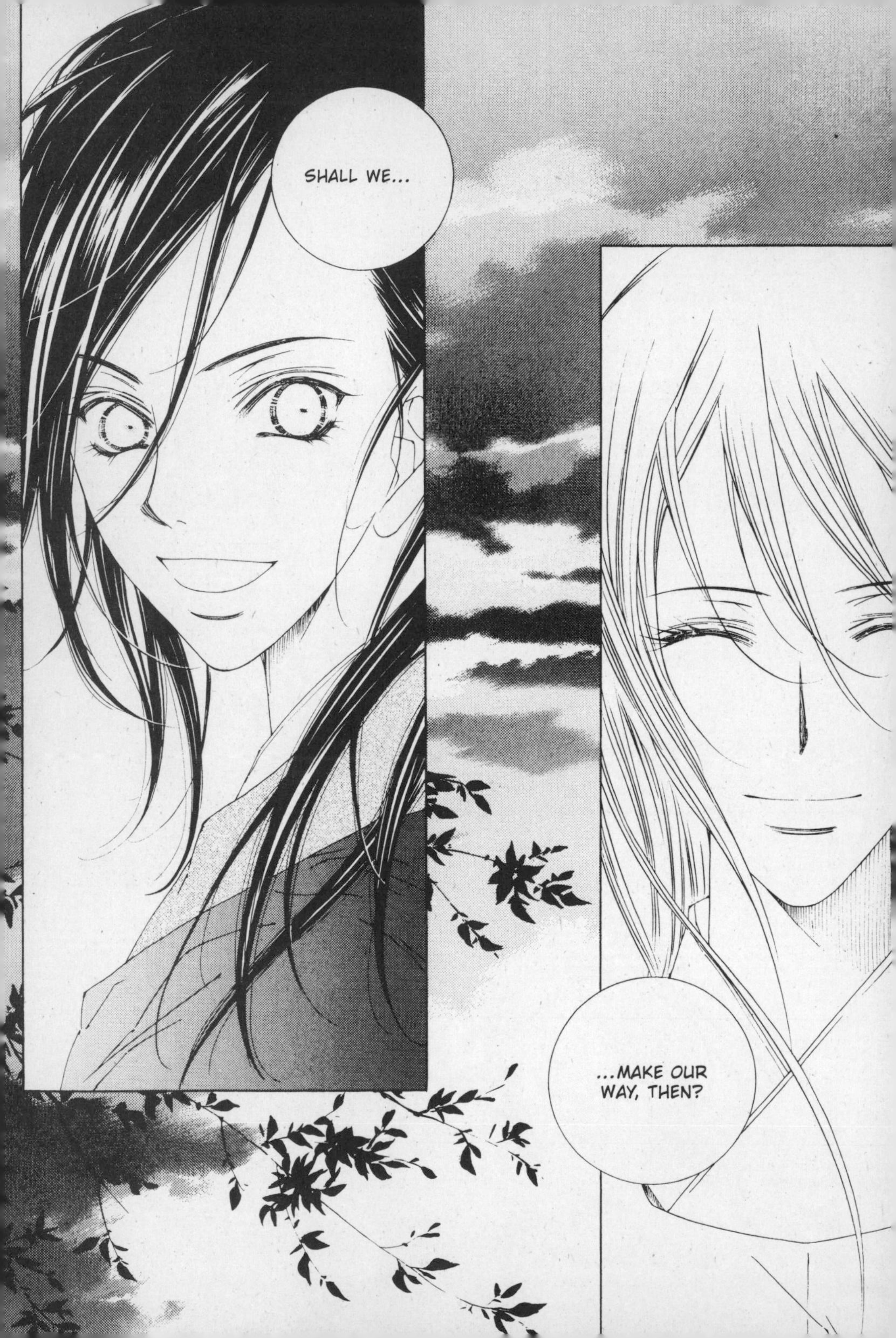
SHALL WE...
...MAKE OUR WAY, THEN?

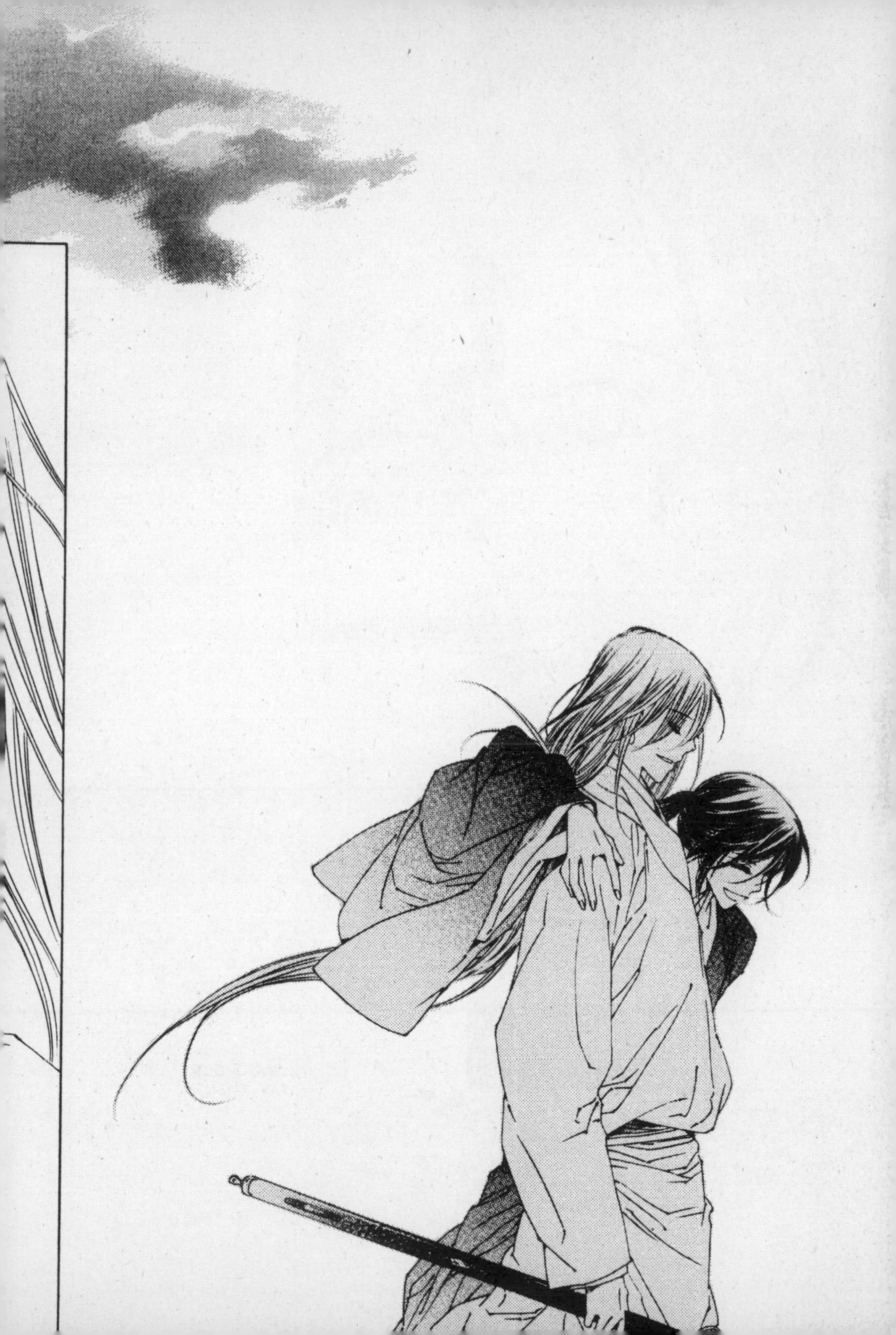

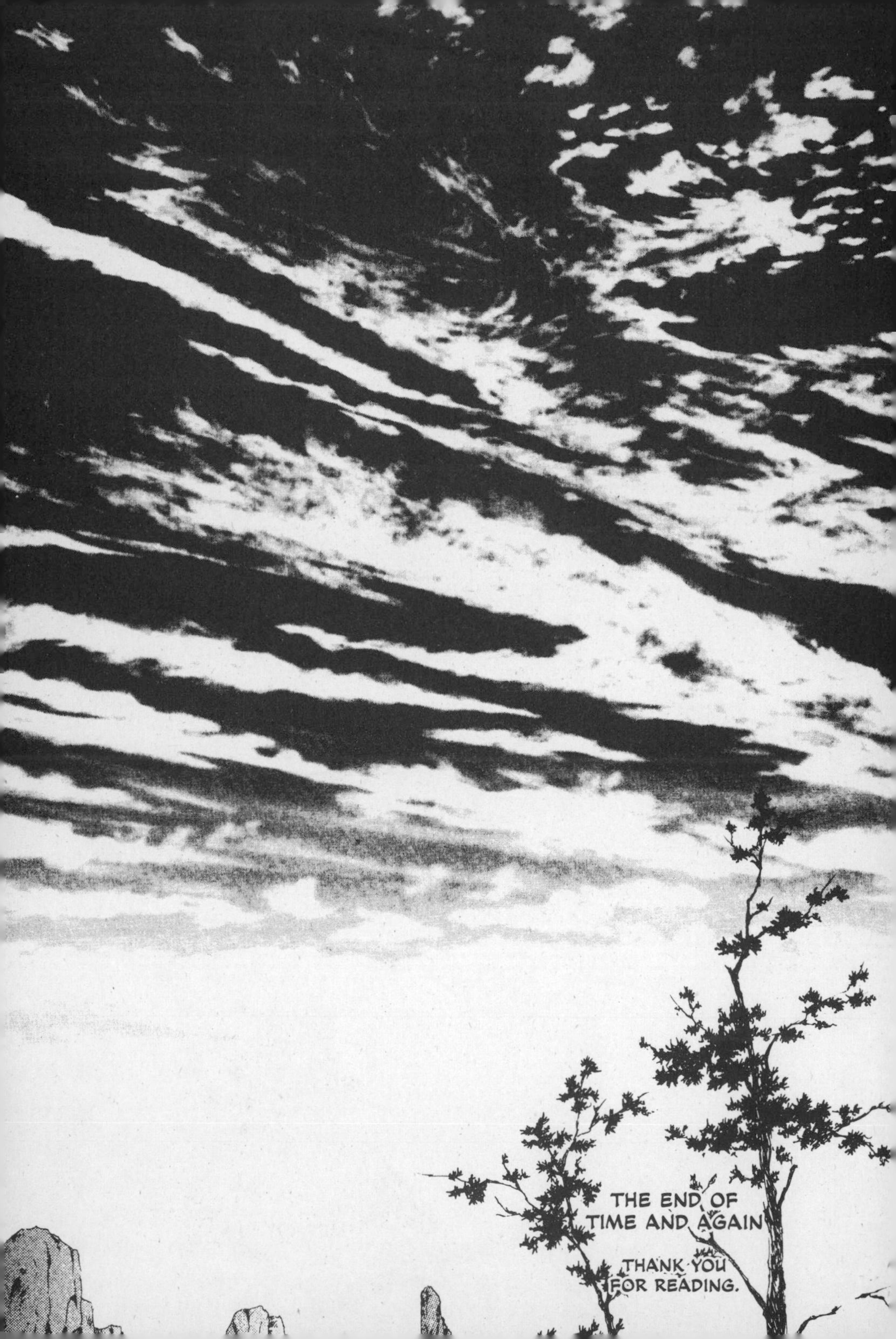
THE END OF
TIME AND AGAIN
THANK YOU
FOR READING.

TIME AND AGAIN

Afterword

STUPID MASTER SON -
ERRORS OBVIOUS TO EVERYONE ELSE: EPISODE 4

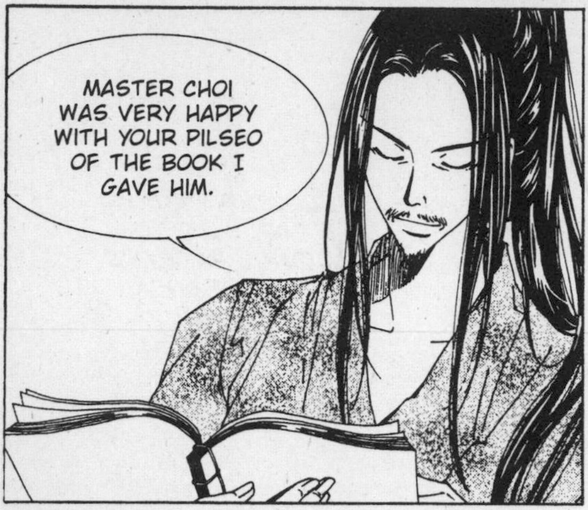
MASTER CHOI WAS VERY HAPPY WITH YOUR PILSEO OF THE BOOK I GAVE HIM.

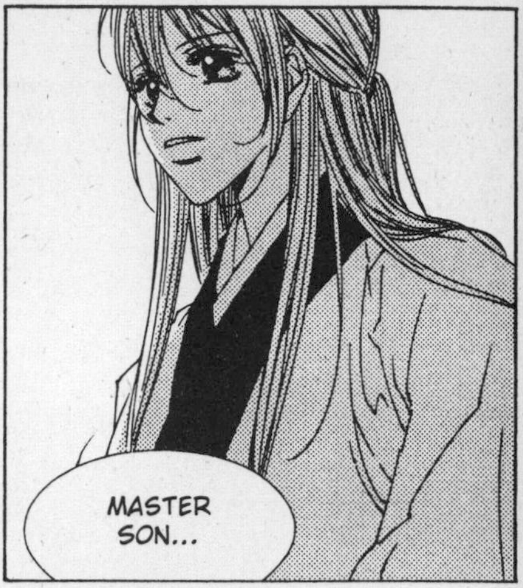
MASTER SON...

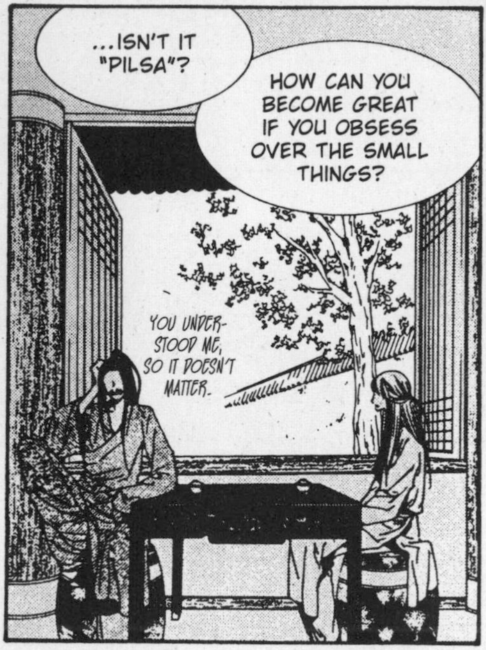
...ISN'T IT "PILSA"?
HOW CAN YOU BECOME GREAT IF YOU OBSESS OVER THE SMALL THINGS?
YOU UNDER-STOOD ME, SO IT DOESN'T MATTER.

- *PILSA: TRANSCRIPTION OF A BOOK BY HAND.*
- *PILSEO: ???*

VOLUME 4, PAGE 51: I CORRECT "PILSEO" TO "PILSA" IN THE KOREAN EDITION. I AM SO SORRY FOR USING A WORLD THAT ISN'T EVEN IN THE DICTIONARY AND FOR NOT REALIZING IT FOR SUCH A LONG TIME. I AM A STUPID PERSON WHO NEVER GETS SMARTER.

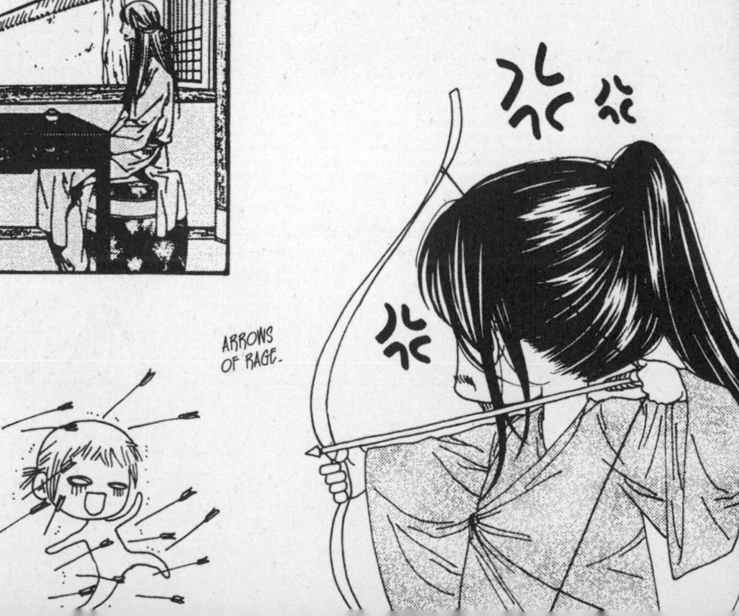
ARROWS OF RAGE.

STUPID WRITER - ERRORS OBVIOUS TO EVERYONE ELSE: EPISODE 5

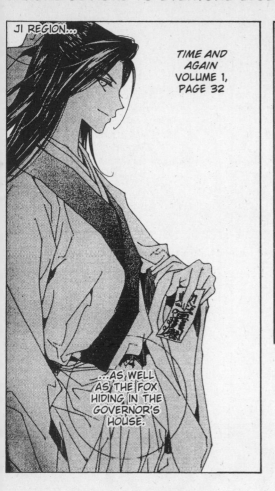

JI REGION...
TIME AND AGAIN VOLUME 1, PAGE 32
...AS WELL AS THE FOX HIDING IN THE GOVERNOR'S HOUSE.

LUOYANG WAS THE CAPITAL, SO IT WOULD NOT HAVE HAD THE TYPE OF LOCAL GOVERNOR MENTIONED HERE.

IF A KIND READER HADN'T TOLD ME, I WOULD NEVER HAVE KNOWN ABOUT THIS MISTAKE. I'M GLAD I FOUND OUT ABOUT THIS WHILE I STILL HAD A CHANCE TO CORRECT IT. THANK YOU SO MUCH.

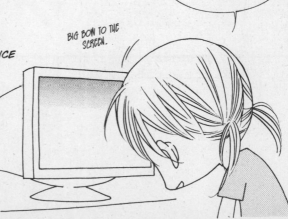

THANK YOU.
BIG BOW TO THE SCREEN.

PLEASE THINK IT WAS SOME OTHER GOVERNMENT OFFICIAL. ♥

ARE YOUR EYES OPEN? - ERRORS OBVIOUS TO EVERYONE ELSE: EPISODE 6

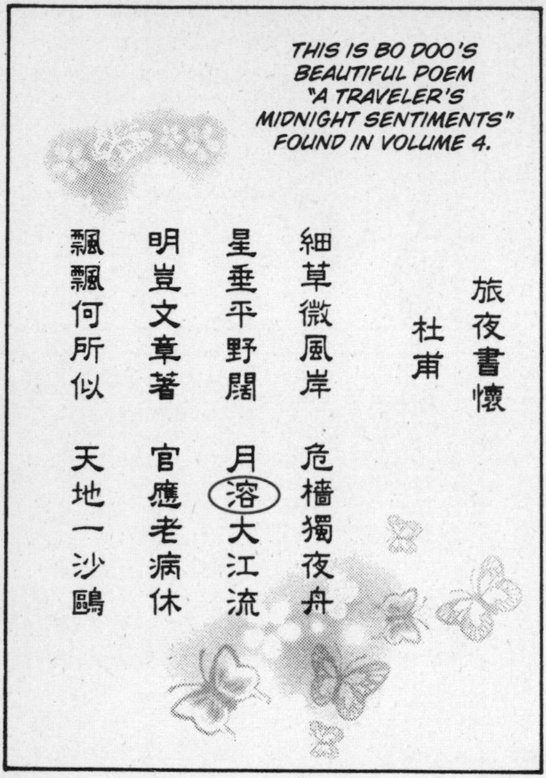
THIS IS BO DOO'S BEAUTIFUL POEM "A TRAVELER'S MIDNIGHT SENTIMENTS" FOUND IN VOLUME 4.
旅夜書懷
杜甫
細草微風岸
危檣獨夜舟
星垂平野闊
月溶大江流
明豈文章著
官應老病休
飄飄何所似
天地一沙鷗

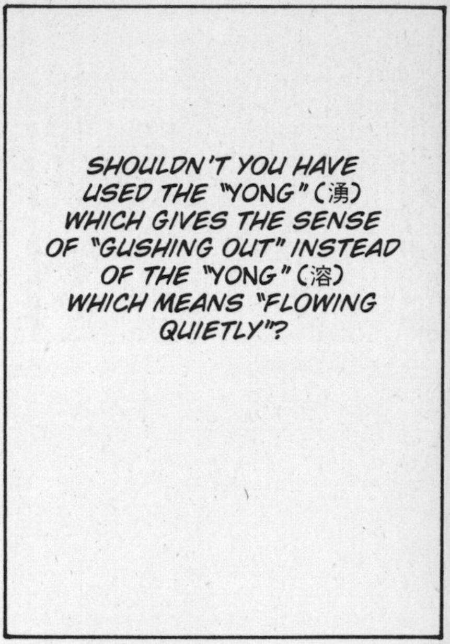
SHOULDN'T YOU HAVE USED THE "YONG" (湧) WHICH GIVES THE SENSE OF "GUSHING OUT" INSTEAD OF THE "YONG" (溶) WHICH MEANS "FLOWING QUIETLY"?

I AM SORRY.
YOU ARE RIGHT.
PLEASE CORRECT IT IN YOUR MIND WHEN YOU READ IT.

IN THE EARLY MORNING ON THE DAY THE PAGES FOR VOLUME 6 WERE DUE, A READER POINTED THIS OUT ON MY PERSONAL BLOG. SO I ADDED THIS PAGE AT THE LAST MINUTE. I AM SO THANKFUL THAT THE READER GAVE ME THE CHANCE TO FIX THIS. PLEASE CALL ME "EYES WIDE SHUT."

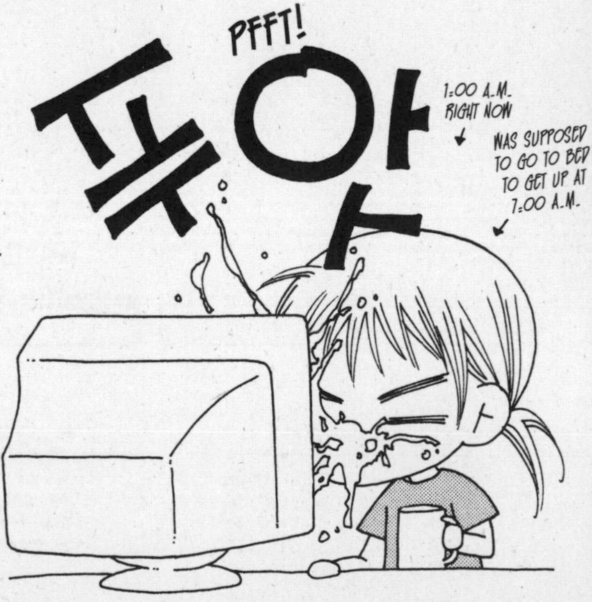
PFFT!
1:00 A.M. RIGHT NOW
WAS SUPPOSED TO GO TO BED TO GET UP AT 7:00 A.M.

CHAPTER NINETEEN

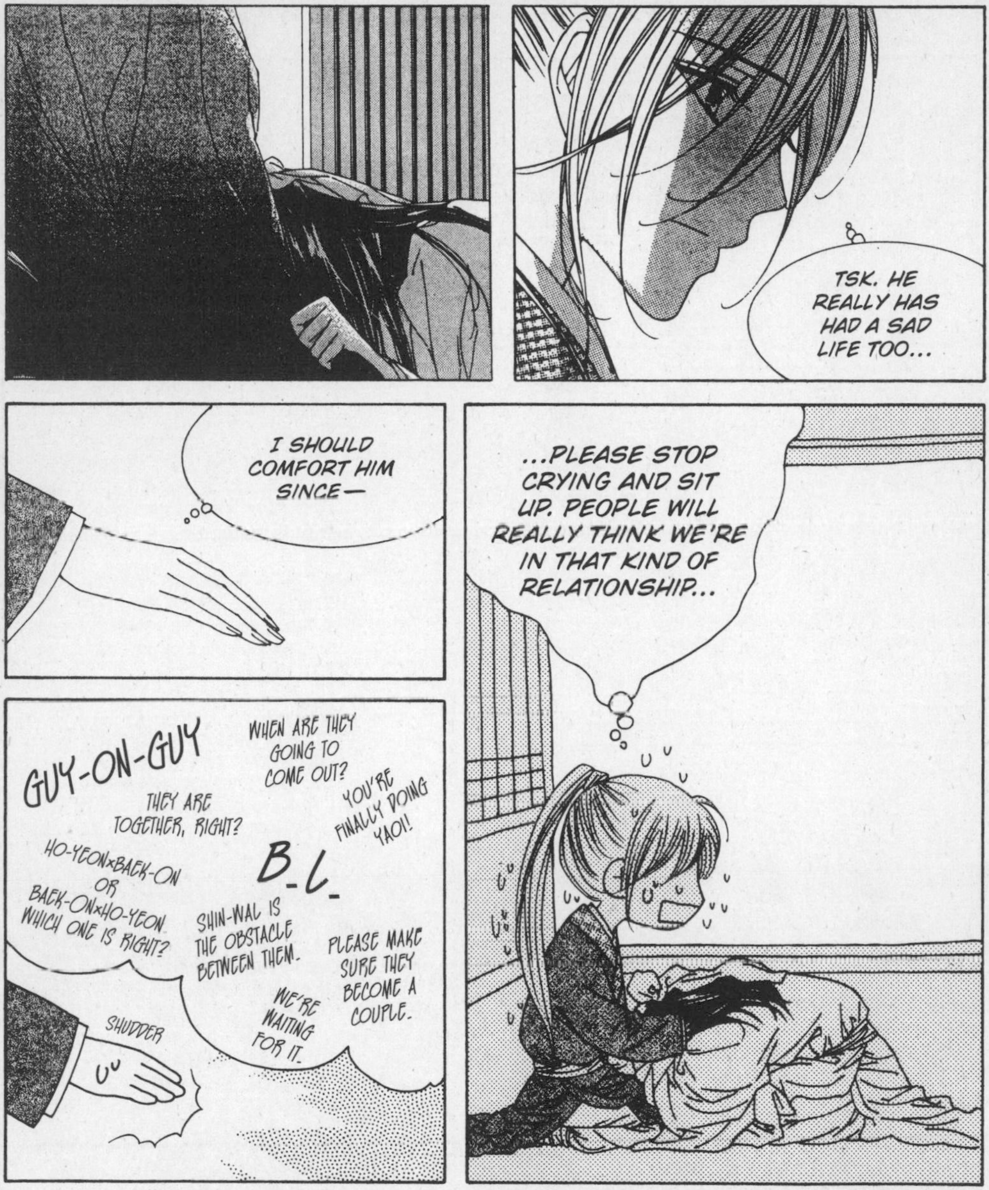
TSK. HE REALLY HAS HAD A SAD LIFE TOO...
I SHOULD COMFORT HIM SINCE—
GUY-ON-GUY
WHEN ARE THEY GOING TO COME OUT?
THEY ARE TOGETHER, RIGHT?
YOU'RE FINALLY DOING YAOI!
HO-YEON×BAEK-ON OR BAEK-ON×HO-YEON WHICH ONE IS RIGHT?
B.L.
SHIN-WAL IS THE OBSTACLE BETWEEN THEM.
PLEASE MAKE SURE THEY BECOME A COUPLE.
WE'RE WAITING FOR IT.
SHUDDER
...PLEASE STOP CRYING AND SIT UP. PEOPLE WILL REALLY THINK WE'RE IN THAT KIND OF RELATIONSHIP...

THAT WAS HOW I FELT WHILE DRAWING IT.

THIS CHAPTER WAS A PRETTY STRAIGHTFORWARD GHOST STORY WITH A WOMAN BECOMING A GHOST AFTER A MAN LEAVES HER. IN MANY CASES, THIS KIND OF STORY ENDS WITH THE GHOST'S REVENGE, BUT I WANTED TO END IT SIMPLY.

I'VE ONLY SEEN A GHOST (I THINK IT WAS A GHOST) ONCE IN MY LIFE. WHEN I SAW THE GHOST, I FELT SAD AND SYMPATHETIC RATHER THAN SCARED. I THINK WE MISUNDERSTAND AND HAVE PREJUDICE AGAINST GHOSTS.

CHAPTER TWENTY

WITH THE EXCEPTION OF SOO-KYUNG, WHO'S ONLY IN A FEW SCENES, EVERYONE IN THIS CHAPTER HAS BLACK HAIR. I WAS ABOUT TO GO CRAZY DRAWING THEIR HAIR.

MY HAND IS ABOUT TO LOSE ALL FEELING. SEVENTEEN HOURS... SEVENTEEN HOURS?

THERE IS A LIMIT TO USING SCREEN TONES.

...SUDDENLY, I REMEMBERED A TEXT FROM MY UPPERCLASSMAN FROM COLLEGE.

RIGHT! THIS IS IT!! MY UPPER-CLASSMAN YOO!

I'M GETTING MARRIED~ YOU ENVY ME, DON'T YOU?

← THE FIRST TEXT SINCE WE GRADUATED.

CONGRATU-LATIONS!! PLEASE BE HAPPY!! AND THANK YOU!!!

HE LOOKED LIKE HE DIDN'T THINK I'D COME.

HUH?

YOU HELPED ME ESCAPE FROM REALITY.

I THINK YOU HAD LONG HAIR, BUT I DON'T REALLY REMEMBER THE DETAILS. SORRY.

ACCORDING TO THE THEORY OF DEATH AND REBIRTH AND KARMA...

- BAD THINGS THAT HAPPEN TO A PERSON BEFORE HE OR SHE IS TWENTY YEARS OLD ARE BECAUSE OF WHAT THE PARENTS HAVE DONE WRONG.

- BAD THINGS HAPPEN BETWEEN 20 AND 34 YEARS BASED ON WHAT YOU DID WRONG IN YOUR PREVIOUS LIFE.

- BAD THINGS HAPPEN BETWEEN 35 AND 49 YEARS OF AGE BECAUSE OF WHAT YOU DID WRONG BETWEEN 20 AND 34 IN THIS LIFE.

- AFTER 50, YOU PAY FOR WHATEVER IS LEFT OF THE WRONG YOU DID IN THIS LIFE, AND WHATEVER YOU DO WRONG DURING THIS TIME WILL BE CARRIED INTO THE NEXT LIFE.

...I'VE CONSIDERED THIS DEEPLY, AND IT CAN'T JUST BE A THEORY. I DETERMINE TO LIVE AS A GOOD PERSON WHEN I THINK ABOUT IT.

OF COURSE, THIS THEORY HAS NOTHING TO DO WITH BAEK-ON'S THEORY.

LORD YUE LAO: HE IS A CHINESE GOD DESCRIBED IN SOKYOOGWEROK. HE HOLDS THE BOOK OF MARRIAGE AND TIES A BOY AND A GIRL WHO ARE SUPPOSED TO MARRY LATER WITH A RED THREAD.

How have you been, mother? Ho-Yeon and I are doing fine.

THEY'RE ALL RIGHT.

Luoyang is still in chaos. I don't think this will end any time soon. Everyone here is having a hard time.

OH NO.

So mother, please send me some money. You can send me as much money as you want.

THAT BRAT!!

AM I YOUR BANK ACCOUNT?

PAK (FWAP)

THIS STORY IS FROM THE KOREAN BOOK CALLED GUMKEPILDAM. THE ORIGINAL STORY HAS A MAN WHO KILLED A MONK BECAUSE THE MONK WAS DOING BAD THINGS. THIS MONK IS REBORN AS THE MAN'S SON TO EXACT REVENGE ON HIM. BUT THE MAN AND HIS WIFE KNEW IT AND WEREN'T SAD WHEN THE CHILD DIED, SO THE MONK COULDN'T HAVE HIS REVENGE. WHETHER THE MONK SUCCEEDED OR NOT, THE STORY IS QUITE CRUEL.

THIS IS THE END OF TIME AND AGAIN. I THOUGHT I WAS DOING THIS BOOK FOR MYSELF, BUT THANK YOU SO MUCH FOR ENJOYING THIS BOOK WITH ME. IT WAS A FUN EXPERIENCE. (I DON'T KNOW WHEN I'LL GET THE CHANCE TO DRAW CLOTHES FROM THE TANG DYNASTY AGAIN...)

TIME AND AGAIN ⑥

JIUN YUN

Translation: HyeYoung Im • English Adaptation: J. Torres

Lettering: Abigail Blackman

Time and Again, vol. 6 © 2008 by YUN Ji-un, DAEWON C.I. Inc. All rights reserved. First published in Korea in 2008 by DAEWON C.I. Inc. English translation rights in USA, Canada, UK and Commonwealth arranged by Daewon C.I. Inc. through TOPAZ Agency Inc.

Translation © 2011 by Hachette Book Group, Inc.

Yen Press
Hachette Book Group
237 Park Avenue, New York, NY 10017

www.HachetteBookGroup.com
www.YenPress.com

Yen Press is an imprint of Hachette Book Group, Inc.
The Yen Press name and logo are trademarks of Hachette Book Group, Inc.

First Yen Press Edition: July 2011

ISBN: 978-0-7595-3063-8

10 9 8 7 6 5 4 3 2 1

BVG

Printed in the United States of America